Nature and Society

Nature and Society looks critically at the nature/society dichotomy – one of the central dogmas of western scholarship – and its place in human ecology and social theory. Rethinking the dualism means rethinking ecological anthropology and its notion of the relation between person and environment. The deeply entrenched biological and anthropological traditions which insist upon separating the two are challenged on both empirical and theoretical grounds.

By focusing on a variety of perspectives, the contributors draw upon developments in social theory, biology, ethnobiology and sociology of science. They present an array of ethnographic case studies – from Amazonia, the Solomon Islands, Malaysia, the Moluccan Islands, rural communities in Japan and north-west Europe, urban Greece and laboratories of molecular biology and high-energy physics.

The key focus of *Nature and Society* is the issue of the environment and its relations to humans. By inviting concern for sustainability, ethics, indigenous knowledge and the social context of science, this book will appeal to students of anthropology, human ecology and sociology.

Philippe Descola is Directeur d'Etudes, Ecole des Hautes Etudes en Sciences Sociales, Paris, and member of the Laboratoire d'Anthropologie Sociale at the Collège de France. **Gísli Pálsson** is Professor of Anthropology at the University of Iceland, Reykjavík, and (formerly) Research Fellow at the Swedish Collegium for Advanced Study in the Social Sciences, Uppsala, Sweden.

European Association of Social Anthropologists

The European Association of Social Anthropologists (EASA) was inaugurated in January 1989, in response to a widely felt need for a professional association which would represent social anthropologists in Europe and foster co-operation and interchange in teaching and research. As Europe transforms itself in the nineties, the EASA is dedicated to the renewal of the distinctive European tradition in social anthropology.

Other titles in the series

Conceptualizing Society
Adam Kuper

Revitalizing European Rituals
Jeremy Boissevain

Other Histories
Kirsten Hastrup

Alcohol, Gender and Culture
Dimitra Gefou-Madianou

Understanding Rituals
Daniel de Coppet

Gendered Anthropology
Teresa del Valle

Social Experience and Anthropological Knowledge
Kirsten Hastrup and Peter Hervik

Fieldwork and Notes
Han F. Vermeulen and Arturo Alvarez Roldan

Syncretism/Anti-Syncretism
Charles Stewart and Rosalind Shaw

Grasping the Changing World
Václav Hubinger

Civil Society
Chris Hann and Elizabeth Dunn

Nature and Society

Anthropological perspectives

Edited by
Philippe Descola and Gísli Pálsson

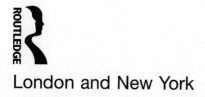

London and New York

First published 1996
by Routledge
11 New Fetter Lane, London EC4P 4EE

Simultaneously published in the USA and Canada

by Routledge
29 West 35th Street, New York, NY 10001

Routledge is an International Thomson Publishing Company

© 1996 Philippe Descola and Gísli Pálsson, selection and editorial matter;
individual chapters, the contributors

Typeset in Times by Routledge
Printed and bound in Great Britain by Redwood Books, Trowbridge,
Wiltshire

British Library Cataloguing in Publication Data
A catalogue record for this book is available from the British Library

Library of Congress Cataloguing in Publication Data
A catalogue record for this book has been requested

ISBN 0–415–13215–0 (hbk)
ISBN 0–415–13216–9 (pbk)

Contents

Illustrations

Contributors

Kaj Århem is Professor of Anthropology at the University of Gothenburg.

Philippe Descola is Directeur d'Etudes at the Ecole des Hautes Etudes en Sciences Sociales, Paris, and member of the Laboratoire d'Anthropologie Sociale at the Collège de France.

Roy F. Ellen is Professor of Anthropology and Human Ecology at the University of Kent.

Bertrand Hell is Professor of Anthropology at the University of Franche-Comté, Besançon.

Alf Hornborg is Professor of Anthropology in the Human Ecology Division at the University of Lund.

Signe Howell is Professor of Anthropology at the University of Oslo.

Edvard Hviding is Lecturer in the Department of Social Anthropology at the University of Bergen.

Tim Ingold is Professor and Chair in the Department of Social Anthropology at the University of Manchester.

John Knight is Lecturer in Social Anthropology at the University of Kent.

Detlev Nothnagel is associated with the universities of Göttingen, Hildesheim, and Munich.

Gísli Pálsson is Professor of Anthropology in the Faculty of Social Science at the University of Iceland and (formerly) Research Fellow at the Swedish Collegium for Advanced Study in the Social Sciences in Uppsala.

Eleni Papagaroufali is Lecturer in Social Anthropology at the University of the Aegean in Mytilene.

Paul Richards is Professor of Anthropology at University College, London, and Chair, Working Group for Technology and Agrarian Development, the Agricultural University, Wageningen, the Netherlands.

Laura Rival is Lecturer in Social Anthropology at the University of Kent.

Guido Ruivenkamp is Research Secretary, Working Group for Technology and Agrarian Development, the Agricultural University, Wageningen, the Netherlands.

Editors' preface

This book focuses on the nature–society interface in anthropology and several ethnographic contexts. The articles are revised versions of papers that were presented at the Third Conference of the European Association of Social Anthropologists in Oslo in June 1994. In her opening address to the Oslo conference, Signe Howell remarked that the organisers had been taken by surprise and that the abstracts submitted, as well as suggestions for themes for workshop discussion, indicated rather unexpected developments; not only had some of the 'established' themes offered by the organisers received little or no response from prospective participants, but some themes generally considered either emptied or outmoded in recent years – including those of ecology and kinship – turned out to be embraced with renewed enthusiasm. Thus, no less than three full sessions focused on nature and the environment. This book gathers together a selection of the papers that were presented in these sessions. The renewed interest in ecological issues which the Oslo conference and this volume reflect is somewhat unanticipated, given the hegemony of textualist theorising in recent years. Apparently, however, nature and the environment refuse to leave the agenda for good, re-emerging this time with more vigour than before. This suggests that the time is ripe for revisiting ecological anthropology on new theoretical terms. After all, a new millennium is almost here, a millennium which no doubt will pose massive environmental problems for humans.

We would like to thank the participants in the sessions we organised at the Oslo conference for their contributions to the lively discussions that took place, in particular the authors of the papers that were presented. Thanks are also due to Stephen Gudeman, who acted as a discussant in one of the sessions, and Agnar Helgason, who helped to prepare the final manuscript. Finally, we are grateful to Roger Goodman for his valuable editorial advice.

Chapter 1

Introduction

Philippe Descola and Gísli Pálsson

The overall theme of this volume – the place of nature and the environment in anthropological theory and social discourse – is not a novel one. From early on, nature was one of the central concerns of anthropology, whether in the field of folk-sciences and cultural ecology or in the study of myths and rituals linked to the environment and subsistence techniques. Nevertheless, in recent years the issue of ecology, in the broadest sense of the term, has tended to be relegated to the margin of anthropological discussions, as post-modernism and culturalist perspectives have dominated the centre stage of theoretical developments in the social sciences generally. This is reflected in the declining supply of (and, presumably, reduced demand for) ecology courses in the curricula of many anthropology departments. However, the situation is changing again, as anthropologists are increasingly returning to the study of environmental issues (see, for instance, McCay and Acheson 1987, Croll and Parkin 1992). Similar developments seem to be taking place in other disciplines, including philosophy, history, and sociology (see, for example, Dickens 1992, Simmons 1993, Attfield and Belsey 1994).

The contributors to this book focus on the nature–society interface from a variety of theoretical and ethnographic perspectives, drawing upon recent developments in social theory, biology, ethnobiology, epistemology, sociology of science, and a wide array of ethnographic case studies – from Amazonia, the Solomon Islands, Malaysia, the Moluccan Islands, rural communities from Japan and north-west Europe, urban Greece, and laboratories of molecular biology and high-energy physics. Among the questions posed by the authors are the following: Are the different cultural models of nature conditioned by the same set of cognitive devices? Are we to replace the historically relative nature–culture dualist category with the more general distinction between the wild and the socialised? Do non-western cultures offer alternative models for rethinking universality and the issue of moral attitudes towards non-humans? Will the blurring of the nature–culture opposition in certain sectors of contemporary science imply a redefinition of traditional western cosmological and ontological categories? And, finally, would the theoretical rejection of the nature–culture dualism merely signify a return to the 'ecological' concepts of the early medieval European world or would it, perhaps, set the stage for a new kind of ecological anthropology? This introduction briefly outlines the themes of the volume, reviews the theoretical frameworks and arguments of the contributors, and defines fields of consensus and areas of disagreement. The discussion is divided into three parts, emphasising the problems posed by the nature–culture dualism, some misguided attempts to respond to these problems, and potential avenues out of the current dilemmas of ecological discourse.

THE NATURE–CULTURE DUALISM

For over forty years the nature–culture dichotomy has been a central dogma in anthropology, providing a series of analytical tools for apparently antithetical research programmes as well as an identity marker for the discipline as a whole. Materialists considered nature as a basic determinant of social action and would import from the natural sciences models of causal explanation which, they hoped, would give sounder foundations and a wider scope to the social sciences. For cultural ecology, sociobiology, and some brands of Marxist anthropology, human behaviour, social institutions and specific cultural features were seen as adaptive responses to, or mere expressions of, basic environmental or genetic constraints. Internal or external nature – defined in the ethnocentric terms of modern scientific language – was the great driving force behind social life. As a result, little attention was paid to how non-western cultures conceptualised their environment and their relation to it, except to evaluate possible convergences or discrepancies between bizarre emic ideas and the etic orthodoxy embodied in the laws of nature.

Structuralist or symbolic anthropology, on the other hand, has used the nature–culture opposition as an analytical device in order to make sense of myths, rituals, systems of classification, food and body symbolism, and many other aspects of social life that imply a conceptual discrimination between sensible qualities, tangible properties and defining attributes. Although the cultural configurations submitted to this type of analysis differed widely from one another, the actual *content* of the concepts of nature and culture used as classificatory indexes always referred implicitly to the ontological domains covered by these notions in western culture. In other words, while each of the two approaches emphasised a particular aspect of the polar opposition – nature shaping culture versus culture imposing meaning on nature – they nevertheless took the dichotomy for granted and shared an identical, universalistic conception of nature.

The epistemological implications entailed by the dualist paradigm are addressed by several contributors to the present volume. A recurring criticism is that the nature–society dichotomy hinders true ecological understanding. Analysing the figure of the 'optimal forager' in human ecology and its relation to 'economic man', Ingold (Chapter 2) shows that whereas economic man is credited with the design of his own strategies of maximisation, foragers are construed as the mere executors of strategies assigned to them by natural selection. The natural domain is characterised by rational choice, while society is reduced to an external normative structure that causes behaviour to deviate from the optimum. Evolutionary ecology has thus created the anti-ecological fiction of a natural being endowed with a set of capacities and dispositions prior to its relation with the environment. Following a similar line of argument, Hornborg (Chapter 3) shows that the present-day opposition between 'dualist' and 'monist' approaches in human ecology echoes the former polarity between formalists and substantivists in economic anthropology. While advocates of dualism stress objectification, conscious choices and decontextualisation, a monist espistemology would emphasise embeddedness, self-regulation and local autonomy. Drawing upon the pioneering work of Roy Rappaport, Hornborg argues that the monist approach is also the only solid premise for a 'contextualist' stance, i.e. one that considers traditional, pre-industrial societies as having something to tell us about how to live sustainably. The dualist paradigm thus prevents a genuine ecological approach to human–environmental relatedness. In Chapter 4, Pálsson suggests that once the ontological separation between nature and society has been posited there is no way out, no escape from the dual 'prison houses' of language and naturalism, whatever the dose of dialectics and interactive language injected into theoretical discourse.

As Descola points out, in Chapter 5, this ontological disjuncture also induces a strange epistemological confusion in the theoretical premises of both materialist and culturalist approaches. Leaving aside the initial comparative ambition of Julian Steward, cultural ecology tends to treat each society as a specific homeostatic device tightly adapted to a specific environment. On the other hand, culturalist perspectives see each society as an original and incommensurate system of imposing meanings on a natural order, the definition and boundaries of which are nevertheless derived from western conceptions of nature. Paradoxically, the purported universality of geographical determinism thus leads to an extreme form of ecological relativism, while self-claimed cultural relativism leaves unquestioned its assumption of a universalistic conception of nature.

The dualist paradigm also prevents an adequate understanding of local forms of ecological knowledge and technical know-how, as these tend to be objectified according to western standards. Making this point, Hviding (Chapter 9) criticises conventional ethnoecology for its incapacity to accommodate alternative 'ethnoepistemologies' and its correlative tendency to reify certain domains of indigenous knowledge so as to make them compatible with western science. These trends, he argues, impede any serious understanding of the role played by certain beliefs and practices – such as 'magic' or ritual – in people's daily engagement with their environment. In a similar vein, Ellen (Chapter 6) questions the close correspondence implied by mainstream contemporary ethnobiology between the Linnaean taxonomic scheme and the structure of folk classifications of plants and animals, noting that the hierarchic conception of nature typified by scientific taxonomy is not one which is readily yielded from his own ethnographic data. Nature as an abstract inventory of things, distinguished by a small number of features, he notes, is more obvious in museums of natural history than in the lived culture of indigenous peoples. As Hviding and Descola also point out, the search for domain-specific universals in the recognition of 'nature's basic plan' (Berlin 1992: 8) impedes taking into serious consideration those entities and phenomena which do not fall within the sphere of the western notion of nature, however important they may be in local conceptions of the environment.

The persistence of the nature–culture distinction in anthropological discourse is all the more surprising as this core dichotomy appears in many respects as the philosophical touchstone of a whole series of typically western binary oppositions which anthropologists have otherwise successfully criticised: mind–body, subject–object, individual–society, etc. Moreover, the nature–culture distinction is challenged by a growing body of evidence from a variety of sources. One kind of evidence relates to studies of biological evolution, comparisons of human and non-human behaviour, and research on the process of hominisation. In the theories of Mendel and Darwin, organisms are presented as both passive and alienated from the environments in which they live, as objects dictated by genes, on the one hand, and selective pressures through a mechanical process of adaptation, on the other. Such models, the theoretical ancestors of a series of neo-Darwinian paradigms, including optimal foraging theory, seem to present substantial theoretical difficulties. For one thing, while the mechanical conception of adaptation was necessary, perhaps, to establish the modern science of biology, it closed other avenues and, thus, has prevented further developments. Indeed, the dominant evolutionary models derived from the so-called 'New Synthesis' of Mendelian and Darwinian theory increasingly contradict the facts of biology; they do not 'stand up under even the most casual survey of our knowledge of development and natural history' (Lewontin 1983: 284). An alternative model emphasises that the organism is empowered to shape its own development, the *subject* of evolutionary forces (see Ho and Fox 1988). Drawing upon such a perspective, some scholars have argued that the relations between organisms and their environments are reciprocal, not one-way. In the process of engaging with the environment, organisms construct their own niches. In other words, the evolving organism is one of the selective pressures acting upon itself; each living being participates in its own making, engaging in cultural or 'proto-cultural' alterations of selective pressures (Odling-Smee 1994: 168). Significantly, the interactive vocabulary of 'co-evolution' and 'niche construction' is emerging in the place of mechanical Newtonian notions of automatic responses to the 'forces' of the alienated environment.

Recent research on the ethology of primates as well as growing evidence on the enormous time-scale entailed by the process of hominisation also tend to invalidate such notions as a clear phylogenetic boundary between nature and culture. Studies of chimpanzees in the wild not only show that non-human primates use and make some of the kinds of stone tools usually believed to be a distinctive feature of *homo faber*; they also indicate that neighbouring bands of chimpanzees elaborate and transmit markedly distinct styles of tools. In the terminology of prehistorians, chimpanzees thus appear to possess different 'traditions' in terms of material culture (Joulian 1994). The complexity of social behaviour among baboons is also well documented (Strum 1987). The fact that an individual may provoke a certain kind of response from another individual in order to influence the behaviour of a third one seems to indicate that baboons are capable of understanding and categorising behaviour in terms of underlying states, not as mere movements of the body. Such an achievement strongly suggests that they have the ability to form meta-representations, i.e. representations of representations, without the help of language. The development of language is probably nothing more than one among many stages in the process of hominisation and, in an evolutionary perspective, it may be seen as a consequence, rather than a cause, of the development of communication made possible by the ability to form meta-representations (Sperber 1994: 61). Culture certainly took a long time to evolve. Did it emerge with the first hominids, some 3 million years ago, or with the first recorded tools, one million years later? Although the first modern humans, *homo sapiens sapiens*, are probably no older than 100,000 years, some form of burials are 150,000 years old and the first hearth is dated 450,000 BC. The very idea that the origin of culture could be dated or ascribed to a single stage in the hominisation process thus appears utterly unrealistic.

A related shift in perspective with respect to the nature–culture dualism has been taking place in ethnographic studies of enskilment and expertise. According to traditional theories of learning, the novice individual gradually becomes a competent person by inter-nalising a cultural code or a superorganic script (Pálsson 1994). The person, in other words, is seen as an alienated container that progressively absorbs increasing amounts of information from the social environment. Recent studies indicate, however, that the radical opposition of person vs. environment and individual vs. society prohibits an adequate understanding of the contextual nature of the learning process. Assuming a constitutive model of the individual, introducing agency and dialogue into the process of learning, Lave (1993) and some others have shown how learning is situated in communities of practice. Such a perspective suggests a radical break with the Cartesian tradition. The proper focus of research is no longer the passive autonomous individual but the whole person acting within a particular context (Ingold and Rival, both in this volume). Anthropological fieldwork is one branch of learning which is currently being recast along those lines. While the experience of fieldwork does involve highly 'personal' moments, it is not simply a solitary enterprise, the monologic reflection of an independent observer. Ethnography is a dialogic product involving colleagues, spouses, friends, and neighbours – the collective result of a 'long conversation' (Gudeman and Rivera 1995).

Modernist critics may argue that the current dissatisfaction with the theoretical dualisms of the past is simply yet another post-modernist fad and that the deconstruction of the nature–society dichotomy has more to do with competition on the academic labour market and trendy rhetorics than with solid evidence and reliable observations of the real world. This kind of criticism is implied in Worster's remark (1990:18) concerning the current popularity of chaos theory; there are 'striking parallels', he argues, between chaos theory in science and post-modern thought. Ethnographic discourse, however, invites a rather different argument. For many anthropologists – including some contributors to this volume – the shift from a dualist to a monist perspective appears to have been triggered by fieldwork among peoples for whom the nature–society dichotomy was utterly meaningless. This is the case, for instance, of the Achuar Jivaro of the Upper Amazon who, according to Descola (1994), consider most plants and animals as persons, living in societies of their own, entering into relations with humans according to strict rules of social behaviour: game animals are treated as affines by men, while cultivated plants are treated as kin by women. A similar situation prevails among the Makuna, another people of the Upper Amazon; for them humankind represents a particular form of life, participating in a wider community of living beings regulated by a single and totalising set of rules of conduct (Århem, this volume; see also Rival, this volume).

Cosmologies such as these are not restricted to native peoples of Amazonia, for other contributions to this volume present remarkably similar pictures. Howell, for instance (Chapter 7), states that the Chewong of the Malay rainforest do not set humans apart from other beings; plants, animals, and spirits are said to be endowed with consciousness, i.e. language, reason, intellect and a moral code. Ontological distinctions between different classes of beings are all the more difficult to establish among the Chewong, as humans and many non-humans are reputedly able to change their appearance at will, so that their real identity is almost impossible to ascertain at first sight. Similarly, Hviding argues that the native inhabitants of the Marovo Lagoon in the Solomon Islands do not see organisms and non-living components of their environment as constituting a distinct realm of nature separated from human society. He shows that the categories they use to describe their environment function as analogic codes rather than binary oppositions, and that these categories are strongly dependent upon the ways in which people see themselves to be engaging with components of their ecosystem. Drawing on his material on the Nuaulu of Seram, Ellen is cautious not to deconstruct completely the notion of nature, arguing that, among this people of Eastern Indonesia, a conceptual space can be construed which presents several dimensions commensurate with what we, in the West, recognise as nature. He strongly emphasises, however, that these dimensions are highly contextual, variable and contingent and that in many other cases the ethnographic data resist the imposition of our own nature–culture dualism.

Not only does the nature–culture dichotomy appear inadequate when trying to make sense of non-western realities, there is also a growing awareness that this type of dualism does not properly account for the actual practice of modern science. As Latour (1994) argues, the reification of nature and society as antithetical ontological domains results from a process of epistemological purification which disguises the fact that modern science has never been able in practice to meet the standards of the dualist paradigm. Since at least the beginnings of modern physics, science has constantly produced hybrid artefacts and phenomena in which material effects and social conventions have been inextricably mixed. Awareness of the artificiality of the dualist paradigm has, of course, been encouraged by alertness to the increasing artificiality of the scientific process itself. Nothnagel argues (in Chapter 14 of this volume), advocating a 'symmetric anthropology' (using data obtained during ethnographic fieldwork at the CERN conglomerate of laboratories in Geneva), that high-tech science reproduces nature; science does not deal with 'naturally occurring' phenomena, but produces its own facts and evidence through the mediation of highly complex technical apparatus and mathematical models.

This point, which was already clear in the physics of elementary particles (see Bachelard 1965), has now reached a wider public as the development of biotechnologies triggers a growing concern with the environmental, philosophical, and ethical consequences of mass-produced new forms of life in 'non-natural' ways. While technology and social science, Richards and Ruivenkamp argue (Chapter 15 of this volume), are often drawn up in an oppositional relationship, such conceptual polarisation is hard to sustain when attention is paid to the generation of technology as a social process. Also, the new techniques of human reproduction (Strathern 1992), transgenic manipulations on animals, and research on xenotransplantation (Papagaroufali, Chapter 13, this volume) tend to obfuscate long-established boundaries between humans and non-humans and alter social representations of kinship ties and of the construction and the deconstruction of the person. Such techniques also further dispel anthropocentric prejudice, as the units of reference are no longer whole individuals but genetic codes and fragmented body parts. Similarly, the research on transgenic crop types and modified organic molecules has led to the fear that the release of genetically-transformed organisms in the environment may greatly increase the risks of biohazards (Richards and Ruivenkamp, this volume). Although biotechnologies, in their crudest forms, predate the domestication of plants and animals, the possibilities opened by the new techniques of genetic engineering have highlighted the fact that nature is not only increasingly becoming an artefact produced by society (Rabinow 1992, Descola, Chapter 5, this volume) but an artefact submitted to the laws of the market. Social scientists are now exploring the 'uneasy case' (Munzer 1994) against recognising property rights in human organs, tissues, fluids, cells, and genetic material. For some, such commoditisation is inhuman and degrading, an offence against personhood and dignity, whereas for others it represents a humanitarian effort, increasing the supply of body parts (Zelizer 1992).

Radical post-modernists are likely to object to some of the arguments presented above on the grounds that the notions of 'fact', 'evidence', and 'empirical verification' are modernist constructs, relics of the Enlightenment and European history. There is, indeed, no such thing as final truth; paradigms and *épistémès* are inevitably social constructs, the products of a particular time and place. Nevertheless, some constructs are less adequate than others for understanding the world, and when they fail to illuminate and are shown to be contrary to experience they should be revised or abandoned.

MISGUIDED ATTEMPTS

Some may argue that the claim about the absence in many societies of any concept corresponding to the western idea of nature is merely a question of semantics and that alternate notions, such as 'wildness', would be more universal and less ethnocentric. It is true that many cultures attribute, explicitly or implicitly, the quality of wilderness to certain portions of their environment, thus identifying a particular space beyond the direct control of humans (Oelschlaeger 1991). Ellen suggests that a cognitive dimension of all emic models of nature could be the spatial definition of the realm outside the immediate living area of humans. He also points out, however, that, for the Nuaulu, the distinction between wild and socialised is highly dependent on context: sometimes *wesie* (uncut primary forest) is non-human, sometimes it is the people; sometimes it is male, sometimes female; sometimes it is portrayed as antagonistic, sometimes as life-nurturing. Hviding makes a similar point when he argues that although some concepts in Marovo may conform to a 'wild–tame' dimension, they do not operate within a binary framework.

Even in cultures which have an explicit concept of wilderness, the distinction between wild and non-wild is not necessarily clear-cut. Analysing the effects wrought by the post-war transformation of Japanese mountain forests into timber plantations, Knight shows that it mixed up an already ambiguous separation between 'wild' and 'domesticated'. While the old forest was considered by mountain villagers as an embodiment of natural order, beautiful and sacred because of its wilderness, the new forest has become a space of radical disorder. Though technically a space of domestication, this forsaken industrial forest retains the wild attributes of the natural forest it replaced, although these attributes have now become wholly negative as the forest has been stripped of its moral values and desocialised. Such a shift, Knight argues (Chapter 12), reflects the fact that, in certain cases, 'wild' environments may be more satisfactorily controlled, socially, technologically and ideologically, than domesticated ones. In a similar way, Hell (Chapter 11) stresses the fundamental ambivalence of the category of the wild as expressed in the values attached to forest hunting in contemporary north-west Europe. In this region, the nature–culture opposition is mediated by an ambivalent attitude oscillating between, on the one hand, an initially positive hunting compulsion defining gender status and male hierarchy and, on the other hand, the ever-present danger of the hunter becoming wild, notably through excessive contact with the 'black blood' of game. As wilderness is both in the forest and within oneself, positively-valued hunting involves the ability to control this ambiguous coexistence of nature and culture. In all these cases, then, it appears that the notion of wilderness fluctuates according to context; it can hardly qualify as a substitute for the ontological concept of nature as it is used in the dualist paradigm.

One response to the criticism of the modernist project and the current division of labour between the natural and the social sciences is to exchange concepts and perspectives across the nature–society divide, emphasising the fundamental similarities of the natural and the social domain. Thus, some of the natural sciences have borrowed the concepts of community and society from social scientists. Likewise, some branches of anthropology have adopted the biological concepts of natural selection and genetic fitness. Richerson, for example, has suggested that 'a theory of human ecology can be readily developed from existing similarities between the theoretical constructs of social and biological sciences and that this approach is very promising' (1977: 2). Much of such conceptual exchange, however, merely underlines the pitfalls of the dualist project. Each camp continues to practise its own form of reductionism, one part of the nature–culture pair colonising the other. Thus, sociobiology insists upon subsuming culture under the 'natural laws' of Darwinian selection.

In the extreme constructivist perspective, which subsumes the environment under the symbolism of tradition and culture, the environment has no active role at all. In anthropology, the frequent reference to culture – the supposedly unique human capacity to store memories, to learn, and to communicate – seems only to reinforce the dualist structures one would like to transcend. To some extent, the constructivist position echoes that of medieval European scholars who saw their task primarily as one of reading the 'book' of nature. For modern textualists, however, the environment is not simply a script in a metaphoric sense: beyond cultural interpretation there is only triviality, if not empty space (see Pálsson 1995). Some of the chief architects of the textualist school converted rather suddenly from environmental determinism and cultural ecology, moving from one extreme to another. Thus, the year before he published his influential textualist treatise *The Interpretation of Cultures* (1973), Geertz wrote an article on irrigation systems that indicates a deterministic environmental outlook. Comparing Bali and Morocco, he suggests that the 'radically different ways in which water is handled in the two settings leads to some general insights into the again strikingly different cultures situated in them' (Geertz 1972: 74). To be fair, Geertz objects, here as in later works, to simple forms of geographical determinism, arguing that 'the familiar split between nature and culture which renders the former a stage upon which the latter performs' is only 'an illusion'. Nevertheless, he argues that the environment is an active and central factor in shaping social life and that 'an established society is the end point of such a long history of adaptation to its environment that it has, as it were, made of that environment a dimension of itself' (Geertz 1972: 87–88). While textualism and sociobiology are sensitive to the growing disillusion with the theoretical dualism of nature and society, neither of them provides a feasible theoretical alternative to the modernist project.

Deconstructing the dualist paradigm may appear as just one more example of the healthy self-criticism which now permeates anthropological theory. After all, burning conceptual fetishes has long been a favourite pastime of anthropologists and very few domains have escaped this iconoclastic trend. If such analytical categories as economics, totemism, kinship, politics, individualism, or even society, have been characterised as ethnocentric constructs, why should it be any different with the disjuncture between nature and society? The answer is that this dichotomy is not just another analytical category belonging to the intellectual tool-kit of the social sciences; it is the key foundation of modernist epistemology. Going beyond dualism opens up an entirely different intellectual landscape, one in which states and substances are replaced by processes and relations; the main question is not any more how to objectify closed systems, but how to account for the very diversity of the processes of objectification.

One may wonder, then, why some anthropologists bother with studies of human–environmental relations at all if they are so disillusioned with conventional ecological anthropology? If nature has become a meaningless category and environmental determinism a thing of the past, how can the understanding of the interactions between humans and other living and non-living components of their surroundings still be a worthwhile pursuit? A first answer is that this topic is now in the forefront of the public agenda, as the place of the environment in human affairs has become a major political and ethical concern of peoples and governments throughout most of the industrialised world. Anthropologists are able to fulfil their roles as citizens and scholars by using their competence to address a series of debated environmental issues: the mechanisms of a sustainable mode of livelihood in non-industrial societies, the scope and status of traditional knowledge and techniques of resource mangement, the shifting taxonomic boundaries entailed by new reproductive technologies, the ideological foundations of conservationist movements, and the commoditisation of many components of the biosphere. Indeed, some of the reasons why anthropologists are revisiting environmental issues have to do with ongoing changes in the nature–society relationship. Not only does modern biotechnology present humans with a 'nature' very different from that experienced by earlier generations (Richards and Ruivenkamp, this volume), but the ongoing process of globalisation, the exponential intensification of worldwide social relations, also has profound effects (Lash and Urry 1994: 294). As the degradation of the environment has escalated with technological advances and expanding economic production, concern for the natural environment has drifted outside the scope of the nation-state. The issue of environmental responsibility, the ethics and politics of nature, refuses to respect any cultural boundaries; witness the recent growth in environmentalist movements on the international scene and the recurring tension between western science and local epistemologies. Nature is no longer a local affair; the village green is nothing less than the entire globe.

In spite of (perhaps *because of*) globalisation, the privatisation and pricing of environmental 'goods' has accelerated; with the expanding rhetoric of consumerism, nature becomes a market-place. A fundamental transformation has been taking place in many societies as a result of the rapid extension of market approaches to natural resources (fishing stocks, forests, etc.) and organic products (including genetic material and body parts) – in response to ideological commitments, technological developments as well as economic and ecological problems. Given the significance of the market and the fascination with economic man in western political economy and environmental discourse (Kopytoff 1986, Friedland and Robertson 1990, Dilley 1992), anthropological studies of the concepts and practices of environmental economics and the commoditisation of the natural environment present an important field of research. Anthropological knowledge and expertise are crucial for spelling out the metaphysics, ethnocentrism, and drawbacks of some of the key concepts frequently applied to the 'economy', including those of the 'market', 'efficiency', and 'production'. Also, the similarities and differences in moral evaluation of commoditisation pose an intriguing theoretical and comparative problem.

Another reason for this continued interest in ecological issues has to do with epistemology. Exploring new avenues does not mean being oblivious of past achievements. The attention paid to the relationship between humans and their environment by such diverse currents of social theory as Marxism, structuralism, phenomenology, cultural ecology and cognitive anthropology points to a basic premise: human history is the continuous product of diverse modes of human–

environmental relations. Admitting such a premise does not mean returning to the pitfalls of dualism and geographical or technical determinism. On the contrary, it implies taking seriously the evidence offered by many societies where the realm of social relations encompasses a wider domain than the mere society of humans. Huaorani hunters know that the animals they hunt communicate, learn, and modify their ways of life in response to humans; humans and animals are social beings mutually engaged in each other's world, and that explains, Rival suggests (Chapter 8, this volume), the correspondence between the ways in which people treat each other and how they treat animals. In such 'societies of nature' (Descola 1992), plants, animals and other entities belong to a sociocosmic community, subjected to the same rules as humans; any account of their social life must perforce include these components of the environment which are perceived as forming part of the social domain. Anthropology can no longer restrict itself to the conventional social analysis of its beginnings; it must rethink its domains and its tools to embrace not only the world of *anthropos*, but also that part of the world with which humans interact.

POTENTIAL AVENUES

It is realistic to assume that the environment matters and that to understand both humanity and the rest of the natural world anthropology, ecology and biology need new kinds of models, perspectives, and metaphors. Such a realisation may necessitate a fundamentally revised division of academic labour; in particular, the removal of the disciplinary boundaries between the natural and the social sciences. We may well have to abandon the current separation of physical and biological anthropology, on the one hand, and, on the other, cultural and social anthropology, giving new life to the old philosophical, anthropological project which focused on the unity of the human being (Ingold 1990, and this volume). The different fields of academic scholarship, it seems, have more in common than disciplinary sectarians normally like to admit. Significantly, similar moralities and metaphors are applied to rather different theoretical contexts (Nothnagel and Pálsson, both in this volume); discourses on nature, ethnography, and cultural translation, for instance, employ similar kinds of imagery, notably the metaphors of hunting and personal relatedness and the theatrical language of irony, tragedy, comedy, and romance.

A reshuffling of the academic cards seems already under way. One of the relevant signs is represented by the widespread current interest in the human body, beyond the narrow confines of physical anthropology. Despite its suppression in modernist social scientific discourse, the body has emerged as a major theoretical theme in social anthropology. This need not be that surprising since the body is a popular topic in many ethnographic contexts (Lock 1993). Clearly, the body does not easily allow for a fixed division of academic labour, nor does it admit a firm boundary between nature and culture. Rival shows (this volume) how, in the process of hunting and gathering, the Huaorani cease to be extraneous bodies, alien to the forest world; they learn to perceive the environment as other animals do, becoming 'dwellers' deeply involved in a conversation with plants and animals (see also Howell, this volume). Another sign of the fragility of the boundary between the natural and the social sciences is the growing interest in landscape in a variety of studies, including anthropology. While previously place and space (classic concerns in geography and the natural sciences) were relegated to a 'black box' in the social sciences (see Hirsch 1995: 1), now they are the focus of extensive comparative research. Again, theoretical developments resonate with much ethnography. A strong attachment to place, 'topophilia' (see Thompson 1990: 113), seems to be quite a common feature of human societies – frequently coloured, in state societies, by ethnicity, nationalism, and related sensibilities. Globalisation does not erase such 'local' concerns, it redefines them.

The recognition that nature is a social construct and that conceptualisations of the environment are the products of ever-changing historical contexts and cultural specificities, presents a difficult challenge to anthropological inquiry. Are we to restrict ourselves to endless ethnographic accounts of local 'cosmologies' or must we look for general trends or patterns that would enable us to replace different emic conceptions of nature within a unified analytical framework? And, in the latter option, on what theoretical foundations would a unified framework rest? To these crucial questions, the contributors to the present volume provide conflicting answers. Some take a decidedly relativist position, emphasising the situatedness of knowledge and doubting that implicit and inextricable local systems of meanings can ever be couched adequately into a meta-discourse. Hornborg thus sees the task of ecological anthropology as understanding the socio-cultural contexts which allow ecologically sensitive knowledge systems to persist and evolve. Such local calibrations, he argues, are at their most efficient when they are not subjected to attempts at encompassment by totalising frameworks. A relativist stance also appears in several papers influenced by textualist approaches. Hell, for example, draws upon Geertz's work to define the culture of hunting in Europe as a 'text', while Papagaroufali characterises representations of reality produced in the West by both scientists and laymen as 'stories', thus stressing the narrative and morality-based nature of these truth claims.

A few contributors advocate an intermediary position: while challenging universalistic models, they are also careful not to close the door on the possibility of meaningful comparisons. Howell thus maintains that her position is not an extreme version of cultural relativism in that she accepts that sociality and intersubjectivity are innate predispositions of humankind. The task of anthropologists, she argues, is first to interpret local cultural systems and then to address the basis for the differentiation of modes of socialities. Similarly, Hviding criticises the privilege awarded to western rationalist presuppositions in the process of translating cultures, advocating instead a meta-language that would be based on the comparison of different 'ethnoepistemologies', including our own. The last step is taken by some authors who, feeling uneasy with the conceptual fragmentation induced by relativist perspectives, venture to formulate alternate analytical models as substitutes for the current dualist paradigm. Employing the oppositions of continuity and discontinuity, on the one hand, and, on the other, of domination and protection, Pálsson thus distinguishes between three kinds of human–environmental relations – orientalism, paternalism, and communalism – each of which would represent a particular stance with respect to 'environmental' issues. In the case of both environmental orientalism and paternalism, humans are masters of nature, he argues, but whereas the former 'exploits' the latter 'protects'. Communalism differs from both in that it involves the rejection of any radical distinction between nature and society and between science and practical knowledge. To reject the notion of mastery and to allow for chaos and contingency in human–environmental relations does not mean that human efforts at 'managing' their lives are insignificant or beside the point; rather it suggests less arrogant policies and greater sensitivity to practical knowledge and ethnography, trying to flow with the current rather than establish complete control.

Ellen also puts forward the hypothesis that the issue of the status of nature can be approached by identifying a minimum number of underlying assumptions upon which pragmatic schemata and symbolic representations are built. Behind all cultural models of nature, he argues, is a combination of three cognitive imperatives: the inductive construction of nature, in terms of the 'things' which people include within it and the characteristics assigned to these 'things'; the spatial recognition of a realm outside the human domain; and the metaphoric compulsion to understand phenomena by their essence. Depending on the contexts of 'prehension' which give rise to particular classifications, designations and representations, the relative weight of each of these axes and their internal asymmetries varies in each conceptualisation of nature and accounts for their specificities. Descola likewise advocates a transformational model to account for the largely implicit schemes of praxis through which each society objectifies specific types of relations with its environment. Each local variation, he argues, results from a particular combination of three basic dimensions of social life: modes of identification or the process by which ontological boundaries are created and objectified in cosmological systems such as animism, totemism or naturalism; modes of interaction which organise the relations between and within the spheres of humans and non-humans according to such principles as reciprocity, predation or protection; and modes of classification (basically the metaphoric scheme and the metonymic scheme) through which the elementary components of the world are represented as socially recognised categories.

While acknowledging the difficulty of translating into general propositions the complexity and intricacy of their own experience of a particular society, most of the contributors to this volume nevertheless show a willingness to go beyond the mere description of local systems of human–environmental relations. Paradoxically, a renewed faith in the comparative project may have emerged from the very richness of the ethnographic experience itself, i.e. from the shared recognition that certain patterns, styles of practice, and sets of values described by fellow anthropologists in different parts of the world are compatible with one's ethnographic knowledge of a particular society. Such a recognition was probably fuelled by far-reaching changes in the style of ethnographic narrative. Forsaking the universalistic categories which structured former monographies, anthropologists now tend to be both more personal and more imaginative in choosing the devices they use to convey their interpretation of a society. Previously unsuspected convergences and affinities thus emerge from what may have seemed at first sight like a chaos of unconnected ethnographic accounts. In other words, ethnography makes one focus on the particular while a lot of ethnographic particulars kindle anew the interest in comparison.

While the contributors to the present volume adopt a variety of perspectives, approaches, and theoretical positions, there is an overall emerging consensus on many important issues. Most importantly, the authors share a concern with the nature–society interface and the theoretical problems it necessarily invites. Anthropology is broad in scope, drawing upon both the natural and the social sciences, but, as we have seen, it is continually troubled with a fundamental contradiction; 'the first part of the story of the human species is couched in evolutionary and environmental terms, the second denies environment a meaningful role in human history' (Crumley 1994: 2). Rethinking the nature–society interface means rethinking ecological anthropology, in particular its notion of the relation between person and environment. The deeply entrenched biological and anthropological traditions which insist upon separating the two are increasingly being challenged on both empirical and theoretical grounds. Bateson identified some of the problems using the example of a blind person with a stick: 'Where do *I* start? Is my mental system bounded at the handle of the stick? Is it bounded by my skin? Does it start halfway up the stick? But these are nonsense questions' (Bateson 1972: 459). Indeed, they are. The point is not simply to determine the exact location of the boundaries of person, technology, and environment, but rather to draw attention to fields of significance, 'mental systems' in Bateson's terminology. Etymologically, the concept of the 'environment' refers to that which surrounds and, therefore, strictly speaking, an environment incorporates just about everything, except that which is surrounded (Cooper 1992). Given the ecological perspective developed by James Gibson, however, it is important to assume some phenomenological notion of *intentional* environment; the 'affordances' of the environment vary from case to case but depending upon its 'meaning' or the way in which it is perceived (see Ingold 1992, Carello 1993). This is not to suggest *multiple* environments in the interpretivist sense; nature is not a series of 'books' nor is its perception (or 'reading') necessarily informed by intermediate cultural 'texts'. Rather, person and environment embrace an irreducible system; the person is part of the environment and, likewise, the environment is part of the person.

Many of the contributors to the present volume argue for an ecological anthropology along these lines. A similar perspective was developed by Bakhtin with reference to language. It was important, he argued, to go beyond the positivist notions of linguistics which depicted the speaker as a passive partner in speech communication. Bakhtin suggested the approach of 'translinguistics', an approach that not only offered a powerful critique of the abstract objectivism of autonomous linguistics but also sought to readdress the embedded nature of language. For him, language was 'social throughout its entire range and in each and every of its factors, from the sound image to the furthest reaches of abstract meaning' (Bakhtin 1981: 259). Rejecting the radical separation of the individual and social, Bakhtin argued that every word in language is the cumulative result of the prior experiences of the speakers and their interactions with the speech community. Perhaps we should draw upon Bakhtin's perspective and speak of 'transecology', to underline the notions of dwelling and embeddedness with respect to the human household, the social nature of the human *oikos*.

REFERENCES

Attfield, R. and Belsey, A. (eds) (1994) *Philosophy and the Natural Environment*, Cambridge: Cambridge University Press.

Bachelard, G. (1965) *L'activité Rationaliste de la Physique Contemporaine*, Paris: Presses Universitaires de France.

Bakhtin, M. (1981) *The Dialogic Imagination: Four Essays by M. M. Bakhtin*, M. Holquist (ed.) trans. C. Emerson and M. Holquist, Austin: University of Texas Press.

Bateson, G. (1972) *Steps to an Ecology of Mind*, Frogmore: Paladin.

Berlin, B. (1992) *Ethnobiological Classification: Principles of Categorization of Plants and Animals in Traditional Societies*, Princeton: Princeton University Press.

Carello, C. (1993) 'Realism and Ecological Units of Analysis', in D. Steiner and M. Nauser (eds) *Human Ecology: Fragments of Anti-fragmentary Views of the World*, London: Routledge.

Cooper, D. E. (1992) 'The Idea of Environment', in D. E. Cooper and J. A. Palmer (eds) *The Environment in Question: Ethics and Global Issues*, London: Routledge.

Croll, E. and Parkin, D. (eds) (1992) *Bush Base–Forest Farm: Culture, Environment and Development*, London: Routledge.

Crumley, L. (ed.) (1994) *Historical Ecology: Cultural Knowledge and Changing Landscapes*, Santa Fe: School of American Research Press.

Descola, P. (1992) 'Societies of Nature and the Nature of Society', in A. Kuper (ed.) *Conceptualizing Society*, London and New York: Routledge.

——(1994) *In the Society of Nature: A Native Ecology in Amazonia*, Cambridge: Cambridge University Press.

Dickens, P. (1992) *Society and Nature: Towards a Green Social Theory*, New York: Harvester Wheatsheaf.

Dilley, R. (ed.) (1992) *Contesting Markets: Analyses of Ideology, Discourse and Practice*, Edinburgh: Edinburgh University Press.

Friedland, R. and Robertson, A. F. (1990) 'Beyond the Marketplace', in R. Friedland and A. F. Robertson (eds) *Beyond the Marketplace: Rethinking Economy and Society*, New York: Aldine de Gruyter.

Geertz, C. (1972) 'The Wet and the Dry: Traditional Irrigation in Bali and Morocco', *Human Ecology* 1, 1: 73–89.

—— (1973) *The Interpretation of Cultures*, London: Hutchinson.

Gudeman, S. and Rivera, A. (1995) 'From Car to House' (Del Coche a la Casa), *American Anthropologist* 97, 2: 242–50.

Hirsch, E. (1995) 'Introduction: Landscape: Between Place and Space', in E. Hirsch and M. O'Hanlon (eds) *The Anthropology of Landscape: Perspectives on Place and Space*, Oxford: Clarendon Press.

Ho, M.-W. and Fox, S. W. (1988) *Evolutionary Processes and Metaphors*, Chichester: John Wiley & Sons.

Ingold, T. (1990) 'An Anthropologist Looks at Biology', *Man* (NS) 25, 2: 208–29.

—— (1992) 'Culture and the Perception of the Environment', in E. Croll and D. Parkin (eds) *Bush Base–Forest Farm: Culture, Environment and Development*, London: Routledge.

Joulian, F. (1994) 'Peut-on Parler d'un Système Technique Chimpanzé: Primatologie et Archéologie Comparées', in B. Latour and P. Lemonnier (eds) *De la prehistoire aux missiles ballistiques: l'intelligence sociale des techniques*, Paris: La Découverte.

Kopytoff, I. (1986) 'The Cultural Biography of Things: Commoditization as Process', in A. Appadurai (ed.) *The Social Life of Things*, Cambridge: Cambridge University Press.

Lash, S. and Urry, J. (1994) *Economies of Signs and Space*, London: Sage Publishers.

Latour, B. (1994) *We Have Never Been Modern*, Cambridge, Mass.: Harvard University Press.

Lave, J. (1993) 'The Practice of Learning', in S. Chaiklin and J. Lave (eds) *Understanding Practice: Perspectives on Activity and Context*, Cambridge: Cambridge University Press.

Lewontin, R.C. (1983) 'Gene, Organism and Environment', in D. S. Bendall (ed.) *Evolution From Molecules to Men*, Cambridge: Cambridge University Press.

Lock, M. (1993) 'Cultivating the Body: Anthropology and Epistemologies of Bodily Practice and Knowledge', *Annual Reviews of Anthropology* 22: 133–55.

McCay, B. M. and Acheson, J. M. (eds) (1987) *The Question of the Commons: The Culture and Ecology of Communal Resources*, Tucson: University of Arizona Press.

Munzer, S. R. (1994) 'An Uneasy Case against Property Rights in Body Parts', in E. F. Paul, F. D. Miller, Jr and J. Paul (eds) *Property Rights*, Cambridge: Cambridge University Press.

Odling-Smee, F. J. (1994) 'Niche Construction, Evolution and Culture', in T. Ingold (ed.) *Encyclopedia of Anthropology*, London: Routledge.

Oelschlaeger, M. (1991) *The Idea of Wilderness: From Prehistory to the Age of Ecology*, New Haven and London: Yale University Press.

Pálsson, G. (1994) 'Enskilment at Sea', *Man* (NS) 29, 4: 901–27.

——(1995) *The Textual Life of Savants: Ethnography, Iceland, and the Linguistic Turn*, Chw, CES: Harwood Academic Publishers.

Rabinow, P. (1992) 'Studies in the Anthropology of Reason', *Anthropology Today* 8, 5 (October): 7–10.

Rappaport, R. A. (1968) *Pigs for the Ancestors: Ritual in the Ecology of a New Guinea People*, New Haven: Yale University Press.

Richerson, P. J. (1977) 'Ecology and Human Ecology: A Comparison of Theories in the Biological and Social Sciences', *Human Ecology* 4: 1–26.

Simmons, I. G. (1993) *Environmental History: A Concise Introduction*, Oxford: Blackwell.

Sperber, D. (1994) 'The Modularity of Thought and the Epidemiology of Representations', in L. A. Hirshfeld and S. A. Gelman (eds) *Mapping the Mind: Domain Specificity in Cognition and Culture*, Cambridge: Cambridge University Press.

Strathern, M. (1992) *Reproducing the Future: Anthropology, Kinship and the New Reproductive Technologies*, Manchester: Manchester University Press.

Strum, S. (1987) *Almost Human: A Journey into the World of Baboons*, New York: Random House.

Thompson, S. (1990) 'Metaphors the Chinese Age By', in S. Thompson (ed.) *Anthropology and the Riddle of the Sphinx: Paradoxes of Change in the Life Course*, London: Routledge.

Worster, D. (1990) 'The Ecology of Order and Chaos', *Environmental History Review* 14: 11–18.

Zelizer, V. A. (1992) 'Human Values and the Market', in M. Granovetter and R. Swedberg (eds) *The Sociology of Economic Life*, Boulder: Westview Press.

Part I

Contested domains and boundaries

Chapter 2

The optimal forager and economic man

Tim Ingold

INTRODUCTION

Enlightenment thought has proclaimed the triumph of human reason over a recalcitrant nature. As a child of the Enlightenment, neoclassical economics developed as a science of human decision-making and its aggregate consequences, based on the premise that every individual acts in the pursuit of rational self-interest. Whether the postulates of microeconomic theory are applicable to humanity at large, or only to those societies characterised as 'western', has been much debated: classic anthropological statements include those of Malinowski – who dismissed as 'preposterous' the assumption that 'man, and especially man on a low level of culture, should be actuated by pure economic motives of enlightened self-interest' (Malinowski 1922: 60); and Firth – who argued, to the contrary, that 'in some of the most primitive societies known ... there is the keenest discussion of alternatives in any proposal for the use of resources, of the relative economic advantages of exchange with one party as against another, and the closest scrutiny of the quality of goods which change hands ... and taking a profit thereby' (Firth 1964: 22, see Schneider 1974: 11–12).

My concern here is not to revisit this old debate. Instead, I want to address the paradox presented by the emergence of an approach within contemporary anthropology which seeks to understand the behaviour of so-called primitive people – or more specifically, hunters and gatherers – not through a direct extension of the principles of formal economics, but through a rather more indirect route. This is to extend to human beings principles already applied in analysing the behaviour of non-human animals, principles that are nevertheless closely modelled on – even to the extent of being identified with – those of economics. The approach in question is known to its practitioners as 'human evolutionary ecology', and it is currently one of the most vigorous areas of research in ecological anthropology.

I aim to show that evolutionary ecology is the precise inverse of microeconomics, just as natural selection is the mirror-image of rational choice. As such, it reproduces in an inverted form the dichotomy between reason and nature that lies at the heart of post-Enlightenment science. But in seeking to account for behaviour in terms of pre-specified and heritable properties of discrete individuals, evolutionary ecology is prevented – despite its claims to the contrary – from developing a truly *ecological* perspective. By this I do not simply mean a perspective that would incorporate external environmental variables as part of the explanation for behaviour. An approach that is genuinely ecological, in my view, is one that would ground human intention and action within the context of an ongoing and mutually constitutive engagement between people and their environments. Yet such an approach, I argue, calls into question the very foundations of the neo-Darwinian explanatory paradigm.

Suppose you were an advocate of economic formalism in anthropology, and that you were concerned to explain why a particular group of hunters and gatherers should choose to concentrate their efforts on harvesting a certain mix of plant and animal resources. By attaching a utility value to each unit of resource, measured in terms of the satisfaction it yields, you would calculate an optimal strategy of resource procurement, that would yield the highest overall utility relative to time and energy expended. You would then compare this strategy with what the people actually do and, finding a nice fit, you would declare that your model has passed the test of empirical confirmation. Anticipating the 'so what?' challenge of the sceptic, you would conclude that what this proves is that hunters and gatherers are just as capable of making informed choices in their own best interests as anyone else. Reason, you would point out, is a faculty common to all humans, not just 'modern western' or 'civilised' ones, and it is ethnocentric to imagine that while *we* decide what to do in any given situation on the basis of rational deliberation, *they* are bound in their actions by blind conformity to the received wisdom of cultural convention.

What, then, of non-human animals? They, too, seem to come out with strategies of resource procurement which would look eminently rational, had they worked these strategies out for themselves. But of course, you say, they have not. The animals have had their strategies worked out for them in advance, by the evolutionary force of natural selection. The logic of natural selection is simply as follows:

individuals with more efficient resource procurement or foraging strategies will have a reproductive advantage over individuals with less efficient strategies, and since these strategies – or more precisely, the rules or programmes for generating them – are encoded in the materials of heredity, the more efficient strategies will automatically tend to become more firmly established in each generation as their carriers bear proportionally more offspring. Now the point of departure for human evolutionary ecology is that the foraging behaviour of human hunter-gatherers, just like that of their non-human counterparts, can be understood as the application, in specific environmental contexts, of decision rules or 'cognitive algorithms' that have been shaped up through a Darwinian process of variation under natural selection. From this premise has been derived a body of theory, known in the trade as 'optimal foraging theory', consisting of formal models which predict how, under given external conditions, a forager should behave, assuming that the overriding objective is to maximise the balance between the energy intake from harvested resources and the energy costs of procurement.

Is the human hunter-gatherer, then, a version of economic man or a species of optimal forager? On the face of it these two figures – both of them, of course, ideal constructs of the analytic imagination – appear diametrically opposed, and their conflation in the archetypal figure of the 'primitive' hunter-gatherer seems to reflect the ambivalent status of this figure, within the discourse of western science, as transitional between the conditions of nature and humanity (see Figure 2.1). Economic man, surely, exercises his reason in the sphere of social interaction, and in so doing advances in culture or civilisation, against the background of an intrinsically resistant nature. The rationality of the optimal forager, by contrast, is installed at the very heart of nature, while the specifically human domain of society and culture is seen as a source of external normative bias that may cause behaviour to deviate from the optimum. Here, then, is the paradox to which I referred at the outset, of an approach which, while explicitly modelling itself on classical microeconomics, is nevertheless considered applicable to human beings only insofar as their behaviour is in some sense comparable to that of non-human animals. How can we hold, at one and the same time, that the faculty of reason is the distinctive mark of humanity, and that the rationality of human hunter-gatherers, by comparison with that of their non-human counterparts, is compromised by social and cultural constraints? I take this question as my point of departure.

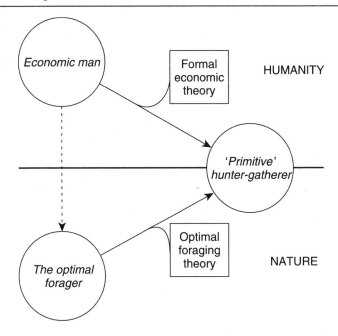

Figure 2.1 The 'primitive' hunter-gatherer conceived as a version of economic man and as a species of optimal forager

CULTURE AND CHOICE

> Hunters-gatherers, or foragers, live in environments characterised by diverse and heterogeneously distributed resources. From the array of potential food species, foraging locations and pathways, the forager can choose combinations which more or less effectively and efficiently procure subsistence. The forager's choices make up a strategy of adjustment to ecological conditions, an adaptive pattern resulting from evolutionary processes and the constraints of situation, time, and chance.
>
> (Winterhalder 1981a: 66)

This lucid statement, by one of the foremost exponents of optimal foraging theory, takes us directly to the core of the problem. It lies in the contradiction between the notions, on the one hand, that the forager's 'strategy of adjustment' is the result of a series of choices about where to go and what to procure, and on the other hand, that as an 'adaptive pattern' it is the product of an evolutionary process. In explicating this contradiction it helps to have an empirical example in mind, and for this purpose I turn briefly to ethnographic material that Winterhalder himself presents, gathered through fieldwork among Cree people of Muskrat Dam Lake in northern Ontario.

The Cree draw for their subsistence on a variety of large and small mammals, waterfowl and fish, distributed rather sparsely and patchily in an environment which consists of a fine-grained mosaic of different types of dominant vegetation. Not only does the abundance of resource species fluctuate markedly and irregularly from year to year, but the vegetational mosaic also changes in response to climatic variations. The result is that the Cree hunter is unlikely ever to encounter the same conditions from one year to the next (Winterhalder 1981a: 80–1). He has, therefore, to work out his tactics as he goes along. One hunting trip described by Winterhalder exemplifies this point very well. In this trip, ostensibly for beaver trapping, he and his Cree companion came across signs of grouse, moose, wolf, hare, beaver, mink, otter and muskrat. At each sign his companion had to make up his mind whether to pursue the animal in question. In the event, the grouse was shot, the moose and wolf were ignored, snares were set for the hare and beaver, and traps for the muskrat and otter. But this hunt, Winterhalder tells us, was an example of an older style of doing things: although the journey from the village to the start of the trail was made by snowmobile, during the hunt itself the companions proceeded on snowshoes. Hunters of the younger generation are making greater use of the snowmobile, not just for getting to the trail but in the course of seeking out animals. The consequent reduction in search times allows them to be far more selective, and to concentrate on taking high-priority species. In the past, the mark of a good hunter was supposed to lie in his ability to handle almost any kind of animal; nowadays, by contrast, younger hunters are said to specialise in hunting just one or two species, and to lack competence in dealing with the others (Winterhalder 1981a: 86–9).

It is clear from this account that hunters are faced with choices, that the choices they make add up to a pattern, and that this pattern changes in response to alterations in the parameters of hunting brought about, for example, by the introduction of new technologies. It is not so clear, however, that the pattern has 'evolved' in the Darwinian sense, or that its emergence has anything to do with the process of natural selection. For the sake of argument let us suppose that in the hunting trip described above, taking account of the expected calorific yield of different resource species and of the energy costs of search and pursuit (or of setting and visiting traps), the hunter's decisions conformed closely to what might be modelled as the optimal strategy for a forager seeking to maximise the net rate of energy gain. And let it also be supposed – rather more problematically – that the households of tactically skilled hunters, being relatively securely provisioned, are also prosperous in terms of the production of healthy offspring: in other words that the hunter's success in the woods is matched by reproductive success at home. There would still be no reason to believe that the successful hunting strategy was the result of an evolutionary process.

It is commonly argued, even by biologists who should know better (e.g. Dunbar 1987), that to show how behaviour of a certain kind has evolved by natural selection, one has only to demonstrate that it contributes positively to the reproductive fitness of those individuals who execute it. This argument is critically incomplete, for it misses out the essential link that closes the loop of Darwinian explanation. Behaviour will only evolve by natural selection if, through its effects on reproduction, it contributes to the representation, in successor generations, of a set of instructions or a 'programme' for generating it. In other words, the behaviour must not only have consequences *for* reproduction but also be a consequence *of* the elements that are reproduced (Ingold 1990: 226 fn.9). So far as non-human animals are concerned, the replicated programme elements are usually assumed to be genes. Whatever the merits of this assumption, once our attention turns to human beings it looks decidedly unrealistic. I know of no recent author who has seriously suggested that the behavioural variability apparent from ethnographic studies of human hunter-gatherers might be attributed to inter-populational genetic differences. Instead it is proposed that the instructions underwriting human foraging behaviour are cultural rather than genetic, encoded in words or other symbolic media rather than the 'language' of DNA. As Winterhalder himself has noted (1981b: 17), in the case of human foragers 'information passed from generation to generation by culture provides much of the strategic framework within which specific choices and options are exercised by individuals and groups'.

Does this enculturation model take us any closer to understanding the behaviour of the Cree hunter in the above example? Although in the account the hunter is described as having made a number of decisions – to shoot this animal, pass up another, lay a trap for a third, and so on – the model would imply that in reality, the scope of his autonomy in decision-making is extremely restricted. He is, after all, merely applying a set of decision rules acquired more or less unselfconsciously from his seniors, and whose prevalence in the society is due not to their perceived efficacy but to the fact that they served his predecessors well, enabling them to bring in the food to support numerous offspring who – following in their fathers' footsteps – reproduced the same strategic steps in their own hunting activities. To put the point in more general terms, if a particular strategy of hunting is inscribed within a cultural tradition, and if that tradition has evolved through a process of natural selection, then all the hunter can do is to carry on in the same way, even if changes in environment or technology have had the effect of wiping out its earlier advantages. This is not to say that behaviour is completely prescribed, for genuine choices may still have to be made. But they are made *within* a received strategic framework, they are not about what framework to adopt.

NEO-DARWINIAN BIOLOGY AND NEO-CLASSICAL MICROECONOMICS

Strangely, however, this view of the human forager as the bearer of evolved cultural propensities that cause behaviour to strain towards the optimum, exists, in the writings of evolutionary ecologists, side by side with a quite different picture. Observing that human behaviour often seems far from optimal, the blame for the discrepancy is placed squarely upon culture itself. Thus Winterhalder explicitly singles out 'cultural goals', situated within systems of belief and meaning, as one of the possible reasons for the disjunction, in the human case, 'between modeled optima and observed behaviors' (1981b: 16). Likewise, Foley (1985: 237) lists, as among the consequences of the human capacity for culture, a number of characteristics that 'may inhibit the achievement of optimality'. Nowhere, however, is the contradiction more blatant than in the recent review of optimal foraging theory in its archaeological and anthropological application to human hunter-gatherers, by Robert L. Bettinger (1991).[1]

Referring back to the classic debate in economic anthropology between the advocates of so-called 'formalism' and 'substantivism', Bettinger reminds us that the terms of the debate have their source in Max Weber's (1947: 184–5) distinction between the formal and substantive aspects of human rationality, the first consisting in the element of quantitative calculation or accounting involved in economic decision-making, the second in the subservience of economic activity to ultimate ends or standards of value of a qualitative nature.

Without denying the salience of the latter in human affairs, Bettinger argues that formal models have the great advantage of providing a 'yardstick of objective economic rationality', against which it is possible to gauge how far actual behaviour is governed by 'rational, self-interested incentives' as opposed to 'cultural norms and ideas' (Bettinger 1991: 106). And this, he maintains, is precisely what the models of optimal foraging theorists enable one to achieve. The ideal typical forager of these models is a creature entirely free from cultural constraint to act out of pure, calculated self-interest; insofar as real human beings are biased by their commitment to 'cultural norms', it is expected that their behaviour will diverge from the optimum.

This puts the Cree hunter in an entirely different light. The received wisdom of his cultural heritage, far from underwriting his ability to come up with an effective strategy, is actually liable to *prevent* him from recognising the best course of action judged in terms of an objective reckoning of costs and benefits. For example, older hunters, strongly committed to the traditional ideal of spreading their effort across a range of species, continue to practise a broad spectrum style of hunting even when the availability of the snowmobile makes it much more profitable to concentrate on a few preferred, high-yield game animals. By contrast, men of the younger generation, whose commitment to traditional cultural values (at least in the eyes of their seniors) is weak, readily opt for a more specialised strategy. It seems perfectly reasonable to suppose that this strategy is a result of the quite conscious and deliberate decision, on the part of these younger men, *not* to imitate the style of their forefathers. But by the same token, it makes no sense at all to regard it as the outcome of a process of variation under natural selection.

One cannot avoid the impression that optimal foraging theorists are trying to have it both ways, taking their cue, as it suits them, either from neo-Darwinian evolutionary biology or from neo-classical microeconomics. Indeed, in Bettinger's view the fact that optimal foraging theory came to anthropology via biology is more or less incidental – 'it might just as easily have been borrowed from economics' (1991: 83). If that were really so, then the theorems of economics should be as applicable to non-human as to human behaviour, and economic man would have his counterpart among the animals. The 'economic muskrat', for example, would place its own self-preservation before the promptings of its genes, and would choose not to visit the traps laid by the Cree hunter. The following passage, however, gives the game away:

> In Darwinian theories... individuals are essential to explanation: their interests cannot be ignored. It is the self-interested individual that must make *real and metaphorical choices* about reproduction and the selective risks associated with different courses of action.
>
> (Bettinger 1991: 152, my emphasis)

Crucially, Bettinger fails to explain what he means by 'metaphorical choices'. We can only surmise that he has in mind the common habit that neo-Darwinian biologists have of speaking *as if* the individual had selected what in fact is built into its *modus operandi* by countless generations of natural selection of which its own constitution is the latest product. The metaphor may have its uses, affording a kind of shorthand, but when reality and metaphor are fused, as they are here, the consequences are disastrous.

Are the Cree hunter's choices real or metaphorical? If they are real, then they have not been 'passed on' as part of any inherited schema, whether genetic or cultural, and appeals to natural selection are irrelevant. If, on the other hand, the hunter's behaviour follows a strategy that has evolved through a process of natural selection, albeit working on culturally rather than genetically transmitted character-istics, then strictly speaking, he exercises no more choice in the matter of where to go or what species to pursue than do non-human creatures whose behaviour is presumed to be under genetic control. 'Why', asks Ernst Mayr (1976: 362), 'did the warbler on my summer place in New Hampshire start its southward migration on the night of the 25th August?' His answer is that the bird has an evolved genetic constitu-tion, shaped up 'through many thousands of generations of natural selection', which induces it to respond in this particular way to a specific conjunction of environmental conditions (a reduction in daylight hours coupled with a sudden drop in temperature). Likewise, the muskrat is drawn compulsively into the hunter's trap. And likewise too, according to this selectionist account, the hunter is predisposed to respond appropriately to signs of the presence of animals, as revealed by their tracks, by pursuing some, laying traps for others, and passing yet others by. He could not have chosen to do other than what he actually does, any more than the muskrat could have chosen not to enter the trap, or the warbler not to migrate. As a product of 'enculturation', the hunter is as stuck with his heritage as are the muskrat and the bird with their respective sets of genes.

In short, to have recourse to neo-Darwinian theory is to show not how individuals design strategies, but how natural selection designs strategies for individuals to follow. Equipped by virtue of its evolutionary past with a programme for generating more or less optimal behaviour, within an appropriate environmental context, the individual is predestined to execute that behaviour; thus its entire life, judged by its reproductive outcome, becomes just one trial in that protracted and ongoing decision process that is natural selection itself. Toulmin (1981) refers to this as a process of *populational* adaptation, by contrast to the *calculative* adaptation that results from rational decision-making. But as he points out, explanations of adaptive behaviour based on rational choice and on natural selection are not incompatible. Indeed it may be argued that the former actually depend on the latter – in other words, that a prerequisite for any theory of calculative adaptation is an account of human nature which must necessarily be couched in populational terms. I present this argument below.

REASON AND NATURE AS AGENTS OF SELECTION

A formal theory of rational choice, as elaborated in classical microeconomics, predicts what people will do, assuming that their deliberate aim is to obtain the greatest benefit from their actions. The relative benefit to be derived from alternative courses of action can, however, only be evaluated in terms of people's own subjective beliefs and preferences. It may, of course, be possible to derive certain 'lower order' beliefs and preferences from 'higher order' ones. But this process of derivation cannot go on indefinitely. Ultimately, if we want to explain where these beliefs and preferences came from in the first place – if, that is, we seek the source of human intentions – then we have to show how they may have emerged through a history of natural selection. Appeal to human intentionality and rational choice, it is argued, reveals only the *proximate* causes of behaviour, while the *ultimate* cause lies in those selective forces that have furnished individuals both with the fundamental motivations underwriting their choices and with the cognitive mechanisms that allow them to be made (Smith and Winterhalder 1992: 41–50). Thus even if strategies are taken to be products of human reasoning, we have still to resort to natural selection to account for the rationality of the strategists.

Does human evolutionary ecology offer such an account? It does not – indeed it *cannot*, so long as it remains committed to its principal tactic of analysing behaviour in terms of its potential reproductive consequences rather than focusing on the effects of differential reproductive success in establishing the psychological mechanisms that give rise to it. As Symons (1992: 148) has put it, evolutionary ecology is concerned with the *adaptiveness* of behaviour, whereas a properly Darwinian account should be concerned with *adaptation*. That is, it should attempt to show how the most basic goals that human beings seek to achieve, and that motivate their behaviour, have been designed by natural selection under the kinds of environmental conditions experienced by ancestral populations in the course of the evolution of our species. Such goals, Symons argues, are both species-specific and inflexible, such that their contemporary pursuit, under environments very different from those of the 'environment of evolutionary adaptedness', can lead to behaviour whose consequences are profoundly maladaptive. A taste for sweet things, for example, may have served our hunter-gatherer ancestors well, in establishing a preference for fruit when it is at its most nutritious. But for the more affluent inhabitants of a modern industrial society it can have the less benign consequences of obesity and tooth decay (Symons 1992: 139).

In recent years an entirely new field of study, known as 'evolutionary psychology', has grown up around the attempt to identify those capacities and dispositions conventionally gathered under the rubric of 'human nature', and to explain how and why they evolved (Barkow, Cosmides and Tooby 1992). This is not the place for a critique of evolutionary psychology, but it is worth noting that its protagonists find themselves at loggerheads with the advocates of evolutionary ecology, despite their common allegiance to the neo-Darwinian paradigm. The difference between them is this: evolutionary ecology seeks to show how behaviour is sensitively responsive to variations in the environment, but lacks a coherent account of human nature; evolutionary psychology seeks to construct just such an account, but in doing so is insensitive to the fine-tuning of human behaviour to environmental conditions. This is not just a difference of emphasis: on behavioural differences as against cognitive universals. The issue is more profound, for behaviour that evolutionary psychology interprets as the product of evolved problem-solving mechanisms in the human mind/brain, is interpreted by evolutionary ecology as the expression of solutions already reached through the mechanism of natural selection, and impressed upon the mind through a process of enculturation. As I intend to argue, neither alternative offers an adequate, ecologically grounded account of how the subsistence skills of hunters and gatherers are acquired and deployed. The problem lies at the heart of the Darwinian paradigm itself.

COGNITIVE ALGORITHMS AND RULES OF THUMB

Let me return for a moment to Winterhalder's ethnography of the Cree of Muskrat Dam Lake. It will be recalled that the environment presents a heterogeneous mosaic of habitat types, which differ in terms of the kinds and relative abundance of the prey species they support. Optimal foraging theory predicts that under these circumstances, hunters will move from patch to patch, sampling what each has to offer, but will drop low-quality patches from their itinerary once it is clear that more is to be gained from concentrating their efforts in high-quality patches despite the extra costs of between-patch travel (MacArthur and Pianka 1966). Where travel costs are high, hunters will tend to be patch-generalists, where they are low they will be patch-specialists. Winterhalder found that the adoption by the Cree of snowmobiles and outboard motors, which greatly reduced the time spent on travel, did indeed favour specialisation. Yet even in the days when everyone moved about on snowshoes, it appears that their itineraries took in relatively few patch types.

To account for this discrepancy, Winterhalder (1981a: 90) proposes that the Cree employ an 'interstice' rather than a 'patch-to-patch' strategy of foraging (see Figure 2. 2). It is a strategy that makes good sense when one is hunting animals, such as moose and caribou, which themselves move frequently from one patch to another, which are not particularly abundant in proportion to the number of patches they are associated with, and which leave tracks or trails that may be used by hunters as evidence for their recent movements and present whereabouts. Moving in the interstices between patches – mainly, that is, on the hard-packed snow of frozen lakes and creeks which in any case makes travel easier – the hunter can expect to intercept the tracks left by animals as they move from patch to patch, and will visit a patch only when the tracks indicate that favoured prey are present there. 'Cree foragers', Winterhalder remarks, 'have developed this technique to a high level of skill' (1981a: 91).

There is no reason to doubt the truth of this remark. My concern is rather with the significance to be attached to the notion of *skill* in this context. For Winterhalder, skill evidently means an ability to produce rapid solutions to ostensibly rather complex problems posed by specific conjunctions of environmental circumstances. Elsewhere, Smith and Winterhalder (1992: 57) suggest that this is done by means of 'rules of thumb'. Clearly, as they point out, the formal mathematical techniques (including geometric tangents, partial derivatives,

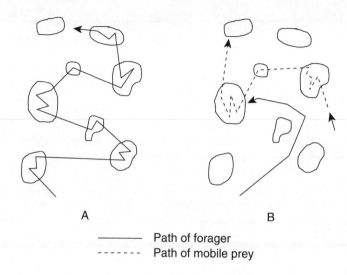

—————— Path of forager
- - - - - - Path of mobile prey

Figure 2.2 Alternative foraging strategies in a patchy environment:
(A) patch-to-patch (B) interstice foraging
Source: Winterhalder 1981a: 91

algebraic inequalities and the like) used in the construction of optimal foraging models are not replicated in the 'everyday decision processes of actors'. Nevertheless, 'simple rules of thumb *or cognitive algorithms* provided by natural or cultural selection may allow them to approach the solution [to a particular foraging problem] quite closely under conditions approximating the environments in which these "short-cuts" evolved' (1992: 58, my emphasis). One such rule, for the Cree hunter, might be stated as follows: 'Proceed along the creek bed until you intercept a track; then, if the track is fresh, search the upland patch to which it leads'. To become skilled, then, the hunter must be equipped with such rules through a process of enculturation.

Now I do not wish to deny that Cree hunters have resort to rules of thumb. I believe, however, that to describe these rules as 'cognitive algorithms' is fundamentally to distort their nature. The notion of cognitive algorithm comes from planning theory, and posits a series of linked decision rules, internal to the actor, which operate on received information to generate plans for subsequent action. As a 'solution' to a perceived 'problem', the plan is supposed to contain a precise and complete specification of the action that is predicated upon it, so that the latter is fully accounted for by the former: to explain what foragers do it is enough to have explained how they decide what to do. The power and utility of rules of thumb, by contrast, rest on the fact that they are inherently vague, specifying little or nothing about the concrete details of action. Invoked against the background of involvement in a real world of persons, objects and relations, rules of thumb may furnish people with a way of talking about what they have done, or about what they mean to do next, but once launched into the action itself they must necessarily fall back on abilities of a quite different kind – namely, on developmentally embodied and environmentally attuned capacities of movement and perception. Rules of thumb, as Suchman (1987: 52) puts it, serve 'to orient you in such a way that you can obtain the best possible position from which to use those embodied skills on which, in the final analysis, your success depends'. In no sense, however, do they substitute for these skills. Nor, as I shall now show, can we understand the acquisition of technical skills, in successive generations, as a process of enculturation.

ENCULTURATION AND ENSKILMENT

If, as evolutionary ecology would claim, the interstice pattern of foraging has evolved by natural selection as an optimal strategy of resource procurement for hunters and trappers in the boreal forest environment, then it must be expressible in the form of rules and representations that can be transmitted across generations. Let me emphasise once again that there is no question of these rules and representations being encoded genetically. The suggestion is rather that the 'formula' for interstice foraging is contained within a body of cultural information that is passed on, in a manner analogous to genetic transmission, from one generation to the next. According to this analogy, the transmission of cultural information must be distinguished from the experience of its application in particular settings of use, just as the transmission of the constituent elements of the genotype must be distinguished from the latter's realisation, within a particular environment, in the manifest form of the phenotype. This distinction is commonly made by means of a contrast between two forms of learning: social and individual (e.g. Richerson and Boyd 1992: 64). Thus in social learning, the novice absorbs the underlying rules and principles of hunting from already knowledge-able members of the community; in individual learning he puts them to use in the course of his activities in the environment.

Given that social learning occupies such a central place in their theory – as central, indeed, as genetic replication – it is rather surprising that evolutionary ecologists have devoted almost no attention to how it occurs. Consequently, as Kaplan and Hill are honest enough to admit, 'we know virtually nothing about...the developmental processes by which children become adult foragers' (1992: 197). Most often, cultural transmission is viewed as a simple process of copying, in which a whole inventory of rules and representations is miraculously downloaded into the passively receptive mind of the novice. It is to precisely this notion of enculturation that evolutionary psychologists have taken exception. Nothing can be acquired, they claim, unless innate processing mechanisms are already in place that serve to 'decode' the signals received from the social environment, and to extract the information contained therein. Thus the traditional model of enculturation, they argue, rests upon an impossible psychology. Not only do innate information-processing mechanisms make the transmission of variable cultural forms possible; they also impose their own structure on what can be learned and how. And it is the evolution of these mechanisms under natural selection, according to evolutionary psychologists, that has to be explained (Tooby and Cosmides 1992: 91–92).

Does this offer an account that is any more convincing? I do not believe that it does, for a very simple reason. Human beings are not born with a ready-made architecture of specialised acquisition mechanisms; to the extent that such mechanisms *do* exist, they could only emerge within a process of ontogenetic development. Thus, even if there were such a thing as a 'technology acquisition device' (analogous to the 'language acquisition device' posited by many psycholinguists), it would still have to undergo formation within the very same developmental context in which the child learns the particular skills of his or her community. And if both are aspects of the same developmental process, it is difficult to see how the learning of the 'acquired' skills can be distinguished from the formation of the 'innate' device (Ingold 1995: 195). However, there is no reason to suppose that anything like a 'technology acquisition device' exists at all. Rather, the learning of technical skills appears to depend on what might be called 'technology acquisition support systems' (Wynn 1994: 153). These systems, as Wynn argues, are not even partly innate. They are rather *systems of apprenticeship*, constituted by the relationships between more and less experienced practitioners in 'hands-on' contexts of activity. And it is on the reproduction of these relationships, not on genetic replication – or the transmission of some analogous code of cultural instructions – that the continuity of a technical tradition depends.

Considering how novice hunters actually learn their trade, two points should be made right away. First, there is no explicit code of procedure, specifying the exact movements to be executed under any given circumstances: indeed practical skills of this kind seem fundamentally resistant to codification in terms of any formal system of rules and representations (Ingold 1995: 206). Second, it is not possible, in practice, to separate the sphere of the novice's involvement with other persons from that of his involvement with the non-human environment. The novice hunter learns by accompanying more experienced hands in the woods. As he goes about, he is instructed in what to look out for, and his attention is drawn to subtle clues that he might otherwise fail to notice: in other words, he is led to develop a sophisticated perceptual awareness of the properties of his surroundings and of the possibilities they afford for action. For example, he learns to register those qualities of surface texture that enable one to tell, merely from touch, how long ago an animal left its imprint in the snow, and how fast it was travelling.

We could say that he acquires such know-how by observation and imitation, but not, however, in the sense in which these terms are generally employed by enculturation theorists. Observation is no more a matter of having information copied into one's head, than is imitation a matter of mechanically executing the received intructions. Rather, to observe is actively to attend to the movements of others; to imitate is to align that attention to the movement of one's own practical orientation towards the environment. Together they lead to the kind of rhythmic adjustment or resonance in the relation between the hunter and his surroundings that is the hallmark of skilled practice.

As I have argued elsewhere (Ingold 1991: 371, 1993: 463), the fine-tuning of perception and action that is going on here is better understood as a process of enskilment than as one of enculturation (see also Pálsson 1994). For what is involved is not a transmission of representations, as the enculturation model implies, but an *education of attention*. Indeed, the instructions the novice hunter receives – to watch out for this, attend to that, and so on – only take on meaning in the context of his engagement with the environment. Hence it makes no sense to speak of 'culture' as an independent body of context-free knowledge, that is available for transmission prior to the situations of its application (Lave 1990: 310). And if culture, in this form, exists nowhere save in the heads of anthropological theorists, then the very idea of its evolution is a chimera.

CONCLUSION

In short, a technique such as interstice foraging is not passed on as part of any systematic body of cultural representations; it is rather inculcated in each successive generation through a process of development, in the course of novices' practical involvement with the constituents of their environment – under the guidance of more experienced mentors – in the conduct of their everyday tasks. The accomplished hunter consults the world, not representations inside his head. The implications of this conclusion cannot be overemphasised, since they strike at the very core of neo-Darwinian theory itself. It is a fundamental premise of this theory that the morphological attributes and behavioural propensities of individual organisms must be specifiable, in some sense, independently and in advance of their entry into relations with their environments, and that the components of these specifications – whether genes or (in humans) their cultural analogues – must be transmissible across generations. It is my contention, to the contrary, that such context-independent specifications are, at best, analytic abstractions, and that in reality the forms and capacities of organisms are the emergent properties of developmental systems (Oyama 1985: 22–3).

We can now see why the attempt to produce a neo-Darwinian evolutionary *ecology* inevitably runs into difficulties. For if morphology and behaviour truly emerge through a history of organism–environment relations, as a properly ecological perspective requires, then they cannot be attributed to a prior design specification that is imported into the environmental context of development. Yet just such an attribution is entailed in the theory of adaptation under natural selection. As we have seen, evolutionary ecologists have tended to evade the problem by focusing on the reproductive consequences of behaviour while remaining agnostic about its developmental causes, thereby substituting the study of adaptiveness for that of adaptation. On the other hand, evolutionary psychologists, adhering more strictly to the neo-Darwinian logic of adaptation, have come up with an account of human nature that is fundamentally *anti*-ecological in its appeal to an 'evolved architecture' that is fixed and universal to the species, regardless of the environmental circumstances in which people happen to grow up.

Let me conclude by returning to the opposition with which I began, between the optimal forager and economic man. Whereas the latter is credited with the capacity to work out his strategies for himself, the former has to have them worked out for him by natural selection. They appear to stand, thus, on opposite sides of an overriding division between reason and nature, freedom and necessity, subjectivity and objectivity. But this is also a dichotomy on which the project of modern natural science depends, and it underwrites the distinction, as it has appeared in the literature of western anthropology, between the scientist, whose humanity is not in doubt, and the hunter-gatherer who, it would appear, is only contingently human. The scientist – in this case the evolutionary ecologist – constructs an abstract model on the basis of which he can calculate what it would be best for the hunter-gatherer to do; this prediction is then 'tested' against what the hunter-gatherer actually does. If observed practice conforms to the prediction, the model is said to provide an ultimate explanation for the hunter-gatherer's behaviour. Natural selection features, in this account, not as a real-world process but as the reflection of scientific reason in the mirror of nature, providing the theorist with the excuse to parade models *of* behaviour as though they were explanations *for* behaviour.

No amount of appeal, however, to 'methodological individualism', the 'hypothetico-deductive method', or other such contrivances in the analyst's bag of tricks (Smith and Winterhalder 1992, Winterhalder and Smith 1992), will get around the fact that the individuals whose behaviour evolutionary ecologists purport to explain are creatures of their own imagination. The scientific image of hunting and gathering, as a naturally prescribed course of fitness-maximisation, is as illusory as the image that science has of its own enterprise, as a monument to the freedom and supremacy of human reason. Far from confronting one another across the boundary of nature, both the people who call themselves scientists and the people whom scientists call hunter-gatherers are fellow passengers in this world of ours, who carry on the business of life and, in so doing, develop their capacities and aspirations, within a continuing history of involvement with both human and non-human components of their environments. If we are to develop a thoroughgoing ecological understanding of how real people relate to these environments, and of the sensitivity and skill with which they do so, it is imperative to take this condition of involvement as our point of departure. Yet to achieve this, as I have shown, will require nothing less than a fundamental overhaul of evolutionary theory itself.

NOTE

1 What follows draws substantially on one section of a review article (Ingold 1992), dealing with Bettinger's book and a selection of other recent hunter-gatherer studies in archaeology and anthropology.

REFERENCES

Barkow, J. H., Cosmides L. and Tooby, J. (eds) (1992) *The Adapted Mind: Evolutionary Psychology and the Generation of Culture*, New York: Oxford University Press.

Bettinger, R. L. (1991) *Hunter-Gatherers: Archaeological and Evolutionary Theory*, New York: Plenum Press.

Dunbar, R. (1987) 'Darwinizing Man: a Commentary', in L. L. Betzig, M. Borgerhoff Mulder and P. Turke (eds) *Human Reproductive Behavior: A Darwinian Perspective*, New York: Cambridge University Press.

Firth, R. (1964) 'Capital, Saving and Credit in Peasant Societies: a Viewpoint from Economic Anthropology', in R. Firth and B. S. Yamey (eds) *Capital, Savings and Credit in Peasant Societies*, London: Allen & Unwin.

Foley, R. (1985) 'Optimality Theory in Anthropology', *Man*(NS) 20: 222–42.

Ingold, T. (1990) 'An anthropologist looks at biology', *Man* (NS) 25: 208–29.

— (1991) 'Becoming Persons: Consciousness and Sociality in Human Evolution', *Cultural Dynamics* 4: 355–78.

— (1992) 'Foraging for Data, Camping with Theories: Hunter-Gatherers and Nomadic Pastoralists in Archaeology and Anthropology', *Antiquity* 66: 790–803.

— (1993) 'Technology, Language, Intelligence: a Reconsideration of Basic Concepts', in K. R. Gibson and T. Ingold (eds) *Tools, Language and Cognition in Human Evolution*, Cambridge: Cambridge University Press.

— (1995) '"People Like Us": the Concept of the Anatomically Modern Human', *Cultural Dynamics* 7: 187–214.

Kaplan, H. and Hill, K. (1992) 'The Evolutionary Ecology of Food Acquisition', in E. A. Smith and B. Winterhalder (eds) *Evolutionary Ecology and Human Behavior*, New York: Aldine de Gruyter.

Lave, J. (1990) 'The Culture of Acquisition and the Practice of Understanding', in J. W. Stigler, R. A. Shweder and G. Herdt (eds) *Cultural Psychology: Essays on Comparative Human Development*, Cambridge: Cambridge University Press.

MacArthur, R. H. and Pianka, E. R. (1966) 'On Optimal Use of a Patchy Environment', *American Naturalist* 100: 603–9.

Malinowski, B. (1922) *Argonauts of the Western Pacific*, London: Routledge and Kegan Paul.

Mayr, E. (1976) [1961] 'Cause and Effect in Biology', in *Evolution and the Diversity of Life: Selected Essays*, Cambridge, Mass.: Belknap Press of Harvard University Press.

Oyama, S. (1985) *The Ontogeny of Information: Developmental Systems and their Evolution*, Cambridge: Cambridge University Press.

Pálsson, G. (1994) 'Enskilment at Sea', *Man* (NS) 29: 901–27.

Richerson, P. J. and Boyd, R. (1992) 'Cultural Inheritance and Evolutionary Ecology', in E. A. Smith and B. Winterhalder (eds) *Evolutionary Ecology and Human Behavior*, New York: Aldine de Gruyter.

Schneider, H. K. (1974) *Economic Man*, New York: Free Press.

Smith, E. A. and Winterhalder, B. (1992) 'Natural Selection and Decision Making: Some Fundamental Principles', in E. A. Smith and B. Winterhalder (eds) *Evolutionary Ecology and Human Behavior*, New York: Aldine de Gruyter.

Suchman, L. (1987) *Plans and Situated Actions: The Problem of Human–Machine Communication*, Cambridge: Cambridge University Press.

Symons, D. (1992) 'On the Use and Misuse of Darwinism in the Study of Human Behavior', in J. H. Barkow, L. Cosmides and J. Tooby (eds) *The Adapted Mind: Evolutionary Psychology and the Generation of Culture*, New York: Oxford University Press.

Tooby, J and Cosmides, L. (1992) 'The Psychological Foundations of Culture', in J. H. Barkow, L. Cosmides and J. Tooby (eds) *The Adapted Mind: Evolutionary Psychology and the Generation of Culture*, New York: Oxford University Press.

Toulmin, S. (1981) 'Human Adaptation', in U. Jensen and R. Harré (eds) *The Philosophy of Evolution*, Brighton: Harvester Press.

Weber, M. (1947) *The Theory of Social and Economic Organization*, T. Parsons (ed.) trans. A. M. Henderson, New York: Oxford University Press.

Winterhalder, B. (1981a) 'Foraging Strategies in the Boreal Forest: an Analysis of Cree Hunting and Gathering', in B. Winterhalder and E. A. Smith (eds) *Hunter-Gatherer Foraging Strategies: Ethnographic and Archeological Analyses*, Chicago: University of Chicago Press.

— (1981b) 'Optimal Foraging Strategies and Hunter-Gatherer Research in Anthropology: Theory and Models', in B. Winterhalder and E. A. Smith (eds) *Hunter-Gatherer Foraging Strategies: Ethnographic and Archeological Analyses*, Chicago: University of Chicago Press.

— and Smith, E. A. (1992) 'Evolutionary Ecology and the Social Sciences', in E. A. Smith and B. Winterhalder (eds) *Evolutionary Ecology and Human Behavior*, New York: Aldine de Gruyter.

Wynn, T. (1994) 'Tools and Tool Behaviour', in T. Ingold (ed.) *Companion Encyclopedia of Anthropology: Humanity, Culture and Social Life*, London: Routledge.

Chapter 3

Ecology as semiotics

Outlines of a contextualist paradigm for human ecology

Alf Hornborg

In this chapter, I would like to connect two recurrent themes in ecological anthropology.[1] One is the epistemological polarisation between 'dualist' and 'monist' approaches to human ecology. The other is the issue of whether or not traditional, pre-industrial human societies have something to tell us about how to live sustainably. As a shorthand for this latter polarity, I will use the categories 'contextualist' (for the position that they do have something to tell us) versus 'modernist' (for the position that they do not). I believe that the interconnectedness of these two polarities deserves to be clarified. As the limitations of dualist and modernist perspectives are inexorably revealing themselves all over the world, I will try to take stock of some of the theoretical foundations on which a normative, monistic and contextualist stance can be articulated.

I choose to speak of 'contextualism' (rather than, say, 'traditionalism') because it suggests, in positive terms, the logical antithesis to *modernity* as defined, for instance, by Giddens (1990). Giddens' observations on the 'disembedding' (i.e. decontextualising) tendencies in modernity subsume a long line of concepts offered by social philosophers such as Weber, Marx, Tönnies, and Simmel. Processes of decontextualisation pervade all aspects of modern society. They are as representative for the construction of scientific knowledge as for the organisation of economic life. Against this background, a 'contextualist' stance is one that denies the capacity of abstract, totalising systems such as science or the market to solve the basic problems of human survival, recognising local and implicit meanings as the essential components of a sustainable livelihood. All this is of much more than academic significance, considering its implications for the role of what is often referred to as 'traditional ecological knowledge' or 'traditional resource management' in the public discussion on 'sustainable development'.

VULGAR MATERIALISM OR HEGELIAN ECOLOGY?

My point of departure in this article is the contextualist position of Roy Rappaport's *Pigs for the Ancestors* (1968). This is not so much to defend his early, cybernetic formulations as to trace briefly the career of a pioneer contextualist message through three decades of shifting anthropological paradigms. Moran (1990: 15) suggests that 'no work has had a greater impact on the development of an ecosystem approach in anthropology' than Rappaport's study, 'nor has any other study attracted as many critics of the ecological approach'. I will discuss only one of his critics (Friedman 1974, 1979) and instead concentrate on the convergences between Rappaport's contributions and more recent components of what could be articulated as an increasingly elaborate, contextualist framework.

In economic anthropology, much of the modernist–contextualist polarity was evident in the debate between formalists and substantivists in the 1950s and 1960s, and many of us will associate the concept of 'embeddedness' with Karl Polanyi. In the 1970s, I would suggest, the same, underlying polarity that had organised the anthropological discourse on economics was projected into its discourse on ecology. Representing the contextualist pole, Rappaport (1968, 1979) suggested that traditional, decentralised social systems tended to develop means of regulating local ecosystems which were better geared to sustainability than modern economies.

Rappaport's urge to bring nature and society into a common framework should be understood against the backdrop of two diametrically opposed approaches to ecological anthropology, the materialist 'cultural ecology' pioneered by Julian Steward and Leslie White, and the mentalist 'ecology of mind' of Gregory Bateson (1972). His argument may be viewed as an attempt at reconciliation, but has been criticised in the very dualist language it had hoped to transcend. Jonathan Friedman, for instance, asserted in 1974 that Rappaport's work belonged to a 'functional ecology... entrenched in the ideological matrix of vulgar materialism' (Friedman 1974: 445). Five years later, Friedman (1979) described the same work as 'Hegelian Ecology', suspended 'between Rousseau and the World Spirit'. To have been charged, for the same work and by the same critic, with both 'vulgar materialism' and Hegelianism, suggests that

Rappaport's attempt at monism may not have been altogether unsuccessful, and that Friedman's two critiques, though contradictory, remain entrenched in the matrix of dualism.

To be sure, a number of formulations in ecological anthropology deserve criticism for their materialist or functionalist bias. Rappaport's own formulations (1968) are not flawless in this respect, as he himself is ready to concede (Rappaport 1979, 1990). In retrospect, however, we may observe that these shortcomings largely derive from a failure to extricate more decisively the contextualist argument from a dualist vocabulary, a task which would have been more demanding in the 1960s than in the 1990s. I hope to show that the underlying intuition which was then couched in the functionalist terms of cybernetics can now be elaborated in the light of more recent paradigms such as post-structuralism and practice theory, and of theoretical developments in areas such as cognitive science, metaphor theory, and semiotics.

HOMEOSTATS AND CONSCIOUS PURPOSE

The positions of Rappaport and Friedman are diametrically opposed with respect to the role of conscious purpose in maintaining social and ecological systems within the 'goal ranges' defining their viability. Rappaport (1979: 169–70) follows Bateson (1972: 402–22) in suggesting that the linear structure of purposive, problem-solving consciousness is incapable of grasping the circular connectedness of living systems, and that explicit knowledge and rationality are insufficient tools for the sustainable management of ecological relations. Both advocate a more holistic human involvement in the natural environment, which includes the engagement of unconscious aspects of the human mind, as in religion, ritual, and aesthetics. Friedman (1979), on the other hand, seems to distrust the regulatory significance of any cultural institution that is not organised by conscious intention.

Whereas Bateson and Rappaport are explicitly concerned with discovering principles for providing human societies with greater capacities for self-regulation and for avoiding catastrophes, Friedman seems to share no such hopes. In his view, offered against the backdrop of I. Prigogine's far-from-equilibrium thermodynamics and of R. Thom's 'catastrophe theory', social systems are inherently and once and for all incapable of self-regulation. This fatalistic view is difficult to reconcile with his warnings that Bateson's and Rappaport's 'religious solution' is 'dangerous, to say the least' (Friedman 1979: 266). One wonders in what sense anything can be more 'dangerous' than regarding catastrophe as inevitable. The paradox here is that in advocating social policies serving to revitalise local, cultural autonomy, Bateson (1972) and Rappaport (1979) emerge as the champions of conscious purpose (though at another level), whereas it could be argued that Friedman's fatalism at times assumes a religious dimension. Again, the problem seems to be Cartesian dualism. Whereas Bateson and Rappaport consistently deal with human cognition and information processing as active aspects of evolutionary processes (which agrees very well with Prigogine's fundamentally optimistic position: cf. Prigogine and Stengers 1984), Friedman's objectivist approach to cycles of social transformations suggests very little scope for human agency.

Another aspect of Friedman's argument that deserves scrutiny is his view on homeostasis. He suggests that the cycle of ritual pig slaughter among the Tsembaga Maring does not qualify as a homeostat, since the reference values which trigger the slaughter (women's complaints) are not identical with the goal ranges set by the carrying capacity of the local ecosystem. Thus, there is 'no homeostatic regulation of the environment but rather the maintenance of certain environmental variables as a *non-intentional* result ... of the ritual cycle' (1979: 256, italics added.) As an instance of a real homeostat, where goal ranges and reference values do coincide, Friedman offers the mechanical thermostat. A thermostat, it seems, qualifies as a homeostat because it is 'a mechanism that must be set by a human regulator' in purposive or teleological fashion (ibid.: 256), and purposiveness or teleology means that 'there exists a sentence in the programme specifying the goal to be attained' (ibid.: 267).

If homeostatic processes are to be defined in terms of conscious intention, as Friedman suggests, at least two major problems arise. The first is whether the myriad of homeostatic processes within living organisms from amoebas to mammals (including their body thermostats) are no longer to be considered homeostatic, and the concept is henceforth to be restricted to human-made machines? Second, the concepts of intentionality and purposiveness defined as the existence of 'a sentence in the programme specifying the goal to be attained' evoke an increasingly outmoded epistemology according to which it would be feasible for us to judge whether or not the 'sentence' stands in some exact relationship to the 'goal'. Conscious purpose would have to be buttressed with an objectivist epistemology in order to justify such a clear-cut distinction between teleology and teleonomy.

Intentionality does not imply transparency. If the goal is as complex as ecological viability, a vast number of different sentences could conceivably work towards that same goal. Traditional cosmologies may codify very relevant observations of (and participation in) ecological processes without corresponding to the vocabulary or even the logic of modern science. If it were not so, the pre-modern human colonisation of every biome on the planet would have been inconceivable. In concentrating on the *adequacy* of cultural models rather than on their literal 'truth' as defined by the categories of modern science, Rappaport's work in 1968 in a sense foreshadowed the postmodern deposition of the master narrative.

Recent studies in cognitive science (Maturana and Varela 1987) serve to downplay the distinction between human intention and other forms of systemic directionality in living systems. Recognising the continuity means not only to acknowledge the complexity of goal orientation in living systems generally, but to deconstruct the illusion of transparency projected by the concept of 'conscious purpose'.

If the crucial issue in defining a homeostat is whether 'there exists a sentence in the programme specifying the goal to be attained', we must ask ourselves on which criteria – other than survival – we could possibly base an assessment of the degree to which the 'sentence' accurately specifies the 'goal'. If we follow the meta-perspective on cognition offered by Maturana and Varela (1987: 136–37), the only way to assess such a correspondence is to approach the relationship between programme and environment from a detached position, like that of people on the shore congratulating a submarine navigator for avoiding reefs that he himself could only detect as indicator readings. Maturana and Varela's (1987: 172–74) pragmatist definition of 'knowledge' does not assume an internalisation of the environment but 'an effective (or adequate) behavior in a given context'. In a nutshell, these authors conclude, 'to live is to know'.

From this perspective, in discussing the prospects for sustainability, the issue is not the exactitude, in terms defined by modern science, of the relationship between programme and goal (reference values and goal ranges), but the feasibility of maintaining some kind of feedback of information which might continuously calibrate one with the other. The crucial issue then becomes the nature (and origin) of the programme that defines the reference values and thus governs local resource use. This is a recurrent theme in Rappaport's (1979) discussion of adaptation versus 'maladaptation'. With the loss of local self-sufficiency, he argues (ibid.: 162), there is also loss of homeostatic capacity. Not surprisingly, he identifies 'all-purpose money' as one of the major causes of such maladaptive trends (ibid.: 130–31, 167). The economic terms in which reference values are expressed 'may be alien to and inappropriate for the systems being regulated' (ibid.: 100). Another, but structurally related, source of maladaptation is the objectivism of modern science, a mode of knowledge construction which apotheosises 'facts' and systematically destroys meanings (ibid.: 128–30): 'Because knowledge can never replace respect as a guiding principle in our ecosystemic relations, it is adaptive for cognised models to engender respect for that which is unknown, unpredictable, and uncontrollable, as well as for them to codify empirical knowledge' (1979: 100–1). Rappaport concludes that the decontextualised rationality of science or the world market is ill-suited to the task of deriving a sustainable livelihood from local ecosystems.

THE MONIST FOUNDATION OF CONTEXTUALISM

Now that over fifteen years have passed since Friedman and Rappaport pitted their modernist versus contextualist arguments against each other, it is interesting to consider the extent to which more recent developments in anthropology, sociology and related fields might serve to solidify a critical, contextualist framework. A brief selection of references will suffice to indicate the thrust of this convergence. Rappaport's concern over the loss of local autonomy, for instance, is shared by a growing number of anthropologists and development theorists addressing the dominance of 'disembedded' over 'embedded' knowledge systems (cf. Gudeman 1986, Apffel Marglin and Marglin 1990, Shiva 1991, Croll and Parkin 1992, Banuri and Apffel Marglin 1993).

The connection between monism and contextualism is particularly evident in the recent collection of articles edited by Croll and Parkin (1992). The argument that people, their indigenous knowledge and their environment exist inseparably 'within each other' (ibid.: i) is fundamental to their critique of external 'scripts' for development. When the environment is 'separated out from human agents and perceived as an exterior non-human habitat', subjugated by specialists imposing outside distinctions and categories in the interests of order, rationality, and standardisation, it is opened to 'appropriation, domination, attack, conquest and domestication' (ibid.: 32). Even as benevolent a discourse as that of 'global' environmentalism, we might add, is largely founded on the same, 'western' inclination towards objectification and decontextualisation (Evernden 1985, Ingold 1993, Hornborg 1993a, 1994a).

If contextualism is served by a monist epistemology, we may conversely conclude that the 'disembedding' tendencies of modernity are part and parcel of Cartesian dualism. The interrelations between the different dimensions of modernity (e.g. market institutions, 'western' personhood, and dualist epistemology) deserve to be more fully illuminated. As I have argued elsewhere (Hornborg 1993b), Croll and Parkin's argument might have proceeded much further in what Bourdieu (1990) has called 'objectifying objectification', i.e. in conceptualising and defamiliarising the 'western' outlook which is undermining the 'inside wisdom' (Croll and Parkin 1992: 22) of traditional ecocosmologies. If their book represents the discovery that people, discourse and environment may be inseparable, it does not reflect back on the discoverers, i.e. on why this should be news to us 'westerners'. It does not in any way connect its concerns with the sociological concepts of modernity and 'disembeddedness', nor even with Polanyi's early observations on the modern economy as being less 'embedded' than pre-modern modes of livelihood. It is a sign of the times that ecological anthropology in the 1990s focuses on the 'difficult, negotiable and contested relationship between person and environment' (Croll and Parkin 1992: 9), but unfortunate that it seems so altogether disengaged from economic anthropology. A more profound understanding of modernity would have provided these crucial links between economy, discourse, personhood, and ecology. Decontextualisation and objectification can be understood as two sides of the same coin. The decontextualisation of social relations, knowledge production and identities can also be expressed as the objectification (and fetishisation) of exchange, language and the self. Moreover, objectification (of the body, the landscape, labour, women, the colonies) can be identified as the ultimate foundation of power, repression and exploitation. Paradoxically, this only becomes visible to us as we turn the logic of modernity against itself, by objectifying objectification, achieving a distanced view of the distanced view, and encompassing the ambition to encompass (Hornborg 1994b).

Post-structuralism, in recognising the unity of discourse and practice, could well serve to buttress the contextualist message which Rappaport delivered in *Pigs for the Ancestors* more than a quarter of a century ago. Indeed, in his more recent articles we find the same underlying message couched in an updated and more persuasive vocabulary. Rappaport writes, for instance, that human

> meanings and understandings [do] not only reflect or approximate an independently existing world but participate in its construction.... Language has ever more powerfully reached out from the species in which it emerged to reorder and subordinate the natural systems in which populations of that species participate.
>
> (Rappaport 1993: 156)

Lines such as these suggest Foucault applied to ecosystems. They also harmonise well with the perspective of cognitive scientists such as Maturana and Varela (1987: 234, 253), who conclude that 'it is by languaging that the act of knowing ... brings forth a world', and that 'knower and known are mutually specified'. A similar view is emerging in the field of environmental history, where 'knowledge' is being recognised neither as a representation of something that exists outside it, nor merely a social construction, but as a negotiated *relationship* with nature that actually reconstructs nature in the process of representing it (cf. Bird 1987).

Such a 'relationist' conception of knowledge offers a middle road between the Scylla of representationism and the Charybdis of solipsism (Maturana and Varela 1987: 133–34), each in its own way a product of the dualist matrix. Beyond the paralysing, late modern stalemate between objectivism and relativism (cf. Bernstein 1983), it suggests a *rapprochement* of subject and object that might restore a sense of involvement and responsibility to the production of knowledge.

Monistic approaches are increasingly explicit in recent, ecological anthropology (e.g. Bennett 1990, Croll and Parkin 1992). Rappaport's own formulations, however, at times seem unnecessarily dualistic. Consider the following distinction between ecosystems and cultures:

> An ecosystem is a system of matter and energy transactions among populations of organisms of various kinds, and between each of them.... Culture is the category of phenomena distinguished from others by its contingency upon symbols.
>
> (Rappaport 1979: 59–60)

My conviction that this dichotomy may be misleading largely stems from the work of Jakob von Uexküll (1982) and from Ingold's (1992) discussion of the significance of von Uexküll's concept of *Umwelt* for ecological anthropology. In the words of Thure von Uexküll (1982: 7),

Umwelt-theory amounts to 'the fact that living organisms (including cells) respond as subjects, i.e. they respond only to signs...' Each organism in an ecosystem lives in its own subjective world (*Umwelt*) largely defined by its species-specific mode of perceiving its environment. 'The question of meaning', says Jakob von Uexküll (1982: 37), is therefore 'the crucial one to all living beings'. The implication is that ecological interaction *presupposes* such a plurality of subjective worlds. Indeed, ecological relations are based on meaning; they are semiotic. Ecosystems, no less than cultures, are contingent upon communication. Rappaport's aspiration to bring the objective and the subjective into a common framework is paralleled by the interdisciplinary field of semiotics, the aim of which is to 'reintegrate the natural and human sciences in the higher synthesis proper to a doctrine of signs' (Anderson *et al.* 1984: 8).

At one point, Rappaport (1979: 158) does concede that 'all organisms behave in terms of meanings' (the crucial difference being that humans 'must themselves construct those meanings'; cf. also Ingold 1992: 43), but apparently this does not prompt him to revise his definition of an ecosystem as fundamentally 'a system of matter and energy transactions' (Rappaport 1979: 59). Here he clearly remains constrained by the categories of dualism. There is really no reason to emphasise the material over the communicative aspect of ecosystems or, for that matter, to do the reverse with respect to human societies. Once we recognise that human subjectivity, along with the subjectivity of all the other species, is an aspect of the very *constitution* of ecosystems, we have a solid foundation for the conclusion that the destruction of meaning and the destruction of ecosystems are two aspects of the same process.

In trying to visualise the process by which meanings and ecosystems are simultaneously dismantled, we come back to the concept of decontextualisation. As Rappaport (1979: 142) suggests, the confusion of hierarchical relations among different levels of understanding (e.g. specific versus general, concrete versus abstract, etc.) may 'lead not only to the destruction of meaning but of the material world as well'. Decontextualising models, such as the universal rationality of the 'Green Revolution' or the formalism of neo-classical economic theory, alter the relationship between person and world by subordinating or eclipsing the non-objectifiable, local specificities which render meanings everywhere so implicit and inextricable. The neo-classical concept of 'utility', for instance, imposes on local worlds everywhere the axiom of universal interchangeability, dissolving complex codifications of resource flows and paving the way for a system, the blind logic of which is simply to reward an accelerating rate of destruction (Hornborg 1992).

The disenchantment with western rationality has a long history. My argument here, however, is that studies in human ecology are now in a unique position to articulate a *rational* critique of that rationality. The contextualist position is not mysticism but a sober recognition of the limitations of totalising institutions and knowledge systems. It is an argument not for regression but for a *recontextualisation* of the production of knowledge. Because of the sheer complexity and specificity of ecosystemic interrelationships and fluctuations, it is not unreasonable to expect that optimal strategies for sustainable resource management are generally best defined by local practitioners with close and long-term experience of these specificities, and with special stakes in the outcome. Yet it is clear that actual management strategies are today generally informed by entirely different sets of conditions. This structural contradiction in the organisation of human society is an adequate point of departure for any anthropological contribution to ongoing deliberations on 'sustainable development'.[2]

METAPHOR, MORALITY AND POLICY

Our argument for a recontextualisation of the production of knowledge relating to local ecological practice necessarily leads on to a consideration of the significance of metaphor. This issue is central to the contextualist argument in as much as it suggests an answer to the general question of what it is in the nature of traditional understandings that might make them more meaningful and at the same time more conducive to sustainable resource use than modern representations. I am not referring here to the capacity of traditional knowledge systems to register complex ecological relations, which has been amply documented (cf. e.g. Johannes 1989, Posey and Balée 1989, Moran 1993), but to their capacity to constitute prescriptive 'models for' sustainable resource use. Rappaport, having traced the complex metaphorical structure of Maring ritual cosmology (1979: 103–16), observes that metaphors do not convey 'information in the digital sense' but meanings which may be 'affectively more powerful' (ibid.: 156–57). In their inclination to codify normative, practical attitudes, metaphorical understandings of nature assume the responsibilities which must always adhere to the very act of 'knowing'.

If 'knowledge' is a *relationship* with nature that is constitutive both of the knower and the known, then metaphor is a mode of knowing that incorporates the very conditions of knowledge.

The connection I want to make here is with Gudeman's (1986) important observation that neo-classical economic theory distinguished itself from all local models of livelihood by its ambition to abandon metaphor. Rather than positioning the knowing subject by investing economic practices with meanings deriving from other spheres of life (e.g. respect for the ancestors), Ricardo's 'derivational' representations turn inward on themselves in a closed, self-referential, and thus ultimately tautological web of concepts. This act of decontextualisation dispelled morality from human livelihood and provided a vocabulary (e.g. 'utility') for engulfing all local systems of meaning.[3]

Metaphor is a mode of knowing that positions the human subject by *evoking* non-objectifiable inner states associated with specific forms of practice. The significance of metaphor for contextualism thus lies in its capacity to activate tacit, practical knowledge based on experience of highly specific, local conditions. This position accommodates Ingold's (1992: 52–53) proposition that cultural constructions of the environment are secondary to practical action ('the practitioner's way of knowing'), while recognising the capacity of such constructions to codify and reinforce a specific, ecological *habitus*, not least in the transmission of such dispositions between generations. A metaphorical, 'cognised model' does not so much encode ecological information as provide 'cues' for the activation of specific, practical repertoires appropriated in the context of action.

Metaphorical understandings of subsistence practices and ecological relationships have been richly documented in the anthropological literature (for general discussions, cf. Gudeman 1986, Ingold 1986, Bird-David 1993). Bird-David (1993: 112, 121) notes that hunter-gatherer culturers all over the world tend to represent 'human–nature relatedness . . . in terms of personal relatedness', within a 'subject–subject' rather than a 'subject–object' frame, and suggests that 'since these tribal peoples share an intimate and time-proven knowledge of their respective natural environments, their representations cannot be dismissed outright in favour of the western one'. The application of social metaphors to practices of livelihood is not limited to hunter-gatherers, but seems to be a pervasive aspect of pre-modern subsistence production. Descola (1994) demonstrates, for instance, how the Achuar conceptualise different subsistence practices in terms of different kinds of social behaviour: 'the women's consanguine mothering of cultivated plants and the affinal charming of game practiced by the men' (ibid.: 327).

Descola further suggests that if social relationships provide the conceptual model for human–nature relationships, a modification of the latter will generally begin with 'prior mutation' of the former (ibid.: 330). It may not be necessary to establish such a generalised priority, among other things because metaphors are known to predicate meanings in a reciprocal manner (cf. Isbell 1985). Descola's observation, however, on the congruity between social relationships and human–nature relationships is clearly relevant to the argument advanced here, that several features of modern life generally treated as distinct (viz., market exchange, 'western' personhood, Cartesian dualism) are but the social and epistemological aspects of a single phenomenon of modernity. Rather than treat plants and animals as categories of kinsmen, a society of strangers will breed 'natural aliens' (cf. Evernden 1985). In other words, a society founded on objectification (of self and others as public *persona*) will tend to project the same, hierarchical subject/object dichotomy onto the relationship between person and (natural) world.

Among the implications of such a conclusion is yet another argument for the post-modern resurrection of 'a renewed fixity' (Giddens 1990: 178) within a local sphere of social life. If the predominant, modern mode of human–nature relationship can only be improved in conjunction with a transformation of the predominant, modern mode of sociability, the discussion on 'sustainable development' will have to incorporate considerations of how to revitalise that aspect of human existence which Tönnies called *Gemeinschaft* (cf. note 2).

Another implication is that our choice of metaphors in the discourse on 'sustainable development' deserves very careful consideration. It is exceedingly interesting to compare the new social metaphors for human–nature interaction, which are being articulated by different parties in this discourse, with their pre-modern counterparts. Whereas traditional subsistence cultures commonly conceptualised human–nature interaction in terms of their own social practices of gift-giving and reciprocity (cf. Ingold 1986, Århem Chapter 10, this volume), the recent discourse on 'ecological economics' suggests that ecosystems are a form of 'capital' which humans should 'invest' in and that they provide humans with 'services' which need to be properly evaluated in monetary terms (e.g. Folke and

Kåberger 1991, Jansson *et al.* 1994). Hitherto unpaid ecosystem services are thus said to have generated, for human society, an ecological 'debt' of immense proportions, and concepts such as 'green taxes' and the 'Polluter Pays Principle' have been advanced to rectify the situation. This is clearly a modern instance of the projection of a social metaphor on human–nature relationships, where the latter are accordingly conceptualised as market transactions. In as much as it serves as a literal understanding of the environmental crisis, however, it is an extremely misleading metaphor, since monetary phenomena such as 'investments', 'services' and 'debts' remain relationships between human beings and could not possibly denote human–nature relationships. Ecosystems are not offering their 'services' on the market, nor do they have any use for monetary compensation. Money is a claim on other people. Thus, contrary to the tenets of conventional discourse, it cannot restore damages to the biosphere, only redistribute them socially. Nevertheless, the metaphorical understanding of nature in terms of 'services' to be paid for serves the crucial ideological function of marshalling the adverse effects of economic 'growth' merely to reinforce our faith in it (WCED 1987).

CONCLUSION

In an otherwise very persuasive critique of modernity, Marglin (1990) at one point draws an unnecessarily sharp line between the domains of what Keynes called 'organic' and 'atomic' propositions, respectively. The former are propositions 'the truth of which depends on the beliefs of agents', whereas the latter are propositions 'the truth of which is independent of these beliefs'. In Marglin's view, 'propositions about the world of things and plants are atomic, while many if not all propositions about the world of human beings, the world of social relationships, are organic' (Marglin 1990: 15).

In the light of the various arguments sketched in this article, such a clear-cut distinction between nature and society should be difficult to maintain. To a greater extent than we normally recognise, even conceptualisations of nature generate propositions 'the truth of which depends on the beliefs of agents'. Rappaport provides a persuasive example:

> In a world in which the lawful and the meaningful, the discovered and the constructed, are inseparable the concept of the ecosystem *is not simply a theoretical framework* within which the world can be

analyzed. It is itself an element of that world, one that is crucial in maintaining that world's integrity in the face of mounting insults to it. To put this a little differently, the concept of the ecosystem is not simply descriptive.... It is also 'performative'; the ecosystem concept and actions informed by it are *part of the world's means for maintaining, if not indeed constructing, ecosystems.*

(Rappaport 1990: 68–69)

In this sense, debates over the self-stabilising capacities of ecosystems (e.g. Friedman 1979, Vayda 1986) are as ideologically committing as the polarisation between proponents of traditional 'environmental wisdom' and those writers who 'now dwell singlemindedly on examples of bad natural resource management among traditional peoples, advancing the opposing notion that traditional environmental practices were basically unsound' (Johannes 1989: 7).

In this chapter, I have explored some of the possible theoretical foundations for the former of these two positions. I have argued that a number of advances in recent social and cognitive science converge in a critique of modernity's *decontextualisation of knowledge,* and that this critique coincides with an increasingly successful ambition to transcend Cartesian dualism. The resultant, 'contextualist' paradigm is of fundamental significance for the contemporary debate on 'sustainable development'.

The discussion on 'traditional ecological knowledge' and 'traditional resource management' (cf. Johannes 1989, Posey and Balée 1989, Gadgil 1991, Moran 1990, 1993, Berkes, Folke and Gadgil 1993, Berkes and Folke 1994) is intrinsically paradoxical to the extent that it hopes for an appropriation and application of local knowledge by the very modernist framework by which such knowledge is continually being eclipsed. In advocating what he calls 'epistemological decentralization', Banuri (1990: 97–99) recognises that an increasing contextuality of knowledge will render 'the expert, trained in universal sciences, an anachronism'. Clearly, an 'expert' in an abstractly conceived field of 'local knowledge' is a contradiction in terms. But this paradox, of course, is a pervasive aspect of the anthropological condition. We can engage in a meta-discourse on the construction of knowledge, but in terms of concrete expertise we can at best become awkward apprentices to specific, local practitioners.

Rather than approach indigenous knowledge as another 'resource' to be tapped, ecological anthropology might concentrate on the socio-cultural contexts which allow ecologically sensitive knowledge systems to evolve and persist over time. There are reasons to believe that the best conditions for such local calibrations are precisely when they are *not* being subjected to attempts at encompassment by totalising frameworks of one kind or another. In recognising implicit and inextricable local meanings as the very stuff of ecological resilience, a critical inquiry into human ecology might begin to confront the agents of destruction by modifying its own ambition to encompass.

NOTES

1 I gratefully acknowledge funding from the Swedish Council for Planning and Coordination of Research (FRN) in support of the work underlying this chapter.

2 A very general conclusion, albeit naive, is that any policy designed to reempower local communities to develop their own strategies for sustainable reproduction would need to find a way of somehow 'immunising' basic subsistence activities against the concepts and the vicissitudes of the world market. In the long run, the only logical solution may be to distinguish, by means of special-purpose currencies, two completely separate spheres of exchange, one devoted to basic local reproduction (e.g. subsistence, shelter) and the other to continued global integration (e.g. telecommunications, advanced medicine). This would be a manifestation, at the institutional level, of a cosmology that recognises that everything is not interchangeable (cf. Kopytoff 1986). In fundamentally reorganising the *conditions* for economic rationality (e.g. the determination of optimal energy inputs in agriculture), it would profoundly transform global patterns of resource management.

3 Gudeman suggests that we should rethink 'imperialism... in terms of who gets to model whom' (1986: 157). The universalist modeler 'rejoins the world of all modelers', and though by definition he could not admit it, his images may in fact 'create their own reality' (ibid.: 154–55). In a review of *Economics as Culture*, Friedman (1987) again illustrates the objectivist, dualist position by deploring that Gudeman does not distinguish between 'discourse about reality and the organization of that reality'. Yet it must run counter to some of the most central tenets of modern anthropology to maintain an ontological (as opposed to analytic) distinction between social relations and their ethno-explication (e.g. between the market and neo-classical economic theory). There is indeed a sense in which the strategy of universalist, conceptual encompassment is synonymous with social domination (Hornborg 1994b).

REFERENCES

Anderson, M., Deely, J. Krampen, M., Ransdell, J. Sebeok, T. A. and von Uexküll, T. (1984) 'A Semiotic Perspective on the Sciences: Steps toward a New Paradigm', *Semiotica* 52: 7–47.

Apffel Marglin, F. and Marglin, S. (eds) (1990) *Dominating Knowledge: Development, Culture, and Resistance*, Oxford: Clarendon Press.

Banuri, T. (1990) 'Modernization and its Discontents: A Cultural Perspective on the Theories of Development', in F. Apffel Marglin and S. Marglin (eds) *Dominating Knowledge: Development, Culture, and Resistance*, Oxford: Clarendon Press.

Banuri, T. and Apffel Marglin, F. (eds) (1993) *Who Will Save the Forests? Knowledge, Power and Environmental Destruction*, London: Zed Books.

Bateson, G. (1972) *Steps to an Ecology of Mind*, Frogmore: Paladin.

Bennett, J. W. (1990) 'Ecosystems, Environmentalism, Resource Conservation, and Anthropological Research', in E. F. Moran (ed.) *The Ecosystem Approach in Anthropology: From Concept to Practice*, Ann Arbor: University of Michigan Press.

Berkes, F. and Folke, C. (1994) 'Investing in Cultural Capital for Sustainable Use of Natural Capital', in A. M. Jansson, M. Hammer, C. Folke and R. Costanza (eds) *Investing in Natural Capital: The Ecological Economics Approach to Sustainability*, Washington, DC: Island Press.

Berkes, F., Folke, C. and Gadgil, M. (1993) 'Traditional Ecological Knowledge, Biodiversity, Resilience and Sustainability', Beijer Discussion Papers No. 31, Stockholm: Beijer International Institute of Ecological Economics.

Bernstein, R. J. (1983) *Beyond Objectivism and Relativism: Science, Hermeneutics and Praxis*, Philadelphia: University of Pennsylvania Press.

Bird, E. A. R. (1987) 'The Social Construction of Nature: Theoretical Approaches to the History of Environmental Problems', *Environmental Review* 11: 255–64.

Bird-David, N. (1993) 'Tribal Metaphorization of Human–Nature Relatedness', in K. Milton (ed.) *Environmentalism: The View from Anthropology*, London: Routledge.

Bourdieu, P. (1990) *The Logic of Practice*, Cambridge: Polity Press.

Croll, E. and Parkin, D. (eds) (1992) *Bush Base–Forest Farm: Culture, Environment, and Development*, London: Routledge.

Descola, P. (1994) *In the Society of Nature: A Native Ecology in Amazonia*, Cambridge: Cambridge University Press.

Evernden, N. (1985) *A Natural Alien*, Toronto: University of Toronto Press.

Folke, C. and Kåberger, T. (eds) (1991) *Linking the Natural Environment and the Economy: Essays from the Eco-Eco Group*, Dordrecht: Kluwer Academic Publishers.

Friedman, J. (1974) 'Marxism, Structuralism, and Vulgar Materialism', *Man* (NS) 9: 444–69.

— (1979) 'Hegelian Ecology: between Rousseau and the World Spirit', in P. C. Burnham and R. F. Ellen (eds) *Social and Ecological Systems*, London: Academic Press.

— (1987) 'Review of S. Gudeman, *Economics as Culture: Models and Metaphors of Livelihood*', *Ethnos* 52: 396–98.

Gadgil, M. (1991) 'Traditional Resource Management Systems', *Resource Management and Optimization* 8: 127–41.

Giddens, A. (1990) *The Consequences of Modernity*, Cambridge: Polity Press.

Gudeman, S. (1986) *Economics as Culture: Models and Metaphors of Livelihood*, London: Routledge and Kegan Paul.

Hornborg, A. (1992) 'Machine Fetishism, Value, and the Image of Unlimited Good: Towards a Thermodynamics of Imperialism', *Man* (NS) 27: 1–17.

— (1993a) 'Environmentalism and Identity on Cape Breton: On the Social and Existential Conditions for Criticism', in G. Dahl (ed.) *Green Arguments and Local Subsistence*, Stockholm: Almqvist and Wiksell.

— (1993b) 'Review of E. Croll and D. Parkin, *Bush Base–Forest Farm: Culture, Environment and Development*', *Ethnos* 58: 394–96.

— (1994a) 'Environmentalism, Ethnicity and Sacred Places: Reflections on Modernity, Discourse and Power', *Canadian Review of Sociology and Anthropology* 31: 245–67.

— (1994b) 'Encompassing Encompassment: Anthropology and the U-turn of Modernity', *Ethnos* 59: 232–47.

Ingold, T. (1986) 'Hunting, Sacrifice and the Domestication of Animals', in *The Appropriation of Nature: Essays on Human Ecology and Social Relations*, Manchester: Manchester University Press.

(1992) 'Culture and the Perception of the Environment', in E. Croll and D. Parkin (eds) *Bush Base–Forest Farm: Culture, Environment, and Development*, London: Routledge.

(1993) 'Globes and Spheres: the Topology of Environmentalism', in K. Milton (ed.) *Environmentalism: The View from Anthropology*, London: Routledge.

Isbell, B. J. (1985) 'The Metaphoric Process: "From Culture to Nature and Back Again"', in G. Urton (ed.) *Animal Myths and Metaphors in South America*, Salt Lake City: University of Utah Press.

Jansson, A. M., Hammer, M., Folke, C. and Costanza, R. (eds) (1994) *Investing in Natural Capital: The Ecological Economics Approach to Sustainability*, Washington, DC: Island Press.

Johannes, R. E. (ed.) (1989) *Traditional Ecological Knowledge: A Collection of Essays*, Cambridge: IUCN, The World Conservation Union.

Kopytoff, I. (1986) 'The Cultural Biography of Things: Commoditization as Process', in A. Appadurai (ed.) *The Social Life of Things: Commodities in Cultural Perspective*, Cambridge: Cambridge University Press.

Marglin, S. (1990) 'Towards the Decolonization of the Mind', in F. Apffel Marglin and S. Marglin (eds) *Dominating Knowledge: Development, Culture, and Resistance*, Oxford: Clarendon Press.

Maturana, H. R. and Varela, F. J. (1987) *The Tree of Knowledge: The Biological Roots of Human Understanding*, Boston: Shambhala.

Moran, E. F. (ed.) (1990) *The Ecosystem Approach in Anthropology: From Concept to Practice*, Ann Arbor: University of Michigan Press.

— (1993) *Through Amazonian Eyes: The Human Ecology of Amazonian Populations*, Iowa City: University of Iowa Press.

Posey, D. A. and Balée, W. (eds) (1989) 'Resource Management in Amazonia: Indigenous and Folk Strategies', *Advances in Economic Botany* 7 (special issue).

Prigogine, I. and Stengers, I. (1984) *Order out of Chaos*, New York: Bantam Books.

Rappaport, R. A. (1968) *Pigs for the Ancestors: Ritual in the Ecology of a New Guinea People*, New Haven: Yale University Press.

— (1979) *Ecology, Meaning, and Religion*, Berkeley: North Atlantic Books.

— (1990) 'Ecosystems, Populations and People', in E. F. Moran (ed.) *The Ecosystem Approach in Anthropology: From Concept to Practice*, Ann Arbor: University of Michigan Press.

— (1993) 'Humanity's Evolution and Anthropology's Future', in R. Borofsky (ed.) *Assessing Cultural Anthropology*, New York: McGraw-Hill.

Shiva, V. (1991) *The Violence of the Green Revolution*, London: Zed Books.

Vayda, A. P. (1986) 'Holism and Individualism in Ecological Anthropology', *Reviews in Anthropology*, Fall 1986: 295–313.

von Uexküll, J. (1982 [1940]) 'The Theory of Meaning', *Semiotica* 42: 25–82.

von Uexküll, T. (1982) 'Introduction: Meaning and Science in Jakob von Uexküll's Concept of Biology', *Semiotica* 42: 1–24.

WCED (1987) *Our Common Future*, Oxford: Oxford University Press.

Chapter 4

Human–environmental relations
Orientalism, paternalism and communalism

Gísli Pálsson

Much anthropological thinking, in different academic settings, representing a wide range of theoretical 'schools' or paradigms, assumes a fundamental distinction between nature and society. Hollingshead, whose ideas influenced the cultural ecology of Julian Steward, expressed one formulation of such a dualism in clear and simple terms, speaking of 'the ecological and sociological orders':

> The former is primarily an extension of the order found everywhere in nature, whereas the latter is exclusively, or at least almost, a distinctly human phenomenon .... The ecological order is primarily rooted in competition, whereas social organization has evolved out of communication.
>
> (Hollingshead 1940: 358)

Dualist theory, it was generally assumed, was on the right tracks: 'now that the problem is recognized and a beginning made', Hollingshead suggested (1940: 358) 'we may expect a solution...'.[1] Such a theoretical beginning was reinforced by a rigid academic divison of labour and massive institutional structures. The sociological order remained the subject of anthropologists and sociologists while the ecological one belonged more properly to professional ecologists.

Having established a fundamental dichotomy, Hollingshead, and many of those who followed him, usually qualified the dualistic thesis, emphasising that nature and society were not to be seen as *totally* separate spheres but dialectically interlinked; each order 'complements and supplements the other in many ways' (Hollingshead 1940: 359). Modern-day ecologists continue to 'compare' the orders of nature and society as if they were separate, autonomous systems, exploring the links between them (Holling *et al.* 1994). Despite the dialectic, interactive language, then, the boundary between society and nature remains a contested interface. During much of the twentieth century social theorists have intensely debated the relative merits of two kinds of determinisms, the 'prison houses' of language and naturalism. In the 1970s, Sahlins quite suitably characterised anthropology, a discipline continually trapped between idealism and materialism, as a 'prisoner pacing between the farthest walls of his cell' (1976: 55), reinventing the allegory of the cave from Plato's *Republic*. In recent years, however, the weary debate of materialist and cultural reason has rather unexpectedly been replaced by a more fundamental one: the distinction between nature and society, one of the key constructs of modernist discourse, has itself increasingly been subject to critical discussion in several fields, including anthropology and environmental history. This development, partly a response to the post-modern, linguistic turn, global environmental problems, modern information technology, the greening of public discourse, and the redrawing of disciplinary boundaries, poses new challenges for social theory and ethnographic practice, setting the stage for a novel kind of ecological anthropology.

One possible avenue in that direction is to extend the Marxian approach, an approach usually restricted to *human* relations, to the analysis of human–environmental relations. Tapper (1988) has argued that in hunting and gathering societies humans and animals engage in the 'mutual production of each others' existence' (1988: 52) and Brightman (1993) similarly alludes to an 'Algonquian labor process' in the case of the Canadian Cree, a process 'in which humans and animals successively participate as producers of the other, the animals willingly surrendering the "product" of their own bodies and the hunters returning it to them as cooked food, all figured in the idiom of "love"' (1993: 188).

Drawing upon such perspectives, my aim is partly to show that similar discourses are applied to rather different theoretical contexts. Discourses on nature, ethnography, and translation, I suggest, extending arguments developed by Donham (1990), Bird-David (1993), and some others, often have much in common, notably the metaphors of personal relatedness and classic rhetorics. More generally, this article argues for the integration of human ecology and social theory, drawing upon perspectives often associated with Marx and Dewey, seeing humans *in* nature, engaged in situated, practical acts. I distinguish between three kinds of paradigms – orientalism, paternalism, and communalism – each of which represents a particular stance with respect to human–environmental relations. The paradigm of communalism differs from both orientalism and paternalism in that it rejects the radical separation of nature and society, object and subject, emphasising the notion of dialogue. While ethical approaches to the environment and human–environmental relations are highly interconnected, I am less concerned with the former than the latter. Merchant (1990) has applied a taxonomy, similar to the one I am suggesting for human–environmental relations, to environmental ethics, distinguishing between egocentric, homocentric, and ecocentric approaches.[2]

THE POLITICAL ECONOMY OF THE ENVIRONMENT

The modern nature–society dichotomy is often taken for granted and it is necessary, therefore, to situate it in a wider historical and ethnographic perspective. In medieval Europe, there was no radical separation of nature and society; if the dichotomy existed it must have been very different from that typical for the modernist project. As Gurevich (1992: 297) argues, in medieval times 'man thought of himself as an integral part of the world.... His interrelation with nature was so intensive and thorough that he could not look at it from without; he was inside it.' Significantly, the medieval term 'individual' originally meant 'indivisible' – that which cannot be divided, like the unity of the Trinity. The change in the meaning of the concept, the adoption of the modern connotation emphasising distinctions and discontinuities, 'is a record in language of an extraordinary social and political history' (Williams 1976: 133). The systematic fragmenting of the medieval world and the 'othering' of nature it entailed first took shape in the Renaissance period, during which the whole western attitude to the environment, knowledge and learning was transformed.

The three-dimensional space established by Italian painters during the fourteenth and fifteenth centuries is one of the key elements of the epistemological revolution of the Renaissance.[3] For early Renaissance painters, trained in the static and holistic world of Aristotelian philosophy and the medieval church, the canvas was primarily decorative space for the glorification of godly designs. By the end of the Renaissance, in contrast, the art of painting consistently focused on cognitive and spatial research, the representation of human activities and their place in nature and history. Renaissance painters were rewarded for their efforts with spectacular artistic success, the laws of perspective (*perspectiva*, or 'seeing through'). In a brief period,

nature became a quantifiable, three-dimensional universe appropriated by humans. This 'anthropocracy', to use Panofsky's term
(1991), represented a radical departure from the enclosed universe of
the Aristotelians constituted by the earth and its seven surrounding
spheres. The Cartesian anxiety of estrangement and uncertainty,
however, of the separation from the mother-world of the Middle Ages
and the nursing earth, was compensated for by the rational ego, the
obsession with objectivity, and a 'masculine' theory of natural
knowledge: ' "She" [nature] becomes "it" – and "it" can be understood and controlled. Not through "sympathy" . . . but by virtue of
the very *objectivity* of the "it" . . . . The "otherness" of nature is now
what allows it to be known' (Bordo 1987: 108).

If nature is an 'Other', it has to be 'translated'; much like the noise
in the ruins of the Tower of Babel it demands close attention and effort
at understanding. Such efforts, however, can take different forms.
Students of literary translation emphasise that although translation
may be seen as a perfect marriage between two different contexts, an
important element in translation proper concerns the relations of
power between 'source' and 'receptor' (Lefevere and Bassnett 1990).
A translation indicates the relative submissiveness or superiority of
the translator and the authority of the receptor *vis-à-vis* the source.
Such a perspective may be applied to the ethnographic enterprise.
How ethnographers, as visitors or guests, meet their hosts (and how
they are met by them), how they manage their lives among them, and
how they report what they experience, varies from case to case
(Pálsson 1993, 1995). Thus, one may speak of different relations of
ethnographic production.

Similarly, emphasising the contrast between domination and
protection with respect to the environment, we may distinguish
between two radically different kinds of human–environmental
relations, environmenal orientalism and paternalism. The key difference between them is that while the former 'exploits' the latter
'protects'. Environmental orientalism suggests negative reciprocity
in human–environmental relations, whereas paternalism implies
balanced reciprocity, presupposing human responsibility. In the case
of both environmental orientalism and paternalism, humans are
masters of nature. Rejecting the radical separation of nature and
society, object and subject, and the modernist assumptions of
othering, certainty and monologue, adding the dimension of continuity and discontinuity, yields a third paradigm which may be
referred to as communalism (see Figure 4.1). This paradigm suggests

generalised reciprocity in human–environmental relations, invoking the notions of contingency, participation, and dialogue.

Analogies of the human world and the natural environment need not be surprising. Humans often treat other human beings and the environment in a similar manner. Indeed, discourses on nature, ethnography and textual translation have much in common. Thus the metaphoric language of classic rhetorics – of irony, tragedy, comedy, and romance – has appeared in a wide range of fields and contexts at different points in time. Donham argues that even though the attempt to construct typologies with the 'dramatic' metaphors of rhetorics 'is bound to result in a certain crudeness, questions of rhetoric nevertheless appear to delineate... the manner in which all social theories proceed from particular moral assumptions' (Donham 1990: 192). Another metaphoric association draws upon the language of personal relatedness, of kinship and sexual relationships; such metaphors, as we will see, have often been used to represent both textual translation and the nature–society interface.

ORIENTALIST EXPLOITATION

The paradigm of environmental orientalism not only establishes a fundamental break between nature and society, it also suggests that people are masters of nature, in charge of the world. In this 'colonial' regime, the world becomes 'a *tabula rasa* for the inscription of human history' (Ingold 1993: 37). If humans are not quite godly beings, at

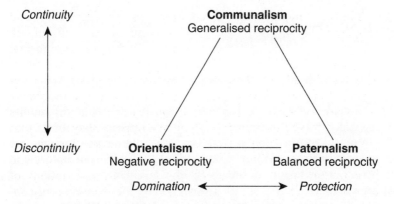

Figure 4.1 Kinds of human–environmental relations

least they compete with God; thus the arrogant statement reported for Carl von Linné, the arch classifier of natural species, that 'while God created Nature, *he* put it in order'. The vocabulary of orientalism is typically one of domestication, frontiers, and expansion – of exploring, conquering, and exploiting the environment – for the diverse purposes of production, consumption, sport, and display. To the extent that one can speak of environmental 'management' in this context, management is simply a technical enterprise, the rational application of Baconian science and mathematical equations *to* the natural world. This typically suggests a lofty stance with respect to the 'object' in question. In the orientalist context, scientists present themselves as analysts of the material world, unaffected by any ethical considerations. This implies a radical distinction between laypersons and experts, another theoretical construct rooted in the innovations of the Renaissance.

Given the persistent othering of the object of modernist scholarship, the Baconian imagery of sexual assault, of 'entering and penetrating... holes and corners' (Francis Bacon, cited in Bordo 1987: 108), is a recurrent one. As Bordo (1987: 171) and Nelson (1992: 108, 1993: 27), among others, have shown, the literature on modern science is replete with passages that describe human–environmental interactions by means of an aggressive, sexual idiom; nature appears as a seductive but troublesome female. Anthropology is not exempt from modernist, sexual jargon and predator–prey metaphors. Malinowski (1972) argued, for instance, that

> the Ethnographer has not only to spread his nets in the right place, and wait for what will fall into them. He must be an active huntsman, and drive his quarry into them and follow it up to its most inaccessible lairs.
>
> (Malinowski 1972: 8)

This is the rhetoric of the classic ethnography produced during the heyday of western colonialism. Orientalist ethnographers colonise the reality they are studying in terms of a universalist discourse, asserting the superiority of their own society in relation to that of the natives. Given that anthropology was the offspring of colonialism, the predominance of the objectivist and orientalist extends over a long period in the history of the discipline. Textual translation has often been rendered in similar terms. Some leading students of translation talk about the relationships between translator and author not only in terms of a predator–prey relationship, they also tend to employ a violent sexual language. The content of the source-text is represented as a passive, female prey to be appropriated by a male translator.

Many examples of the industrial exploitation of 'wild', undomesticated species illustrate the characteristics of environmental orientalism. The literature on fishing economies, for example, often attests to an aggressive stance; the expansive Icelandic fishing economy is one case in point. In the competitive fishing of most of this century, the chief criterion used for evaluating the social honour of a skipper was the relative size or the volume of catch, not the relative value of what was landed. The hero of fishing was the brave skipper who might risk the crew for extra tonnage, not so much fishing 'by diligence' (*af lagni*) as 'by force' (*af krafti*). During this period, the sea represented a gigantic, continuous mass of energy to be worked upon actively and offensively by humans, 'by force' – more specifically, by daring males almost at war with the ecosystem (see Pálsson 1991).[4]

To capture the morality of evironmental orientalism and its impractical consequences, the rhetorical metaphor of irony may be a useful one. The producers naïvely expect to be in total control and yet by their own practices they seriously undermine their mastery, sometimes bringing the species they exploit to near depletion. To act in terms of concepts that have such unintended consequences is, indeed, rather ironic. Even more ironically, faced with the realities of resource depletion people sometimes adopt the fatalistic attitude that depletion is simply an inevitable ingredient of economic progress. The metaphor of irony, however, has probably enjoyed far less popularity, at least in academic circles, than the one of tragedy; witness the exponential growth in the literature on the 'tragic' theory of the commons. Governmental authority or privatisation, it is often assumed, are the only alternatives to individual greed and environmental abuse. In one sense, however, the orientalist regime has no drama at all; there is no environmental problem to solve, no need for corrective measures and scientific, ecological or social expertise.

PATERNALISTIC PROTECTION

While the paternalistic paradigm shares some of the modernist assumptions of orientalism (it, too, implies human mastery and a distinction between laypersons and experts), it is characterised by relations of protection, not exploitation. This involves privileging scientific expertise, an inversion in the relative power of experts and laypersons. In the modern, environmentalist view, humans have a particular responsibility to meet, not only to other humans but also to members of other species, to fellow inhabitants of the animal kingdom, and the ecosystem of the globe. Precisely because of its radical stance, however, with respect to human–environmental relations, the environmentalist movement tends to fetishise nature, thereby setting it apart from the world of humans. Humans, it is argued, are acting on behalf of nature. The issue of animal rights among radical ecologists 'becomes something akin to the activities of the left revolutionaries of the nineteenth century, only now Nature, not the oppressed proletariat, is the beneficiary' (Bennett 1993: 343). Moreover, trapped in objectivist, western discourse on science and the Other, animal rights activists (oriental environmentalists, if you will) often make a fundamental distinction between 'them' (indigenous producers) and 'us' (Euro-Americans). In other words, only *some* segments of humanity properly belong to nature, those reported to love animals and take care of their environment, variously called 'primitives', the 'children of nature', or *Naturvölker*. 'We', it is assumed, left 'the state of nature' long ago. Similar notions, by the way, have often surfaced in anthropology; thus, deterministic, ecological models are sometimes presumed to apply only to some societies, notably hunting and gathering societies.

Again, an equivalent morality may be revealed in ethnographic practice. In some cases, ethnographers idealise and relativise the world of their hosts, representing their relations in terms of a protective contract. Despite the argument of protection, such a position only maintains the orientalist distinction between the observer and the native. Rosaldo suggests that the protectionist invocation of 'my people' in many ethnographic accounts simply represents an ideological denial of actual relations of hierarchy: 'It seems fitting', he claims, with reference to Evans-Pritchard's work on the Nuer, 'that a discourse that denies the domination that makes its knowledge possible idealizes, as alter egos, shepherds rather than peasants. Pastoralists, like individual tourists . . . exercise domination less readily than peasants, missionaries, or colonial officials' (Rosaldo 1986: 96). Similar themes emerge in the academic discourse on textual translation. The idea of the marital contract, as already indicated, is a persistent theme in the works of many literary scholars; thus, the frequent notions of the 'fidelity' and 'faithfulness' of translation; such constructs even manage to survive the most deconstructive onslaughts. Derrida speaks of the 'translation contract', defined as 'hymen or marriage contract with the promise to produce a child whose seed will give rise to history and growth' (1985: 191). Johnson (1985: 143) takes the analogy between translation and matrimony into a similar territory, arguing that the translator may be regarded 'not as a duteous spouse but as a faithful bigamist, with loyalties split between a native language and a foreign tongue', adding that, perhaps, the project of translation is best described as incest.

Peasants often seem to think of human–environmental relations in terms of protection and reciprocity. Bourdieu gives the impression of a metaphorical extension from the domain of kinship to the sphere of human–environmental relations among Kabyle peasants in Algeria. Kabyle say that the land 'settles its scores' and takes revenge for bad treatment and, by extension, the 'accomplished peasant "presents" himself to the land with the stance befitting one man meeting another, face to face, with the attitude of trusting familiarity he would show a respected kinsman' (Bourdieu 1990: 116). Significantly, the relationships between humans and their land are modelled on the social bonds among *distant* relatives characterised by respect and formality, by balanced, not generalised, reciprocity.

In the case of Icelandic fishing, the paradigm of paternalism is represented by the current application of scientific rationality to fisheries management. This rationality, largely the product of the cod wars with Britain and West Germany in the 1970s and the threat of overfishing in recent years, operates with the harvesting orientation of homeostatic fisheries. The first serious limitations on the fishing effort of Icelandic boats were temporary bans on fishing on particular grounds, but later on, by 1982, stronger measures were introduced to prevent the imminent collapse of the cod stock, the most important national resource, and make fishing more economical. A quota system was introduced in 1983 to deal with the problem. While fishermen continue to appropriate their prey, in the sense of removing it *from* the natural domain, a world separated from that of humans, with scientific management extraction has been subject to protective measures (*fiskvernd*) and stringent regulations. Consequently, fishermen have become increasingly dominated by techno-scientific knowledge and the agencies of the state. The chief architects of the paternalistic regime of protective fishing and the present system of individual transferable quotas (economists, biologists, and other policy makers) often remain firmly committed to a modernist, objectivist stance.[5] One example is their suppression of the issue of inequality and social distribution, a distracting, ethical subject, an irrelevant externality in the study and management of 'economic man', perhaps comparable to the category of 'society' in structural linguistics.

Given that, within the moral framework of paternalism, people are aware of the ecological consequence of their actions and that they seek to organise themselves to redress the 'balance', the metaphor of the comic plot may seem an appropriate one. The metaphor of comedy has, indeed, been used by several scholars to draw attention to the potential of collective action for corrective environmental purposes. McCay (1995) suggests, for instance, that such a metaphor captures the narrative style of economistic approaches to the question of the commons informed by game theory. She emphasises, however, that while such approaches represent an important shift in economistic assumptions about human nature, the comic plot is still 'squarely modernist' (McCay 1995: 109) in the sense that it fails seriously to address the larger contexts of history, power, and culture. Several anthropologists and economists have raised doubts with respect to the neoclassical and androcentric assumptions of economic theory and the general attempt to separate economics from politics, ethics, and culture (Gudeman 1992, England 1993).

COMMUNALISM

The paradigm of communalism differs from those of orientalism and paternalism in that it rejects the separation of nature and society and the notions of certainty and monologue, emphasising instead contingency and dialogue. Unlike paternalism, communalism suggests generalised reciprocity, an exchange often metaphorically represented in terms of intimate, personal relationships. The need to develop an 'ecological' theory along such lines, a theory that fully integrates human ecology and social theory, abandoning any radical distinction between nature and society, is often recognised nowadays. The outline, however, of such a theory was proposed early on in the writings of the young Marx, who insisted that humans could not be separated from nature, and, conversely, that nature could not be separated from humans. Nature, he argued, 'taken abstractly, for itself – nature fixed in isolation from man – is *nothing* for man' (1961: 169).

The recent development of a theory of practice, informed by both the writings of Marx and the perspectives of pragmatism, including that of Dewey, draws upon these insights. Not only does such a theory provide a perspective that resonates with the paradigm of communalism, dismissing the dualism of experts and laypersons, it also offers a compelling view on how people acquire the skills necessary for managing their lives, starting, as Dewey put it (1958: 23), 'from knowing as a factor in action and undergoing'.[6] The theory of practice draws attention to whole persons, master–apprentice relations, and the wider community of practice to which they belong, decentring the study of human action (Gudeman 1992, Pálsson 1994). Such a perspective provides a useful antidote to methodological individualism. The proper unit of analysis is no longer the autonomous individual separated from the social world by the surface of the body, but rather the whole person in action, acting within the contexts of that activity. Similar perspectives have been developed with respect to the notion of the 'separative' self in some other disciplines. England (1993) argues that the neoclassical idea of the self and subjective utility – an idea which logically excludes the possibility of interpersonal utility comparisons, of 'translating one's own and another person's metric for utility' – must be replaced by the notions of empathy and connectedness.

Recognising the importance of trust and communalism, anthropologists engage themselves in a serious ethnographic dialogue with the people they visit, forming an intimate rapport or communion. The communalism of fieldwork may be characterised as a project in which anthropologists and their hosts engage in meaningful, reciprocal enterprises, as the inhabitants of a single world (Pálsson 1993, 1995). Such a notion has much in common with what Habermas refers to as the discourse ethics of the 'ideal speech situation', a general communicative strategy for recognising differences and solving conflicts (Habermas 1990: 85). Fieldwork, Gudeman and Rivera (1990) emphasise in a similar vein, is a long conversation; anthropologists produce their ethnography *with* a responding people. Once again, there are obvious parallels in literary discourse. Neild (1989: 239) suggests an hermeneutic approach to translation which underlines the reciprocal nature of the enterprise; thus, if the process of translation is to be described as a love affair, an adequate theory of translation must recognise the role of empathy and seduction. The author 'reaches out' to the translator, altering his or her consciousness just as the translator alters the text.

Judging from many ethnographies, hunting and gathering societies nicely represent the principles of communalism. In such societies, it is often pointed out, relations with wild animals are characterised by close cooperation. Bird-David (1993) shows how many groups of hunters and gatherers metaphorically extend the communalism of relations among humans to the realm of environmental relations, thereby projecting an image of the 'giving environment'. Just as a child may expect the care of its parents, the environment provides its *unconditional* support, irrespective of what happened in the past. In hunting and gathering societies, then, human–environmental relations may be described in terms of generalised reciprocity. As the Nayaka of South India say, 'forest is as parent'. Similarly, the Canadian Cree sometimes speak of themselves as being in communion with nature and animals (Brightman 1993). Hunting activities are frequently regarded as love affairs where hunters and their prey seduce each other; hunters must enter into relationships with game animals in order to have any success and *vice versa*. To kill an animal is to engage in a dialogue with an inhabitant of the *same* world; animals are social persons and humans are part of nature. In the hunter's view, there is no fundamental distinction between nature and society.

While the classic ethnographic examples, perhaps, of the paradigm of communalism are those of hunters and gatherers, others may be relevant as well. Consider the ancient Scandinavians and their relations to the land. Gurevich (1992) points out that in ancient Scandinavia people were so indissolubly linked with the land they cultivated that they saw in the land an extension of their own nature: 'the fact that a man was thus personally linked with his possessions found reflection in a general awareness of the indivisibility of men and the world of nature' (1992: 178). Social honour, then, was embodied in the land, the *óðal* (hence the German *edel*). A pertinent modern example is the 'economy of livelihood' described by Gudeman and Rivera (1990) for rural Colombia. Here, too, the force of the human body is embodied in the land. If the land (and, by extension, the human body) is not replenished, the 'base' will erode and people leave for the cities. Therefore, 'caring for' (or 'managing') the base is a major concern. For rural Colombians, the base is not simply an economic 'resource', in the narrow meaning of the word; it is nothing less than life itself, a seamless *oikos*. Such views are echoed by some western, academic economists (Nelson 1993: 33) who argue for a 'provisioning' definition of economics that considers humans in relation to the world.

To return to the context of fishing, there may be good grounds for exploring, in the spirit of communalism, to what extent the practical knowledge of fishermen could be brought more systematically into the process of resource management and how this knowledge differs from the textual knowledge of professional biologists. I have argued

(Pálsson 1994) that skippers' extensive knowledge of the ecosystem within which they operate, the collective product of apprenticeship, is the result of years of practical enskilment and that it may be wise for management purposes to pay closer attention to this knowledge, allowing for extreme fluctuations in the ecosystem, relaxing at the same time the modernist assumption of predictability associated with the ecological project of sustainability. Some scholars argue that multi-species fisheries are chaotic systems with too many uncertainties for any kind of long-term control (interestingly, in a critical commentary on the idea of 'sustainability', focusing on the history of fisheries management, Ludwig, Hilborn, and Walters (1993: 17) make the observation that it may be 'more appropriate to think of resources as managing humans than the converse'). But if marine ecosystems are deterministic *and* chaotic regimes, those who are directly involved in resource-use on a daily basis are likely to have the most reliable information as to what goes on in the system at any particular point in time. In the Icelandic management regime there are few attempts to utilise the knowledge that skippers have achieved during years of practical engagement. There are, however, some interesting signs of change in this respect, one of which is the so-called 'trawling rally', whereby a group of skippers regularly fish along the same, pre-given trawling paths (identified by skippers and biologists), in order to supply detailed ecological information.

It is not quite clear, on the other hand, what the empowering of the practitioner's knowledge entails. While it is true that an extensive body of local knowledge has often been set aside, if not eliminated, in the course of western expansion and domination and there are good grounds for attempting to recapture and preserve what remains of such knowledge, the reference to the 'indigenous' and 'traditional' in such contexts tends to reproduce and reinforce the boundaries of the colonial world, much like earlier notions of the 'native' and the 'primitive'; 'natives' and 'primitives' have a tendency to congregate in particular times and locations. Where does a particular skill or body of knowledge have to be located to be classified as 'indigenous'? How old does it have to be to count as 'traditional'? Another contested issue relates to the concept of knowledge itself. Practical knowledge is sometimes presented as a marketable commodity, a thing-like 'cultural capital', for instance when encoding indigenous knowledge for the protection of intellectual property rights and defending legal claims about patents and royalties. Much of the practitioner's knowledge, however, is tacit – dispositions acquired in the process of direct engagement with everyday tasks. In reifying practical knowledge we fall into the trap of Cartesian dualism that we may be trying to avoid, separating body and mind.

Given the paradigm of communalism, and the contingent nature of human life, the overly pessimistic plot of tragedy is hardly the appropriate theatrical metaphor for capturing human–environmental relations. Nor is the overly optimistic plot of comedy a convincing one. The members of the human household are not simply greedy Robinsonades (to borrow a Marxian label) who inevitably destroy the ecosystems of which they are a part, nor are they necessarily able to work in harmony for a well-defined common good. The metaphor of romance may be more realistic, allowing for some degree of future hope, in a world with contesting perspectives, conflicting interests, and unexpected turns. In romance, as McCay suggests (following Donham 1990):

> conflict drives the narrative and is not overcome in the manner of neoclassical analyses.... Romance implies...complex development of character, situation, and plot and hinges upon the tension of not knowing what the outcome will be, but hoping for the best.
>
> (McCay 1995: 110)

'As a literary metaphor', she concludes, romance 'comes closer to the anthropological endeavor.'

CONCLUSION

I have distinguished three kinds of paradigms with respect to human–environmental relations: orientalism, paternalism, and communalism. Some of the modernist assumptions of orientalism (notably the conjecture of human mastery, the nature–society interface, and the distinction between laypersons and experts) are shared by the paternalistic paradigm – both paradigms are, indeed, the intellectual heirs of the Renaissance, the Enlightenment, and early positivist science (developed by, among others, Descartes and Francis Bacon), all of which instituted a series of decisive dualisms. But while relations of domination characterise the former, protective relations distinguish the latter. Moreover, whereas orientalism suggests the absence of reciprocity in human–environmental relations, the latter typically presupposes human responsibility and balanced reciprocity. Finally, the paradigm of communalism differs from both orientalism and paternalism in that it rejects the notions of certainty and monologue and the radical separation of nature and society. Unlike paternalism, it emphasises the *generalised* reciprocity of human–environmental relations, an exchange frequently modelled on close, personal relationships. As we have seen, similar relations are evident in ethnographic practice and textual translation. Thus, discourses on environmental management, ethnography, and textual translation have much in common, including the metaphors of personal relatedness and sexual intercourse and the language of theatre, the metaphors of irony, tragedy, comedy, and romance.

Social discourse is often, if not always, polyphonic. In modern Iceland, for instance, one can easily elicit evidence for the presence of *all* of the paradigms discussed (Pálsson 1995). To take another example, speaking of Cree representations of human–animal relations Brightman (1993: 194) points out that some indigenous accounts, including the ones of seduction, attest to mutualism and communion in human–animal relations while others indicate hierarchy and domination; such accounts, he claims, can be placed along a 'continuum between reciprocity and exploitation'. This suggests that paradigms of management should not be regarded as bounded regimes or discursive islands in either time or space. 'Operatively speaking', as Dewey remarked, echoing the Malinowskian idea of the 'long conversation', 'the remote and the past are "in" behavior making it what it is' (1958: 279). But if Icelanders themselves, or the Cree for that matter, do not seem to be able to make up their minds individually or to agree collectively on crucial ethnographic points – nor, indeed, the ethnographers who have written about them (the issue of 'whether Crees believe one or the other model to possess greater validity is exceptionally difficult to address' Brightman (1993: 200) concludes) – how are those with only second-hand ethnography at their disposal to issue a single, final verdict? To this question I can only offer a simple, pragmatic answer: if the problem of ethnographic disagreement needs to be resolved, it has to be approached, much like environmental problems, by means of some form of communicative ethics or a moral standard that allows for free and unrestricted dialogue.

In the early modernist project, with the discovery of the laws of perspective and the triumph of visualism, science became a passionate and aggressive search for truth and knowledge. Later, modernism was exposed as childish and vulgar scientism by critics of various kinds. The project of the Enlightenment was rendered as a metaphysical illusion. Panofsky, who generally emphasised the *successes* of the

Renaissance project and its contribution to science, seems to have anticipated some of these developments, suggesting that one may reproach perspective, the 'mathematization' of visual space, for 'evaporating "true being" into a mere manifestation of seen things' (Panofsky 1991: 71). Nowadays, westerners increasingly think of themselves as an integral part of nature as modern environmental discourse seems characterised by a 'post-modern condition', a discourse that emphasises, much like pre-Renaissance thought, the interrelatedness of nature and society, the 'individual' nature of human life, in the original, unified sense of the term.

The paradigm of communalism, with its emphasis on practice, reciprocity, and engagement, I suggest, provides an avenue out of the modernist project and current environmental dilemmas. It is true that critics of the modernist project often bask in nostalgia and utopia. The concepts of the perfect society and its antithesis, frequent themes in western thought, have taken many forms, all of which assume, as Berlin (1989) points out, a Golden Age when 'men were innocent, happy, virtuous, peaceful, free, where everything was harmonious' followed by some kind of catastrophe, 'the flood, man's first disobedience, original sin, the crime of Prometheus, the discovery of agriculture and metallurgy, primitive accumulation, and the like' (Berlin 1989: 120). To adopt the dialogic perspective of communalism is not, however, simply to return to the pre-Renaissance medieval world and indulge in naïve romanticism, but rather to embrace a *more* realistic position, shunning the ethnocentric preconceptions of the modernist project. Treating nature, non-human animals, and 'other' cultures as mere museum pieces for academic and theoretical consumption, is both unrealistic and irresponsible, given the fact that our lives and activities are inevitably situated in larger ecological and historical contexts. Anthropology was led astray by the radical separation of nature and society, what Hollingshead (1940: 358) referred to, in highly modernist terms, as a proper theoretical 'beginning'.

In the age of post-modernity, Sahlins's image (1976: 55), referred to at the outset, of anthropology as a prisoner pacing between the 'walls' of idealism and materialism, seems increasingly irrelevant. A more appropriate image of contemporary anthropology would be that of a former convict scratching his or her head in the open air, liberated from the Platonian cave, puzzled by the ruins of the prison house – its perceptual illusions, its strict codes of conduct, and its bizarre architectural design. Not only must such ex-prisoners wonder, in

Kafkaesque fashion, why they were locked up in the first place and how they eventually got out, but more importantly, how they could possibly enjoy the new freedom in the apparent absence of any kind of idealist agenda but faced with unavoidable materialist constraints and an ecological crisis.

ACKNOWLEDGEMENTS

The study on which this chapter is based is part of a collaborative research project – 'Common Property and Environmental Policy in Comparative Perspective' – initiated by the Nordic Environmental Research Programme (NERP). Work on this chapter has been supported by several other programmes and institutions, including the Nordic Committee for Social Science Research (NOS-S) and the Icelandic Science Foundation.

NOTES

1 In social theory, the organic individual has often been contrasted with collective social life; the former, it is assumed, is part of nature while the latter is superorganic. Such a distinction is illustrated by Mauss's famous analysis of the seasonal morphology of Inuit identity (Pálsson 1991: 68). For Mauss, the rhythm of the congregation and dispersion of game, during winter and summer, respectively, determined the relative importance of the natural and the social being in the life of the Inuit.

2 The egocentric approach, Merchant suggests, is grounded in the self and laissez faire capitalism, the homocentric one is grounded in society and the notion of stewardship, and, finally, the ecocentric approach addresses the whole cosmos, assigning intrinsic value to non-human nature.

3 Elsewhere, I have discussed in more detail the nature of this revolution and its implication for anthropology (see Pálsson 1995, especially Chapter 1).

4 Examples of the discourse I have associated with environmental orientalism are likely to be found also in the literature on the human use of domesticated animals (Tapper 1988).

5 The arguments for quota systems, informed by neoclassical economics, are seductive and powerful in the modern world. First, the resource is appropriated by regional or national authorities and later on the total allowable catch for a season is divided among producers, often the owners of boats. At a still later stage, such temporary privileges are turned into a marketable commodity.

6 Dewey's position with respect to environmental issues is a matter of some current debate (see Pepperman Taylor 1990).

REFERENCES

Bennett, J. W. (1993) *Human Ecology as Human Behavior: Essays in Environmental and Developmental Anthropology*, New Brunswick: Transaction Publishers.

Berlin, I. (1989) *Against the Current: Essays in the History of Ideas*, Oxford: Clarendon Press.

Bird-David, N. (1993) 'Tribal Metaphorization of Human–Nature Relatedness', in K. Milton (ed.) *Environmentalism: The View from Anthropology*, London: Routledge.

Bordo, S. (1987) *The Flight to Objectivity: Essays on Cartesianism and Culture*, New York: State University of New York Press.

Bourdieu, P. (1990) *The Logic of Practice*, trans. R. Nice, Cambridge: Polity Press.

Brightman, R. (1993) *Grateful Prey: Rock Cree Human–Animal Relationships*, Berkeley: University of California Press.

Derrida, J. (1985) 'Des Tours de Babel', in J. F. Graham (ed.) *Difference in Translation*, Ithaca: Cornell University Press.

Dewey, J. (1958 [1929]) *Experience and Nature*, New York: Dover Publications.

Donham, D. L. (1990) *History, Power, Ideology: Central Issues in Marxism and Anthropology*, Cambridge and Paris: Cambridge University Press and Editions de la Maison des Sciences de l'Homme.

England, P. (1993) 'The Separative Self: Androcentric Bias in Neoclassical Assumptions', in M. A. Ferber and J. A. Nelson (eds) *Beyond Economic Man: Feminist Theory and Economics*, Chicago and London: University of Chicago Press.

Gudeman, S. (1992) 'Markets, Models and Morality: the Power of Practices', in R. Dilley (ed.) *Contesting Markets: Analyses of Ideology, Discourse and Practice*, Edinburgh: Edinburgh University Press.

— and Rivera, A. (1990) *Conversations in Colombia: The Domestic Economy in Life and Text*, Cambridge: Cambridge University Press.

Gurevich, A. (1992) *Historical Anthropology of the Middle Ages*, J. Howlett (ed.) Oxford: Polity Press.

Habermas, J. (1990) 'Discourse Ethics: Notes on a Program of Philosophical Justification', in S. Benhabib and F. Dallmar (eds) *The Communicative Ethics Controversy*, Cambridge, Mass.: MIT Press.

Holling, C. S., Gunderson, L. and Peterson, G. (1994) 'Comparing Ecological and Social Systems', paper presented at the Beijer International Institute of Ecological Economics, The Royal Swedish Academy of Sciences, Stockholm, 29–30 August.

Hollingshead, A. B. (1940) 'Human Ecology and Human Society', *Ecological Monographs* 10, 3: 354–66.

Ingold, T. (1993) 'Globes and Spheres: the Topology of Environmentalism', in K. Milton (ed.) *Environmentalism: The View from Anthropology*, London: Routledge.

Johnson, B. (1985) 'Taking Fidelity Philosophically', in J. F. Graham (ed.) *Difference in Translation*, Ithaca: Cornell University Press.

Lefevere, A. and Bassnett, S. (1990) 'Introduction: Proust's Grandmother and the Thousand and One Nights: the "Cultural" Turn in Translation Studies', in S. Bassnett and A. Lefevere (eds) *Translation, History and Culture*, London: Pinter.

Ludwig, D., Hilborn, R., and Walters, C. (1993) 'Uncertainty, Resource Exploitation, and Conservation: Lessons from History', *Science* 260: 17, 36.

McCay, B. M. (1995) 'Common and Private Concerns', *Advances in Human Ecology* 4: 89–116.

Malinowski, B. (1972 [1922]) *Argonauts of the Western Pacific: An Account of Native Enterprise and Adventure in the Archipelagoes of Melanesian New Guinea*, London: Routledge and Kegan Paul.

Marx, K. (1961 [1844]) *Economic and Philosophical Manuscripts of 1844*, Moscow: Foreign Language Publishing House.

Merchant, C. (1990) 'Environmental Ethics and Political Conflict: a View from California', *Environmental Ethics* 12, 1: 45–68.

Neild, E. (1989) 'Translation is a Two-Way Street: a Response to Steiner', *Meta* 34, 2: 238–41.

Nelson, J. A. (1992) 'Gender, Metaphor, and the Definition of Economics', Economics and Philosophy 8: 103–25.

— (1993) 'The Study of Choice or the Study of Provisioning?: Gender and the Definition of Economics', in M. A. Ferber and J. A. Nelson (eds) *Beyond Economic Man: Feminist Theory and Economics*, Chicago and London: University of Chicago Press.

Pálsson, G. (1991) *Coastal Economies, Cultural Accounts: Human Ecology and Icelandic Discourse*, Manchester: Manchester University Press.

— (1993) 'Introduction', in G. Pálsson (ed.) *Beyond Boundaries: Understanding, Translation and Anthropological Discourse*, Oxford: Berg Publishers.

— (1994) 'Enskilment at Sea', *Man* (NS) 29, 4: 901–27.

— (1995) *The Textual Life of Savants: Ethnography, Iceland and the Linguistic Turn*, Chur, CES: Harwood Academic Publishers.

Panofsky, E. (1991 [1927]) *Perspective as Symbolic Form*, trans. C. S. Wood, Cambridge, Mass.: Zone Books.

Pepperman Taylor, B. (1990) 'John Dewey and Environmental Thought: a Response to Chaloupka', *Environmental Ethics* 12, 2: 175–84.

Rosaldo, R. (1986) 'From the Door of his Tent: the Fieldworker and the Inquisitor', in J. Clifford and G. E. Marcus (eds) *Writing Culture: The Poetics and Politics of Ethnography*, Berkeley: University of California Press.

Sahlins, M. (1976) *Culture and Practical Reason*, Chicago: University of Chicago Press.

Tapper, R. L. (1988) 'Animality, Humanity, Morality and Society', in T. Ingold (ed.) *What is an Animal?*, London: Unwin Hyman.

Williams, R. (1976) *Keywords: A Vocabulary of Culture and Society*, Glasgow: Fontana.

Chapter 5

Constructing natures

Symbolic ecology and social practice

Philippe Descola

Many anthropologists and historians now agree that conceptions of nature are socially constructed, that they vary according to cultural and historical determinations, and that, therefore, our own dualistic view of the universe should not be projected as an ontological paradigm onto the many cultures where it does not apply. Such a revision was triggered in part by an internal critique of western metaphysics and epistemologies (see, among others, Rosset 1973, Horigan 1988, Latour 1994). It was also the product of ethnographic studies conducted by anthropologists who realised that the nature–culture dichotomy was an inadequate or misleading tool to account for the ways in which the people they studied were talking about and interacting with their physical environment. Not only would these people commonly attribute human dispositions and behaviours to plants and animals – one of the oldest anthropological puzzles – but often they would also expand the realm of what are, for us, non-human living organisms to include spirits, monsters, artefacts, minerals or any entity endowed with defining properties such as conscience, a soul, a capacity to communicate, mortality, the ability to grow, a social conduct, a moral code, etc. In many cultures where the distinctions between living kinds, artefacts and chimeras appear fuzzy, and where non-humans seem to share many specificities of humankind, the common criteria of morphological or behavioural homology used in eliciting native taxonomies were found to be excessively narrow: by ignoring native classificatory criteria, they simply restricted the conceptualisation of beings to the classes of objects that we expect to find in the western category of nature.

The results of this naturalistic prejudice have been clearly visible in the anthropological division of labour: while most ethnobiologists still confine their ambitions to studying the folk taxonomies and nomenclatures of 'naturally' existing living kinds, 'symbolic' anthropology has devoted its attention to elucidating the logic of native cosmologies which do not appear to classify their components in conformity with the rules of domain-specificity. According to the purported homogeneity or heterogeneity of their contents, classifications have thus been defined and treated in quite different ways, an extraordinary anomaly for a discipline which assumes the unity of humankind.

This theoretical dualism also favoured the persistence of such binary oppositions as the one between the natural and the supernatural, whatever fashionable guise it may now take. When nature is assumed to be a transcultural and transhistoric domain of reality, no phenomenon or entity which is said to depart from ordinary physical possibilities can escape being labelled supernatural. However, as Durkheim argued almost a century ago (1960), the idea of a supernatural order is necessarily derived from the idea of a natural order of things, the former being but a residual category for all those phenomena which appear incompatible with the rational working of the laws of the universe. The nature–supernature opposition was formed in the course of the mathematisation of the physical world and though it has long been, from Lucretius to Marx, the main weapon of materialist philosophies against the illusions of religion, it can hardly qualifiy as an anthropological universal.[1] Modern self-claimed materialist approaches, such as cultural ecology or some brands of Marxist anthropology, did not pay heed to Durkheim's demonstration when they attempted to reduce the social construction of nature to a mechanical reflection in the mind of physical and technical determinations. In these perspectives, conceptions of nature were nothing but ideologies, i.e. distorted representations of those 'objective' material forces – be they arbitrarily selected limiting factors of the ecosystem or poorly defined 'levels of productive forces' – that purportedly shaped the structure and evolution of societies (Descola 1988). This fetishisation of nature led to an extreme form of ecological relativism in which every society was the exclusive product of a narrow adaptation and thus irreducible to any others, including those which appeared to share very similar environments.

However, the nature–culture dichotomy has sometimes proved to be quite fruitful, in structural anthropology for instance, where Lévi-Strauss has used it in a variety of contexts. It is hardly convincing in *Les structures élementaires de la parenté* (1949), where it functions as the hypothetical premise on which to rest the explanation of the incest

taboo as the origin and condition of marriage exchange and, therefore, of social life. Not only can this preliminary demonstration be
logically divorced from the principles of alliance theory set forth in the
rest of the book – which, in my opinion, stand on their own – but the
sudden emergence of culture from a state of nature also appears
highly implausible in the light of current accounts of the process of
hominisation (see Descola and Pálsson, this volume). In other works,
Lévi-Strauss has tended to downplay the dualism of the nature–
culture opposition, particularly in 'Structuralism and ecology' (1972)
where he advocates a remarkably naturalistic conception of the
working of the mind as a filtering device decoding sets of contrasts
already present in nature. In the *Mythologiques* (1964, 1966, 1968,
1971), however, the nature–culture distinction reappears as the
central device for the ordering, in semantic matrixes, of contrastive
properties and attributes expressed in mythological discourse. In spite
of the fact that the native societies of the Americas from which Lévi-
Strauss has drawn most of his mythological material do not
distinguish nature from culture in the way we do – if they do so at
all – most of the oppositions he draws on that axis make sense for
anthropologists familiar with the area. Furthermore, these oppositions are heuristic in that they permit valid inferences from new
material gathered in the same or neighbouring societies. The key to
this paradox is perhaps that the nature–culture distinction is little
more than a blanket label under which Lévi-Strauss has conveniently
organised contrasted sets of sensible qualities which may be ethnographically relevant, although the Amerindians do not feel the
necessity to subsume them, as we do, under two different ontological
domains.

BEYOND UNIVERSALISM AND RELATIVISM

That nature is socially constructed poses, however, a formidable
question: must we restrict ourselves to describing as best as we can the
specific conceptions of nature that different cultures have produced at
different times, or must we look for general principles of order
enabling us to compare the seemingly infinite empirical diversity of
nature–culture complexes? I am reluctant to adopt the relativist
position because, among other reasons, it presupposes the existence
of what needs to be established. If every culture is considered as a
specific system of meanings arbitrarily coding an unproblematic
natural world, which everywhere possesses all the features that our

own culture attributes to it, then not only does the very cause of the nature–culture(s) division remain unquestioned, but, declarations to the contrary notwithstanding, there can be no escape from the epistemological privilege granted to western culture, the only one whose definition of nature serves as the implicit measuring rod for all others.

Supposing, then, that there exist some very general patterns in the way people construct representations of their social and physical environment, where do we start looking for traces of their existence and *modus operandi*? Such a quest cannot rest, at least not exclusively, on the study of ethnobiological taxonomies. For one thing, the classification of plants and animals is only a limited aspect of the social objectivation of nature, this process by which each culture endows with a particular salience certain features of its environment and certain forms of practical engagement with it. To understand such a process, one must also take into account such dimensions as local theories of the working of the cosmos, sociologies and ontologies of non-human beings, spatial representations of social and non-social domains, ritual prescriptions and proscriptions governing the treatment of, and the relation with, different categories of beings, etc. Furthermore, strong doubts have been cast on the supposed universality of taxonomical structures stressed by evolutionary ethnobiologists: these doubts range from an acknowledgement of the extreme variability of the types of semantic determinants defining folk taxa (Friedberg 1986, 1990) and of the artificiality of taxonomic artefacts (Ellen 1993) to a radical challenge to the very existence of natural species (Ellen 1979) and of the hierarchical ordering of ethnobiological classifications (Howell 1989). Finally, even if one accepts that there may be domain-specific semantic universals reflecting perceptual discontinuities among living kinds, the question remains: how will knowledge of these universal patterns contribute to a better understanding of the actual diversity of the conceptualisations of non-humans? In other words, if all cultures classify plants and animals according to identical procedures, but if each of them endows living kinds with specific attributes and social values and conceives its relations with them in its own fashion, it must be because ethnobiological taxonomies play a subsidiary role in that process of diversification.

A common feature of all conceptualisations of non-humans is that they are always predicated by reference to the human domain. This leads either to sociocentric models, when social categories and relations are used as a kind of mental template for the ordering of the cosmos, or to a dualistic universe, as in the case of western cosmologies where nature is defined negatively as that ordered part of reality which exists independently from human action. Whether it operates by inclusion or by exclusion, the social objectivation of non-humans thus cannot be disjoined from the objectivation of humans; both processes are directly informed by the configuration of ideas and practice from which every society draws its concepts of self and otherness (Descola 1992: 111). Both processes imply establishing boundaries, ascribing identities and devising cultural mediations. This is not to say that the organic and inorganic environment of humans is a symbolic artefact which would only exist, in Berkeleyan fashion, because it is perceived through the prism of specific cultural codes. Giving excessive weight to explicit social classifications in the conceptual ordering of nature would be as misleading as reducing it to a species-specific, genetically engineered, perceptual and computa-tional process. It would easily lead to a renewal of the old Durkhei-mian dualism wherein nature is merely a phantasmagoric analogon of society, a static projection of explicit social categories, impervious both to the influence of practice and to the incidence of physical factors on the way people use and perceive their environment.

Furthermore, except in the western scientific tradition, representa-tions of non-humans are not usually based on a coherent and systematic corpus of ideas. They are expressed contextually in daily actions and interactions, in lived-in knowledge and body techniques, in practical choices and hasty rituals, in all those little things that 'go without saying' (Bloch 1992). Anthropologists reconstruct these mainly non-verbal mental models of practice from bits and pieces, from all sorts of apparently trifling acts and disconnected statements which they weave together so as to produce meaningful patterns (Descola 1994a). Are these meaningful patterns represented as guidelines for action in the mind of the people we study, or are they merely a blueprint for our own ethnographic interpretations? My reason for favouring the first option is that, although most members of any given community will find themselves unable to state explicitly the elementary principles of their cultural conventions, they never-theless appear to conform their practice to a basic set of underlying patterns.[2]

Now, these underlying patterns which seem to organise the relations between humans, as well as the relations between humans and non-humans, are not in my view universal structures of the mind which operate independently of cultural and historical contexts. These schemes or schemata of praxis, as I like to call them, are simply objectified properties of social practices, cognitive templates or intermediary representations which help to subsume the diversity of real life under a basic set of categories of relation. But since patterns of relations are less diverse than the elements which they relate, it seems obvious to me that these schemes of praxis cannot be infinite in number. This is why I believe that the mental models which organise the social objectivation of non-humans can be treated as a finite set of cultural invariants, although they are definitely not reducible to cognitive universals. I may explain my position better by using the analogy of kinship systems. This sphere of social practice is structured by a combination of rules of marriage alliance, ordering principles of the social domain by terminologies and modes of behaviour, and ideas about compatibility and incompatibility between bodily substances and between discrete elements defining the ascription and transmission of rights and identities, both collective and individual. Kinship systems thus organise modes of relation, modes of classification, and modes of identification in a variety of combinations which are far from having been exhaustively described and understood, but which many anthropologists are willing to treat as a finite group of transformation. It seems to me that the social objectivation of non-humans is equally structured by a combination of modes of relations, modes of identification and modes of classification and I believe it may be amenable to a similar treatment.[3]

SYMBOLIC ECOLOGY

Modes of identification

Modes of identification define the boundaries between self and otherness as expressed in the treatment of humans and non-humans, thus giving shape to specific cosmologies and social topographies. I have argued elsewhere that the opposition between 'totemic systems' and 'animic systems' reflects two such modes of identification (Descola 1992). While totemic classifications make use of empirically observable discontinuities between natural species to organise, conceptually, a segmentary order delimiting social units (Lévi-Strauss 1962), animism endows natural beings with human dispositions and social attributes. Animic systems are thus a symmetrical inversion of totemic classifications: they do not exploit the differential relations between natural species to confer a conceptual order on society, but rather use the elementary categories structuring social life to organise, in conceptual terms, the relations between human beings and natural species. In totemic systems non-humans are treated as signs, in animic systems they are treated as the term of a relation. It should be emphasised that these two modes of identification can very well be combined within a single society (see Århem's discussion of the Makuna, Chapter 10, this volume). Totemic systems are linked to a segmentary organisation and are thus conspicuously absent among societies which lack descent groups, while animist systems are found in cognatic as well as in segmentary societies. However, in societies where both systems are present, a common case among native Americans, there is often a clear distinction between two separate domains of non-humans, one being objectified through totemic classification and the other through animism.[4]

A third mode of identification, more familiar to us, is naturalism. Naturalism is simply the belief that nature does exist, that certain things owe their existence and development to a principle extraneous both to chance and to the effects of human will (Rosset 1973). Typical of western cosmologies since Plato and Aristotle, naturalism creates a specific ontological domain, a place of order and necessity where nothing happens without a reason or a cause, whether originating in God (such as Spinoza's famous 'Deus sive natura') or immanent to the fabric of the world ('the laws of nature'). Since naturalism is our own mode of identification and permeates our common sense as well as our scientific practice, it has become for us a 'natural' presupposition structuring our epistemology and, in particular, our perception of other modes of identification. In this context, totemism or animism appear to us as intellectually interesting but false representations, mere symbolic manipulations of that specific and circumscribed field of phenomena that we call nature. Viewed from an unprejudiced perspective, however, the very existence of nature as an autonomous domain is no more a raw given of experience than are talking animals or kinship ties between men and kangaroos.

Nor is the fact that, ever since Galileo, modern science has been increasingly efficient in describing and explaining the inner workings of reality, proof of the ultimate truth of our dualist cosmology. Indeed, as Latour convincingly argues (1994), the increased artificialisation of nature which has characterised the operations of science and technology from the seventeenth century onwards, was only made possible in practice because of a reinforcement of the polar opposition between nature and society. A dualist *épistémè* which prevented the conceptualisation of ontological hybrids actually favoured their phenomenological proliferation. The naturalistic explanations of social institutions favoured by sociobiologists are a contemporary illustration of this paradox: when nature, in the guise of DNA, reputedly drives social relations by maximising its reproductive potential, it operates as the *homo œconomicus* of Adam Smith and Ricardo would in an open market of scarce means and infinite ends (Sahlins 1976, Ingold, Chapter 2, this volume). In that respect, naturalism is never very far from animism: the former constantly produces actual hybrids of nature and culture which it cannot conceptualise as such, while the latter conceptualises a continuity between humans and non-humans which it can produce only metaphorically, in the symbolic metamorphoses generated by rituals.

Modes of relation

But animism, totemism and naturalism are only abstract topological grids distributing specific relational identities within the collectivity of humans and non-humans. These identities become differentiated, and thus anthropologically significant, when they are mediated by modes of relation, or schemes of interaction, which reflect the variety of styles and values found in social praxis. I have defined two such modes of relation under the labels of predation and reciprocity (Descola 1992). Both were isolated, within the general framework of animism, in two different cultures of the Upper Amazon very similar in their technology, settlement pattern and division of labour.

As evidenced by the cosmology of the Tukanoan Indians of eastern Colombia, reciprocity is based on a principle of strict equivalence between humans and non-humans sharing the biosphere, the latter being conceived as an homeostatic closed circuit. Since the amount of generic vitality present in the cosmos is finite, internal exchanges must be organised so as to return to non-humans the particles of energy which have been diverted from them in the process of food procurement, especially during hunting. Energetic feedback is ensured, among other methods, by the retrocession of human souls to the Master of Animals and by their subsequent transformation into game animals. Humans and non-humans are thus substitutes for one another and they contribute jointly, by their reciprocal exchanges, to the general equilibrium of the cosmos. The social organisation of the Tukanoan tribes is based on a similar principle of punctilious reciprocity. Despite linguistic diversity, each tribe, each local group, conceives of itself as an element integrated into a regional metasystem, owing its continuity to regulated exchanges of women, symbols and artefacts with the other parts of the whole.

Predation, on the other hand, appears to be the dominant value of the Jivaroan tribes of eastern Ecuador and Peru. Here also, non-humans are considered as persons (*aents*) sharing some of the ontological attributes of humans, with whom they are linked by ties of consanguinity (for the domesticated plants) or affinity (for forest animals). However, they do not participate in a network of exchange with humans, and no counterparts are offered for taking their lives. Non-humans try instead to take revenge, manioc by sucking the blood of women and children, game animals by delegating to the Masters of Animals the task of punishing excessive hunters by snakebite (and cannibalistic ingestion, in mythical discourse). This reciprocal predation also regulates relations between humans. Head-hunting between Jivaroan tribes, and constant feuding within (combined with the abduction of women and children), express the necessity of compensating each loss of life by the capture of real or virtual identities among closely related neighbours. Revenge is expected in that case, but it is not intended. Thus, mutual predation is the unintentional result of a general rejection of reciprocity, rather than a deliberate exchange of lives through bellicose intercourse. As contrasted modes of relation to humans and non-humans, reciprocity and predation constitute dominant schemes permeating the ethos of a culture. However, they do not preclude the presence of their opposite in specific niches: balanced reciprocity governs normal marriage alliance among the Jivaro, while the Tukano, who sometimes indulge in wife-raiding, are quite aware of their intermediary position in a cosmic food-chain (see Århem, Chapter 10, this volume). In other words, reciprocity encompasses predation among the Tukano, while the reverse is true of the Jivaro.

A similar type of hierarchical inclusion may be found in a third mode of relation: protection. It prevails when a large collection of non-humans are perceived as dependent upon humans for their reproduction and welfare. This collection may be composed of only a few species of domesticated plants and animals which are so closely linked to humans, on a collective or an individual basis, that they appear as genuine components either of the whole society (e.g. cattle for pastoralists) or of a more reduced kinship unit (family pets, sacred animals as ancestral figures, etc.). The bond of dependency is often reciprocal and somewhat utilitarian, as the protection of non-humans usually ensures beneficial effects. It may guarantee a basis of subsistence, fulfil a need for emotional attachment, provide currency for exchange, or help to perpetuate a link with a benevolent divinity. Even at its most altruistic level, as in contemporary conservationist movements, the protection of non-humans is not devoid of self-gratification. It transfers the Cartesian mastery and ownership of nature to another plane, a small enclave where guilt is alleviated and domination euphemistically transmuted into patronising preservation and aesthetic entertainment.

Protection is not only mutually profitable, it often implies a cascading chain of dependencies linking different ontological levels by a reduplication of asymmetric relations. In some cultures, the benevolent patronage bestowed by humans upon plants and animals also defines the attitude towards humans held by representatives of another group of non-humans, to wit, divinities. These divinities, who may themselves be an hypostasis of a plant or animal particularly important in the local economy, are perceived as founding ancestors and protectors of humans, as well as ultimate providers – and sometimes direct genitors – of the non-humans that the humans use and protect. Protection can thus become the encompassing value of a system of relation which combines a form of predation (taking the life of animal or vegetal non-humans without offering direct counter-parts) and a form of reciprocity (oblation to divine non-humans in exchange for the perpetuation of a successful domination over animal and vegetal non-humans). While this set of terms is now organised in a hierarchy, the social objectification of non-humans is still structured by a relation of analogy.

Modes of categorisation

Conceptualising the world of humans and non-humans also implies distributing its elementary components in such a way that these can be objectified in stable and socially recognised categories. However, categorisation should not be reduced to mere taxonomic classification (see Quéré 1995). For Aristotle as well as for contemporary mainstream ethnobiology, the classification of natural kinds amounts to a predicative inference or the subsumption of an object under a class. In such a perspective, the classified items are conceived as substances, distinguished from one another by contrastive features and generally by a specific linguistic marking; they are thus treated as individual mental representations, endowed with a distinctive autonomy as a result of a reputedly homogeneous perceptual salience. Since taxonomic classification operates on contents which may already be given in nature, or which may result from specific cognitive and perceptual constraints, it is not surprising that the inner architecture of ethnobiological folk-taxonomies should present a few, probably universal, defining characteristics (Atran 1990, Berlin 1992).

But the categorisation process can be viewed more broadly, in the tradition of Kantian schematism, as the ordering of a dynamic space by a methodical determination of singularities. In such a perspective the constitution of categories is a function of their relative position, and their relational identities are constructed through largely implicit procedures. The classification of illness in ayurvedic medicine (Zimmermann 1989) or the organisation of social attributes among the Zafimaniry of Madagascar (Bloch 1992) provide excellent anthropological illustrations of such classificatory principles. This type of ordering, which is sometimes known as paradigmatic (Petitot 1985), is thus based on a logic of relations, while taxonomic classification is based on a logic of predicates. The distinction is not new. Kant distinguished between the scholastic division, which provides a systematisation for the use of memory, and the natural division, which distributes living creatures according to laws of combination rather than ranking them under established labels (Kant 1947). If we follow Tort, however, these two classificatory schemes need not be considered as antithetical; using the vocabulary of the classification of tropes devised by Du Marsais in the eighteenth century, he argues that the metaphoric scheme, which classifies by likeness, and the metonymic scheme, which classifies by attributes or properties, are jointly constitutive of any classificatory device (Tort 1989). The domination of one of these schemes is never absolute, since the apparent order it establishes is always subverted by that inherent to the other scheme.

Standard folk-taxonomies of plants and animals are thus often organised according to the principle of similarity, i.e. by a metaphoric scheme. However, if only the semantic dimensions of nomenclatures are considered, it is often a metonymic scheme which governs the attribution of names, especially at the level of subgeneric taxa where many specifying determinants refer to the qualities or uses of the classified items. Conversely, symbolic or totemic classifications are based on a metonymic scheme, since they correlate classes of humans and classes of non-humans either by linking them through a chain of interlocking properties or by positing that the organisation of the contrast set in one of the domains is a reflection of, or a conceptual model for, the organisation of the other (see Durkheim and Mauss (1903) for the sociocentric version, and Lévi-Strauss (1962) for the converse). But the principle of association at work in symbolic classification may itself be obliterated by a principle of similarity, for instance when a resemblance is stressed between the essential qualities of a totemic species and those ascribed to the members of the descent group which bears its name. It may even be that the lack of distinction between the metonymic and the metaphoric schemes – which operate simultaneously in many symbolic classifications, but at different logical and contextual levels – is the main reason for the resilience of that anthropological fetish which Lévi-Strauss called the totemic illusion (1962).

Each culture, each historical *épistémè*, articulates these two classificatory schemes to produce specific combinations, the nature of which vary according to the dominant type of scheme, to the number of levels encompassed by this scheme, and to the type of classificatory mode privileged by each of the schemes at each level of classification. These modes are quite diverse: for instance the metaphoric scheme may classify by morphological resemblance (e.g. mainstream botany since Adanson), by analogy (of structures, designs, intellectual faculties or moral dispositions), or by a matrix of contrastive features (as in structural phonology, cladistics or racialist physical anthropology). As for the metonymic scheme, it may classify by properties or uses (e.g. pre-classical western botany), according to a relation of spatial contiguity (classification by habitats in folk ethnobiological taxonomies or by *topoi* in folk cosmologies) or according to a relation of temporal contiguity (such as the genealogical principle at work in evolutionary biology or in the folk classification of certain descent groups). I believe – rather as a prospective act of faith – that studying these hierarchical combinations of classificatory schemes and modes of classification may shed some light on the different types of categorisation of humans and non-humans. Such an endeavour might at least provide an escape from the two options between which ethnoscience has been oscillating for some time, that of the incommensurability of cultural grammars and that of an artificial universality of the ordering of living kinds stemming from the sole consideration of taxonomic classifications.

COMBINATIONS

Given the hypothetical nature of the propositions presented here-tofore, it seems fair to illustrate their scope and potential applications by providing a few ethnographic examples. For lack of space, I will consider only some types of objectivation of non-humans resulting from various combinations of modes of identification and modes of relation, leaving aside modes of classification.

Animic variations

As a mode of identification, animism can be specified by at least three dominant types of relation: predation, reciprocity and protection. The Jivaro have already provided us with an example of predatory animism, but this trait also applies to many warlike societies, especially in the Americas, for whom the capture and the incorporation of persons, identities, bodies and substances form the touchstone of a cannibalistic social philosophy: for instance among the Mundur-ucú of Brazil (Murphy 1958), the Nivacle of the Gran Chaco (Sterpin 1993) or the Southwestern Chippewa of the Great Lakes area (Ritzenthaler 1978).

Reciprocity is an inversion of predation and it defines those animic systems in which the relations between humans, as well as the relations between humans and non-humans, are fuelled by a constant exchange of services, souls, food or generic vitality. The dominant belief in such systems is that humans have a debt towards non-humans, notably for the food the latter provide. Although humans may try to dodge their obligations, they also readily admit that it is legitimate for non-humans to try re-establish the balance of reciprocity by capturing components of the human person, by partaking of their food or by tapping a part of their vitality. Besides the aforementioned Tukanoan societies of Northwestern Amazonia, this type of conception has been well documented among peoples of the Arctic and subarctic areas of North America, such as the Inuit (Blaisel 1993), the Montagnais-Naskapi (Speck 1935), the Northern Ojibwa (Hallowell 1981) and the Cree (Tanner 1979, Brightman 1993), or among certain people of Southeastern Asia, such as the Chewong (Howell 1989, see also this volume, Chapter 7) or the Ma 'Betisek of Malaysia (Karim 1981).

As a dominant mode of relation, protection is seldom associated with animic systems, since these are most common among societies in which hunting constitutes the main focus of mediation between humans and non-humans. Protection, on the other hand, implies a direct and permanent contact with the protected species and a type of dependency of non-humans upon humans which are more typical of the interactions with domesticates. However, Hamayon clearly describes a case of protective animism in her analysis of the 'pastoral shamanism' practised by the Exirit-Bulagat of Southern Siberia (Hamayon 1990: 605–704). Among these people, the symbolic status of domestic animals (cattle, horses and sheep) derives from the standard conception of Siberian hunters wherein humans and animals share a similar essence. But while the Buriat hunting societies conceive their relation with game animals and the Spirit of the Forest as one of equality and alliance, the Buriat herders favour a hierarchical relation between humans, protected non-humans (cattle) and the non-human protector of the two former categories, a figure called the Lord-Bull. It is with this hypostasis of cattle that a relation of exchange is established through the sacrifice of animals intended as counterparts for ensuring the continuous mastery of humans over non-humans.

Totemic variations

The modes of relation between humans and non-humans typical of totemic systems are necessarily dichotomised. In such systems, non-humans provide a repertory of labels for social classification; they are the signs that a society uses to conceptualise its segmentation and, as such, they cannot constitute the terms of social relations with humans. But since the meaning and function of non-humans is not limited to their role in social classification, other aspects of their practical or symbolic potentialities may be emphasised in other spheres of social life. A predatory relation with a totemic species is thus possible only if a clear distinction is made between the species as a classificatory concept and the individual members of this species. This appears to be the case among Australian aborigines, where hunting is not conceived as an exchange, or the product of a covenant, between humans and animals, but rather as a quite mundane activity of food procurement (Testart 1987). Contrary to what prevails in many Amerindian and Siberian cosmologies, where the relation to hunted animals is presented as one of affinity or alliance with individuals of equal status, Australian hunters do not consider their prey as an *alter ego* whose death should be compensated for. The relation of predation appears to be quite literal and it does not carry a specific cosmological meaning. Falling outside the scope of hunting, the ritual treatment of animals emphasises an abstract lineal continuity between the community of non-humans and the community of humans, in a ceremonial organisation oriented towards the celebration of the solidarity and the complementarity of the different segments forming the social whole. Depending on context, then, animals are either good to eat or food for thought, but they are never social partners.

A relation of reciprocity with totemic non-humans is no more possible than a relation of predation, since totemic species, being simple signifiers of social segmentation, cannot enter into a reciprocal relation with humans. However, pure totemic systems are rather exceptional outside Australia, and they are often combined with animic systems which allow the expression of a relation of reciprocity with at least a fraction of non-humans. Such is the case among the Bororo of Brazil (see Note 4 at end of chapter).

The combination between a totemic system and a relation of protection also implies a relative dichotomy of the modes of interaction between humans and non-humans. However, this dichotomy is less marked than in the other modes of relation inasmuch as the protected non-humans, without necessarily forming part of the set of totemic species, may nevertheless be endowed with a totemic function, i.e. they can be used as markers of social status and relations. The Nuer offer a good example of the latter case: besides having an entirely orthodox totemic system, in which certain non-humans (mammals, birds, reptiles, trees) serve to conceptualise lineage segmentation, the Nuer also 'tend to define all social processes and relationships in terms of cattle' (Evans-Pritchard 1940: 19). This aspect is particularly emphasised in ritual life, for instance in male initiation ceremonies during which each young man takes his 'ox-name' which he will retain long after the particular ox from which the name is derived ceases to be in his possession (Evans-Pritchard 1956: 250–57). In the Nuer case, cattle is good to protect,[5] it is good to think of as a marker of individual and collective identities, and it is good to socialise as a direct substitute for humans in the various spheres of exchange.

Naturalistic variations

Of all the modes of identification, naturalism is obviously the most familiar to westerners, even if some of its expressions result in antinomies and are thus condemned to remain in the domain of utopia. This is the case, for instance, with the dream of positing a relation of reciprocity between humankind and nature, conceived as partners or entities of equal status, an aim impossible to achieve since, in a naturalist cosmology, there can be no common ground between humans and non-humans: either they are perceived as belonging to interconnected communities, and naturalism loses its predicative role, or they remain confined in separate ontological domains, and the dialectics of reciprocity amount to no more than a metaphor in which to couch an impossible aspiration to supersede dualism. Expressions of this aspiration have been common in philosophical and literary discourse: in one form or another they have been voiced by such diverse spokesmen as Schelling (in his philosophy of nature), romantic poets such as Lamartine or Goethe, Engels (in his *Dialectics of Nature*) or, more recently, Michel Serres (1990).

As for predatory naturalism, it is less a value than an old European practice, born in the Middle Ages when large tracts of forest where cleared for cultivation; a practice which acquired its legitimacy with Cartesian philosophy, and its full expression with the mechanisation of the world – in the physical as well as in the technical sense of the expression; a practice which then transformed into the historical destiny of Europe, under the name of production, when bourgeois society managed to conceive itself as the embodiment of a natural order. A desire to protect nature could not fail to emerge from such a state of affairs; it took the guise of an ideology which extended to wild species and natural landscapes the type of sensibility and behaviour already experienced in relation to certain domestic animals, and in the development of pleasure gardens (Thomas 1983). By fetishising nature as a transcendental object, the control of which would be displaced from predatory capitalism to the rational management of modern economics, the conservationist movements, far from questioning the foundations of western cosmology, tend rather to perpetuate the ontological dualism typical of modern ideology. However, the programme set forth by environmental activists will perhaps lead, unintentionally, to a dissolution of naturalism, since the survival of a whole range of non-humans, now increasingly protected from anthropic damage, will shortly depend almost exclusively upon social conventions and human action. The conditions of existence for blue whales, the ozone layer or the Antarctic will thus be no more 'natural' than they are presently for wild species in zoos or for genes in biological data banks. Drifting away from its time-honoured definition, nature is less and less the product of an autonomous principle of development; its foreseeable demise, as a concept, will probably close a long chapter of our own history.

CONCLUSION

Because of its very vagueness, the idea of nature has been the main prop in a series of dichotomies which constitute the building blocks of the history of western thought: nature–culture, nature–supernature, nature–art, nature–history, nature–mind, etc. However, as Heidegger rightly pointed out (1968), nature has been much more than the basic term of a series of antithetical notions; in all those distinctions it functions as an encompassing totality defining the very character-istics of each of the notions it opposes. What is distinguished from nature receives its determination from it, so that most metaphysical themes appear to draw their existence from an endeavour to transcend a notion which, in itself, has very little meaning. The conclusion seems inescapable: suppress the idea of nature and the whole philosophical edifice of western achievements will crumble. But this intellectual cataclysm will not necessarily leave us facing the great void of Being which Heidegger ceaselessly denounced; it will only reshape our cosmology and render it less exotic for many cultures who are on the verge of embracing the values of what they believe is modernity. Globalisation may then take a very different meaning: neither the abolition of all differences between 'them' and 'us' nor our return to the principles of Augustinian theology, but a new common ground that will render 'us' closer to 'them', as we strive, in our own way, to cope with an hybrid universe in which humans and non-humans can no longer be comfortably managed by two entirely different sets of social devices.

Whether such a reshuffling of the cards will eventually come about, and whether it will produce a better world, is not for me to predict. However, its epistemological consequences for anthropology are clearly foreseeable. The main one is the obsolescence of the debate between universalism and relativism, itself a relic of the nature–culture dichotomy, and its attempted transcription into antithetical programmes. Going beyond universalism and relativism implies ceasing to treat society and culture, as well as human faculties and physical nature, like autonomous substances, thus opening the way to a true ecological understanding of the constitution of individual and collective entities. Whether they are self ascribed or externally defined, whether they are crafted by humans or only perceived by humans, whether they are material or immaterial, the entities of which our universe is made have a meaning and identity solely through the relations that constitute them as such. Although relations precede the objects that they connect, they actualise themselves in the very process by which they produce their terms. A non-dualistic anthropology would then amount to a kind of structural phenomenology in which local systems of relations are described and compared, not as functional networks differing by their scales and types of connection – as in the symmetric anthropology advocated by Latour (1994) and Callon (1991) – but as variations within a group of transformations, i.e. a set of combinations structured by compatibilities and incompatibilities between a finite number of elements. Among these elements would figure relations of objectivation of humans and non-humans (Descola 1994b), modes of categorisation, systems of mediation and types of technical and perceptual 'affordances' (Gibson 1979) geared to specific environments. Once the ancient nature–culture orthogonal grid has been disposed of, a new multi-dimensional anthropological landscape may emerge, in which stone adzes and quarks, cultivated plants and the genome map, hunting rituals and oil production may become intelligible as so many variations within a single set of relations encompassing humans as well as non-humans.

NOTES

1   Stating that the natural–supernatural opposition is culture-specific does not exclude the hypothesis that there may exist a set of assumptions concerning every day physical phenomena which are shared by everyone in every culture, nor does it exclude the related hypothesis that religious ideas may result from the explicit violation of some of these, possibly universal, physical intuitions (see Boyer 1993). There is a huge difference, however, between assuming the universality of a domain-specific mental tool-kit for the cognition of a restricted set of physical phenomena (gravity, tangibility, visibility, etc.) and assuming the universality of a notion of 'nature' qualified as an ontological domain which would everywhere be conceived as having the same discrete boundaries and as being activated by the same laws.

2   That such a conformity to underlying patterns is not confined to preliterate societies can be ascertained by a measure of reflexivity. For instance, while I have been operating efficiently within the French academic system for some time, I nevertheless had to wait for Bourdieu's *Homo Academicus* (1992) to become fully aware of some of the principles which determined my position and guided my actions in this specific social and cultural field.

3   The propositions outlined in this chapter are but a rough sketch of the arguments of a book in progress on the comparative anthropology of the relations between humans and non-humans.
4   This is the case, for instance, among the Bororo of Eastern Brazil, who make a clear distinction between, on the one hand, *aroe* species (the jaguar and most felidaes, aras, aquatic birds, the harpy eagle, etc.) that are associated with totemic classifications, social order and nominal essences and, on the other hand, *bope* species (vultures, deers, the tapir, the capybara, peccaries, catfish, etc.) which embody life processes, both positive and negative, and which exchange vital energy with humans in a complex system of reciprocity (see Crocker 1985).
5   'The cow is a parasite of the Nuer, whose lives are spent in ensuring its welfare' (Evans-Pritchard 1940: 36).

REFERENCES

Atran, S. (1990) *Cognitive Foundations of Natural History. Towards an Anthropology of Science*, Cambridge and Paris: Cambridge University Press and Editions de la Maison des Sciences de l'Homme.

Berlin, B. (1992) *Ethnobiological Classification: Principles of Categorization of Plants and Animals in Traditional Societies*, Princeton: Princeton University Press.

Blaisel, X. (1993) *Espace Cérémoniel et Temps Universel chez les Inuit du Nunavut (Canada). Les Valeurs Coutumières et les Rapports Rituels entre Humains, Gibiers, Esprits et Forces de l'Univers*, Doctoral thesis in anthropology, Ecole des Hautes Études en Sciences Sociales, Paris.

Bloch, M. (1992) 'What Goes Without Saying: the Conceptualization of Zafimaniry Society', in A. Kuper (ed.) *Conceptualizing Society*, London and New York: Routledge.

Bourdieu, P. (1992) *Homo Academicus*, Paris: Editions de Minuit.

Boyer, P. (1993) *Cognitive Aspects of Religious Symbolism*, Cambridge: Cambridge University Press.

Brightman, R. (1993) *Grateful Prey: Rock Cree Human–Animal Relationships*, Berkeley: University of California Press.

Callon, M. (1991) 'Techno-Economic Networks and Irreversibility', in J. Law (ed.) *A Sociology of Monsters*, London: Routledge.

Crocker, J. C. (1985) *Vital Souls: Bororo Cosmology, Natural Symbolism and Shamanism*, Tucson: University of Arizona Press.

Descola, P. (1988) 'L'explication Causale', in P. Descola, G. Lenclud, A. C. Taylor and C. Severi (eds) *Les Idées de l'Anthropologie*, Paris: Armand Colin.

— (1992) 'Societies of Nature and the Nature of Society', in A. Kuper (ed.) *Conceptualizing Society*, London and New York: Routledge.

— (1994a) *In the Society of Nature: A Native Ecology in Amazonia*, trans. Nora Scott, Cambridge: Cambridge University Press.

— (1994b) 'Pourquoi les Indiens d'Amazonie n'ont-ils pas Domestiqué le Pécari? Généalogie des Objets et Anthropologie de l'Objectivation', in B.

Latour and P. Lemonnier (eds) *De la Préhistoire aux Missiles Balistiques. L'intelligence Sociale des Techniques*, Paris: La Découverte.

Durkheim, E. (1960 [1912]) *Les Formes Élémentaires de la Vie Religieuse. Le Système Totémique en Australie*, Paris: Presses Universitaires de France.

— and M. Mauss (1903) 'De quelques Formes Primitives de Classification. Contribution à l'Étude des Représentations Collectives', *Année Sociologique* 6: 1–72.

Ellen, R. F. (1979) 'Introductory Essay', in R. F. Ellen and D. A. Reasons (eds) *Classifications in Their Social Context*, London: Academic Press.

— (1993) *The Cultural Relations of Classification. An Analysis of Nuaulu Animal Categories from Central Seram*, Cambridge: Cambridge University Press.

Evans-Pritchard, E. E. (1940) *The Nuer: A Description of the Modes of Livelihood and Political Institutions of a Nilotic People*, Oxford: Clarendon Press.

— (1956) *Nuer Religion*, Oxford: Clarendon Press.

Friedberg, C. (1986) 'Classifications Populaires des Plantes et Modes de Connaissance', in P. Tassy (ed.) *L'ordre et la Diversité du Vivant. Quel Statut Scientifique pour les Classifications Biologiques?*, Paris: Fondation Diderot/Librairie Fayard.

— (1990) *Le Savoir Botanique des Bunaq. Percevoir et Classer dans le Haut Lamaknen (Timor, Indonésie)*, Paris: Muséum National d'Histoire Naturelle.

Gibson, J., J. (1979) *The Ecological Approach to Visual Perception*, Boston: Houghton Mifflin.

Hallowell, A. I. (1981 [1960]) 'Ojibwa Ontology, Behaviour and World View', in S. Diamond (ed.) *Culture in History. Essays in Honor of Paul Radin*, New York: Octagon Books.

Hamayon, R. (1990) *La Chasse à l'Âme. Esquisse d'une Théorie du Chamanisme Sibérien*, Nanterre: Société d'ethnologie.

Heidegger, M. (1968) 'Ce qu'est et Comment se Détermine la Physis', in *Questions II*, Paris: Gallimard.

Horigan, S. (1988) *Nature and Culture in Western Discourses*, London: Routledge.

Howell, S. (1989 [1984]) *Society and Cosmos: Chewong of Peninsular Malaysia* (2d edn), Chicago and London: University of Chicago Press.

Kant, E. (1947 [1775–77]) 'De la Diversité des Races en Général', in *La Philosophie de l'Histoire*, Paris: Aubier.

Karim, W.-J. (1981) *Ma'Betisek Concepts of Living Things*, London: Athlone.

Latour, B. (1994) *We Have Never Been Modern*, Cambridge, Mass.: Harvard University Press.

Lévi-Strauss, C. (1949) *Les Structures Élémentaires de la Parenté*, Paris: Presses Universitaires de France.

— (1962) *Le Totémisme Aujourd'hui*, Paris: Presses Universitaires de France.

— (1964) *Mythologiques, I. Le Cru et le Cuit*, Paris: Plon.

— (1966) *Mythologiques, II. Du Miel aux Cendres*, Paris: Plon.

— (1968) *Mythologiques, III. L'origine des Manières de Table*, Paris: Plon.

— (1971) *Mythologiques, IV. L'homme Nu*, Paris: Plon.

— (1972) 'Structuralism and Ecology', *Gildersleeve Conference*, Barnard College: Barnard Alumnae.

Murphy, R.F. (1958) *Mundurucú Religion*, Berkeley and Los Angeles: University of California Press.

Petitot, J. (1985) *Morphogenèse du Sens*, Paris: Presses Universitaires de France.

Quéré, L. (1995) 'Présentation ', in B. Fradin, L. Quéré and J. Widmer (eds) *L'enquête sur les Catégories: de Durkheim à Sachs*, Paris: Editions de l'EHESS.

Ritzenthaler, R. E. (1978) 'Southwestern Chippewa', in B. G. Trigger (ed.) *Handbook of North American Indians, vol. 15, Northeast*, Washington, DC: Smithsonian Institution.

Rosset, C. (1973) *L'anti-nature: Eléments pour une Philosophie Tragique*, Paris: Presses Universitaires de France.

Sahlins, M. (1976) *The Use and Abuse of Biology: An Anthropological Critique of Sociobiology*, Chicago and London: University of Chicago Press.

Serres, M. (1990) *Le Contrat Naturel*, Paris: Editions François Bourin.

Speck, F. J. (1935) *Naskapi: The Savage Hunters of the Labrador Peninsula*, Norman: University of Oklahoma Press.

Sterpin, A. (1993) 'La Chasse aux Scalps chez les Nivacle du Gran Chaco', *Journal de la Société des Américanistes de Paris* 79: 33–66.

Tanner, A. (1979) *Bringing Home Animals: Religious Ideology and Mode of Production of the Mistassini Cree Hunters*, St John: Memorial University of Newfoundland.

Testart, A. (1987) 'Deux Modèles du Rapport entre l'Homme et l'Animal dans les Systèmes de Représentation', *Études Rurales* 107–8, 171–93.

Thomas, K. (1983) *Man and the Natural World: Changing Attitudes in England (1500–1800)*, London: Allen Lane.

Tort, P. (1989) *La Raison Classificatoire: Quinze Études*, Paris: Aubier.

Zimmermann, F. (1989) *Le Discours des Remèdes au Pays des Épices. Enquête sur la Médecine Hindoue*, Paris: Editions Payot.

Chapter 6

The cognitive geometry of nature

A contextual approach

Roy F. Ellen

INTRODUCTION

That conceptions of nature vary historically and ethnographically, and are, therefore, themselves intrinsically cultural, is so widely asserted nowadays that it is often assumed to have become a self-evident anthropological truth. Perhaps the best example of this in popular environmentalist discourse, as in some anthropology, is the opposition drawn between the holistic systemic vision of 'traditional', 'tribal' or 'archaic' societies and the dualism of the modern scientific and dominant Judaeo-Christian tradition. How conceptions of nature vary beyond such abstractions is well-demonstrated in individual studies, both historical (e.g. Collingwood 1945, Thomas 1983, Horigan 1988, Torrance 1992) and ethnographic. In particular, much attention has been given to how these might arise from particular *practices* of environmental interaction (e.g. Ingold 1992, Bird-David 1993), and how these in turn might sustain, or (e.g. Schefold 1988) be sustained by, particular social ideologies.[1] As Philippe Descola puts it:

> each specific form of cultural conceptualisation also introduces sets of rules governing the use and appropriation of nature, evaluations of technical systems, and beliefs about the structure of the cosmos, the hierarchy of being, and the very principles by which living things function.
>
> (Descola 1992: 110)

But empirical demonstrations of such relativity – many of which find their origin in the claim by Leach (1964: 34–35) that nature is no more than some topological grid imposed upon a continuous world – have led to an almost indignant rejection of the very idea of nature. Indeed, it has become increasingly awkward and misleading to carve out from these implied 'representations' or 'constructions', a conceptual space which is linguistically, cognitively and symbolically coherent. The new consensus has thus given rise to new problems: that of commensurability between different conceptions of nature (including the assumption that *our* nature always exists as a category comparable to *their* nature); the implication that each culture has a single ruling (and unambiguous) conception of nature, which it is our task to locate, excavate and describe; and the problem as to how those collective notions of nature which we can claim to exist are 'constructed' or 'negotiated'. I shall argue that we can approach the question of the categorical status of nature in two – superficially antithetical – ways.

The first is a continuation of what the relativists and deconstructionists are arguing; namely that any one population may, depending on the circumstances, generate conceptions of nature which are fuzzy and variable – which may indeed be inconsistent and contradictory – and that such variability may reveal itself at the level of individual praxis and at the level of collective representations, or in some combination of the two. Consequentially, it is difficult to speak of 'societies' and 'cultures' (that is, second-order constructs) as having a single conception of nature, and an exaggeration to claim that it is even true of empirically identifiable local populations. Indeed, it may be claimed that some peoples have no concepts of nature whatsoever.

The second way is to buck this trend and identify a minimum number of underlying assumptions upon which pragmatic schemata and symbolic representations are built, and which ultimately constrain human conceptual permutations (cf. Boyer 1993).[2] If I interpret him correctly, this is what Descola (1992: 110) means by 'the social objectification of nature [being] implemented through a limited number of operative schemes', and his acknowledgement that 'modes of representation of relations to nature present certain similar characteristics' (ibid.: 123). Such widely-observed 'similar characteristics' may be accounted for if we hypothesise that underlying all models of nature are three cognitive axes or dimensions, which will, when the cultural devices they permit are combined in different ways, generate particular representations, all recognisably transformations of some ur- or proto-nature. The first axis is that which allows us to construe nature *inductively* in terms of the 'things' which people include within it, and the characteristics assigned to such things. The second is that which allows us to define nature *spatially*, assigning it to some realm outside humans or their immediate living (cultural) space. The third is that which allows us to define nature in *essentialist* terms, as some force which is exogenous to human will but which can to varying degrees be controlled. To the extent that these three cognitive axes make an equal contribution to representations, they may be predicted to approach that multi-faceted, ambiguous, but ultimately recognisable idea which we in the West recognise as nature; whereas the more asymmetry is introduced into the model the less familiar the construction becomes. And to the degree that each of these axes dominates a conceptualisation characteristic of a particular context, so it also becomes a 'definition' of nature.

I focus here on examples drawn largely from my own work on the Nuaulu, a people of Seram in eastern Indonesia whose mode of subsistence may be summarily typified as a combination of hunting, sago extraction and swidden cultivation. There are no new data, though the way I have used them is different. Thus, I start by asking how we might begin to identify cultural phenomena which best approximate each of the three cognitive axes specified above, and by exploring the extent to which they permit us to infer the existence of nature as a domain. I then examine how combining cultural ideas derived from each of the axes generates *intrinsic* ambiguity, and how this is reflected in the variation accompanying different practical and symbolic contexts.

NATURE AS KINDS OF 'THING'

Let us first examine how far the first axis, the inductivist (nature as 'things') model, assists us in generating an approximation, or one dimension, of some hypothetical Nuaulu conceptualisation of nature. In cultural modifications of this model, particular 'things', by virtue of their resemblance to other things, are – once aggregated – seen as *part of* nature. Thus, through induction, nature itself becomes a thing which can then be the conceptual starting point of deductive reasoning. It has been suggested (Ingold 1986: 3, 1992: 44) that the fact that we see 'things' at all is what distinguishes *Homo sapiens* from other animals: birds may perceive functional objects such as anvils or missiles, but only humans can perceive something as abstract as 'a stone'. Hence the human environment consists of neutral objects waiting to be ordered, an orientation which is closely linked to the tendency to view animals and plants as physical objects, things of nature. Such a view is – for example – implicit in Lévi-Strauss's theory of totemism.

If nature is the sum total of its parts then we must begin by examining what these constituents might be, and the most accessible evidence here is ethnobiological. It is now well-established that all peoples work with a concept of *natural kind*, whether as a 'common sense kind of phenomenal substance', or as an 'ontological entity with an underlying nature' (Atran 1990: 86, 94). There is some dispute as to whether basic categories always occur at a particular level of abstraction, and concerning the detailed way they map onto phylo-genetic templates. The extent to which we can represent and account for more-or-less inclusive categories is contested; but the fact that all human populations engage in such activity is hardly in doubt (Ellen 1993b). What is more controversial is the claim by Berlin (1992) and Boster (1996) that natural kinds have a different perceptual character from cultural forms, fashioned by selective pressure. As the biological world has radiated, so the human capacity to recognise the basic order in that radiation has co-evolved. Thus, in this view (with which I am in basic sympathy), nature itself – or, at least, 'the biological world' – is the product of human cognitive evolution.

A formal expression for this kind of model would be simple incremental linear aggregation:

$$n1 + n2 + n3 \ldots = N,$$

where *n* is a culturally agreed natural kind, and *N* nature as a totality. But most peoples that we know of also recognise more inclusive conceptual domains such as 'plant', 'animal', 'rock' and so on, such that an aggregative model of nature should intuitively have a structure something like: animals + plants + other living things + non-living things = nature, which we might express formally as:

$$(n1 + n2 + n3 \ldots) = N + (\ldots)N + (\ldots)N + \ldots = N.$$

In order to demonstrate the plausibility of such a model we have to show that

1 each of these generic component parts (*N*) is recognised;
2 they share common characteristics; and
3 there is evidence to show that they are linked together to form a conceptual whole (*N*) – an over-arching category in other words.

We can explore 1 and 2 by examining the Nuaulu category which glosses most closely with English *animal*. The existence of such a category, what Brent Berlin calls a 'unique beginner', can in principle be inferred from the presence of specific terms whose reference can be shown to be coterminous with the semantic content of the domain, or, where such terms are absent, from various linguistic and cultural markers, or (up to a point) by employing sorting experiments.

There is no one commonly-used or widely-acknowledged Nuaulu term for all animals, though there are three possible, partial and rarely-used candidates (Ellen 1993b: 96–97). So, in effect, we might say that the category is, terminologically, 'covert', or at least 'semi-covert'. But even in the absence of an unambiguous domain label we may infer the existence of a cognitive prototype marked out from other domains, and also from humans. Thus, when speaking of animals, their qualities and relationships, Nuaulu employ a discourse which can be distinguished in certain small but significant respects from other discourses. It differs both lexically and in terms of appropriate semantic relationships. Thus, there are different words for killing an animal (*ihunui*) and for killing a human (*atoria*), for a human voice (*mo'nyom*) and an animal call (*nioke*); and for human head hair (*hua*) and bodily hair, animal feathers or fur (*hunue*). In some cases the differences amount only to slight phonological shifts, as in *anai* (human child) and *anae* (animal young). There is also a specialised lexicon for specific activities relating to animals (e.g. *atinai*, 'to hunt cuscus'; *asakaka*, 'to call a cuscus'), and many special anatomical terms (e.g. *mata hunua*, mollusc and insect antennae; *kihene*, wings and fins), in addition to about forty-seven such terms which humans and other animals share. That forms in core animal categories are clearly similar in multiple respects, and often overlap; that the terms are often expressed as contrast sets, while animal partonyms ('head', 'heart', and so on) and other linguistic usages are present, goes some way to imply the existence of a category 'animal' (cf. Taylor 1990: 47–51). Such differences not only help to locate and maintain separate domains, in the interests of effective linguistic communion, but also serve the purposes of symbolic contrast. The core of the domain is clearly regarded as being bound by polythetic affinities, such that the unique beginner is not as arbitrary as some (Hunn 1977: 44) have suggested, although its borders may occasionally be difficult to determine.

We could undertake a similar exercise for the domain 'plant', or indeed for any other conceptual domain which aggregates identifiable parts of the human environment on the basis of similar characteristics or overall form, simply by drawing inferences from linguistic utterance and cultural practice. Once this has been done we might then order the domains themselves into more inclusive contrastive categories, using distinctive features such as those which Taylor (1990) has suggested for the Tobelo: living–non-living, sexual–non-sexual, breathing–non-breathing, and so on. Such abstract distinctions are also discernible among the Nuaulu (Ellen 1993b: 95), but have little practical bearing on their lived culture, are of no prominent symbolic significance, and certainly cannot be held to be a starting point for their classification of the natural world. In this instance, I suspect they are examples of that genre of elicited but quite ungeneralisable contrasts which are happily provided by willing informants, and at which the ethnographer is tempted to grasp in some vain attempt to impose order on what otherwise looks like utter chaos.

In short, the hierarchic conception of nature typified by scientific taxonomy, and its folk-semantic extension which includes at its more-inclusive levels contrasts between unique beginners, and life and non-life, is not one which is readily yielded from the Nuaulu data. But we do not need to rely on such abstractions, irrespective of whether or not they can convincingly be shown to be emically-rooted, in order to model an aggregated or integrated concept of natural things, as conceptual domains can also be linked through their overlap (especially the overlap of their peripheries), by what various authors (e.g. Hays 1976: 502) have described for less inclusive categories as 'chaining', or 'linking'. Thus, if *a* is linked to *b*, *b* to *c* and *c* to *d* then this implies the existence of a 'group' *a-b-c-d*: an instance of polythetic resemblance.

Certain Nuaulu life-forms which are regarded as animals in phylogenetic terms have no obvious affinities with any other category. These include sponges, which are grouped with 'fungi'. Molluscs and starfish, however, are firmly perceived as animals for a combination of behavioural and morphological reasons. There is no sharp division between animals and plants and other domains, either in linguistic or conceptual terms (Lévi-Strauss 1966: 138–39, Morris 1976: 542). Some invertebrates are ambiguously animals and plants, some plants (e.g. certain fungi and lichens) are ambiguously plant and inert material; different life-forms merging together to strongly permit the inference of a *life* category, which itself may merge with non-life. Thus, despite the cognitive imperative to distinguish domains in terms of a small number of features or cognitive prototypes, in practice there are always going to be 'problems', some of which may be culturally manifest as anomalies; and it is precisely these which serve to link domains into more inclusive groupings.

If nature is an inventory of things in this sense, then this must be linked to rules about how these things are to be identified and related: that is *order*, and this order has to find some cultural legitimation. Nuaulu acknowledge that there is (indeed, must be) order in the world, an order which is in general terms comparable to the pre-Darwinian 'great chain of being'. Non-directive evidence for this might first be sought in that part of Nuaulu origin mythology which speaks of the time when the first Matoke (Lord of the Land) descended from the sky and walked throughout the earth where each natural kind was represented only by a single organism – one snake, one betel palm, one hornbill, and so on. As the Matoke came by each of these, so he named it, saying: 'This is a snake', 'This is a betel palm', 'This is a hornbill' and so on. And as he did so, the many emerged from the singular. But this is not to say that Nuaulu readily expound, even less agree upon, the principles for order, and certainly not the identification or classification of animals for pragmatic purposes. They will simply admit to not knowing it, or at least large parts of it (Ellen 1993b: 94). Less modest individuals might dispute among themselves, but every disputed classification itself exists within an axiomatic field, the coordinates of which are assumed to be quite fixed. And the *primus inter pares* of axioms is that nature itself is finite, and that all animals have names – even if they remain unknown. In Nuaulu theory at least, names are not given arbitrarily, for economy of thought; they reveal part of an order which was laid down at the beginning of the world, but which is only partially known about, and even less understood.

Nature as an inventory of things reaches its apogee in modern western classifications. The 'great chain of being' has already been mentioned, but it is also there in the concept of species, in the taxonomic schemes of Linnaeus and their Darwinian reinterpretation; it is there in the very idea of 'natural history', embedded within the notion of exhibitions to display nature as these emerged from cabinets of curiosity to become museums of natural history, herbaria, botanical and zoological gardens, during the eighteenth and nineteenth centuries. What is additionally significant here, and which comes through well in static displays, is that they are concerned as much with minerals (which have never lived) as with life; and equally with dead plants and animals, and the ambiguous classificatory material presented in the form of bones, fossils and the mineral

extrusions and excretions of living things (e.g. coral). The conceptualisation of nature as a collectivity of things is, therefore, most obvious
in the representations generated by western science and those
generated by anthropologists investigating the folk classifications of
the natural world, where the western paradigm is the implicit or
explicit reference point. It is there also, supremely so, commoditised
both in its parts and its entirety, in the slogans of environmentally-
inspired marketing and in the politics of ecology and biodiversity.

NATURE AS SPACE WHICH IS NOT HUMAN

Nature is often understood less as some abstracted inventory of its
contents (in which items are cognitively detached from their habitat
and reorganised according to a limited number of morphological or
functional criteria), than in terms of its predominant spatial or
phenomenological manifestation. It is this definition which is implicit
in many ethnographically-reported instances of the semantic congruence between forest and nature. But for different peoples, using
different subsistence strategies, living in different environments, the
semantic congruence may be with some alternative topography ('sea'
or 'desert', say, or 'mountains'); all of which have in common what is
perhaps best (provisionally) construed as the quality of 'wilderness'.
But 'wilderness' is the apogee of something closer and more familiar,
though different. So, although for the Nuaulu the congruence is
archetypically exemplified by 'forest', more routinely, perhaps, in this
spatial sense, nature is 'that which is not of the village', or 'that which
is not of the village or gardens'.

The 'natural otherness' of the Nuaulu concept of forest is
encountered in its most mundane sense in adjectival qualifiers for
animals or plants: as in the contrast between the geckoes *imasasae
numa* ('house') and *imasasae ai ukune* ('tree top, tree branches, far
forest'), for *Hemidactylus frenatus* and *Gekko vittatus*; or in the
contrast between the murids *mnaha numa/niane* ('house/village') and
mnaha wesie ('forest'), for *Mus musculus* and *Melomys*. It is also
evident in the symbolic organisation of village space (Ellen 1986), and
in the differential attitudes to language and behaviour within and
without the village. Thus you may 'joke', mock or use expletives
involving certain animals in the village, but you may not do so outside.
Among such exclamatory phrases are: *ikae nawe*, 'long fish', *mau
(w)anae*, 'kitten', *asuwani anae*, 'young cassowary', and *hahu onate*,
'large pig'. In the village (and by extension in the gardens as well) these

expletives are used extensively in ordinary discourse; in the forest they anger the spirits and bring on heavy rain. While an individual may try to escape the consequences of his utterances, he runs the risk of being swallowed up by the earth (Ellen 1993b: 175–76). Interestingly, the oath *masi mokota*, 'let the earth open up', is subject to the same taboo. The same – village (permissible) : forest (prohibited) – rule applies to a wide range of other expressions, among which are included expletives derived from the names of spirits (e.g. *painakite raia*). This is significant given the classificatory similarities between animals and spirits, to which I shall turn shortly.

But it is insufficient to contrast forest and village in the abstract, since the usual personal experience is that forest, bush, or whatever its semantic approximation might be, *surrounds*, or encompasses the village, and ultimately the self; and it is in this sense that nature comes closest to what in the western scientific tradition has become 'environment'. Thus, nature is always constructed by reference to the human domain, and is in the last instance informed by ideas and practices concerning 'self' and 'otherness'. This is not merely symbolic analogy, but an *homology* of experience. This should not worry us since it is a matter of fact that what is experienced and represented around us homologously is at key moments, in significant contexts, symbolically transformed into abstract binary oppositions which permit more formal analogy. Thus the Nuaulu *experience* of living within houses which are located within village spaces, which are in turn located within forest, is easily transformed into various abstract linear oppositions between, say, house and forest or village and forest, which in turn may be drawn into more complex symbolic linkages through analogy (Ellen 1986).

NATURE AS INNER ESSENCE

The third dimension of the concept of nature is its sensation as an inner essence or vital energy or force, outside human control. This is the most intangible of the three. We can perceive and touch 'things' and walk through 'spaces', but inner essence is usually only experienced in terms of its sensate consequences, usually through some combination of the first two axes. However, the best physical manifestations of inner essence are those fluids and pulses associated with living things, with bodily function: blood, sweat and tears, semen, breast milk; heart-beat, breath, excretion, movement; or more generally in the environment: flow of water, heat and cold, wind, noise, growth. And this is not confined to life narrowly-construed. Thus, Tournefort could identify the act of creation in both seeds and mineral crystals (Atran 1990: 230). In certain clearly defined circumstances the generic cultural character of essence or energy will be clear; thus with respect to human passion, we often speak of it as 'animal nature'. This is embedded in the western notion of natural instinct, nature as opposed to nurture; Islamic *hawa nafsu* as opposed to *akal* (reason), and the widespread Indonesian idea that the process of socialisation is the progressive controlling of natural forces. But nature within need not primarily be an allusion to animality; the dynamic properties may rather be experienced as consubstantial in any number of different 'kinds of' nature. It need not be a metaphor for the social, and sometimes it might be better to speak of both natural and social phenomena – as, say, reflected in physical maturation – as wholly comparable outcomes of similar processes (Bloch 1992).

The idea of nature as an essence or force within may everywhere have associations of uncontrollability, but we cannot prescribe in advance whether its cultural expression will be positive, negative or neutral. This will very much depend on the cultural metaphors which draw upon the imagery. One set of metaphors which do so, and which have been examined extensively in the literature, are those linked to gender (MacCormack and Strathern 1980, Atkinson and Errington 1990, Valeri 1990). As it happens, the Nuaulu data fit well with the 'male is to female as culture is to nature' motif, females treated as representing a danger to the male order, the intrusion of nature into culture often physicalised with reference to menstrual blood and the act of childbirth.

BOUNDARY PROBLEMS AND CONTRADICTIONS

Each of the three axes – or, if you will, dimensions or definitions – outlined is insufficient in itself to generate or define any one cultural construction of nature: all three are necessary to even begin to map out its underlying geometry. Moreover, my presentation so far has been fundamentally artificial in that I have ignored boundary problems and inner contradictions which arise once we juxtapose two or more of the axes, which is of course how we culturally experience nature. It is true that I have had to anticipate some of these, as no ethnographic data known to me present the conditions in any other way, but I have tried to limit these in the interests of clarity of exposition. It may help in reviewing these issues to imagine the three axes as related in three-dimensional space. I shall first consider the conflation of the first axis (nature as an aggregation of things) with the second (nature as outer space); I shall then consider the conflation of the first with the third (nature as inner essence); and finally, conflation of the second with the third. The justification for this order will, I hope, become apparent. Of course, there are some contexts in which all three axes have a direct bearing on what is going on.

The conflation between one and two (things and the spatial other) is best exemplified by the universal cultural recognition that humans themselves might possibly be 'things' of nature, comparable to other natural things, that the inventory of nature is not confined to *the other* (a version of the so-called subject–object problem); and by the recognition that humans physically intrude into the space of nature. We can explore this idea in relation to Nuaulu animal classification.

In general terms, people are regarded by the Nuaulu as being in many respects like animals. People share anatomical and physiological similarities with animals, but more than this myths inform us that animals, like their human counterparts, have societies. In the case of some species, they are represented as reflecting basically human organisation and values (e.g. Ellen 1972: 233); they are spoken of in the idiom of kinship. Animal societies too are bound by the Patalima–Patasiwa, 'Five group'–'Nine group', division of Seramese peoples (the Nuaulu themselves being Patalima), while totemic traditions and a rich mythology underscore the idea that animals may change into humans, and vice versa (Ellen 1993b: 163–76). In short, humans impose a social classification on the world of animals. Many terms referring to behaviour and appearance which are used for humans are also used for animals. In some instances shared terms may be understood as consubstantial, while in others the allusion – at least – is to a metaphorical extension from humans. The exceptions occur – and we have examined some of these already – where there is no human model, as with 'wing', 'beak', 'tail' and so on. And, of course, none of this prevents Nuaulu from defining the domain of animals essentially in contrast to humans. Taylor (1990: 51) reports that in Tobelorese language and concepts humans are treated quite differently from 'animals'. He regards this as problematic, since 'humans' meet the defining features of the Tobelo category 'fauna'. Rather than being problematic this seems to me to be an understandable feature of all people's conceptual universes. We might ask if humans are 'animals' in British or French folk classification. The answer, of course, is that it depends, and in this respect Nuaulu beliefs are like those of many other peoples. An extension of the same problem is encountered when we consider the place in any inventory of natural things of domesticated species, or any humanly-modified part of nature (Descola 1992: 111).

The conflation between one and three (things and essences) is best exemplified in the attribution of essence to particular parts of nature. A widespread version of this idea is associated with animism – a kind of 'social objectification of nature' (Descola 1992: 114), and I have shown elsewhere (Ellen 1988) that the attribution of life to the inanimate (most commonly through anthropomorphism) is basic to all human conceptualisations of the world. It is the continuity of natural kinds, as discussed above, which must, in all cultures, give plausibility to the idea that *all* nature is animate: animal, vegetable and mineral; the humanly-modified and the humanly-unmodified.

A particular aspect of this continuity is evident in my Nuaulu data dealing with the consubstantiality of spirits and animals. Nuaulu recognise spirit categories in much the same way as they recognise categories of animal; indeed, spirits are treated *as* natural kinds, as equally significant parts of their environment (Ellen 1993b: 176–79). People claim to hear and 'see' spirits all the time and I have on occasions been present when the alleged discovery of a particular spirit in a tree, or in a bush, has created scenes of some excitement. Some Nuaulu spirit forms appear to describe real animals; for example *sinne inae* (certain scarab and long-horned beetles, including *Oryctes rhinoceros* and *Mulciper linnaei*), (*kau*) *kama nahune* (edible long-horned beetles such as *Gnoma giraffa* and *Glenea corona* – *kama nahune* being the spirit of a person killed by falling from a tree in the throes of hunting cuscus), *inararai* (the frog *Litoria amboinensis*), and *rikune* (various kinds of bugs and beetles, including *Mictis*, *Oncomeris* and *Euphanta*). Perhaps we should not be surprised if it is insects which are most likely to be redefined as spirits (cf. Dentan 1968: 26–27). Other categories, such as *naka*, which refers to those mythical creatures we call dragons, are used by the Nuaulu to label certain real world animals which they have heard of but never seen, in this case the Komodo 'dragon'. Domains become even more blurred when spirits enter the bodies of animals influencing their behaviour, as when a *sakahatene* enters the jaws of the death adder *nanate* (*Acanthophis antarcticus*). Other spirits are modelled on particular animal proto-types to the extent that experiences of paired entities seem at times to be conflated. Thus, *masenu* are compared with *tuku tuku* (probably *Otus magicus*), and *ahone* with *sakoa* (*Ninox squamipila*) in their vocalisations. These are both owls and consequently nocturnal, which is itself significant. Some animals are held to be derived from spirits, such as *isanone* ants from *isanone nanie*. So not only are there sometimes no simple breaks at domain boundaries in what we might construe as the 'real' world, there are even areas of overlap between the objectively visible and invisible.

The conflation between two and three (space and essence) is no better summed-up than in the notion of 'the wild', and its cognates. The natural other is not always chaotic or malign and for some peoples it might most faithfully be expressed as some kind of 'culture of the beyond' (Schefold 1988). However, as far as the Nuaulu are concerned, it is unpredictable, difficult to control and with a fundamentally moral character; there are right and wrong ways in which to engage with forest, which arise in part from the specific social histories of parts of it, but also from its intrinsic mystical properties. This natural 'other' is reflected in the inferential symbolic opposition between 'nature' and 'culture' evident in most ritual, in the specific rituals conducted prior to cultivating forest, in the charms which are used to protect travellers in the forest, in the prohibitions on certain behaviours and utterances while in the forest, in the correct ritual disposal of its products. When humans enter the forest they carry with them what amounts to an 'aura' of culture, and when ritual is conducted in the forest, it is as if islands of culture are created to ensure its efficaciousness. Thus, in Nuaulu male initiation ceremonies platforms are erected which mimic that entity which most epitomises (indeed physicalises) culture, namely the house. Individual neophytes at this ceremony are required to stand upon blocks made of five logs as if preventing contamination from the forest. Similar structures are used when performing land-clearing and other routine rituals. The same meeting of nature as inner force and as outer space is reflected through the prism of gender concepts in the symbolic layout of Nuaulu villages. Here, females are associated – through the location of their menstruation and birthing huts – with the outer rim of the village (nearest the forest). What is, therefore, universally significant about this conflationary aspect of nature is that it becomes a condition for knowledge, by controlling the relation between what is taken as internal nature and what is taken as external nature (Strathern 1992: 194), that which is natural and that which is of nature.

CONTEXTUAL VARIATION

We can see, therefore, that *logically* the functional association of any two, or all three, of the cognitive axes specified results in conceptual complications which greatly extend and enhance the richness of the symbolic imagery of nature. But what is intriguing about human cognitive and social behaviour generally is that logical inconsistencies can be suppressed in particular circumstances, and different aspects of a multi-dimensional idea privileged at the expense of other aspects in any one context. Let us take a few rather different Nuaulu examples of these: forest, animal spirits and ritual killing.

As we have seen, the archetypal Nuaulu representation of the collective natural other is *wesie*, uncut primary forest (Ellen 1993a: 138–40). However, this contrasts in different ways with other land types, depending on context. It may contrast with *wasi* (owned land, which may sometimes display very mature forest growth), emphasising a jural distinction; with *nisi* (garden land), emphasising human physical interference; or with *niane* (village), emphasising land-forms: empty as opposed to well-timbered space, inhabited (dwelt) as opposed to uninhabited space, untamed as opposed to tamed space, all with various symbolic associations and practical consequences for Nuaulu consumers. Although there are no Nuaulu words for either 'nature' or 'culture', it is in the various and aggregated senses of *wesie* that the Nuaulu come closest to having such a term, and from which the existence of an abstract covert notion of 'nature' can reasonably be inferred (cf. Valeri 1990).

Thus, in particular contexts, the meaning of *wesie* as a natural other may be sharply dichotomised, only to appear in a different guise elsewhere. As Croll and Parkin (1992: 3) argue, most peoples ascribe a somewhat capricious agency to their environment which they are obliged to interpret and negotiate, and which they commonly regard themselves as inseparably part of. In some contexts, even for the Nuaulu, the forest *is* the people, in the same way as the ancestors are, in a sense, extensions of the living. Negotiations and renegotiations take place regarding the meanings of forest and village, cleared and uncleared, cultivated and uncultivated, wild and tame (Croll and Parkin 1992: 16). Oppositions are set up only to be transcended or merged; sometimes forest is male, sometimes female; sometimes portrayed as antagonistic, sometimes life-nurturing. These all provide alternative modes of identification (ibid.: 16).

Similarly, the juxtaposition of classifications of spirits and animals not only serves to show the structural similarities and the conceptual bases of categories and their relationship to each other, but also reminds us of an important difference: that spirits are in the normal way experientially incorporeal while animals are first experienced as things, even though the Nuaulu 'know' that spirits have bodies and bodies have spirits. The logic of this in one direction is that the Nuaulu must claim to see spirits for them to exist, and in the other that animals must have spirits because of the prohibitions and beliefs surrounding them. But the notion that animals have spirits is problematic if you have to kill them, and Nuaulu culture provides a very practical response to this, in rituals connected with wooden meat skewers or *asumate*.

When an animal is butchered it is generally skewered on a sharpened wooden stake, and a chip from the pointed end kept and afterwards tied to the pole. This piece is traditionally employed to butcher the killed animal, and represents its spirit; the re-tying to the pole is thus supposed to represent the re-uniting of the soul and body of the animal killed. The purposes of the *asumate* are: to inform the ancestors that meat has been killed and that they should come and partake of it; to confer prestige, the *asumate* being placed where everyone can see it; to return the spirit to the cosmos, and therefore to ensure that finite stocks are not depleted and that hunting prospects remain good. Every time a hunter fails to plant an *asumate* the wild stock of that species is thought to be depleted by a factor of one. Such practical steps, however, if taken to their logical extreme, become highly inconvenient in the normal daily round. Far better to rely upon periodic strategic amnesia and operate with two contradictory conceptions of the animal world: one which stresses unity with humankind (and the privilege of taking life for food) and another which stresses the fundamental differences between humans and animals and which legitimates and makes easier their exploitation as food (cf. Wazir-Jahan Karim 1981: 188). Of course, any cosmology motivated by animism must generate respect for other species, a respect often reinforced by prohibitions of various kinds. But this need not be inconsistent with hunting, and I suspect that there may long have been a contradiction between the doctrine of infinite renewal and the recognition that hunters could exterminate animals locally (Brightman 1987: 137).

My final example conveniently follows on from our consideration of *asumate*. All Nuaulu killing in the course of hunting takes place outside the village, in the natural other. That killing which takes place as a culmination of hunting not only takes place *in* nature, it involves *a part* of nature, and exemplifies the control of natural forces: the domination of culture over nature in nature. By contrast, animal sacrifice takes place in the village (is therefore controlled, cultural, killing), the domination of nature in culture. In the first, the offering is a consequence of a killing for some other purpose (usually for food); in the second the food (where it is consumed) is a consequence of the offering. But meat killed outside the village is not just any kind of meat, it belongs to recognised animal categories, specific natural things. The most important of these are *peni* (the collective term for pig, deer and cassowary), which is simultaneously natural and cultural. *Peni* (creatures of the forest) pass, therefore, from a natural (uncontrolled) condition into a cultural (controlled) condition, and in an important dual sense sustain the possibility of 'culture', being identified with the descent group and the house in which their accumulated mandibles have been stored (culture-within-nature). Animals of sacrifice, by contrast, are of domestic stock (chickens – preferably cockerels) or of the village realm by metaphoric association, as in the case of the cuscus (phalangers), which resemble humans and which, through historical convenience, have become a substitute for human heads. Such animals are, therefore, nature-within-culture (Ellen 1996a).

CONCLUSION

Nature is definitely not a *basic* category. It is more a 'higher order' category in Rappaport's sense (Rappaport 1971: 33–34), and for many peoples it would appear to have no clearly bounded categorical status at all. As with more inclusive units in the Linnaean hierarchy, non-basic folk categories cannot be objectively defined, and no firm distinction between perceptual and social can be sustained. Indeed, it is inconceivable that classification might proceed in ways which, to follow Geertz, 'externalise culture'. Conceptualisations of nature are not the inventions of individuals (in which case they would more closely reflect cognitive process), but arise through historical contingency, linguistic constraints, metaphorical extension, ritual prohibitions and so on. As parts of belief systems, they are the productions of interactions, accretions, elaborations and condensations. That contradictions and inconsistencies exist is because nature is simultaneously an abstract symbolic and a non-basic cognitive category, variously a model 'of' the world (a representation) and a model 'for' (a plan for action) (Geertz 1966). It is precisely this ability to switch between one and the other, to engage with the environment and disengage from it, which distinguishes us from non-human primates.

Our understandings of nature are rooted in particular situations which, when their common meanings are distilled, provide us with something which has a provisional, abstract and emergent quality. Such notions of nature are the consequence of what I have elsewhere (Ellen 1993: Chapter 8) called *prehension*: those processes which through various cultural and other constraints give rise to particular classifications, designations and representations. People bring to situations in which classifying activity takes place, and from which verbal statements about classifying behaviour result, information of diverse kinds acquired through both informal and formal socialisation experience, of the world in general and of earlier classifying situations. How they then classify depends upon the interplay of this past knowledge (including prescriptions and preferences with regard to particular cognitive and linguistic idioms) with the material constraints of the classifying situation, the purposes of the classifying act, and upon the inputs of other inter-penetrating ones.

In addition, it is important to recognise that the processing and storage of information in the brain is imperfect, and communication of that information less perfect still. Paradoxically, there is a connection between this shortcoming and the considerable capacity of the human mind to re-order information in different ways, replacing irrelevant information with that of greater and more immediate utility. As Sperber (1985: 31) has remarked, 'mental representations have a basically unstable structure: the normal fate of an idea is to become altered or to merge with other ideas; what is exceptional is the reproduction of an idea'. Following Lévi-Strauss, he insists that any epidemiology of ideas is, therefore, as much concerned with transformation as persistence. That understandings of nature are messy, cross-cutting and changing is a reflection of this. Concepts are often used, operationalised, without defining them. The efficient practice which precedes theory does not require self-reflection on the operation while performing it, and much of what we learn, in fact, is learning *not* to think about operations that once needed to be thought about (Medawar 1957: 138).

All of this is to emphasise the contextual, variable and contingent way in which we use those cultural abstractions which in terms of our own emic conventions we find convenient to represent as 'nature'. But, of course, in order for communication to take place classification must have at least some intersubjective structure, agreed cultural rules, some 'doxa' (Bourdieu 1977). Much of this is possible simply because there is *sufficient* agreement about cultural conventions, but this is not to endorse '*a grammar* of the variety of ways in which nature is socialised' (Descola 1992). Everything I have said here suggests that a grammatical analogy would be quite false, as would any attempt to confine discussion to a linguistic level of expression. Very few languages have words which easily translate as 'nature', yet some focal notion in terms of the three cognitive dimensions examined here is always present. Sometimes, as in the Nuaulu case, the resemblance to global etic nature is sufficiently close for it to be recognisable; in other cases – as among many hunter-gatherers – the resemblance is much weaker. Language only mediates – and then rather inadequately – between the many cultural appearances and the three underlying cognitive axes which generate the possible coordinates: the objectification of the world, the spatial other, and inner essence. And such a model of the cognitive geometry of nature as I have offered here is consistent with recent attempts – such as those of Bloch and Ingold – to go beyond linguistic representation and to situate perception within actions on the world (non-mediated forms of knowledge), and – paradoxically – to resist the imposition of our own nature–culture dualisms on data.

ACKNOWLEDGEMENTS

Earlier versions of this chapter were presented to a seminar at the Muséum National d'Histoire Naturelle in Paris, sponsored jointly by the CNRS and the Laboratoire d'Ethnobiologie-Biogéographie, and as a Munro Lecture at the University of Edinburgh. I would like to thank Claudine Friedberg, Cecile Barraud and Anthony Cohen for the opportunity to explore the ideas presented here in a revised and shortened form. All of the Nuaulu data referred to has been published before in the works cited, where full acknowledgement of permissions and funding bodies may be found.

NOTES

1 I provide here only a few indicative references. Further examples, together with a more extensive discussion of the 'cultural construction of nature' are to be found in Ellen 1996b.

2 In a sense, my aim is to examine the extent to which it is possible to identify a category innocent of morality at a time when the prevailing inclination is to emphasise the intrinsically moral character of nature. One might, of course, demur that ultimately all categories imply rules, and all rules imply the moral force of 'right' and 'wrong'. In this I would agree.

REFERENCES

Atkinson, J. M. and Errington, S. (eds) (1990) *Power and Difference: Gender in Island Southeast Asia*, Stanford: Stanford University Press.

Atran, S. (1990) *Cognitive Foundations of Natural History*, Cambridge: Cambridge University Press.

Berlin, B. (1992) *Ethnobiological Classification: Principles of Categorization of Plants and Animals in Traditional Societies*, Princeton, NJ: Princeton University Press.

Bird-David, N. (1993) 'Environment, Metaphor and Culture: Hunter-Gatherers in Asia, Africa, Australia and North America Compared', in K. Milton (ed.) *Anthropological Perspectives on Environmentalism*, ASA Monograph 31, London: Routledge.

Bloch, M. (1992) 'What Goes Without Saying: the Conceptualization of Zafimaniry Society', in A. Kuper (ed.) *Conceptualizing Society*, European Association of Social Anthropologists, London: Routledge.

Boster, J. (1996) 'Human Cognition as a Product and Agent of Evolution', in R. F. Ellen and K. Fukui (eds) *Redefining Nature: Ecology, Culture and Domestication*, London: Berg.

Bourdieu, P. (1977) *Outline of a Theory of Practice*, trans. R. Nice, Cambridge Studies in Social Anthropology 16, Cambridge: Cambridge University Press.

Boyer, P. (1993) *Cognitive Aspects of Religious Symbolism*, Cambridge: Cambridge University Press.

Brightman, R.A. (1987) 'Conservation and Resource Depletion: the Case of the Boreal Forest Algonquians', in B. M. McCay and J. M. Acheson (eds) *The Question of the Commons: The Culture and Ecology of Communal Resources*, Tucson: University of Arizona Press.

Collingwood, R.G. (1945) *The Idea of Nature*, Oxford: Clarendon Press.

Croll, E. and D. Parkin (1992) 'Cultural Understandings of the Environment', in E. Croll and D. Parkin (eds) *Bush Base–Forest Farm: Culture, Environment and Development*, London: Routledge.

Dentan, R.K. (1968) 'Notes on Semai Ethnoentomology', *Malayan Nature Journal* 16: 17–28.

Descola, P. (1992) 'Societies of Nature and the Nature of Society', in A. Kuper (ed.) *Conceptualizing Society*, European Association of Social Anthropologists, London: Routledge.

Ellen, R.F. (1972) 'The Marsupial in Nuaulu Ritual Behaviour', *Man* (NS) 7: 223–38.

— (1986) 'Microcosm, Macrocosm and the Nuaulu House: Concerning the

Reductionist Fallacy as Applied to Metaphorical Levels', *Bijdragen tot de Taal-, Land- en Volkenkunde* 142, 1: 1–30.

— (1988) 'Fetishism', *Man* (NS) 23, 1: 1–23.

— (1993a) 'Rhetoric, Practice and Incentive in the Face of the Changing Times: a Case Study of Nuaulu Attitudes to Conservation and Deforestation', in K. Milton *Environmentalism: The View from Anthropology*, London: Routledge.

— (1993b) *The Cultural Relations of Classification: An Analysis of Nuaulu Animal Categories from Central Seram*, Cambridge: Cambridge University Press.

— (1996a) 'Cuscus and Cockerels: Killing Rituals and Ritual Killing amongst the Nuaulu of Seram', in S. Howell (ed.) *For the Sake of Our Future: Sacrificing in Eastern Indonesia*, Leiden: Koninklijk Instituut voor Taal-, Land- en Volkenkunde.

— (1996b) 'Introduction', in R. F. Ellen and K. Fukui (eds) *Redefining Nature: Ecology, Culture and Domestication*, Oxford: Berg.

Geertz, C. (1966) 'Religion as a Cultural System', in M. Banton (ed.) *Anthropological Approaches to the Study of Religion*, Association of Social Anthropologists, Monograph 3, London: Tavistock.

Hays, T.E. (1976) 'An Empirical Method for the Identification of Covert Categories in Ethnobiology', *American Ethnologist* 8: 489–507.

Horigan, S. (1988) *Nature and Culture in Western Discourses*, London: Routledge.

Hunn, E. (1977) *Tzeltal Folk Zoology: The Classification of Discontinuities in Nature*, London: Academic Press.

Ingold, T. (1986) *The Appropriation of Nature: Essays on Human Ecology and Social Relations*, Manchester: Manchester University Press.

— (1992) 'Culture and the Perception of the Environment', in E. Croll and D. Parkin (eds) *Bush Base–Forest Farm: Culture, Environment and Development*, London: Routledge.

Leach, E.R. (1964) 'Anthropological Aspects of Language: Animal Categories and Verbal Abuse', in E. Lenneberg (ed.) *New Directions in the Study of Language*, Cambridge Mass.: MIT Press.

Lévi-Strauss, C. (1966) *The Savage Mind*, London: Weidenfeld and Nicolson.

MacCormack, C. and M. Strathern (eds) (1980) *Nature, Culture and Gender*, Cambridge: Cambridge University Press.

Medawar, P.B. (1957) *The Uniqueness of the Individual*, London: Methuen.

Morris, B. (1976) 'Whither the Savage Mind? Notes on the Natural Taxonomies of a Hunting and Gathering People', *Man* (NS) 11: 542–57.

Rappaport, R. (1971) 'Ritual, Sanctity and Cybernetics', *American Anthropologist* 73: 73–76.

Schefold, R. (1988) 'De Wildernis als Cultuur van Zijde; Tribale Concepten van de "Natuur" in Indonesië', *Antropologische Verkenningen* 7, 4: 5–22.

Sperber, D. (1985) *On Anthropological Knowledge*, Cambridge: Cambridge University Press.

Strathern, M. (1992) *After Nature: English Kinship in the Late Twentieth Century*, Cambridge: Cambridge University Press.

Taylor, P.M. (1990) *The Folk Biology of the Tobelo People: A Study in Folk*

Classification, Smithsonian Contributions to Anthropology No. 34, Washington DC: Smithsonian Institution Press.

Thomas, K. (1983) *Man and the Natural World: Changing Attitudes in England, 1500–1800*, London: Allen Lane.

Torrance, J. (ed.) (1992) *The Concept of Nature: The Herbert Spencer Lectures*, Oxford: Clarendon Press.

Valeri, V. (1990) 'Both Nature and Culture: Reflections on Menstrual and Parturitional Taboos in Huaulu (Seram)', in J. M. Atkinson and S. Errington (eds) *Power and Difference: Gender in Island Southeast Asia*, Stanford: Stanford University Press.

Wazir-Jahan Karim (1981) 'Ma Betisek Concepts of Humans, Plants and Animals', *Bijdragen tot de Taal-, Land- en Volkenkunde*, 137: 35–60.

Part II

Sociologies of nature

Chapter 7

Nature in culture or culture in nature?

Chewong ideas of 'humans' and other species

Signe Howell

In western moral philosophy since Classical times, humans have been set apart from – and above – all other animals according to some essential criteria (e.g. Ingold 1988). This separation has been justified on grounds of moral superiority and reinforced by the Cartesian separation between mind and body, associated with thinking and feeling, respectively. The properties of these dualities have not been held to be of equal value: humans are superior to animals, mind is superior to body, just as thinking is to feeling (Skultans 1977). Furthermore, the mind and mental processes have been regarded as characteristically male qualities and bodily and emotional concerns as female ones. When we further consider a dominant strand of thinking which holds that mind is cultural and body is natural, we find ourselves within the familiar western schema. Such a view is, of course, to be regarded as just one ethnographic example of how humans may construct meaning about their own identities and environments. It is, however, an approach which has universalistic ambitions and it has proved peculiarly resistant to challenges.

Debating a similar topic, Ingold states, '[e]very generation has recreated its own view of animality as a deficiency in everything that we humans are uniquely supposed to have, including language, reason, intellect and moral conscience' and '[we discover afresh regularly that]...human beings are animals too and...it is by comparison with other animals that we best can understand ourselves' (Ingold 1994: 15). As I read him, Ingold advocates a full analytic acceptance of human animality. These and similar statements by others provoked me into reconsidering my perceptions and earlier interpretations of the views on humanity and environment held by the Chewong, a small group of aboriginal people of the Malay tropical rainforest.[1] I shall argue that the Chewong include animals, and other 'natural' species such as trees, plants, rivers, stones, etc. in their construction of meaning about humanity and personhood, but that they do so in very different ways from that which Ingold claims 'we' (western educated humans) do, i.e. by using perceived animal deficiencies to promote our own excellence. First, they do not set humans uniquely apart from other beings which they regard as sentient, be they spirits, animals, plants, or things. Second, separation between mind and body, thinking and feeling, are not meaningful to them. Third, within their own environment of the forest they do not oppose a natural world with a cultural world, although their constructions of self and others within the forest environment are anthropocentric (cf. Descola, Chapter 5, this volume). They do, however, make a distinction between the forest and the outside world of other (and feared) humans, namely that of Malays and Chinese. I nevertheless argue that it is inappropriate to designate that world as nature.

The Chewong thus constitute an empirical counter-example to several universalistic models. Some of the more important of these in the current context are those that make categorical distinctions (whether evaluative or not) between nature/culture, humans/other species, mind/body, mind/emotion, ideology/practice, ritual/mundane, sacred/profane, society/cosmos. What is particularly interesting is not only that such strong oppositional categories, so integral to western discourses, are not present among the Chewong, but also that such distinctions are not used as vehicles for metaphorically creating meaning, or value, in other categories or conceptual domains.

This is far from the first time an ethnographic example has been marshalled to disprove universalistic philosophical claims about human nature, epistemology and ontology. For example, we have been flooded in recent years with ethnographically founded denials of operative oppositions between nature and culture. There is no need to flog this particular dead horse. But even among the multitude of counter-examples, the Chewong provide certain unusual constellations which bring out the issues in slightly novel ways. As such they may prove interesting for rethinking the parameters of the discussions – with regard both to current ecological debates and to comparative anthropology. Before I proceed, it is important to state that my position is not an extreme version of cultural relativism. Rather, I fully accept a psychic and cognitive unity of humanity in so far as one may posit a series of innate predispositions, predilections and constraints – sociality and inter-subjectivity in the construction of awareness and meaning, being, from an anthropological point of view, the most arresting of these. I agree with Lukes' critique of Durkheim's theory of knowledge when he says:

> No account of relations between features of a society and the ideas and beliefs of its members could ever explain the faculty, or ability, of the latter to think spatially and temporally... this is [together with the other categories of mind] what thinking *is*.
>
> (Lukes 1975: 447)

However, having said that, I maintain that, for comparative purposes the use of substantive categories like nature does not get us very far. But more abstract approaches may be helpful. For example, to make another theoretical point clear, in my opinion it is an anthropological truism to maintain that, minimally, people are committed to a description – or sets of descriptions – of their world and that every description presupposes some (often implicit) theory. As Descola suggests (Chapter 5, this volume), people appear to conform their practice to a set of structural rules. Our job is to uncover and interpret the description(s), the theories, and the structural rules. Then one may be able to address the basis for differentiations, for the relations between self and others, and for the different modes of socialities.

FROM NATURE TO ENVIRONMENT AND ECOLOGY – AND BACK AGAIN?

In recent years we may detect a rekindling of an anthropological interest in questions concerning the social construction of nature or the environment (e.g. Ellen 1982, Ingold 1988, 1993, Willis 1990, Milton 1993, Descola 1994). Lévi-Strauss's insistence on the universal dichotomisation of nature versus culture proved a fruitful basis for many for a long time, but the exclusive focus on the classificatory aspects of this dichotomy, and the realisation that it was a far from simple opposition in the way he had assumed, led to its virtual abandonment as a topic for ethnographic investigation. However, many have returned to such issues with an interest in the comparative study of indigenous ideas concerning the environment, coupled with a new focus on questions pertaining to indigenous ideas of human nature, but from different starting points and with different ends in mind. One may simultaneously note a shift in the vocabulary employed. Previously, 'nature' was the standard word, in its implications contrasted to something called 'culture'. Now the wider, more inclusive, terms 'environment' and 'ecosystem' are more common. However, whichever term is employed there is a tendency to assume that one is studying something which is objectively given and separate from humans. For anthropologists, the questions have tended to be 'How do the X perceive or exploit or interact with nature, their environment – their ecological world?' So when we find ourselves in a society where not only is it difficult to establish a nature (environment)–culture (society) dichotomy, but also where a meaningful notion of nature appears not to be constructed, we may still feel compelled either to provide a plausible reason for the *absence* of such a category, or to seek for one through unusual approaches, rather than concentrating on what actually is going on. To suggest that the Chewong do not classify their world in such a manner as includes a meaningful category of nature, is not to say that the Chewong do not construct meaningful categories. In the present context, a more apt characterisation would be to suggest that their main differentiations are those between conscious and unconscious beings. With the exception of human beings, however, the membership of these two categories is not stable, but dependent upon contingent circumstances.

What is becoming clear from recent research is that any claim for ecological determinism cannot be upheld in scientific discourses. Descola has argued with regard to the Amazonian rainforest, '[t]here is no predictable correspondence between specific ecosystems and specific schemes of practice', and 'these schemes are ultimately informed by ideas and practices concerning "self" and "otherness"' (Descola 1992: 111). In other words, one cannot predict what may be construed as problematic or unproblematic in any one social setting.

My aim will be to investigate some implications of the above statements and relate them to Chewong perceptions, concepts, and categories. Because of limited space, my presentation may give the impression of a reified culture imprisoned both temporally and spatially. However, this does not reflect my basic approach to the study of other forms of socio-cultural life, and I refer interested readers to earlier published ethnographic details (Howell 1982, 1985, 1989, 1994, 1995, 1996).

CHEWONG IDEAS OF SPECIES

Chewong understanding of species is integral to their world view, to their views of themselves and of others. However, while they do not employ an evaluative categorisation between humans, animals or plants, there is a class of beings which is constituted on the basis of presence or absence of consciousness – in the sense of language, reason, intellect and moral conscience or knowledge (cf. Ingold 1994). Consciousness in this sense makes one a 'personage' (*ruwai*[2] in Chewong) – an expression I prefer to 'human' – regardless of one's outer shape (or 'cloak' in Chewong parlance) be it that of gibbon, human, wild pig, frog, rambutan fruit, bamboo leaf, the thunder being, a specific boulder or whatever. Absence of consciousness, on the other hand, does not entail membership of another encompassing category, such as animal or plant. It follows from this that there are no general characteristics of 'animality' or 'vegetability' which are used as a basis for evaluative comparisons. Rather, the Chewong think in terms of a series of species-grounded conscious and unconscious beings each with a different shape and adhering to their own particular social and – in the case of conscious beings – moral codes. In other words, one may not discern the familiar western conceptual opposition of 'animality' and 'humanity'; no human behaviour may be classed as animal-like.

I suggest that this may constitute a reason why the Chewong do not have an overarching category of 'animal', but rather a whole series of named species which are not encompassed in a taxonomic classifica-tion schema. This is consistent with their tendency to enumerate rather than to order things – or concepts – hierarchically according to clusters of perceived similarities. This is not to say that they are incapable of classifying according to such principles. For example, there are indigenous categories for bird, snake, flower and tree. But these are very shallow indeed, constituting an umbrella under which all the species are enumerated. Those who speak Malay appear to understand and use the Malay word for animal (*binantang*) while not incorporating it into Chewong language. I have argued elsewhere (Howell 1985, 1989) that theirs is a schema predicated on identifying and naming rather than on clustering, and that the underlying ordering principle is equality, not hierarchy. This is manifest in the symbolic as well as the socio-political order.

CHEWONG

Although the Chewong engage in some simple form of shifting cultivation, their self-perception is constructed around hunting and gathering and their cosmology and social practices draw heavily on a hunting and gathering idiom. They define themselves as 'jungle people' (*bi brete*) and as 'digging people' (*bi bai*). The latter appellation refers to the fact that they dig for wild tubers, i.e. they are foragers rather than cultivators. Individual and collective existential orientations are focused upon, and derive their meanings from, the jungle. The jungle in its totality as a material and spiritual world is, I shall argue, cultural space, not natural. They move around in it with confidence derived from understanding and knowledge. It is full of signs which they know how to interpret – historically, practically, cosmologically. These may be paths made by animals, a fruit tree planted by an ancestor, stones which are inhabited by potentially harmful beings, fallen tree-trunks, the place where an event in a particular myth took place, etc. Nothing in the forest is semantically neutral. The tree fell because someone somewhere laughed near an animal, rain during sunshine indicates the presence of spirits who are hunting for meat which would include the human *ruwai* were they to encounter it, and so on. Like other hunting and gathering people, the Chewong display a detailed and intimate knowledge of the forest in which they live which goes far beyond any practical requirements, and they are engaged in a series of meaningful relationships with it. However, the principles of the symbiosis can only be understood by stepping back and placing it within their cosmological constructions.

QUESTIONS OF CONSCIOUSNESS AND MORAL IMPERATIVES

In view of the above considerations, I prefer to place interpretative emphasis on the constituting significance of meaningful practice rather than on an abstract concept like 'nature'. The Chewong may be regarded as a prime example of a cultural constitution of embodied knowledge, or embodied imagination, in the words of Johnson. However, they have not 'put the body back in the mind' (Johnson 1987: xix): the two were never separated. Moreover, I wish to go a bit further than Johnson and suggest that the reverse relationship also pertains and that, to coin a phrase, bodies are minded. Furthermore, the exclusive concentration upon the mind – the cognitive – should be modified by also giving interpretative status to the affective. This becomes manifest when we examine their understanding of personage and speciesness. The main ingredients of Chewong embodied knowledge include body, *ruwai* ('soul', see below); eyes – as the seat for perceiving reality, or realities; odour; liver – as the medium for emotions and intellect. Although differentiated and named, each of these qualities is not separable into unconnected parts or qualities. Illness, for example, is not simply bodily or mental–psychological. It may be caused by a sore, a broken leg, by the lost *ruwai* or odour, or by inappropriate emotionality. Symptoms by themselves are not informative, causes have to be elicited by shamanic practices before curing activities can take place.

Personages may literally be anything. Whether or not a particular species is a personage may, or may not, be visible to the ordinary human 'hot' eye, but it is always apparent to the 'cool' shamanistic one. While there are essential qualities necessary in order to be characterised as a personage – which are formally identical in all cases – actual manifestations of these and the precepts of morality are species dependent. Much of Chewong morality is expressed through directives involving food which in turn are predicated upon how each species actually sees reality. This is directly attributable to the quality of their eyes, which are subtly different in each case. The way one species sees another is dependent upon what constitutes food for them. Thus, when human beings see a monkey's body they see it as meat; when a tiger sees a human body it sees it as meat. A *bas* (a group of harmful spirits) upon seeing human *ruwai* perceives it as meat, and so on. All mortal beings who live in the jungle have to eat meat in order to stay alive, and in order to do so they have to kill. What actually constitutes meat in each case is dependent upon the habits of the particular species of being.[3] However, the social demand to share food is equally maintained among all groups of personages; eating alone being regarded everywhere as the ultimate anti-social act. Food is thus not a question of biology, but of morality. All personages act culturally and socially and as long as one behaves in conformity with the moral premises of one's own species, one may not be in any sense condemned for one's actions even when these harm other species. Humans (and others) will make every effort to avoid encountering beings known to be harmful because it is assumed that they will behave in their species-bound way and attack. The Chewong are relativists; for them each species is different, but equal.

RUWAI AS PERSONAGE

It is, of course, possible to be alive without being a personage. The Chewong concept *ruwai* has various levels and specificity of meaning. In the broadest sense, all humans, trees, animals, rivers, have *ruwai* in the sense of a vital principle that distinguishes them from dead things. As such it is associated with breath and moisture. The second level of meaning of *ruwai* is in the sense of 'soul' or consciousness. Thus all animals and plants have *ruwai* in the general sense of being alive, but only some 'are people', i.e. are conscious beings or personages. To state that the gibbon for example 'has *ruwai*', is to state that gibbons are personages, sharing in the specifically gibbon version of conscious attributes common to the species.

The third level of meaning is that of spirit-guide, and of having a relationship with one such. In such contexts, to say that one 'has *ruwai*' is to say that one has a relationship with a non-human personage. It is the second level of meaning of *ruwai* that I am concerned with in this chapter, but I think it is significant that the same word is used for all three aspects of 'life', linking them metonymically together in an overall conceptual schema.

What does it mean to be a personage? Primarily it means having rational capacities, with all this entails of language, intentionality, reasoning, emotionality, movement, and to participate in a shared mode of sociality. In other words, personages think, feel, judge and act according to some external moral criteria. However, our notion of consciousness has to be expanded to include physiological aspects, not just mental ones. Each species also has its special body – 'cloak' – and odour, both of which are also integral aspects of their status as personage. Movement, breath and smell are thus part of Chewong notions of consciousness (Howell 1989, 1996). From the point of view of principle all these qualities are necessary, but they are all manifested differently in each species. Adept shamanising beings have had much contact with members of other conscious species. They have many spirit-guides and their *ruwai* can wander into all worlds, and their 'cool' eyes mean that they may see through all deceptions, and see reality for what it really is.

All the aspects of consciousness are constituted in relation to each other and together they make the personage. This means that there is a correct body for the correct *ruwai*. While it is possible to put on the body of another species, this can only be done for short periods and it is a risky business. When in a trance, the *ruwai* (of any conscious being) leaves its body, but it is vital that it returns to the correct one. When the *ruwai* is lost or taken by a harmful being, the person becomes ill, just as a bad physical injury affects the *ruwai*. In either case, healing must be carried out – the balance between the parts restored – or the person dies. While the Chewong acknowledge a divide between *ruwai* and its cloak, they nevertheless insist that these are not truly divisible. Each is constituted through the other, creating a totality which can be separated only temporarily. The qualities of a human *ruwai* are, as it were, imprinted upon the quality of the human cloak and *vice versa*. These in turn affect, and are affected by, the quality of the liver, the eyes, and the odour. Species-bound knowledge and emotions are thus embodied knowledge in a very real sense.

CHEWONG ETHICALITY

Chewong epistemology is thus grounded in an understanding about natural species which entails that those species who are personages participate in their own version of a moral universe – a moral universe embracing daily 'practical' behaviour. I turn now to the question concerning species-informed moral sense, by which I mean awareness of self in the world, in meaningful relationships with others.

The relationship between the body – the 'cloak' – and the *ruwai* is not always either clear-cut or in obvious correspondence. Deception is part of the game. Thus an encountered creature may have the body of a frog, but may in fact be a human – and *vice versa*. The last point is of particular interest in view of what is, after all, an anthropocentric view of the world. It is possible for a spirit or a plant to don a human shape, just as it is possible for a human being to don a plant or animal shape. It is also possible that the fact of temporarily living in an alien kind of body may result in losing one's original species adherence. Again, this applies to humans who have inhabited an animal body as well as to an animal or spirit having inhabited a human body. In such cases, a true metamorphosis occurs and the being sees the world with the eyes of the host species, and experiences and senses like them. Memories of past identity are forgotten. There is thus a very real sense in which one may talk of mind–emotion–body fusion. Chewong notions, therefore, contradict a basic premise of Johnson's suggestions, namely that the body is a stable given from which we are never separated (1987: 206). To the Chewong, bodies are parts of a bigger whole that constitutes the person as a member of a species, and it is perfectly possible to move between bodies – albeit temporarily.

The forest and everything in it is not 'nature'. Rather, the forest environment constitutes the limits of the Chewong cultural domain and as such a potential for manifestations of personages. Until something has revealed itself as a personage, the Chewong have an agnostic attitude to every plant, stone, or moving creature in the forest. If one were to employ old-fashioned concepts, it would not be misleading to state that the Chewong have a dualistic conception of their world, one that can be predicated upon absence or presence of consciousness. However, it is important to stress that there are no absolute boundaries between these – either temporally, spatially or categorically. With the exception of the human category, the species status of a personage is neither finite nor stable, just as the relationships between the various aspects of personhood are not stable. Species move in and out of being categorised as personages, dependent upon contingent circumstances.

Furthermore, the notion that 'nature' is there to be exploited or controlled by humans would be absurd to the Chewong way of thinking, just as it would be absurd to suggest that mind should control the body, or men control women, or some individuals control the rest. People interact with the forest, their sociality is directly engaged in relationships with other conscious beings as well as with the parts of the forest that are not envisioned as personages.

Species-bound identities within an encompassing environment, made up of numerous social and moral universes, are thus the key to understanding Chewong conceptions. It is from this perspective that I base my claim that their social world consists only superficially of the 350-odd individual human beings, but must be extended to be coexistent both with the forest and with their cosmos. A clear perception of how relationships are maintained through processes of exchange underlies Chewong ideas in this regard. All actors and potential actors in their universe are placed relationally. Chewong individuals have no difficulties in understanding the idea of mutuality. Their ontological understanding is founded on such ideas. In a society which can only be characterised as extremely loosely organised – with cognatic kinship, with no formal political institutions or leaders, where the egalitarian ethos truly is lived experience – what constitutes the semantics of society, the moral reference points for individuals, becomes a pertinent question. My suggestion is that society for the Chewong is bounded by those personages with whom they stand in a relationship of obligation, responsibility and rights and with whom these demands are expressed in relations of exchange in some form. For example, all game animals are singed before being partitioned. The smell of the fur goes to the land of the particular animal and represents a kind of return of fecundity. Another way of putting it would be to say that the Chewong are in continuous dialogue with the jungle and jungle occupants and, like all meaningful dialogue, this is carried out within a shared set of premises, values, and concepts.

So while, from one point of view, Chewong society may appear static, this would be misleading. Their ideological constructs are very flexible, and they incorporate those new ideas, material objects, and practices from outside which provoke some cultural resonance (Howell 1995) and make sense of them in conformity with existing principles.

SOURCES OF EVIDENCE

Three main sources may be drawn upon in order to substantiate the above claims. The first two consist of a large body of myths and shamanistic songs, and a range of prescriptions and proscriptions, all of which inform and constitute subjectivity and social behaviour. These two domains are embedded within the third: Chewong cosmology. Many of the cosmological vectors can be found through examining the former two; together these three sources of knowledge constitute the principles that structure daily life, shamanistic practices and the moral code. I will give a very brief presentation of all these, starting with some pertinent Chewong cosmological ideas (for detailed examination, see Howell 1986, 1989).

Cosmology

Schematically one may present Chewong cosmology as eight worlds placed in layers. Earth Seven (*te tujuh*) is that of the forest and the beings who live in it as well as of the Malays and Chinese (and now also the English). This is a hot world, where humans and animals are hot because they shed blood through hunting and eating meat. All creatures are mortal because of this. Below is Earth Eight which is the Afterworld – a foggy island about which the Chewong neither know nor care much – and above is Earth Six which is the home of the 'original beings'. They are still immortal; a state of affairs which is directly attributable to the cool environment caused by their not eating anything but fruit and dew. Between Seven and Six are several worlds of various species of spirits, and the first five earths are not significant. Intermingled, as it were, with Earth Seven are also various other worlds inhabited by various cool and immortal beings who live in, or near, rivers or in flowers and their food is dew. Most beings, whether animal or spirit, have the potential for both harming and helping human beings.

Whenever they cause harm, however, this is never premeditated or malicious, but usually the result of some human misdemeanour (see below). Alternatively, they seek to alleviate their hunger and hunt humans (body or *ruwai*) – just as humans hunt various animals.

Prescriptions and proscriptions

There are no explicit rules that inform the Chewong not to steal or kill, or to avoid other commonly sanctioned behaviour, and there are no socio-political institutions that may punish those who do. Normative behaviour is predicated upon numerous prescriptions and proscriptions that deal with every day behaviour, and the sanction is attack from some non-human being, whether personage or not. The rules cover three main areas: the performance of seemingly mundane tasks, the injunction to share, and the control of emotionality. Repercussions fall within a small range in all instances: the occurrence of illness or mishap, or a 'natural' catastrophe caused by some non-human being. An examination of the rules reveals a strong preoccupation with relations and sociality of all kinds; between humans, spirits, and the general environments and between humans themselves. For example, not to share food, however small an amount there might be, is to expose to danger those who have not given anything; when tying house-beams together, the rattan used must be aligned in a certain way so as not to imprison its spirit; extreme care must be taken when cooking so as not to mix the flesh or smell from different animals. The injunctions on expressive emotional behaviour, e.g. laughing at animals, shouting in the face of misfortune, whistling, expressing (or even experiencing) anticipation or desire, further emphasise individuals' responsibility to control themselves. Some of these forms of action cause landslides, thunderstorms or other 'natural catastrophes' whereas others cause illness or accidents to individuals. It is of particular interest to note that actual repercussions may affect either the offender's body (or that of the victim in the case of being denied a share of food) or some other aspect of his or her consciousness, whether this be *ruwai*, liver, odour or eyes. Similarly, there are cases where a specific animal is the agent of vengeance. For example, a tiger or poisonous millipede – the visible animal or its *ruwai* – bites the body, or the *ruwai*, of those who express a desire for a cigarette when there is no tobacco around.

Disease and accident causation are thus intimately involved in perceptions of individual responsibility, relationship with other species and the forest environment, and an acknowledgement that there is no separation between the body and the mind.

Myths and songs

There is a large body of myths which are well-known to all Chewong (Howell 1982). They all contain some cosmological information, and they demonstrate the intimate entanglement of humans and forest. One of the instructive points about the myths for the Chewong themselves is that they provide information about species identity. Thus, whenever I would ask if a particular species was personage, they would pause to think if there was a myth to that effect. One category of myths may be regarded as exemplars for the correct handling of the self, and contain theories of both cause and effect.

A large number of the myths concern deceptive relations between different species of personages. Thus there are stories in which human personages appear in the cloak of animals, and stories where animals, plants, or spirits appear in human cloak. An added complication is that non-human personages may appear in human bodies when they are 'at home', in 'their own land', thus expressing the fundamental equality between all species of personages. Two major scenarios may be detected in these myths; those in which the masquerading character returns to his or her own species, and those in which they become metamorphosed into the species which they pretend to be. Many of the stories involve sexual relations across species boundaries, but with the illegitimate character deceiving his or her partner. Upon detection, depending upon their behaviour while still in alien guise, they may or may not return to their native kind. If their behaviour has strayed too far from the norms of the codes of their own species, they have no choice and are metamorphosed automatically. Alternatively, upon being found, they return permanently to their true body. Bodies are part of the larger whole that constitutes the person as a member of a species, and while it is possible to move between different bodies, this can only be done for short periods.

The following abbreviated myth demonstrates how inappropriate behaviour among humans leads to a rejection from the human world and a forced return to the character's natal species.

A dog had married a woman. He pretended to be a man. Nobody knew his true identity. Whenever he went hunting with his brothers-in-law, he would find a pretext to return to the spot where the game had been butchered before it was brought home. Here he would eat the intestines and the blood. When this was discovered, he returned to his doghood and dogs lost their status as personages.

Chewong religious practices are shamanistic. People meet spirits in dreams or during trance states and are given songs which must be sung whenever they perform a seance. The songs consist of a multiplicity of voices which are intermingled. Various spirits take turns in singing and telling about their worlds and their activities, the singers also interject their own voices into the song over time, recounting experiences from their soul-journeying. New songs come into existence as the result of individuals' encounters with different spirits, while old songs may die with their owners. The songs are thus a continuous source of details concerning the various spirits and their worlds, as well as being the main medium for maintaining active communication across species boundaries (for a more detailed discussion of Chewong songs, see Howell 1994).

In the present context, four points can be derived from Chewong myths and songs. First, they demonstrate a non-hierarchical inter-connectedness between human beings and other beings – conscious and unconscious – in their world. Second, they express Chewong morality through the exemplars of prescriptions and proscriptions and correct behaviour. As such they have pedagogic normative functions as well as metaphorically constructing a world view. Third, they emphasise both the universality and the species-boundedness of morality, thereby creating distinctions between the various species without evaluating their relative significance. Ritualised action is thus that which is predicated upon the rules. Fourth, Chewong notions of personhood stress both embodied knowledge and 'minded' and 'emotioned' bodies. So my argument is that the Chewong self is engaged in its existential reality through the continuous performance of rituals which, in and by themselves, express the structure of dependence and mutuality. Individuals in such societies are not delimited or bounded by their bodies. The soul, spirit, ego – whatever one wishes to call it – is distributed throughout a much larger social field, and individuals are part of a larger system of relations which define parameters of illness, mishaps, 'natural' catastrophes, fertility and barrenness, etc.

CONCLUSION

Chewong views cannot help western scientists or moral philosophers in their quest for establishing essential differences and similarities between humans and other animals, and ethologists and others arguing for or against the theory that various animals have 'culture' or 'language' must look elsewhere for evidence. Western construction of nature and culture, and the posited boundaries between these concepts, are embedded within a culture-specific ideology and philosophy and have a long intellectual history. They cannot be changed except by posing questions which employ relevant concepts and categories found within western philosophical and scientific discourses. In her book *Primate Visions*, Haraway makes the pertinent point that there can be no pre-discursive encounter with biology or, more generally, nature: 'Natural sciences do not necessarily get closer and closer to an objective "nature" to be materially and symbolically appropriated, but are themselves social activities, inextricably *within* the processes that give them birth' (Haraway 1989, cited in Wade 1993: 18).

Ingold suggests that the question 'What is an animal?' may be answered in many ways, but that 'every. . . paradigm has some view of animality deeply embedded, and often only dimly recognised, within most of its most fundamental assumptions'; 'what links the contributions [of the authors of the edited volume] is not a theory, but a question' (Ingold 1988: 15). I am sure that he is right when applied to western discourses, but equally sure that the question 'What is an animal?' would not be a meaningful one to the Chewong were it posed in such terms. A notion of 'animality', or even more of 'bestiality', is not part of their cognitive map of the world. I suggest that this is also why there is no word for 'animal' in their language. I would further suggest that it is inappropriate to search for a covert category of animal in Chewong classification of the world. My argument has been that, while theirs is an anthropocentric world view, it is more apposite to argue that the symbolic contrasts that they make are anchored in the distinction between those beings, plants, and objects which are personages and those which are not. It is in this sense that they resolve what I take to be a human predilection, namely to lay down premises for distinguishing between self and other. While the Chewong do not make categorical distinctions of the order nature–culture or mind–body, they do nevertheless differentiate between 'us' and 'them'. The continuity, or extension, of humanity is, as it were, moving in and out and around the numerous named and enumerated beings and objects in their environment – in the many worlds that they maintain exist in the forest. What is of interest, however, is that such boundaries are far from absolute, and 'us' is a fluid category. Moreover, reality is not divisible into material and spiritual, into mind and body, emotion and intellect. Rather, it is perceived as being made up of endlessly mutually interacting, and fluid beings and qualities.

The Chewong, then, have no difficulties in accepting that beings other than humans may be self-conscious subjects with thoughts and feelings of their own. However, unlike members of various western ecological movements, the Chewong would not accept that human beings have some *a priori* moral responsibility towards other such living beings, or that every being is in principle of equal importance and with equal rights. The Chewong allow for the possibility that members of any natural species may be, or become, personages, but this is a matter of taking each case as it comes. While they would accept that everything in their environment has the potential for meaningful interaction with themselves – both positively and nega-tively – such views cannot be divorced from their cosmology. The whole forest, including the numerous invisible worlds within and above it, is thus cultural space. Ellen has suggested (Chapter 6, this volume) that one way to identify a universal construction of nature is to look for the way that nature is defined as something separate from us spatially, 'assigning it to some realm outside humans or their immediate living (cultural) space'. But for this to occur, some kind of distinction has to be made between the village and the forest with which humans interact in structured ways. This is not applicable to the Chewong. It is, however, my suggestion that the worlds outside the forest, those of Malays and Chinese, are contrasted to the forest and that they are perceived as unknown and dangerous – possibly wild. However, this world outside the forest may not usefully or adequately be described as nature. Certainly, it is treated with extreme caution, and in their dealings with it the Chewong foster timidity as an integral and positive aspect of their personhood (Howell, 1989, 1996). However, not being participants in the Chewong social universe of humans and non-humans in the forest – in the great chain of being – the kinds of relationships that the Chewong engage in with such people are non-reciprocal. Unlike the significant parts of the forest with which the Chewong are engaged in continuous exchange relations – a gift economy – modes of relating with the unknown worlds outside have no significance beyond actual encounters.

Having said that, I wish to end on a more general note. Chewong cosmology and theories of being in the world mean that their understanding about themselves, each other, and the numerous significant others, guide and constitute them as knowing and acting subjects according to consistent principles and according to different modes of sociality. While they do not ascribe to categorisations that coincide with western ones, this does not mean that they do not differentiate. For a comparative study of ontologies and epistemologies, a good starting point would be an exploration of indigenous principles of differentiation and modes of relating.

NOTES

1 Fieldwork was conducted with the Chewong of Pahang, Malaysia from 1977 to 1979 and was supported by a grant from the Social Science Research Council (UK). Briefer visits were made in 1981, 1990 and 1991. An earlier version of this chapter was presented as a paper to the Department of Sociology and Anthropology, University of Keele. Several of the insightful comments given by staff and students there have been incorporated. The paper was revised while I was enjoying the hospitality extended to me as Visiting Scholar in the Department of Social Anthropology, University of Cambridge. I am grateful to all my colleagues in both these departments.
2 This word is found, in one form or another, among all the Senoi and Semang aboriginal groups in Peninsular Malaysia. It is usually translated as 'soul'. I find this both too narrow and too imprecise to denote the meanings that the Chewong attribute to the word. Personage is the closest I can come to it in English.
3 The fact that a general category of meat (*ai*) exists might be thought to indicate an implicit knowledge about animals. But *ai* includes fish (for which there is a word, *kiel*) and does not include the many animals which are not eaten by the Chewong.

REFERENCES

Descola, P. (1992) 'Societies of Nature and the Nature of Society', in A. Kuper (ed.) *Conceptualizing Society*, London: Routledge.
— (1994) *In the Society of Nature: A Native Ecology in Amazonia*, Cambridge: Cambridge University Press.
Ellen, R. (1982) *Environment, Subsistence, and System: The Ecology of Small-Scale Social Formations*, Cambridge: Cambridge University Press.
Haraway, D. (1989) *Primate Visions: Gender, Race and Nature in the World of Modern Science*, London: Routledge.

Howell, S. (1982) *Chewong Myths and Legends*, Kuala Lumpur: Royal Asiatic Society, Malaysian Branch, Monograph 11.

— (1985) 'Equality and Hierarchy in Chewong Classification', in R. H. Barnes *et al.* (eds) *Contexts and Levels*, Oxford: JASA Monograph 4.

— (1989) *Society and Cosmos: Chewong of Peninsular Malaysia*, Chicago: University of Chicago Press (first published 1984: Oxford University Press).

— (1994) 'Singing with the Spirits and Praying to the Ancestors', *L'Homme* XXXIV, 4: 15–34.

— (1995) 'Whose Knowledge and Whose Power? A new perspective on cultural diffusion', in R. Fardon (ed.) *Counterworks: Managing the Diversity of Knowledge*, London: Routledge.

— (1996) 'A Timid Liver: the Moral Force of Chewong Embodied Emotionality', unpublished manuscript.

Ingold, T. (ed.) (1988) *What is an Animal?* London: Unwin Hyman.

— (1994) 'Humanity and Animality', in T. Ingold (ed.) *Companion Encyclopedia of Anthropology*, London: Routledge.

Johnson, M. (1987) *The Body in the Mind*, Chicago: University of Chicago Press.

Lukes, S. (1975) *Emile Durkheim, his Life and Work, a Historical and Critical Study*, London: Allen Lane.

Milton, K. (ed.) (1993) *Environmentalism: the View from Anthropology*, London: Routledge.

Skultans, V. (1977) 'Bodily Madness and the Blush', in J. Blacking (ed.) *The Anthropology of the Body*, London: Academic Press.

Wade P. (1993) 'Race, Nature, and Culture', *Man* (NS) 28: 17–34.

Willis, R. (ed.) (1990) *Signifying Animals: Human Meaning in the Natural World*, London: Unwin Hyman.

Chapter 8

Blowpipes and spears

The social significance of Huaorani technological choices

Laura Rival

This article argues that hunting technology can shed new light on the interface between society and nature. It examines the social relations existing between the Huaorani, a group of Amazonian hunter-gatherers, and the animals they hunt. It discusses Huaorani extensive ethological knowledge, the social relations through which weapons are made and used, and those through which game is shared, prepared and consumed. Each of these aspects illuminates the principles which structure Huaorani social organisation and ensure its reproduction. Huaorani hunting techniques, which are based on a profound knowledge of animal life, bring about specific social relations, and produce distinctive social identities. It is shown that the blowpipe and the spear, which constitute two contrasting ways of killing and relating to game animals, monitor social distance in myths. Their mythical function thus reveals a striking homology between the way in which Huaorani people treat each other and the way in which they treat animals. It is concluded that hunting technology might be a better guide to the social objectification of nature than animal symbolism.

If we accept the proposition that technical processes are socially meaningful (Lemonnier 1994), we must see hunting technology as a key area for understanding the interface between nature and society. Few ethnographers of hunting societies have failed to comment on the accurate and extensive ethological knowledge possessed by indigenous hunters. And most of them have assumed – if not explicitly stated – that success in the hunt must be attributed primarily to hunters' expert tracking and skilled imitations of animal cries. Why is it, therefore, that studies have tended to ignore the practical knowledge of the living habits of animal species, focusing instead on semiological and ethical aspects of animal symbolism (Nelson 1973, Ridington 1982, Bird-David 1993)?

Studies of Amazonian hunting have discussed environmental adaptation (Gross 1975, Ross 1978, Hawkes *et al*.1982, Redford and Robinson 1987), technical efficiency (Hames and Vickers 1983), or religious beliefs (Reichel-Dolmatoff 1976, Descola 1992). These studies have raised three questions: is small prey hunting adapted to Amazonian ecology? Are traditional weapons more efficient than shotguns? Is ecological balance achieved through shamanic practice? Like most Amazonian anthropology, these studies overlook the lived experience derived from actively engaging with non-human agents sharing one's environment (see Descola 1986 for a notable exception). This can in part be attributed to the extreme polarisation of views on indigenous hunting, explained as expressing either environmental limitations or semiological constraints. I am aware of no work discussing, for instance, the great variety of hunting techniques found in groups operating under similar ecological conditions. This article discusses the fact that Huaorani people hunt almost exclusively monkeys, birds and white-lipped peccaries (*Tajassu peccari*) with essentially two kinds of weapons, the blowpipe and the spear. As I hope to show, criteria other than technical efficiency may have dictated this choice of weapons, deeply embedded in social relations.

THE ETHNOGRAPHIC CONTEXT OF HUNTING

Huaorani history is characterised by a conscious attempt to avoid being inserted in regional networks and to escape from concomitant political alliances. To the best of our knowledge, they have lived for centuries in the interstices between the great Zaparo, Shuar and Tukanoan nations of the Upper Marañon, where they have constituted nomadic and autarkic enclaves fiercely refusing contact, trade, and exchange with powerful neighbours. Their drastic isolationism has found various cultural expressions. For example, Huaorani language cannot be attached to any known phylum. Moreover, non-Huaorani cultural traits were literally absent when the Summer Institute of Linguistics (SIL) first contacted them in the early 1960s.

As I have shown elsewhere (Rival 1992, 1993), such isolationism corresponds to a highly endogamic system, albeit flexible enough to accommodate relatively large demographic variations. When

demographically stable, the overall population is divided into dis-
persed networks of inter-marrying longhouses separated by vast
stretches of unoccupied forest. For greater security and autonomy,
longhouse residential groups tend to isolate themselves from most
other groups. A higher degree of solidarity and unity exists between
longhouses exchanging marriage partners. These loose aggregates,
sometimes called *huaomoni* ('we-people'), maintain relations of latent
hostility with all other groups, which they call 'others' or 'enemies'
(*huarani*). Longhouses not related by marriage avoid meeting, and
often ignore each other's exact location. However, personal relationships between kin living in non-allied longhouses enable the periodic
renewal of alliances between *huarani* groups, without which Huaorani
society could not continue to exist as a separate entity. If the need to
keep *huarani* alliances open ensures overall tribal cohesion, it is the
cultural preference for brother–sister alliances which structures
huaomoni groups. Cross-sex siblings pair themselves from an early
age, and seek to remain socially and spatially close throughout their
lives. They are united by strong and lasting bonds even after they
marry. Marriage is uxorilocal. Most marriages take place between
cross-cousins (with a significant proportion of double cross-cousin
marriages), and many unite pairs of brothers and sisters in sequence.
Expressed in more general terms, the cultural preference is for a
brother and a sister to remain part of the same *huaomoni* group and to
marry some of their children to each other.

The traditional system of social alliances, based on a strict closure
of the Huaorani social world onto itself, as well as on the partial
isolation and mutual avoidance of the regional groups, corresponds to
a particular mode of subsistence and use of the forest. House groups
regularly move between their longhouses (built on hilltops) and a
series of secondary residences and hunting shelters. There is a clear
dietary preference for fruit – particularly the peach palm (*Bactris
gasipaes*) fruit. Birds and monkeys, the favoured game, are arboreal
species which feed mainly on fruit.[1] When abundant, fruit becomes
the main staple, and hunting is discontinued. Fruit trees, a legacy of
past generations, are slow-growing plants whose bounty turns the
forest into a giving environment.

Before the introduction of shotguns in the mid-1970s, birds and
monkeys were exclusively hunted with blowpipes, and white-lipped
peccaries (*Tajassu peccari*) with spears.[2] The white-lipped peccary, the
only ground animal to be eaten, was hunted only occasionally. There
was no other weapon – no traps, bows and arrows or clubs – and most

other animal species were tabooed. Fishing, an activity undertaken more by women and children than by men, was marginal.[3] Except for children, who hunt in bands, hunters usually pursue small arboreal species alone in day time. There is at least one longhouse member hunting each day. Hunters rarely come back without game. In fact, returns are high, and everyone eats at least 200 grammes of meat every day. The meat is immediately shared, cooked and consumed. Meat, which is as praised as fruit, is generally boiled and often eaten with nothing else. There are no particular rules as to who should get which part. Yost and Kelley's (1983) survey of 867 hunts (yielding 3,165 kills) corresponds to my own observations and records: monkeys, especially the woolly monkey (*Lagothrix lagotricha*), but also the howler monkey (*Alouatta seniculus*) and the spider monkey (*Ateles paniscus*), curassows (*Mitu salvini*) and Spix guan (*Penelope jacquacu*), are the most appreciated and most often hunted species.

KNOWING GAME PRACTICALLY

Both men and women have a great knowledge of the habits, habitats and feeding cycles of most arboreal species. Inferring from fruiting cycles, weather conditions, and many other signs, they can predict animal behaviour and locate animals they cannot see. With developed sensorial abilities – especially hearing and smell – they feel the presence of animals and anticipate their next move. Children acquire this knowledge largely among themselves, as they explore the forest (never beyond an approximate four kilometre radius around the longhouse) with older children. Men, women and children spend hours slowly exploring the forest along their trails. They do not merely hunt and gather (two activities which are relatively undifferentiated in practice), but *walk*, observing with evident pleasure and interest the movements of animals, the progress of fruit maturation, or simply the growth of vegetation. When walking in this fashion (a style of displacement markedly different from the one used when going on a visit or when transporting food from one place to another), one does not get tired, or lost. One's body takes the smell of the forest and ceases to be extraneous to the forest world. One learns to perceive the environment as other animals do. One becomes a 'dweller' deeply involved in a silent conversation with surrounding plants and animals (Ingold 1993b). Walking in the forest day after day with Huaorani informants, I began to appreciate that, by interpreting the environment from an animal's perspective, they were recognising the animal's capacity for will and purpose. Birds and monkeys, in particular, show intention and purpose in their quest for food.

Documenting this practical knowledge is far from easy. Informants answer questions about animal behaviour with reluctance, as if their knowledge was not verbalisable. Animal behaviour cannot be explained or taught; it must be observed and experienced practically. Formal interviews, therefore, did not yield any substantial data on animal behaviour, but they made me see some of the principles organising Huaorani practical knowledge. For instance, informants clearly separated observed data from hearsay. When unsure, they openly admitted ignorance. If an informant rewarded my insistence with some (unfounded) generalisation, there was always someone to dismiss it with a counter-example. Finally, animal behaviour was invariably described by means of anthropomorphic expressions (this, according to Kennedy 1992, seems to be a common occurrence among western ethologists too). It was by participating in forest expeditions that I learnt the little I know about animal behaviour and Huaorani perceptions of animal behaviour. Informal conversations, which proceeded at a good pace both during and after a hunt, were also far more instructive than interviews.

Hunting stories are shared with those who stayed behind. Hunters must answer numerous questions, and state precisely which trail they took, how far they went, what the hunted animal was eating, where it was hit, and so forth. Interpretations of animal behaviour are constantly put to the test, and assertions disputed. When telling about a failed approach, hunters are criticised for not having adopted better tactics. A lively discussion ensues, as hunters try to justify their actions on the basis of previous, successful hunts. Women, who accompany hunters and often hunt themselves, fully participate in these conversations. Children listen carefully to these accounts of freshly experienced, observed and remembered interactions between hunters and game. Like their adult kin, they immerse themselves in shared practical knowledge with great delight.

After having participated in a number of hunting trips and heard countless conversations on hunting, I formed the impression that knowledge of, and interest in, monkeys and birds is particularly developed. I have, however, gathered more information on monkeys. From what I could observe and hear, it seems that hunters have a fairly intimate knowledge of the individuals composing a monkey troop (males are recognised from females, adults from young). They plan in advance which individual will be hunted down on any given trip.

Occasionally, the targeted animal makes its 'soul' visible, and 'speaks with its eyes', pleading for its life to be spared. If such communication occurs, the hunter targets a different animal.[4]

Monkeys are by far the most favoured game. Of the three largest monkeys, the woolly monkey is especially praised. Woolly monkeys, which are hunted in large numbers, are considered more prolific than spider and howler monkeys. Their sense of territoriality is said to be highly developed. Their social habits are compared with those of humans. Like humans, they live in stable groups, which are called *nanicaboiri*, a term also used to refer to house groups. I see no totemic operation, and no metaphorical assimilation in this linguistic fact, but, rather, the recognition of the similarity between woolly monkey and Huaorani social organisation (this is, perhaps, why woolly monkeys set the standards by which the two other species are judged). For example, the fact that they reproduce during the peach palm season (a time when marriage ceremonies are held) is highly significant.

A real concern for animal and human population dynamics is built into this detailed knowledge of inter- and intra-species. When human settlements become too large or too sedentarised, arboreal animals flee away. A balance must be found between human groups and the animals they hunt. This is achieved in two ways, one pragmatic, the other symbolic. Food resources – particularly fruit – are consciously shared with hunted species. A fruiting tree is never entirely tapped; some fruit must be left 'for birds and monkeys'. The shamanic adoption of jaguar 'sons' corresponds to the same logic of keeping game close. When visiting their 'parents' during shamanic trances, adopted jaguars, who are said to control the distribution of animals, and attract troops of monkeys or flocks of birds close to human settlements, indicate where hunters can find abundant game.[5]

Efforts to keep close those animals which are naturally limited in their distribution and ecological requirements are all the more remarkable when compared with the complete lack of interest in controlling peccary distribution. The most important characteristic of white-lipped peccaries (*Tajassu peccari*, *urè* in Huaorani) seems to be that they roam in large herds of a hundred or more. Whereas monkeys are recognised as individuals, peccaries form an anonymous crowd. The second significant trait of behaviour is their absence of territory. Wandering over extensive areas, they eat indiscriminately food from different ecozones. They are all-devouring, and their fatty, soft and bland flesh is almost the opposite of monkey flesh, which is

tough, chewy and muscular. Moreover, they eat fallen fruit rotting on
the forest floor. Given the insalubrious environment in which they
live, they are said to be infected with a series of skin and intestinal
parasites (see Reichel-Dolmatoff 1985: 133 for a similar perception by
the Vaupes Indians).

The obvious lack of interest in peccaries struck me as being related
more generally to an aversion to the forest floor, especially the
swampy areas where peccaries wallow in mud. In addition, their
scent gland produces a nauseating and repellent odour which is
associated with the smell of rot and decay. These ground animals, with
their preference for lowlands, swamps and natural clearings, inspire
repugnance in people who live on hilltops and ridges, and never leave
the canopy cover.[6] Finally, when passing in the vicinity of a longhouse,
peccaries leave behind them a trail of destruction. Never sought after
in a hunt, but killed whenever detected near a settlement, they are seen
as aggressive invaders. Huaorani knowledge of peccary social
organisation is limited – to say the least. Given that white-lipped
peccaries are highly social (Sowls 1984), this is somewhat surprising.
It may be that first-hand experience of these animals is minimal. They
are rarely observed in primeval forest, and contact with them seems to
be restricted to collective hunts during which the objective is not to
observe social habits, but to kill as many animals as possible.
However, I was left with the impression that in addition to such
objective reasons, peccaries were seen as sociologically less interesting
than monkeys. If knowledge of animals is primarily guided by direct
involvement – and hunting is the Huaorani's most common form of
involvement with animals – it is also shaped by the cultural (should we
say political?) choice of being more, or less, involved with certain
species.

WEAPONS IN THE MAKING

Huaorani weapons are efficient, functional and well adapted. However, alternative weapons, such as bows and arrows, or different
hunting techniques, such as trapping, would be equally efficient. The
Huaorani have effectively exercised a choice in technology. Bows and
arrows are spread more widely than blowpipes in Amazonia, and
some groups hunt peccaries with blowpipes. I contend that Huaorani
hunting technology, the product of cultural selection, is functional
not only physically, but also socially.

The same basic material, palm wood, is used for blowpipes and spears alike. Whereas blowpipes are made of two pieces of *tepa*, spears are carved in the much harder *tehue*.[7] Huaorani blowpipes are made by splitting a long palm wood rod and grooving each half, then binding the two parts together, sealing them with beeswax (to prevent air leakage), and entirely wrapping them with vine bark. Slightly longer than blowpipes, their spears are thin pieces of wood with fire-hardened points. Double-handed, they end in two heads of a triangular shape. The heads, of which one is usually notched, are as sharp and cutting as metallic blades. They can be sharpened again, but generally break off in the victim's body. Unlike the blowpipe, which is made to be used over and over again, the spear is made for one kill. In warfare, spears must be left in the bodies of dying enemies.

Blowpipes come in different lengths, and some are much better crafted than others. In a good blowpipe, the two grooves match exactly and make a straight canal, with a perfectly smooth surface. This is obtained by putting sand inside the canal, and then smoothing up and down with a long slim fishing lance of very hard *tehue* wood. Hunters may spend weeks making their blowpipes, especially the full length ones, which may measure up to 12 feet (just over 3 metres) and weigh over 9 pounds (4 kilogrammes). As the work required is minute and tedious, no more than a few hours are spent on it, every other day. Spears are not as difficult to make. A spear is good if its ends are well pointed, if its shaft has a good grip, and if it weighs enough for good penetration impact, but not so much as to be cumbersome during transport and charging. It is not considered a finished product until the surface, polished to a smooth grain, is decorated with feathers and distinctive designs made of thin bands of vine. If blowpipes are all very similar – except for a more or less skilled manufacture – spears are individualised. Decorative patterns and the shape of the notches are distinctive markers by which owners can be identified unambiguously.

Blowpipes are used to propel light arrows or darts tipped in curare poison.[8] Arrows, which are stored in bamboo quivers, come from the stem of palm leaves cut to length and whittled sharp. Hunters can easily prepare forty arrows or more in a day. Preparing them is a popular occupation, especially when conversing with visitors. Men make their own curare; it is never traded. Its preparation, which does not take more than a few hours, is easy and straightforward. More-over, the poison keeps for several months if stored in a dry, relatively cool place – usually in a pot hanging from the palm roof, in an empty corner of the longhouse. When needed, sections of the poison vine are cut in the forest by men or women, and brought back to the longhouse. Curare poison, simmered over the conjugal hearth where all cooking takes place, is prepared in the midst of other domestic activities. No particular behaviour is expected from women (not even when menstruating) or from children. I observed no taboo or ritualised behaviour relating to the preparation of curare.

Spears are made in a few hours. Unlike blowpipes, their production is not constrained by an elaborate manufacturing process; it is limited by the scarcity of *tehue* wood. Peach palms are grown for their fruit, in family-owned forest groves. Only old, non-producing trees are normally available for spears. Felling young palms – a common occurrence in war time – is seen as a potential threat to social order. Whereas men make blowpipes at their leisure, when they need one, spear making is 'collective', in the sense that spears tend to be prepared all at once, each man working on his own. Blowpipes are often worked outside the longhouse, in full sunlight. They are made in the midst of other activities, with friends and relatives observing, commenting and giving advice on their progress. Spears, by contrast, are usually worked in the forest, or in the isolation of deserted longhouses (when most residents have left to garden, collect or hunt). While working, men chant war songs which warn everyone of their intentions; spear making is motivated by the wish to spill blood and make many killings.

Blowpipes stand upwards and erect in the centre of the longhouse, readily available for anyone who needs them. They are lent liberally to kin, sometimes for extended periods of time. Under no condition would they be traded, however. Well-made blowpipes are praised for the evenness of their bores, and the quality of their shafts, which are perfectly flat and oval, and widen smoothly at the mouthpiece. Good blowpipe makers are greatly admired, not only for their skill and mastery, but also for their sense of fine proportions and aesthetics. If bigger and heavier blowpipes are technically more efficient (more reliable against false movements, they are designed to aim at monkeys from the ground), they are more 'social' as well. Their size and weight is associated with full-fledged adulthood. It is because they embody important social qualities – achieved maturity, controlled force, artistry, a sense of balance – that these beautiful weapons are sought after. Whereas blowpipes are used by others than their owners, spears can only be held by those who made them. Women, in particular, never touch the spears of their male kin. Every man keeps five or six spears ready in the thatched roof of the longhouse. To leave a spear leaning against the wall would warp the shaft. But more importantly, spears are dangerous, they are not to be seen on a daily basis. In some longhouses, all spears are stored side by side, but in others, each man keeps his own in a separate part of the roof. Men also keep spears hidden in the forest. Quantities of new spears are made whenever needed; typically, after a white-lipped peccary hunt (one or two spears are needed for each animal), before a drinking ceremony organised by non-kin (at which male guests must offer three to five spears as gifts to the male host), or after a killing raid (spears are left in the bodies of enemies). Although rarely used today, spears are still made collectively and offered as gifts to outsiders (governmental officials, oil engineers, tourists, or leaders of indigenous organisations). Homicide is now rare, but it is still perpetrated with spears; shotguns are never used to kill enemies.

'WE BLOW-HUNT AND WE SPEAR-KILL'

A weapon, like any tool, prolongs the body in its effort to know the world by relating to it (Ingold 1993a). Blowpipe hunting, which secures the most regular supply of meat, tends to be a solitary activity. Women, who borrow their fathers', brothers', or husbands' blowpipes, tend to hunt birds rather than monkeys, and, to the best of my knowledge, do not put curare poison on the arrows they themselves prepare. Conversely, spear hunting, which provides large quantities of meat, is communal. However, it only occurs from time to time, when a herd of white-lipped peccaries is detected near a settlement.

Using a blowpipe, like manufacturing it, requires apprenticeship. Boys learn both arts simultaneously, starting with small models.[9] Young children, including girls, are actively taught by older children, as well as by adults. Children learn animal calls, then they learn to aim at small mammals and birds with poisonless arrows from the first limbs of a tree. As they receive increasingly bigger and heavier blowpipes, they gradually develop the right bodily movements. These become increasingly more precise, controlled and co-ordinated, until full efficacy is finally reached. Adolescents in their late teens hunt bigger tree species with force and accuracy. They have learnt to blow with a jolt of the entire body. Monkeys are normally shot from a distance of 17–30 metres. Whereas youths shoot at a 24–31-metre distance, adult hunters can reach a prey at a distance of 39–41 metres (Yost and Kelley 1983: 194–96).

The composure of someone hunting with a blowpipe cannot escape the observer. Animals are not tracked or pursued, but approached. To detect a prey does not occasion any surprise or excitement. Calmly and slowly, hunters prepare their arrows. These are retrieved without rush from the quiver, one by one. Kapok is spun in a butt around each arrow (this makes it fit tightly into the blowpipe) which is then nicked on a piranha jaw (this ensures that the poisoned head will break and remain in the animal's body). The arrows are then propelled as air is blown through the blowpipe held almost vertical with the two hands firmly placed around the mouthpiece. For a spider monkey, as many as twelve arrows may be needed, and thirty minutes may pass before the poison becomes effective. Death ensues, silent and practically painless. Hunting arboreal animals with a blowpipe is 'to carry dead flesh back home' (*oõinga èenqui po*), or to 'go blowing' (*oõnte go*). Only jaguars and harpy eagles kill arboreal animals. Huaorani, the true human beings, 'blow' them. The velocity of non-poisoned arrows may kill small birds, but due to their lightness, their impact is insufficient to kill monkeys. It is not hunting (the action of blowing) that causes the monkey's death, but curare poison.

'Killing' is *hueno tenongui*, literally, 'causing someone to die by spearing'. One can only kill by wounding, spilling blood, and tearing organs with a spear. As in many other cultures (Blackmore 1971: 84–90), there is no difference between hunting and raiding spears. Spearing is a violent and dangerous business. To kill with a spear, the hunter must thrust his weapon violently, and inflict a large wound at close range. Whereas success in blowpipe hunting depends on lung power and throat control, success in spear killing demands strength, endurance, and great physical dexterity, particularly with the arms. Qualities required for successful peccary hunting – and warfare – are not control, movement co-ordination, restraint and the careful choice of the targeted victim, but blind courage and ferocity.

Although I have not witnessed a peccary hunt during fieldwork, I have witnessed people's behaviour at the (false) alert of a herd's approach, and heard many stories of memorable peccary hunts. When a herd approaches a longhouse, its residents run out with great excitement. The proximity of peccaries is enraging; it drives the men to kill. While they fetch their spears, women and children shoo the herd towards them. Each man, armed with five or six spears carried on the shoulder, tries to slaughter as many animals as possible, whatever their age or sex. Once a spear is thrust, it cannot be recovered easily. This is due as much to the way it is designed as to the strength with which it is thrust.

Peccaries are aggressive, they do not flee but charge, causing deep wounds in hunters' legs. In a peccary hunt, therefore, both the hunter and the prey are wounded and shed blood. Death is painful, messy, violent and noisy. The hunt is thought of and carried out as a killing raid, a war expedition. Both peccaries and human enemies are killed with peach palm wood spears, in a fit of driving rage (*pïï inte*), a mixture of courage, fearlessness, anger, and force – both moral and physical. Peccaries, however, are not sought after like human enemies; they are killed whenever they invade longhouse territories. They are unpredictable: they come in packs of anonymous 'others', and must be eliminated. A peccary hunt is the confrontation between a group of humans (the longhouse unit) and a group of animals (the herd). To kill off the enemy, with which no personal relationship can exist, is a collective undertaking. Like the making of spears which demands men's collective undertaking and individual participation, the hunt requires the collaboration of all the group's members, men, women and children. The hands of young children are applied to the fur of the palpitating and bleeding carcasses before they are skinned, so as to absorb their force and energy.

The peccary hunt, therefore, is special; it is a collective slaughter followed by a feast. Hides are not kept for trade, meat is not smoked for later consumption. Baby peccaries are never adopted as pets, but killed and eaten. Peccary meat, the meat of an omnivorous animal with an uncontrolled appetite, is considered highly intoxicating and can only be consumed infrequently, in a kind of orgy, by the *huaomoni* group in whose territory the herd was hunted (I once visited a group who had organised a peccary feast three days earlier; they were still lying, half-sick, in their hammocks).

THE MYTHICAL CHOICE OF WEAPONRY

The way in which blowpipe and spear are incorporated into mythical discourse further demonstrates their social meaning. In myth, as in reality, the two weapons are used to structure two contrasting social relationships, which, I contend, represent two complementary responses to the problem of exchange and alliance. In myth, however, they operate more as regulatory mechanisms than as weapons, and mediate between humans, rather than between humans and animals. A popular myth involving a blowpipe, two brothers and their sister, illustrates the dilemma of social proximity:

A brother and a sister, who have always been very close, sleep in the same hammock. In his sleep, the brother turns into a mosquito, and unwillingly penetrates his sister's mouth. She is awakened by the tickling and soon realises with horror that her face is stained with genipa [a sign that her brother has 'annoyed' her; this is a euphemism for sexual intercourse]. The young man [in some versions of the myth], mortified and terribly ashamed, asks his younger brother to propel him to heaven with his blowpipe. [In other versions, the younger brother, made furious by his siblings' misdemeanour, decides to punish his older brother by sending him to heaven.] The incestuous brother becomes the moon. The younger brother and his sister become close allies. Chagrined by her son's absence, and heart-broken by the irreparable distance [her son will never return] their mother watches the moon every night.

The myth clearly exposes the dilemma faced by this endogamous and uxorilocal society: only one brother can remain close to his sister and marry within the endogamous nexus. Cross-cousin marriage, as practised by the Huaorani, reinforces ties between brothers and sisters, but fosters enmity between brothers. The dispersal and departure of marrying sons, which is almost inevitable, affects primarily the mother. While her married daughters stay at home, her sons must marry out. Second, the myth illustrates well the potential risk contained in the brother–sister relationship. Brothers and sisters are encouraged to form pairs from an early age, to remain close, and to exchange their children in marriage. But if they are too close, they become incestuous, i.e. they form the union that should be made by their children. Brothers who get too close to their sisters threaten the social order in the same way as monkeys who try to ape humans (a number of myths deal with the social catastrophes caused by monkeys who are either too close or too distant from humans). The blowpipe is used to re-establish the right distance. The third lesson of the myth is that the blowpipe monitors social distance between kin. Its action in monkey hunting is the exact reversal of its effect in the myth. In one case, a not-so-distant animal is brought closer spatially and socially. In the other, a relative, who is too close, is made utterly distant – both socially and physically.

The blowpipe, which can either bring closer (if too far), or remove (if too close), is a powerful instrument for monitoring social closeness. It puts men in a position of control, as defenders of endogamous relationships. Both incest and open exchange threaten endogamy, epitomised by the privileged alliance between a brother and a sister, and the symbiotic relationship between a *huaomoni* group and a troop of woolly monkeys. I am tempted to suggest that the particular shape of the Huaorani blowpipe, which, incidentally, is called *oö mena* ('two halves that blow'), corresponds to restricted exchange between equivalent cross-sex siblings.

A myth involving the use of spears to solve inter-ethnic conflicts parallels the myth of the blowpipe as a means for sorting out family matters. In both cases, we find Huaorani imagination making use of hunting weapons to regulate social distance. But whereas the blowpipe links or dissociates close kin living in the same longhouse, the spear associates Huaorani and non-Huaorani people. The myth explains the origin of hardwood and of deadly spears. At the beginning of their history, Huaorani people had only spears made of balsa wood, which were too blunt and soft to kill. They were at the mercy of numerous cannibals, and under the constant threat of being killed off. Their only protection against these powerful enemies was to live in hiding. One day, the son of the sun visited them, and taught them the existence of peach palms. Having learnt to make hard wood spears, they were able to defend themselves, and survive as a separate group. Without peach palm wood spears, Huaorani people would have succumbed to the genocidal actions of over-numerous 'others'. These spears, which are used for internal warfare as well, are also necessary for the continuity of *huaomoni* groups. The spear, in sum, is a violent and powerful instrument that draws social boundaries between 'us' and 'others' as well as between 'true humans' and 'cannibals'.

These two myths confirm that society exists through its objectification of nature (Descola 1992), and that technology is best understood as one of the processes by which social structures are institutionalised (Latour 1994). Conceptualised as the objectification of the privileged tie which unites brothers and sisters, hunting with a blowpipe represents the choice of a close, non-aggressive relationship with arboreal species – of which the woolly monkey is an epitome. This form of hunting, which is not considered violent, is practised by women and children as well. Full-size blowpipes, made by married men living uxorilocally, are widely shared within the longhouse. Associated with the continuity of *huaomoni* groups and of peach palm groves, they help perpetuate an endogamous and autarkic social world based on sharing rather than on reciprocal exchange. Spears, on the contrary, are boundary-making instruments that defend the inside from the predatory outside. Spear hunting is about spilling blood and killing off the enemy. Never shared, highly individualised, and ritually given away to enemies, spears wound unrelated people and animals. Spears are designed to slaughter those others with whom alliances are not possible. In sum, the blowpipe – a technology of inclusion – and the spear – a technology of exclusion – contribute in two different ways to the making of the same moral, symbiotic community: the endogamous *huaomoni* group with its associated palms and tree animals.

CONCLUSION

Huaorani hunting technology is the product of social choices, manifest in the way in which weapons are designed, made and used. The blowpipe and the spear have been created within – and have participated in the reproduction of – a distinctive world of social relations and myths. Moreover, they are linked to different ways of knowing game animals and relating to them. Contrary to Yost and Kelley (1983) who attribute Huaorani preference for arboreal game to technological powerlessness (most ground species were traditionally taboo because no one knew how to hunt them before the introduction of shotguns), I have argued for a non-deterministic view of Huaorani hunting technology. To look at hunting technology in terms of efficiency does not allow us to answer the questions: why is it that the blowpipe was chosen over the bow and arrow, a common weapon in Amazonia? Why is it that no clubs or traps (two other familiar Amazonian weapons) are found in this culture? Why is it that many Amazonian groups eat some of the ground species tabooed by the Huaorani?[10] In fact, when compared cross-culturally, the Huaorani way of hunting peccaries sporadically and exclusively with spears appears quite exceptional. Many Amazonian groups do not wait for peccary herds but regularly track them, and hunt them with poison darts shot from blowpipes. Other groups attack peccaries at close range with clubs, or kill them with long bows (Sowls 1984: 180–82). Some groups have used dogs and shotguns for several centuries (Grenand 1995), and traded hides for ammunition (Descola 1986: 275). Similarly, the view that blowing poisoned darts and spearing represent two completely separate and incompatible hunting techniques is far from universal. South-East Asian blowpipes, for instance, which are often fitted with spear blades lashed to the muzzle, can be used to hunt ground animals such as wild pigs, *as well as* arboreal game (Blackmore 1971, Sellato 1994). Each of these methods signals substantial differences in the way hunters relate socially to game animals, their communities and outsiders.

The hunting technology developed by a particular society must, therefore, be understood in relation to a complex set of historical, social and cultural factors. To determine the specific combination of factors which has led to the adoption of one technology instead of another is of course an extremely risky undertaking (Pfaffenberger 1988: 244). One should be especially wary of substituting an 'instrumental' for a 'substantive' theory of technology (Feenberg 1991). As I have discussed them here, Huaorani hunting techniques appear to correspond to the following conditions and choices.

At one level, hunting techniques are conditioned by historical events – in particular, by the political rejection of all types of contact or exchange with non-Huaorani. The transformation of Huaorani hunting in recent years has been caused primarily by a change of policy towards outsiders. By consenting to live with the SIL missionaries, Huaorani people have agreed to form communities led by powerful outsiders capable of 'attracting' large flows of free manufactured goods. Pushed to adopt a more sedentary lifestyle in semi-permanent villages along rivers (a biotope richer in ground animals), and to intensify horticulture by planting larger manioc gardens which attract rodents, tapirs and collared peccaries, they are increasingly practising 'garden hunting' (Linares 1976) and killing previously tabooed species, whose meat they both consume and trade for ammunitions. If the shotgun enables the hunter to obtain meat supplies by means of the traditional solitary hunt, it also creates a certain dependence *vis-à-vis* outsiders. More isolated groups, by contrast, use blowpipes with more frequency and privilege relations with birds and monkeys, which they continue to attract through constant moving and careful management. This example illustrates that the shotgun, like other weapons and hunting techniques, participates in the constitution of social relationships. It is subjected to social constraints as much as it is adapted to environmental conditions. Huaorani hunters do not perceive the shotgun as a technical improvement over the spear or the blowpipe. They have adopted it as part of a *different* way of life. If spears and blowpipes are today less used in hunting than shotguns, spears have not been replaced as weapons for raids or gifts for 'enemies' which could become potential allies, nor have blowpipes been traded or exchanged with outsiders; as in the past, they are offered as gifts to close kin exclusively.

At another level, hunting techniques reflect the practical knowledge that shapes concrete interactions between humans and animals through direct perception and engagement in the world. The political choice of radical isolationism has led to the formation of close relationships based on trust and respect with certain animals, while violently excluding others, defined as predatory. It is through hunting, a skilled practice which occupies many hours of their daily lives, that hunters acquire knowledge of the species which they consider 'close'. Familiar co-sharers of the same environment, these animals are recognised as having feelings, volition and a certain degree of consciousness. Hunters know from experience that animals communicate, learn, and modify their habits and ways in response to humans. Humans and the animals they hunt, therefore, are social beings mutually engaged in each other's world. This explains the correspondence between the ways in which people treat each other and treat animals.

Finally, the instrumental function of the blowpipe and spear is exploited symbolically at the mythical level. Hunting is practical knowledge on the basis of which common inferences are formed and shared. It is therefore not surprising that hunting serves as an experiential ground from which other types of social experience and relations are imagined or represented. In the Huaorani myths commented on earlier, the two hunting weapons symbolise (indexically rather than metaphorically) two complementary social relationships, endogamy and autarky. In this sense, Huaorani hunting symbolism could be fitted in previous studies of animal symbolism, in which animals personify social groups (Lévi-Strauss 1964), social persons (Urton 1985), or the relationship between humanity and animality (Willis 1990). But, in contrast to these representational systems largely based on cosmological constructs, Huaorani technological symbolism is informed by a direct and practical relationship to the world. Is it because Huaorani people, instead of appropriating nature symbolically (Ingold 1988: 13), prefer discovering its affordances?

ACKNOWLEDGEMENTS

Fieldwork among the Huaorani (carried out between January 1989 and June 1990) was made possible thanks to the generous support of the Wenner-Gren Foundation for Anthropological Research. I am very grateful to Philippe Erikson, Stephen Hugh-Jones, Michael

O'Hanlon and Roy Ellen who commented on earlier drafts, and to
Gísli Pálsson for his helpful editorial comments.

NOTES

1   As far as I know, there is no general term for 'animals'. Game is *oingairi*,
    literally, 'hunted, therefore edible, game'. When pushed hard, informants
    will – not without some reluctance – mention inclusive terms such as
    'monkeys', 'fish' and 'birds', which they form by extending the meaning
    of a 'prototype' species. For example, *gata*, the term for 'woolly monkey'
    can refer to all monkeys.

2   Shotguns were introduced by the SIL. Today widely used, they are rarely
    purchased, as men get them through exchange or as gifts from various
    institutions and oil companies. Some women still hunt with their
    husbands' or sons' shotguns. Although dogs were introduced at the
    same time as shotguns, they are rarely used for hunting.

3   Small fish are stunned with a variety of plant poisons, and then scooped
    out in nets knotted by women. Men sometimes use a long, flexible lance
    made of palm wood to spear bigger fish in water pools. They use these
    fish spears to smooth the canal of their blowpipes after boring.

4   Hunters who have told me of such incidents seem to imply that it is in
    their quality as living organisms that certain animals (and trees) have the
    power to move humans to compassion. Such personal relationships are
    established through eye contact. They are highly conjectural. The same
    animal, met again, might show no sign of awareness and, if found
    indifferent to its fate, will be killed. To the best of my knowledge, there
    is no idea of sacrifice, or of exchange of souls between animals and
    humans.

5   Unlike Tukanoan shamans (Reichel-Dolmatoff 1976) who use their
    power to ensure the constant regeneration of game, Huaorani shamans
    are primarily concerned to attract game animals and control their spatial
    distribution.

6   Although this was never explicitly stated by my informants, I soon
    became aware that the preference for walking along ridges (hunting trails
    invariably follow ridge tops, and rivers and swampy areas are avoided as
    much as possible), where the ground is dry and 'clean', is linked to a
    profound aversion to mud and rotten leaves. Whenever possible, the
    forest floor itself is avoided altogether, and replaced by a form of
    'walking' from one tree to the next. Trees are also climbed to cross rivers.

7   *Tehue* (literally 'hard wood') is the term used for *Bactris gasipaes* wood
    (see Rival (1993) for a discussion of the cultural importance of this
    wood). I am not sure of the signification of *tepa*. Informants have told me
    that *tepa* refers to the softer wood of a young *Bactris gasipaes* palm.
    However, Lescure *et al.* (1987: 298) classify it as a separate, unidentified
    palm species of the *Arecaceae* family.

8   The Huaorani call the poison *oome*, the plant (*Curarea tecunarum*) *oonta*,
    and the vine *dahuaoontame*. The vine is abundant throughout Huaorani
    land. When asked about the poison's origin, informants respond that

curare making is an ancient knowledge which came from experimenting with various poisonous plants. Huaorani ancestors observed that some animal species poisoned their prey – particularly spiders and scorpions. They tried to imitate them. They first attempted to use the liquid obtained from crushed spiders. This method failed, so they continued to experiment – equally unsuccessfully – with numerous leaves, barks and plants, until the day they realised that no animal ever ate the fruit of the *oonta* vine. They tried to prepare poison with it, and it worked.

9 Learning to make a blowpipe is a long and gradual process; the craft is only mastered by married adults. I do not know with certainty how children learn to make and throw spears. I observed spear games on several occasions (I only saw boys), but could not determine whether they were peccary hunts or killing raids.

10 For Yost and Kelley (1983), Huaorani hunting technology is efficient in terms of adaptation to the environment, but inefficient in terms of energy capture, for it does not allow them to tap all existing protein sources.

REFERENCES

Bird-David, N. (1993) 'Tribal Metaphorization of Human–Nature Relatedness', in K. Milton (ed.) *Environmentalism: The View from Anthropology*, London: Routledge.

Blackmore, H. (1971) *Hunting Weapons*, London: Barrie & Jenkins.

Descola, P. (1986) *La Nature Domestique*, Paris: Ed. MSH

— (1992) 'Societies of Nature and the Nature of Society', in A. Kuper (ed.) *Conceptualizing Society*, London: Routledge.

Feenberg, A. (1991) *Critical Theory of Technology*, Oxford: Oxford University Press.

Grenand, P. (1995) 'De l'Arc au Fusil: Un Changement Technologique chez les Wayãmpi de Guyane', in F. Grenand and V. Randa (eds) *Transitions Plurielles: Exemples dans Quelques Sociétés des Amériques*, Paris: Peeters-SELAF (forthcoming).

Gross, D. (1975) 'Protein Capture and Cultural Development in the Amazon Basin', *American Anthropologist* 77: 526–49.

Hames, R. and Vickers, W. (eds) (1983) *Adaptive Responses of Native Amazonians*, New York: Academic Press.

Hawkes, K., Hill, K. and O'Connell, J. (1982) 'Why Hunters Gather: Optimal Foraging and the Ache of Eastern Paraguay', *American Ethnologist* 9: 379–98.

Ingold, T. (1988) 'Introduction', in T. Ingold (ed.) *What is an Animal?*, London: Unwin Hyman.

— (1993a) 'Epilogue: Technology, Language, Intelligence and the Reconsideration of Basic Concepts', in K. Gibson and T. Ingold (eds) *Tools, Language and Cognition in Human Evolution*, Cambridge: Cambridge University Press.

— (1993b) 'Building, Dwelling, Living: How Animals and People Make Themselves at Home in the World', Paper delivered at the ASA Decennial Conference.

Kennedy, J. S. (1992) *The New Anthropomorphism*, Cambridge: Cambridge University Press.

Latour, B. (1994) 'Ethnography of a "High-Tech" Case: About Aramis', in P. Lemonnier (ed.) *Technological Choices: Transformation in Material Cultures since the Neolithic*, London: Routledge.

Lemonnier, P. (1994) 'Introduction', in P. Lemonnier (ed.) *Technological Choices: Transformation in Material Cultures since the Neolithic*, London: Routledge.

Lescure, P., Baslsev, H. and Alarcón, R. (1987) *Plantas Utiles de la Amazonía Ecuatoriana*, Quito: ORSTOM.

Lévi-Strauss, C. (1964) *Totemism*, London: Merlin Press.

Linares, O. (1976) 'Garden-Hunting in the American Tropics', *Human Ecology* 4: 331–49.

Nelson, R. K. (1973) *Hunters of the Northern Forest*, Chicago: Chicago University Press.

Pfaffenberger, B. (1988) 'Fetishised Objects and Humanised Nature: Towards an Anthropology of Technology', *Man* (NS) 23, 2: 236–52.

Redford, K. and Robinson, J. (1987) 'The Game of Choice: Patterns of Indian and Colonist Hunting in the Neotropics', *American Anthropologist* 89: 650–67.

Reichel-Dolmatoff, G. (1976) 'Cosmology as Ecological Analysis: a View from the Rain forest', *Man* (NS) 11: 307–18.

— (1985) 'Tapir Avoidance in the Colombian Northwest Amazon', in G. Urton (ed.) *Animal Myths and Metaphors in South America*, Salt Lake City: University of Utah Press.

Ridington, R. (1982) 'Technology, World View and Adaptive Strategy in a Northern Hunting Society', *Canadian Review of Sociology and Anthropology* 19: 469–81.

Rival, L. (1992) *Social Transformations and the Impact of Schooling on the Huaorani of Amazonian Ecuador*, unpublished PhD thesis, University of London.

— (1993) 'The Growth of Family Trees: Understanding Huaorani Perceptions of the Forest', *Man* (NS) 28, 4: 635–52.

Ross, E. (1978) 'Food Taboos, Diet, and Hunting Strategy: the Adaptation to Animals in Amazon Cultural Ecology', *Current Anthropology* 19: 1–19.

Sellato, B. (1994) *Nomads of the Borneo Rainforest: The Economics, Politics and Ideology of Settling Down*, Honolulu: University of Hawaii Press.

Sowls, L. K. (1984) *The Peccaries*, Tucson: University of Arizona Press.

Urton, G. (ed.) (1985) *Animal Myths and Metaphors in South America*, Salt Lake City: Utah Press.

Willis, R. (1990) 'Introduction', in R. Willis (ed.) *Signifying Animals: Human Meaning in the Natural World*, London: Unwin Hyman.

Yost, J. and Kelley, P. (1983) 'Shotguns, Blowguns and Spears: the Analysis of Technological Efficiency', in R. Hames and W. Vickers (eds) *Adaptive Responses of Native Amazonians*, New York: Academic Press.

Chapter 9

Nature, culture, magic, science

On meta-languages for comparison in cultural ecology

Edvard Hviding

This chapter addresses certain problems in the foundations of anthropological inquiry, concerning the 'empiricist' appropriation of certain concepts prevalent in 'rationalist' discourse (cf. Leach 1976). Turning a critical eye on certain epistemological practices in anthropology, I focus on received wisdom concerning relationships between people and their environment, particularly the often-presumed universal conceptual dualism of 'nature' and 'culture' (cf. Lévi-Strauss 1966). I shall elaborate on the position that the nature–culture dualism forms part of western 'ethnoepistemology' and derives from a non-universal ontological basis. Further, some epistemological contexts of the concepts 'magic' and 'science' are investigated with particular reference to their dualist usage in anthropological discourse and to wider philosophical debates. Through a discussion of ethnographic material from Melanesia, some alternative, non-dualist ontological and epistemological contexts will then be exemplified, and some of their analytical implications explored.

ON EPISTEMOLOGICAL PRIVILEGES IN ANTHROPOLOGY

Much discussion has taken place within and beyond anthropology about whether or not western rationalist presuppositions can be taken as representative of human universals, and whether they can be accorded an epistemologically privileged position in cultural translation. It has become rather widely held that Cartesian dualism and other metaphysics characteristic of western ontological presuppositions have dominated anthropological analysis to a degree that may obscure multiple orderings of reality. As expressed in a critique from feminist anthropology, 'social scientists must guard against the tendency to use the dominant discourse of European culture to universalise our categories, thus rendering ourselves deaf to other ways of structuring the world' (MacCormack 1980: 21). Such universalisation has centred not least on the presumed dualism of 'nature' and 'culture', as discussed by a range of critics. Wagner argues that 'although we allow... that other cultures comprise sets of artefacts and images which differ in style from our own, we tend to superimpose them on the same reality – nature as we perceive it' (Wagner 1975: 142). Strathern (1980) draws on Wagner to state the seemingly simple point that 'there is no such thing as nature or culture. Each is a highly relativised concept whose ultimate signification must be derived from its place within a specific metaphysics' (M. Strathern 1980: 177).

Lévy-Bruhl (1985) explored the 'pre-logical mentality' of 'primitive peoples' which he saw as non-governed by logical relations. His work attacks notions about the psychic unity of humankind, advocating instead a cognitive relativity. However, among subsequent generations of anthropologists, the search for demonstrable human universals (whether as in the empiricist functionalism of Malinowski (1948), the rationalist structuralism of Lévi-Strauss (1963), or the interpretive project of Geertz (1973)) has relegated Lévy-Bruhl to the shelves of obscurity and disfavour. This is not due sheerly to academic disagreement, but also to the rather heavy ideological implications of Lévy-Bruhl's evolutionary scheme of pre-logical and logical levels of mentality as associated with 'undeveloped' and 'developed' peoples.

In a more recent encounter between philosophy and, in this case, first-rate ethnography, Winch (1977) discussed and criticised Evans-Pritchard's classic study of witchcraft and magic among the Azande (1976). As pointed out by Tambiah (1990: 117), Winch's critique deserves to be regarded as historic in that this 'was an occasion when modern philosophers dipped into exotic anthropological ethnography to argue their philosophical discussions'. One of Evans-Pritchard's well-known arguments relates to the notion that there is a context-independent 'reality' against which the rationality of Zande notions about witchcraft, magic and oracles could be judged. Further, he assumed that this context-independent reality can only be established by science: 'Our body of scientific knowledge and logic are the sole arbiters of what are mystical, common-sense, and scientific notions' (Evans-Pritchard 1976: 229).

Thus Evans-Pritchard may safely argue that judged by the criteria of western science, witchcraft does not really exist, despite the observed and recorded 'fact' that Zande notions about witches and their doings display a consistent logic all on their own. Winch (1977), however, building on his critique of logical positivism in social science (1957) and drawing on the late writings of Wittgenstein (1983) on 'language games', argues that Zande notions about witchcraft cannot be compared with western science. Each set of notions, Zande and 'western scientific', are based on the language games of a given community and cannot be judged according to an independent reality or a meta-language. Thus western scientific logic cannot constitute a context-independent truth or sole arbiter according to which Azande magical beliefs and practices can be judged.

A number of critiques of anthropological analysis from within the discipline have argued that the habit of privileging certain 'domains' as more or less given, as is the case notably for kinship, economy, politics, and religion (Schneider 1984) in innumerable ethnographies (and undergraduate university curricula), in fact does nothing but mirror major ontological presuppositions, and political mainstreams, in western (bourgeois) culture. Still another reaction, though of a rather different and less explicitly relativist nature, has been the proliferation of branches of 'ethnoscience'. Since the late 1950s there have been many sub-branches of anthropological investigation bearing the prefix 'ethno'. Most belong under a loosely defined umbrella concerning cognitive approaches to 'the native's point of view' with regard to specific sub-branches of western science. Thus there is, at the very minimum, 'ethnoscience', which in normal anthropological discourse refers not only generally to 'native' points of view, but also to the rigorous methodological approach taken in cognitive anthropological studies of systems of classification and taxonomic structures found in 'other cultures' (cf. e.g. Berlin *et al.* 1974, Ellen, Chapter 6, this volume). Thus we have not only ethnobiology, ethnobotany, ethnoecology, and ethnomedicine, but even, as listed alphabetically almost to the point of involuntary parody in a recent dictionary of anthropology (Seymour-Smith 1986), ethnomathematics, ethnomusicology, ethnopharmacology, ethnophilosophy, ethnopsychiatry and ethnopsychology.

ETHNOSCIENCE AND OTHER SCIENCES

The strong empiricism of diverse branches of ethnoscience is tied to the emic side of the emic–etic distinction originally coined by Pike

(1954) and elaborated upon by scores of cognitive anthropologists. It is notable that 'ethno' is in most cases used to prefix names of disciplines that western epistemology considers to be 'objective science' based on the rigors of hypothetical-deductive method (cf. Popper 1980). On the other hand, little attention has been shown to 'ethnophilosophy', and 'ethnohistory' was chiefly in vogue during times when history was typically considered an objective domain of knowledge; later the past was seen to be 'invented' (e.g. Hobsbawm and Ranger 1983). Moreover, with changing political climates, tribal peoples' histories were treated as history proper (cf. Wolf 1982, Stannard 1990). Thus the prefix 'ethno' is indeed likely to indicate a field of 'native' knowledge whose status is relative to a canonical counterpart within non-'ethno', western science. Along with this goes reification of domains of indigenous knowledge so as to make them compatible with western science, as seen in some of the recent attention given to 'traditional ecological knowledge' (cf. Berkes 1989, Hornborg, Chapter 3, this volume).

Ethnoecology has to do with the study of indigenous knowledge of natural resources and their exploitation (cf. Ellen 1982), and the prefix 'ethno' thus indicates that the specific field of knowledge is that of the observed rather than of the observer (Conklin 1954), following the widely-accepted notion that 'we see [objective] nature in terms of [subjective] cultural images' (Ellen 1982: 206). Drawing upon the western discipline of 'ecology', recently defined by one of its pioneers as 'the study of the earth's life-support systems' (Odum 1989: 24), ethnoecology remains tied to notions about a 'natural environment'. Emphasis is given to studying people's cultural maps of a natural environment whose given attributes are defined by western science. Cultural meaning is seen as interacting with the 'laws' that regulate nature.[1] Echoing Evans-Pritchard's views on Azande witchcraft, ethnoecology is likely to presuppose the existence of a context-independent reality against which the rationality of indigenous 'ecological' knowledge may be evaluated. Notions held and 'truths' established by western biological and ecological science retain epistemological privilege.

Proceeding from ontological constructs in which the dualism of nature and culture dominates, the conventional study of ethnoecology tends to imply that a subjective grid of 'culture' is imposed upon the objective reality of 'nature'. Methodologically, this approach generates much information on taxonomic representations but less on environmental processes and relations as perceived by the people in question, since those processes may well be viewed *a priori* by the anthropologist through western scientific knowledge about the reality of 'nature'. Further, analytical endeavours tend to emphasise the levels of convergence between ethnoecology and ecology, and ethnobiological classification and biological (Linnaean) classification. The evaluation of indigenous knowledge in terms of its compatibility with western science easily becomes a major further task. Studies of indigenous ecological knowledge often emphasise that taxonomic categories and criteria for classification do not correspond to those of western science and that indigenous perceptions of ecological linkages are not consistent with western postulates on causality (cf. Johannes 1981, Berlin 1992).[2]

Berlin, a founder of ethnobiology, has recently argued that widespread regularities in the classification and naming of animals and plants among non-literate, traditional peoples reflect similarities in people's largely unconscious appreciation of 'nature's basic plan' (Berlin 1992: 8). He advocates the universalist claim that

> while human beings are capable of recognizing many distinct patterns in nature's structure in general, in any local flora or fauna a single pattern stands out from all the rest. This overall pattern has been referred to by systematic biologists as the *natural system* ... [people's] pattern-recognizing ability is probably innate.
>
> (Berlin 1992: 9, original emphasis)

However, by thus privileging 'natural laws' and insisting on an innate relationship between natural patterns and people's recognition of them, phenomena and domains that are not in 'nature' according to science (or to western ontology) may well be precluded from having 'real' explanatory value in the analysis of cultural–ecological relations. Thus taxonomic categories, chains of implications and causal linkages as perceived locally may be severely misrepresented by the anthropological observer, leading to inadequate levels of contextualisation. This is not, of course, to postulate that there are no patterns or regularities at all in the environments of, for example, rainforest, savannah, coral reef, desert, or tundra, but rather that the emphases given to patterns within any one type of environment show considerable cultural variation which has to be recognised. A single-minded search for patterned order and universals in classification tends to obscure this. Closer attention to the practice in which humans engage with the environment, rather than positivist pursuit of cognitive models, mainly of taxonomic representations, may lead the way into expanded approaches to cultural ecology and a reversal of the long-running neglect of ethnobiology by mainstream anthropology (cf. Ellen 1993).

ALTERNATIVE EPISTEMOLOGIES: SOLOMON ISLANDS EXAMPLES

I shall turn now to how people living around a coral lagoon in the Melanesian western Pacific relate to the environments of sea, coral reef, and rainforest on which they depend for their material and spiritual sustenance. The Marovo Lagoon, located in the New Georgia area of Western Province, Solomon Islands (see Figure 9.1) is an ecologically diverse environment dominated by 700 square kilometres of coral reef, delimited by a long chain of raised barrier reef and backed by high volcanic islands with rainforest. Around 10,000 people live in villages mainly on the lagoon coasts of the high islands. Household-based production is centred on shifting cultivation of root crops (mainly sweet potatoes), reef and lagoon fishing, and a small but diverse cash sector. Adherence to Christian churches, mainly Methodist and Seventh-day Adventist and with often conspicuous syncretism, is universal in Marovo (Hviding 1996). By early 1995 the Marovo Lagoon with its 'natural and cultural wonders' was proposed for enlisting as a UNESCO World Heritage Site.

Ontological premises prevailing in Marovo hold that the organisms and non-living components of the environment, subsumed in the concept of *puava* (land-and-sea territory and 'all things therein'), do not constitute a distinct realm of 'nature' or 'natural environment' separate from 'culture' or 'human society'. Reefs, sea and forest and the living things therein are not viewed by Marovo people as 'an environment of neutral objects' (Ingold 1992: 53). In Marovo, as among the Baktaman of inner New Guinea, 'one is prepared to be one with an environment in which all places, species and processes are understood as being basically of one unitary kind, agreeable to man' (Barth 1975: 195). To be sure, there are basic concepts in Marovo that do conform to a 'wild–tame' dimension. But these concepts are a matter of degree and function as analogic codes rather than binary oppositions; they are related rather than contrasted and do not constitute an equivalent to a nature–culture dichotomy (see M. Strathern 1980 for a somewhat similar case from the New Guinea Highlands). The transformational relations between the concepts point directly to processual, non-dichotomising ontological premises.

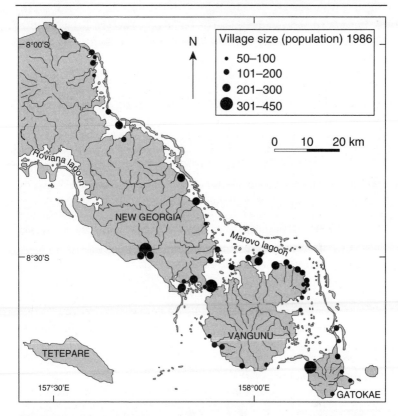

Figure 9.1 The Marovo area, showing settlement pattern according to 1986 census
Source: University of Bergen, 1991

A closer examination of Marovo epistemology illuminates some fundamentally processual and hypothesising attributes of Marovo people's beliefs and knowledge with regard to the environment. Such indigenous notions of the construction, validation, transmission, and practical utility of knowledge about the environment pose a number of challenges to anthropological analysis. Referring to the ontological precepts whereby Marovo people do *not* act in the environment from a dichotomy between 'their' 'culture' and a 'nature' exploited by them through means afforded by that culture, a primary question is how to analyse people's relations to the environment from a basis of information that is not, and cannot be, ordered according to a 'nature–culture' dualism. 'Nature' may be an analytical category to us, but not to Marovo people. The latter do, however, behave rather analytically in their encounters with the environment, but from a position of practical engagement.

In the processual, hypothesising epistemology that prevails in Marovo, several successive states apply to the acquisition and validation of 'knowledge' (*inatei*): from 'hearing about' something (*avosoa*), a state of 'knowing' (*atei*) is obtained. Previous and subsequent knowledge as well as the social context of knowledge transmission determines whether or not this 'knowing' entails 'believing' (*va tutuana*, literally, 'imbuing with truth'), a state that through repeated verifying instances of 'seeing for oneself' (*omia*) is transformed into 'trusting' (*norua*, literally, 'to be convinced of efficacy') and the state of 'being wise' (*tetei*). An example from a very immediate realm of human presence in a potentially dangerous environment may serve to illustrate these relational epistemological processes and mutualist ontological premises.

Six days every week, an average of 200–300 men of Marovo spend most or part of the day diving on the deep outer reefs facing the ocean, for spearfishing and collecting shells for commercial purposes. This presence of people in seas populated by fairly large numbers of potentially dangerous sharks very rarely leads to any form of attack by sharks on swimming humans. It is frequently pointed out that the only divers who have ever been killed by sharks in Marovo came from descent groups (*butubutu*, cf. Hviding 1993) that do not stand in a totemic relationship to these sole man-eaters in the Marovo environment (with the exception of the dreaded saltwater crocodile, to which certain *butubutu* have a similar totemic relationship). For a number of historical reasons, shark totemism (entailing a prohibition against harming, provoking, killing and, most of all, eating sharks) is only associated with and practised by a limited number of the localised *butubutu* of Marovo, especially those with a maritime-oriented history and ancestral territorial holdings (*puava*) of mainly reefs and sea. The observation that sharks tend mainly to attack people from non-totemist, land-oriented groups – a common postulate in coastal areas of the Solomon Islands – is regarded by Marovo's fishermen as a validation of the belief that ancestrally-imposed respect shown to the shark will in return give protection from attacks in the present. Remembered instances of fatal attacks are considered to be the 'test' or 'trial' (*chinangava*) of the ancestrally-derived belief in the efficacy of shark totemism, and 'believing' (*va tutuana*) in the idea one becomes convinced and elevates it to the level of 'trusting' (*norua*).[3]

Such mutualist ideas about the relationship between people and the surrounding environments of sea, land and beyond permeate a great many fields of activity and concern in Marovo. For example, today's disordered state of formerly synchronised menstrual cycles among the women of any particular village is reckoned by many old women to be an outcome of younger women's increased travel to the capital Honiara, where they lose contact with the cyclical rhythms of village life, centred on the lunar periodicity of fishing and agriculture, and on the fact that all women 'traditionally' started menstruating around the night of the new moon (*taomi paleke*, literally, 'to behold the moon', a common term for menstruation). Older women lament that young women's increasing lack of attention to the moon and diminished participation in village activities have eroded female commensality and sociability. This argument also follows a widely-documented Melanesian pattern of emphasising collectivity and shared substance through shared work, residence and, particularly, the consumption of food obtained and cultivated in a common territory (cf. A. Strathern 1973).[4] Thus the argument of the old women of Marovo is not one of a one-sided causal effect of the moon on human lives, but a much more complex one incorporating several levels of causality in people–environment and people–people relationships, with no boundaries along a 'culture–nature' dualism.

Marovo people's relationships with the environment also involve manipulation of the latter through often standardised and widely-known acts of intervention that should – by Evans-Pritchard's (1976) views on the epistemological privilege of science – be seen as belonging to the category of 'magic'. Nevertheless, these acts appear in daily life as highly pragmatic, observable 'tools' in handling problems posed by the environment – in a Pacific Islands context applied not least to the role of weather for maritime travel. If heavy breakers make it impossible to launch a canoe from village beaches on the open sea 'weather' coasts, certain elders may be summoned to carry out the act of *va bule* ('to calm'). This act involves calming the sea for a brief moment (enough to launch the canoe) by chanting a spell and throwing a knotted length of a creeping beach plant into the waves. Practical magic is also used during sea voyages. If a feared *ivori* wind (a form of small tornado) is seen approaching during canoe travel in stormy weather, most adult men or women know how to perform an act that will sever the black column of spinning clouds and send the two parts disappearing down into the sea and back up into the clouds, respectively. This act, *seke ivori* (literally, 'give the death blow to the *ivori* wind') involves reciting a brief spell while making circular motions with a bushknife (invariably carried in canoes) or alternatively hammering together two stones (less often carried at sea).

These acts are integral to Marovo people's practical engagement with the environment, and of their own perception of constraints posed by the environment on human activity. Thus Marovo people's relationships with the environment appear not necessarily constrained by the 'laws of nature'. The efficacy of practical magic to overcome what would in western scientific terms be considered 'natural constraints' is verified regularly by use.[5]   The puzzling dualities of magic as a false technical act but a true social act, as either 'bad science' (according to Tylor, Frazer, and Evans-Pritchard, among others) or 'rhetorical art' (according to Malinowski (1948) and others),

> will disappear only when we succeed in embedding magic in a more ample theory of human life in which the path of ritual action is seen as an indispensable mode for man anywhere and everywhere of relating to and participating in the life of the world.
>
> (Tambiah 1990: 83)

COMPARATIVE EPISTEMOLOGY: THE CASE OF MARINE TURTLES

To address questions of comparison more directly, we shall move to a field of Marovo knowledge which involves direct epistemological confrontation with western science. The seasonal capture of nesting turtles is based on a complex body of knowledge about life cycles, nesting habits and hatching periods of two species of marine turtles.[6] The current major guardian of this domain of maritime practice is David Livingstone Kavusu (b. 1926). During fieldwork in 1986 I had the privilege of being invited by Kavusu to join him on the annual pre-Christmas turtle-hunting expeditions, on the condition that I allowed him to 'make [me] knowledgeable' (*va atei*) before departing for the Hele Islands. Kavusu expressed some of his epistemological foundations as follows:

> All this about turtles came from Tetepare [a large uninhabited island southeast of Marovo], because those people there were

people of the ocean . . . . My father . . . wanted me to know [*atei*] all about turtles so that I would keep that knowledge. I did believe [*va tutuana*] what he told me. But I couldn't trust it [*norua*] until I had seen [*omia*] it all myself. So I went out there to the Hele islands, and I found some turtle nests, and I dug up the eggs and counted them, and I examined those eggs well to mark the time when those turtles would return.[7] Then I went back to the mainland, but when it was time for the first of the turtles to return I was back on that island at Hele. And, they came up, first one, and then the others that I had marked. Then I knew that it worked, what my father had told me. And I could trust it.

The details of examining nests and eggs and thereby accurately predicting the time and place of a turtle's return to the nest again are too complicated to be described here. However, it should be noted that the people of the four small villages of Vangunu's weather coast during each November–February season between them 'mark' and capture as many turtles as they require for the end-of-year cycle of Christmas, New Year and wedding celebrations. There appears to be a near total correlation between mark and capture.[8] People also point out that, since the Hele islands are a full day's paddling from the villages, it would not be worthwhile to go out there at all if they could not trust their own predictions. From a sceptical point of view one might argue that so many turtles come up to nest anyway, and that what is regarded as one 'marked' turtle could in fact be any one. But the Hele beaches are not of the type where thousands of turtles nest, and the overall numbers of turtles and human visitors during any season are much too small for chance encounters to be frequent.

The axiomatic point regarding turtle eggs is that according to received Marovo wisdom they take exactly twenty-one days to hatch. That is to say, since turtles always come ashore to lay their eggs at night, the eggs will hatch on the twenty-first subsequent night (any hatchlings emerging late, in daytime, would be devoured by seabirds and countless other predators). Having been educated by Kavusu to the level of knowing this, I was puzzled some months later to find that in a number of technical reports and authoritative reviews the hatching time of eggs from those same turtles was stated to range from fifty-five to seventy days (e.g. Vaughan 1981, Carr 1984). In mid-1987 I told Kavusu about these assessments based on research in a range of tropical locations (including parts of the Solomons), and asked him what his thoughts were about the grave discrepancy. His immediate reaction was, 'That is either a lie, or they are different turtles!' I assured him that the species were the same, by referring to identifications given in reports on marine turtles in the Solomon Islands (e.g. McElroy and Alexander 1979). This produced the following inspired response, in direct translation and only partly abridged so as to retain the full explanatory effect:

I do not know how those people have found this out ... But as I see it, it is a great lie! Me, I would probably be able to tell you a lie or two on things like fish or stories about *kastom* [tradition], because some of that I do not know very well. But turtles! – what I know about turtles is right there inside my heart, turtles are inside my life, and what I tell you about turtles is true – and I know it is true. ... The old men told me that juvenile turtles come out of the eggs after twenty-one days, and I did believe in what they said, but that was not enough for me. I had to go and see it with my eyes, for myself. So I went out to Hele, and I found a new nest, and I checked the eggs to find out when the turtle would come back, but I didn't dig them all up – I left them there. So I tied the knots [referring to tying a number of knots on a bark string corresponding to the number of nights left until the predicted return of the turtle; one knot is then removed after each night]. And I stayed there on that little island ... and one Sunday came, and two Sundays came, and that turtle came up again to lay new eggs after fourteen days, just how I had marked and tied the knots, following what my father had taught me. And I checked the eggs of the first nest of that turtle, and they hadn't hatched yet, but there were tiny turtles inside. So I waited, and on the seventh night after the return nesting, on the twenty-first night after that first nest was made, baby turtles came out. They made a hole in the sand and then they came out one by one, and a long line of them ran down across the sand into the sea. I have seen this, and I know that when I tell you twenty-one days, it is true. Not once, but twice have I stayed for days and days at Hele to watch this. So I tell you: after seven days, when the *suko* [a calcified spot spreading out over the shell of a new egg, see Note 7] covers the whole egg, that egg is all white. And from this day, blood is inside that egg. Seven days more and we come to fourteen days. The mother turtle will come up again, if she is a *vonu pede* [hawksbill turtle; green turtles are known to have slightly different cycles], and now you can see a small turtle inside the eggs of the first nest if you break one. It is a real turtle with head, eyes, legs. It is a turtle, but it is not ready to come out yet. Seven more days of your knots, and that night is the time for that small turtle to come out and run to the sea. One or two days before that, the shell of the egg has started to break. And on this twenty-first night, it has to be at night, the new turtles dig their way up and they run to the sea, everyone from one nest together. This is how I know it is...

I don't think those scientists have really gone to the islands and lived there for a long time to count all their fifty or sixty days. They have used their mind to find this out. They haven't seen it, I think. Maybe, one of them went to one island and found a nest and put a mark on that nest. But he didn't watch over that nest day and night all the time. No, he had to go back to his office, and then when he came back to check on the nest he had marked some other turtles had disturbed the mark. You know how big turtles make a mess out of the beach when they come up. So they made a mess out of his mark which became stuck in the sand by another nest. And then he didn't see those first eggs, that the baby turtles in them came out on the twenty-first night. Somehow, he thought that when he came out after fifty days... and the nest with the mark was empty, that the eggs took so many days to break open. But he got it all wrong. This is how I think it happened. But as for me, the Hele Islands and turtles belong to me, and I know what I say is true, because I have seen it myself! It is finished now.

The empiricist deductive approach taken by David Livingstone Kavusu in his explanation of the validity of his own knowledge is striking. I can only admit that I find Kavusu's case for a hatching period of twenty-one days at least as convincing as the presentation of the fifty-five to seventy days' hatching period documented in biological reports. The discrepancy is nevertheless so high as to create a major puzzle which cannot be solved here. However, what we may note is that Kavusu's reflections extend all the way into comparative epistemology. When his views are challenged by information from the field of western science, Kavusu ponders over what are the mental processes and methodological constraints that may have produced the, in his view, erroneous notion held by western turtle biologists, and suggests what may have led to misinterpretation.

COMPETING PARADIGMS

Identifying the epistemology of Marovo, as represented by a recognised expert thinker like Kavusu, as fundamentally of an 'empiricist' orientation does not imply any necessary correspondence with a canonical paradigm of western science. Indeed, Kavusu's exposition of this body of practical knowledge is a scientific paradigm on its own. Indigenous theory and anthropological theory, the latter in this case including 'natural laws' as identified by western biology, may be seen as alternative paradigms, possibly in competition. It is not my aim to argue for or against the privilege of any one paradigm in the understanding of what turtles do. My point is rather that an understanding of what people do (which is basically anthropology's project) in relation to turtles, and to other things of the environment, cannot be reached through sole reliance on a comparison of indigenous knowledge with western science, by giving epistemological privilege to the latter.

Another problematic of anthropological research is outlined by the empirical examples. Not only does Marovo epistemology operate from an absence of a nature–culture dichotomy – indeed, from an absence of concepts equivalent to these twin categories – but in processual chains of observations of causal linkages which tend to be deduced and postulated with little or no separation of the 'magic' from the 'real'. This could seem logical, since if there is nothing 'natural' in the western sense, then there can be no 'supernatural'. Furthermore, 'magic' and 'science' are not distinct theories of why and how things come to be (cf. Tambiah 1990). Thus, we have to take the challenge and analyse epistemological processes that include phenomena, even observed by ourselves as fieldworkers (such as interfering with the weather), that would normally be classified by western concepts as belonging to the diffuse, negational realm of the supernatural. On the level of social interaction, too, there are analytical problems in handling knowledge that cannot be incorporated into existing schemes about culture, nature, magic, or science. Compared to more relativist interpretive orientations in anthropology (in particular, feminist approaches to gender relations and to the metaphorical usages of nature–culture dualisms (cf. MacCormack and Strathern 1980, Moore 1988)), studies in 'cultural' or 'human' ecology seem to have been slow to grasp these issues, owing to the embeddedness of these approaches in axiomatic postulates about the cultural ordering and cognitive classification of nature's 'reality', about the universality of the culture–nature dichotomy, and about the need to proceed analytically from an objective baseline. Since the separation of society from nature is so much a part of our own ontological constructs as westerners and intellectuals, it may be difficult to grasp that the social and the subjective may need to be extended well into what might initially be seen as the natural and the objective.

META-LANGUAGES FOR COMPARISON

The above examples indicate that Marovo 'ethnoepistemology' regarding the environment shows striking parallels to a Kuhnian hypothetical-deductive method, while simultaneously dealing with subject matter way beyond the given facts of nature as defined by western science. It seems clear that anthropological studies of relationships between people and their environment must emphasise the comparative analysis of epistemologies proper. The people of Marovo, while having thirteen taxonomic terms for various size stages of the one Linnaean fish species called *Katsuwonus pelamis* (skipjack tuna), subsume more than a hundred Linnaean species of small, colourful fish living among coral in the single taxonomic category of *kepe*. This is because all those little fishes are of virtually no pragmatic or symbolic significance to Marovo people. On the other hand, the skipjack tuna is of immense value as ceremonial food, as the most sacred being of the sea, and as a focus of seasonal ritual activities.

In this sense Berlin's thesis (1992) that people recognise a class of organisms independently of its usefulness or symbolic significance does not seem to apply to Marovo. Taxonomic complexity appears to be strongly tied to the different ways in which people see themselves to be engaging in some form of interaction with different living and non-living components of the environment. Those forms of interaction do not necessarily correspond with western presuppositions about the ecological relationships between people and the environment. The study of 'ethnoecology' in such contexts encompasses far more than identifying 'cultural frames' imposed on the environment to classify it, and must include a more general investigation of ontological boundaries and epistemological criteria.

It may be argued that assumptions about a universal nature–culture dualism cannot constitute a meta-language for the comparative analysis of relations between people and the environment. Nor does the nature–culture dualism constitute a 'language of perspicuous contrast in which we can understand their practices in relation to ours' (Taylor 1981: 209). Rather, a language of comparison in this context has somehow to comprise both the disjuncture between nature and culture inherent in western ontology, and alternative ontologies representing more integrative, interactional approaches. In line with this, what I am advocating here is not an extreme relativism and incommensurability through 'radical alterity' (Keesing 1994), but rather the view that expanded analytical tools not so firmly grounded in western ontology and 'ethnoepistemology' are needed for a proper comparative grasp on relations between people and the environment.

Interactional and relational views may be a foundation for such a meta-language. By focusing on people's interactions with the environment from which they derive multiple forms of sustenance, processual rather than classificatory perspectives gain prominence. The notion of a disjuncture between people's 'culture' and the 'objective reality' of 'nature' may thus yield to a mutualist perspective, along the lines proposed by Ingold (1992). The study of such interactions needs to go beyond the conceptual framework of 'ecological niche' such as pioneered in anthropological analysis by Barth (1956). Now, it should be clear from the preceding discussion that what constitutes 'the total environment' cannot be assumed *a priori* without regard to indigenous notions. Not only may different peoples classify similar environmental components differently; they may also maintain notions about linkages between people and the environment that range beyond 'natural laws'.

Thus the so-called 'ecological determinants' of the social process are not constituted solely by the objective opportunities and constraints posed by 'nature' and people's 'technical tools' for utilising opportunities and overcoming constraints. Rather than restricting itself to a few paragraphs on 'ecological conditions', or, at best, to a chapter on 'ecology' including elements of indigenous classification, the cultural–ecological perspective in anthropology needs to take into account the deeper ontological foundations of human practice in the world, and to follow the implications of these foundations wherever they go. When investigating the webs of environmental relations within which human beings are 'enmeshed' (Ingold 1992: 39), we should avoid reification (as a product of our own 'ethnoepistemology' and interpretive stance) not just of 'ecological systems', but also of 'nature'.

Finally, a meta-language for comparison and analysis in cultural ecology that emphasises engagement rather than disengagement

(Ingold 1992) and builds on interactional views, may encourage a non-essentialist search for prototype-structured categories and scenarios of people–environment relationships. By 'conceiving of each category in terms of its clear cases rather than its boundaries' (Rosch 1978, in D'Andrade 1995: 118), our analysis of people's environmental engagements may thus highlight relationality rather than *a priori*-defined disjunctures, and indeed expand the focus towards the social contexts of environmental knowledge and practice. On a general level, an emphasis on environmental categorisation through prototypes rather than through the properties possessed by 'objects that exist objectively in the world' (Johnson 1993: 8, cf. Lakoff 1987) may move cultural–ecological analysis more strongly towards analytical headings like process, 'fuzziness', flexibility and open-ended interaction. This would in turn highlight oscillations and relations among domains often seen as analytically in disjuncture – such as nature, culture, magic and science.

ACKNOWLEDGEMENTS

For discussion and critiques of drafts of this chapter I thank Harald Grimen and Reidar Grønhaug (at an initial stage) and Gísli Pálsson and Philippe Descola (at the Third EASA Conference, Oslo, 1994). For teachings and discussions about the epistemological complexities of marine turtle capture and weather magic, I am most grateful to David Livingstone Kavusu, Chief of Ninive village in Marovo Lagoon, Solomon Islands. Bob Johannes supplied me with published and unpublished reports by various authors concerning marine turtles in the South Pacific. The empirical material on which this essay is based derives from twenty-eight months of fieldwork in the Solomon Islands (1986–87, 1989–90, 1991–92, 1994), funded by the Research Council of Norway, the Institute for Comparative Cultural Research (Oslo), and the University of Bergen. For permission to carry out this work I thank the Solomon Islands Government and the Marovo Area Council.

NOTES

1 Compare the distinction made by Rappaport (1979) between 'operational' (as defined by the laws of nature) and 'cognized' (as defined by culture) models of the environments of any human population.

2 Present debates about 'indigenous knowledge' and 'community-based management' of environment and resources seem caught in long-running debates between overly-romantic and overly-cynical interpretations (see the contributions in McCay and Acheson 1987 and Berkes 1989).
3 The anthropologist could, of course, point out that evidence on fatal shark attacks in Marovo since around 1950 indicates direct correlation along these lines.
4 In addition, western science appears to support an argument about a synchronisation of menstrual cycles among women who live or work closely together (see McClintock 1971).
5 It is worth pointing out that there are degrees of recognised magical efficacy in this regard. In characteristic fashion, following the egalitarian distribution of knowledge of all kinds in Marovo, those who practise magic on a given occasion may be challenged by observers.
6 Green (*Chelonia mydas*) and hawksbill (*Eretmochelys imbricata*) turtles nest throughout the year in the Hele Islands, but with a marked peak in the November–January period. The leatherback turtle (*Dermochelys coriacea*) nests only on beaches of black volcanic sand, in Marovo found only on the southwest weather coast of Vangunu Island.
7 The age of any given turtle nest is established by picking up a few eggs and examining the state of a white, calcified spot that spreads across the shell during the first seven days after the egg has been laid. After seven days, when the entire shell has been calcified and the egg is all-white, the age of the nest is determined by breaking an egg open and examining the embryo.
8 That virtually all turtles whose return has been 'marked' are actually captured is emphatically stated by the people involved. Moreover, my own quantitative data from the turtle seasons of 1986–87 and 1989–90 strongly substantiate this argument.

REFERENCES

Barth, F. (1956) 'Ecological Relationships of Ethnic Groups in Swat, North Pakistan', *American Anthropologist*, 58, 6: 1079–89.
— (1975) *Ritual and Knowledge Among the Baktaman of New Guinea*, Oslo: Norwegian University Press/New Haven: Yale University Press.
Berkes, F. (ed.) (1989) *Common Property Resources: Ecology and Community-based Sustainable Development*, London: Belhaven Press.
Berlin, B. (1992) *Ethnobiological Classification*, Princeton, NJ: Princeton University Press.
— ,Breedlove, D. E., and Raven, P. H. (1974) *Principles of Tzeltal Plant Classification*, New York and London: Academic Press.
Carr, A. (1984 [1967]) *The Sea Turtle: So Excellent a Fishe*, Austin: University of Texas Press.
Conklin, H. C. (1954) 'An Ethnoecological Approach to Shifting Agriculture', *Transactions of the New York Academy of Sciences*, 17: 133–42.

D'Andrade, R. (1995) *The Development of Cognitive Anthropology*, Cambridge: Cambridge University Press.
Ellen, R. F. (1982) *Environment, Subsistence and System*, Cambridge: Cambridge University Press.
— (1993) *The Cultural Relations of Classification*, Cambridge: Cambridge University Press.
Evans-Pritchard, E. E. (1976 [1937]) *Witchcraft, Oracles, and Magic among the Azande*, abridged from 1937 edition, with an introduction by Eva Gillies, Oxford: Oxford University Press.
Geertz, C. (1973) *The Interpretation of Cultures*, New York: Basic Books.
Hobsbawm, E. and Ranger, T. (eds) (1983) *The Invention of Tradition*, Cambridge: Cambridge University Press.
Hviding, E. (1993) 'Indigenous Essentialism? "Simplifying" Customary Land Ownership in New Georgia, Solomon Islands', *Bijdragen tot de Taal-, Land- en Volkenkunde* 149: 802–24.
— (1996) *Guardians of Marovo Lagoon: Practice, Place, and Politics in Maritime Melanesia*, Pacific Islands Monograph Series, 14, Honolulu: University of Hawaii Press.
Ingold, T. (1992) 'Culture and the Perception of the Environment', in E. Croll and D. Parkin (eds) *Bush Base–Forest Farm: Culture, Environment and Development*, London: Routledge.
Johannes, R. E. (1981) *Words of the Lagoon: Fishing and Marine Lore in the Palau District of Micronesia*, Berkeley: University of California Press.
Johnson, M. (1993) *Moral Imagination: Implications of Cognitive Science for Ethics*, Chicago: University of Chicago Press.
Keesing, R. M. (1994) 'Theories of Culture Revisited', in R. Borofsky (ed.) *Assessing Cultural Anthropology*, New York: McGraw-Hill.
Lakoff, G. (1987) *Women, Fire, and Dangerous Things*, Chicago: University of Chicago Press.
Leach, E. R. (1976) *Culture and Communication*, Cambridge: Cambridge University Press.
Lévy-Bruhl, L. (1985 [1926]) *How Natives Think*, with a new introduction by C. S. Littleton, Princeton, NJ: Princeton University Press.
Lévi-Strauss, C. (1963) *Structural Anthropology. Vol. 1*, New York: Basic Books.
— (1966) *The Savage Mind*, Chicago: University of Chicago Press.
McCay, B. J. and Acheson, J. M. (eds) (1987) *The Question of the Commons: The Culture and Ecology of Communal Resources*, Tucson: University of Arizona Press.
McClintock, M. K. (1971) 'Menstrual Synchrony and Suppression', *Nature* 229: 244–45.
MacCormack, C. P. (1980) 'Nature, Culture and Gender: a Critique', in C. P. MacCormack and M. Strathern (eds) *Nature, Culture and Gender*, Cambridge: Cambridge University Press.
MacCormack, C. P. and Strathern, M. (eds) (1980) *Nature, Culture and Gender*, Cambridge: Cambridge University Press.
McElroy, J. K. and Alexander, D. (1979) *Marine Turtles of the Solomon Islands Region*, SPC-MFMS/Turtles/WP 11, Noumea: South Pacific Commission.

Malinowski, B. (1948) *Magic, Science and Religion and Other Essays*, Illinois: The Free Press.

Moore, H. L. (1988) *Feminism and Anthropology*, Cambridge: Polity Press.

Odum, E. P. (1989) *Ecology and our Endangered Life-Support Systems*, Sunderland, Mass.: Sinauer Associates.

Pike, K. (1954) *Language in Relation to a Unified Theory of the Structure of Human Nature*, Glendale: Summer Institute of Linguistics.

Popper, K. R. (1980 [1959]) *The Logic of Scientific Discovery*, tenth impression, revised, London: Unwin Hyman.

Rappaport, R. A. (1979) *Ecology, Meaning, and Religion*, Berkeley: North Atlantic Books.

Schneider, D. M. (1984) *A Critique of the Study of Kinship*, Ann Arbor: University of Michigan Press.

Seymour-Smith, C. (1986) *Macmillan Dictionary of Anthropology*, London: Macmillan Press.

Stannard, D. E. (1990) *Before the Horror: The Population of Hawai'i on the Eve of Western Contact*, Honolulu: University of Hawaii Press.

Strathern, A. (1973) 'Kinship, Descent and Locality: Some New Guinea Examples', in J. Goody (ed.) *The Character of Kinship*, Cambridge: Cambridge University Press.

Strathern, M. (1980) 'No Nature, No Culture: the Hagen Case', in C. P. MacCormack and M. Strathern (eds) *Nature, Culture and Gender*, Cambridge: Cambridge University Press.

Tambiah, S. J. (1990) *Magic, Science, Religion, and the Scope of Rationality*, Cambridge: Cambridge University Press.

Taylor, C. (1981) 'Understanding and Explanation in the *Geistenwissenschaften*', in S. H. Holtzmann and C. M. Leich (eds) *Wittgenstein: to Follow a Rule*, London: Routledge & Kegan Paul.

Vaughan, P. W. (1981) *Marine Turtles: A Review of Their Status and Management in the Solomon Islands*, Honiara: Ministry of Natural Resources.

Wagner, R. (1975) *The Invention of Culture*, New York: Prentice-Hall.

Wilson, B. R. (ed.) (1977) *Rationality*, Oxford: Basil Blackwell.

Winch, P. (1957) *The Idea of a Social Science and Its Relation to Philosophy*, London: Tavistock.

— (1977) 'Understanding a Primitive Society', in Bryan R. Wilson (ed.) *Rationality*, Oxford: Basil Blackwell.

Wittgenstein, L. (1983 [1953]) *Philosophical Investigations*, Oxford: Blackwell.

Wolf, E. R. (1982) *Europe and the Peoples Without History*, Berkeley: University of California Press.

Chapter 10

The cosmic food web

Human–nature relatedness in the Northwest Amazon

Kaj Århem

Among Amerindians of the Amazon the notion of 'nature' is contiguous with that of 'society'.[1] Together they constitute an integrated order, alternatively represented as a grand society or a cosmic nature. Humankind is thus seen as a particular form of life participating in a wider community of living beings regulated by a single and totalising set of rules of conduct. Following Croll and Parkin (1992) I adopt the concept of eco-cosmology to refer to such integral models of human–nature relatedness.[2] The concept is related to the classical anthropological notions of 'totemism' and 'animism'. Totemism, in Lévi-Strauss' formulation (1966), refers to an intellectual system of classifying social units on the basis of the classification of natural species. As such, totemism thus exploits observable discontinuities in nature to confer a conceptual order on society. Animism, as Descola (1992) has pointed out, may in significant respects be considered the symmetrical inverse of totemism: a mode of conceptually organising the relationship between human beings and natural species on the basis of the system of social classification. Animic systems endow natural beings with human dispositions and social attributes; sometimes, as in the case examined below, animals are attributed with 'culture' – habits, rituals, songs, and dances of their own. If totemic systems model society after nature, then animic systems model nature after society.

   The analytical separation of totemic and animic systems tends, however, to conceal that the two schemes have fundamental properties in common: both imply a relationship of continuity between nature and society with compelling experiential and behavioural implications (cf. Willis 1990). Intellectually, totemism and animism are complementary and commensurate strategies for comprehending reality and relating humans to their environment; the one making use of natural images to make sense of human society and the other using sociological representations to construct order in nature. Experientially they form part of totalising eco-cosmologies, integrating practical knowledge and moral values. As holistic cultural constructs, eco-cosmologies engage and motivate; they mould perception, inform practice, and supply meaningful guidelines for living.

This chapter explores a particular Amazonian eco-cosmology, displaying features of both totemic and animic systems. To the Makuna of the Colombian Amazon, all beings – spirits, humans, animals, and plants – participate in a field of social interaction defined in terms of predation and exchange. The central feature of their eco-cosmology is that they construe human predation as a revitalising exchange with nature, modelled on the rule of reciprocity between affines and the shamanically mediated exchanges between men and gods. This chapter focuses on Makuna ideas about hunting, fishing and animal food consumption, and how these ideas are integrated into a wider cosmological framework, supplying individuals with a moral and existential basis for interaction with the environment. The case exemplifies general and persistent features of indigenous eco-cosmologies, thus adding to the comparative, anthropological understanding of the society–nature interface.

THE MAKUNA

The Makuna, a small Eastern Tukanoan-speaking group in Northwest Amazonia, are contemporary inheritors of an ancient tropical forest culture previously spread over large parts of the Amazon basin.[3] Living in widely scattered multi-family longhouses and small villages along rivers and streams, the Makuna subsist on shifting cultivation, fishing and hunting in the interfluvial forest.[4] Bitter manioc is the staple, and – in line with the general Amazonian pattern – women are gardeners and men hunters and fishermen. Traditional political life centred on the longhouse (*maloca*) and its 'owner', the headman of the group inhabiting it. Ritual specialists – notably two classes of shamans (*cumua, yaia*) but also chanters and dancers – were socially and politically influential owing to their religious knowledge and ritual skills. Clusters of interspersed longhouses, related by agnatic kinship and marriage alliances, formed loosely bounded local and territorial groups under the frail and episodic authority of particularly prominent headmen.

The wider Tukanoan society, of which the Makuna form a part, is organised into named, patrilineal clans (or 'sibs') associated with ritual property, a distinct language, and geographically defined ancestral territories, centred on the mythical birth places of the various clan ancestors. The ritual property includes ceremonial instruments and ornaments, ritual substances (coca, tobacco, red paint, and bees wax), chants, songs, and a set of personal names. In its 'essential', spirit-form, this ritual property is associated with the birth place of the clan ancestor which is also the 'home' and ultimate destination of the 'souls' of all clan members. The ancestral home of the clan is called the 'waking-up-house' of the ancestors; upon death, the souls of deceased clan members travel to this invisible house, where they are said to 're-awaken' as spirit people.

The clans are organised, in order of seniority, into wider exogamous units modelled on a group of agnatic brothers. The exogamous units, in turn, are interrelated by marriage and affinity according to the principle of direct exchange. The ideal form of marriage, as expressed in the idiom of the agnatic ideology, is the balanced exchange of women between two sets of affinally related men. The system is grounded in a 'two-line' (Dravidian) relationship terminology which also provides the basic exchange-model for interaction with 'nature': an alliance between two socially defined categories – 'self' and 'other' – perpetuated by a continuous series of reciprocal exchanges. The Makuna identify themselves as Water People (*Idemasa*), descending from the eponymical clan ancestor Water Anaconda (*Ide hino*). The Water People intermarry closely with another exogamous group, consisting of various clans which identify themselves as Yibamasa or Children of Yiba, alluding to their stipulated descent from an ancestral being associated with the forest. Together Water People and Yiba People form a single linguistic community, speaking the original language of the Water People and inhabiting a continuous territory. This wider spatial and language-bearing social unit may also be referred to – in a broader sense – as Makuna. It is in this latter sense that the term is used in this article. When speaking exclusively of the Idemasa clan I use the native term or its literal translation, Water People.

OUTLINE OF MAKUNA ECO-COSMOLOGY

Among the Makuna, hunting, fishing and gardening – just as almost every other routine work or practical operation, including the everyday consumption of food – are accompanied by ritual or shamanic acts, grounded in Makuna cosmology and constitutive of their particular way of life. Fundamental to this cosmology is the distinction between the visible, physical and changing reality of everyday experience and the invisible, unchanging and transcendental realm of gods and ancestral spirits which the Makuna gloss as the *he*-world – the world of the life-giving and predatory *he*-spirits. Every material form and practical activity has its counterpart in the *he*-world. Indeed, material forms and physical operations in the visible world instruct human beings about the hidden reality of the spirit-world, and thus of the deeper significance of existence.

In this dual reality, all beings and things have a 'phenomenological form' and 'spiritual essence'. In their essential aspect, human beings, (non-human) animals and plants are undifferentiated; they belong to the same ontological category of mortal beings. In shamanic discourse they are contextually classified as *masa* (people).[5] Within the inclusive category of *masa* different classes of beings are distinguished by specific traits (referred to as 'weapons') which are associated with the mythic origin of the class and its specific reproductive and food habits. In this inclusive society of mortal beings, one class of beings readily transforms into another: humans become animals, animals convert into humans, and one class of animals turns into another. The underlying idea is that the spirits of plants, animals and humans can take a variety of material shapes and thus penetrate various life worlds and manifest themselves as different classes of beings. Essence, then, reveals itself in different forms of vitality. All living beings partake of a generic vitality which has the capacity to 'flow' or circulate among different life worlds. The shaman's task is to regulate this vital flow, and to ensure the ordered reproduction of the distinct classes of beings populating the Makuna cosmos.

In shamanic discourse the universe of living beings is construed as a cosmic food web of 'eaters' and 'food'. From the point of view of any class of beings all others are either 'predators' or 'prey'. Thus, from the point of view of human beings (*masa*), this trophic universe is divided into human food (*masa bare*), including all plants and animals which are food for men, and 'man-eaters' (*masa bari masa*), including those predators which, according to Makuna, feed on men. In shamanic language the 'predator' category is labelled after the supreme predator, the jaguar (*yai*), and the 'food' category after the prototypical animal–food, fish (*wai*), thus forming a tripartite system of cosmic classification, based on the food chain:

eater   — food/eater — food
YAI   → *MASA*   → *WAI*
'jaguar' — 'people'   — 'fish'

This is a hunter's universe; the world seen from a male, 'predatory' point of view. The limits of the system are defined, at one extreme, by the supreme predators, who prey on all living beings but are prey to none; and, at the other extreme, edible plants which, in relation to the other life forms in the system, are only food. The intermediate trophic level comprises most life forms, including human beings, who are at the same time both eaters and food. And since all animals – in their essential aspect – are 'people', the scheme applies to any animal: from the point of view of game and fish, men are included in the category of 'predators', while fruits, seeds, insects, and plant detritus are included in their 'food' category. The supreme predator category, comprising jaguars, anacondas, and the major raptors, also includes the gods and predatory *he*-spirits, thus turning the system into a truly cosmic ecology. Just as the human hunter slays and consumes his prey, the gods kill and consume humans. But – and this is the key to the whole system – through killing and consuming human beings, the gods also allow men to reproduce. Analogously, by preying on game and fish, the human hunter enables the animals to breed and multiply. Predation, then, is a 'male' mode of procreation.

When a human being dies, the soul is captured ('consumed') by the gods and returned to the birth house of the clan to be reborn as a complete spirit person. Similarly, when a human hunter kills and consumes his prey, he returns the spirit of the slain animal to its place of origin – the 'birth house' of the animals. By shamanic means he empowers the species to reproduce and multiply. Killing for food, in the Makuna view, involves an act of reciprocity: life and vitality on the level of the individual are exchanged for renewal and essential continuity on the level of the category (clan, species). This, in a nutshell, is the Makuna philosophy of life: predation, reconstrued as exchange, explains death and accounts for the regeneration of life:

YAI		*MASA*		*WAI*
	$\rightarrow$		$\rightarrow$	
	$\leftarrow$		$\leftarrow$	
Predatory spirits		Human beings		Edible animals/plants

In their creative (and destructive) capacities, shamans are identified with predatory spirits, and are called *yaia*. Jaguars, anacondas and raptors are natural manifestations of the predatory spirits, and shamans are their human counterparts. They are all 'cosmic hunters' in different guises, readily changing shape and moving freely between the various layers and domains of cosmos. Through their predatory activities, the cosmic hunters mediate between different life worlds and ensure the continuity and ordered reproduction of all classes of beings in the world.

The Makuna describe animals as 'persons'. Game animals and fish are endowed with knowledge, agency and other human attributes. They are said to live in malocas in the forest and the rivers, in salt-licks, hills and rapids. When animals roam in the forest or swim in the rivers they appear as fish and game, but as they enter their houses they discard their animal guises, don their feather crowns and ritual ornaments, and turn into 'people'. They have gardens where they gather their food, and ports by the river where they collect water and bathe. Every house and community has its owner and headman, who guards and protects its inhabitants. The Fathers of the Fish are the anacondas and sting rays dwelling in the depths of rivers and lagoons. Similarly, every species of game animal has its own particular spirit guardian, and foremost among them are the Spirit Tapirs, the owners of the tapir houses. Animal communities are organised along the same lines as human societies, and human interaction with animals is modelled on the interaction among different groups of people in the human life world. Indeed, each species or community of animals is said to have its own 'culture', its knowledge, customs and goods by means of which it sustains itself as a distinct class of beings. In the sense, then, that the living world is construed as a cosmic society of interacting 'peoples' and 'communities' with their own distinct 'cultures', Makuna eco-cosmology forms a totalising, animic system as defined by Descola (1992).

However, there is also an evident totemic aspect to Makuna eco-cosmology. As noted, the Makuna-speaking clans are divided into Water People and Yiba People, the descendants of Water Anaconda and the mythical forest being, called Yiba. The social division between Water People and Yiba People thus corresponds to a distinction between natural and cosmic domains: river and forest, water and land, edible fish (*wai*) and game (*wai bttctt*, literally 'old fish'). The Water Anaconda is the Spirit Owner of the underwater maloca at Maneitara, the mythical birth place and waking-up-house of the Water People. He is also the Father of the Fish that spawn at

Maneitara. The waking-up-house of the Water People is thus at the same time the birth-and-dance house of the fish population inhabiting the river system which defines the territory of the Water People. Similarly, Yiba is associated with the fruit-eating animals of the forest. They are described as his 'workers' and children. There is a particularly close connection between Yiba and tapirs. Yiba created the salt-licks where tapirs drink and browse, and salt-licks are described as the birth-and-dance houses of the tapirs. But the salt-licks are also the waking-up-houses of the Yiba People; each named salt-lick in the forest is associated with the origin of a particular clan of the Yiba People. The named and personified ancestors of the different Yiba clans are represented as anacondas-turned-tapirs – Spirit Tapirs – guarding and protecting their human and animal descendants.

Here, then, are the minimal elements of a full-fledged totemic system: an analogy between two classificatory orders, and a notion of 'essential relatedness' between units of the two orders. The social division between Water People and Yiba People thus corresponds to a distinction between cosmic domains and two prototypical classes of animals (fish, on the one hand, and fruit-eating game animals, epitomised by tapirs, on the other), each associated with a specific natural domain. The notion of essential relatedness is formulated in terms of shared ancestry and a common origin (see Figure 10.1).

In this cosmic society, where all mortal beings are ontological 'equals', humans and animals are bound by a pact of reciprocity. The categorical distinction between 'eater' and 'food' – or hunter and prey – seems to override the bond of totemic 'kinship' between humans and animals; all animal 'others' are treated as 'essential affines'. The relationship between the human hunter and his prey is thus construed as an exchange, modelled on the relationship among

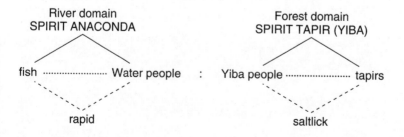

Figure 10.1 The totemic scheme

affines. Men supply the Spirit Owners of the animals with 'spirit foods' (coca, snuff, and burning bees wax). In return, the spirits allocate game animals and fish to human beings. This exchange, mediated by shamans, involves three different sets of relationships: between men and spirits (shamans and Spirit Owners); between spirits and animals (Spirit Owner and his protégé animals); and between men and animals (the human hunter and his prey).

Each of these dyads has a distinct sociological content. The shaman relates to the Spirit Owners of the animals as to a male affine; it is a relationship of equality and reciprocity but also one of potential danger and violence. If the arrangement negotiated by the shaman is violated by the hunter, the Spirit Owner takes revenge by sending death and disease upon the offender and his community. The hunter, on the other hand, relates to his prey as a man to his female affine (i.e. a woman of the prescribed marriage category). The hunter is thus explicitly said to attract and seduce his prey. The behavioural analogy in the social domain is apparent: men tend to behave assertively and are manifestly aggressive towards their potential spouses, while women are expected to behave submissively and furtively towards their male affines. The Spirit Owners, finally, are depicted as Chiefs or Fathers of the animals. The paradigmatic case of this relationship is that between a father and his marriageable daughters, or between a (senior) brother and his (junior) sisters: i.e. one of authority, protection and allocation. Fathers/senior brothers allocate their daughters/ sisters to suitable husbands, just as the Spirit Owners of the animals allocate their 'animal children' to human beings.

In short, the Makuna explicitly exploit the sociological model of marriage exchange in conceptualising the interaction between men and animals. And, just as in the social domain, this 'affinal' relationship is gendered: in their spiritual aspect animal Others are 'male' (Spirit Owners); in their physical aspect they are 'female' (prey). Underlying this sociological exchange model is the cosmological notion linking predation to regeneration. Death is seen as instrumental for the reproduction of life. An animal must be killed for another to be born, just as a human being must die – i.e. be killed, processed and consumed by the gods – for another to be born. The perpetuation of cosmic order – encompassing all varieties of *masa* – requires 'male' predation as well as 'female' fertility, and social life is predicated on the continuous exchange of individual vitality for categorical essence.

The sociological model of exchange is most clearly expressed in hunting shamanism. Hunting, particularly in preparation for large-scale rituals, typically involves an element of active 'negotiation' between the shaman and the Spirit Owners of the game animals. For every category of game, the shaman asks the Spirit Owner for 'cultivated food', which in the veiled language of shamanic discourse is a metaphor for meat. The Spirit Owner, for his part, requests 'spirit foods' (coca and snuff) in return for the game he allots. If one replaces the word 'food' with 'women', the passage provides a perfectly accurate account of the actual negotiations taking place between affines in preparation for a marriage exchange.

The image of exchange between men and fish is different. Fish are the prototypical animal–food for human beings. The proper relationship to fish involves a generalised and continuous offering of spirit foods to the Fathers of the Fish. But there is no active element of negotiation, no asking for permission. The shamanic interaction with the Spirit Owners appears to be modelled on the principle of generalised rather than balanced reciprocity. Indeed, this may be indicative of the 'prescriptive' food-status of fish. In myths, fish are generally presented as a by-product of the gods' creative works, while game animals appear as avatars of the gods themselves, powerful co-actors in the drama of creation. Forest animals figure in myth and shamanic discourse as individuals or individualised species; rarely are they treated as a generic class or compounded into a shamanic food-category such as that of the fish. Game animals, in short, appear as active agents, the equals of gods and men; they are 'persons', and therefore dangerous to kill and consume. In order to become proper food for humans, slain animal-persons have to be deprived of their 'humanity' through food shamanism.

THE SHAMANIC SYSTEM

To the Makuna all food is radically ambivalent and powerful. Food contains the primordial substances from which the world was made and through which it is continuously recreated; it sustains life and gives strength but also kills and causes illness. By means of food shamanism, Makuna men – and men only – convert potentially harmful beings and substances of nature into life-sustaining food for humans. Food blessing is thus a prominent part of the process of food preparation, a male counterpart to women's cooking. At all times and in every place men silently chant and blow spells over a piece of food or a gourd of liquid. Virtually every edible plant or animal brought from the forest or the river is blessed before being eaten.

The conceptual framework and symbolic repertory of food blessing are founded in myth. The blesser must know and in his silent chanting recount the mythic origin of each class of food. In the process of creation each class of being received its particular powers (conceptualised as 'weapons') which allow it to sustain and defend itself in its appropriate habitat. Each distinctive set of 'weapons' (wooden splinters, feathers, poison, saliva, blood, semen) objectifies the creative powers that brought the species into being and define its generic identity. In the case of animals these substances and powers are continuously incorporated through the foods they eat, and thus successively re-incorporated at ascending levels in the food chain. To each form of life there is a prescribed category of proper food (*wai*), amounting to a kind of prescriptive food system. For the Makuna, eating thus becomes a metaphysical act of incorporating the creative powers of the gods, infused as it were into all creatures at the time of creation. Eating involves a process of partial consubstantiation and contextual identification between eater and food – and therefore also the potentiality of the eater being 'consumed' by the very food consumed. Eating is a battle in which the eater conquers and overcomes the defences of the food (or rather, its living source) but at the constant risk of being defeated himself by its lethal weapons.

In the cosmic food web human beings occupy a unique position. As distinct from other living beings, who consume their preordained food 'naturally' as it were, men eat by means of food shamanism. By blessing their food, human beings turn animal-persons into human food and thereby assert their humanity. This shamanic capacity allows humans to overcome the dangers inherent in 'nature' while at the same time incorporating the life force it contains.

Makuna food shamanism forms part of a wider set of ideas and practices constituting a 'shamanic system'. In simplest terms this system is made up of four semantic domains defined by two cross-cutting dimensions or axes. Along one axis the Makuna distinguish between preventive (*queare*) and curative (*quenore*) shamanism; along the other they differentiate between protective, regenerative shamanism (*wanore*) and destructive and potentially lethal sorcery (*rohare*) (see Figure 10.2).

Food blessing is carried out by most adult men. Only food shamanism in connection with exceptional ritual events (such as the

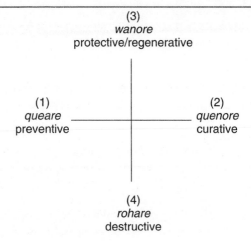

(3)
wanore
protective/regenerative

(1)
queare
preventive

(2)
quenore
curative

(4)
rohare
destructive

Figure 10.2 The shamanic system

male initiation ceremony) requires the services of protective shamans (*cumua*). The same holds for curing. In any community, there are men with partial curing abilities, some even specialising in the treatment of particular ailments and illnesses. More serious illness, however, is treated by recognised shamans, either *cumua* or *yaia*. The *yaia* are considered the most potent healers. Only they are credited with the ability to 'suck out' (*jutire*) diseases caused by predatory spirits and enemy shamans. The *cumua*, on the other hand, specialise in protective and life-sustaining *wanore* shamanism. Owing to their potent knowledge, however, the *cumua* are also called upon to treat a range of illnesses resulting from snake bites, the consumption of harmful foods or infractions on ritual restrictions.

An overview of the four domains in Figure 10. 2 summarises key features of Makuna cosmology and shamanic practice:

1 Due to the powerful substances and objects ('weapons') they contain, all natural foods are inherently dangerous to human beings. Through the blessing of food (*bare queare*) these harmful substances are removed from the food. In his mind, the blesser collects the weapons contained in the food, ties them together, and returns them to their source and place of origin.
2 The notion of species-specific 'weapons' not only accounts for the practice of food blessing, but also forms the basis for native theories of illness and curing. According to the Makuna, most

diseases come from eating unproper or unblessed food. Shamanic curing (*quenore*) generally involves the removal of the pathogenic 'weapons' contained in unblessed food, visualised in the victim's body as bundles of darts, wooden spines or splinters. The curing shaman (*yai*) 'sucks' the entangled objects from the patient's body, unties them, and 'spits' them out. The whole process can be seen as creation in reverse.

3   The life-sustaining powers of every species – what could be glossed as its generic essence or soul – are intimately (and apparently causally) connected with the reproduction and continuity of the species as a distinct class of beings. As the food blesser removes the 'weapons' from the food and sends them back to their origin, he performs an essentially regenerative act: he returns the 'soul' of the killed and cooked animal (or edible plant) to its birth house, and thereby enables its subsequent rebirth. Food blessing thus has a fundamentally creative aspect which partly subsumes it under the domain of *wanore* shamanism: the protective, regulatory and life-sustaining shamanism which ensures the renewal of cosmos and the ordered reproduction of all beings. However, not only must the 'essential' and regenerative properties of each class of animal be returned to its birth house, but the protective shaman (*cumu*) must constantly offer shamanic foods (coca, snuff, and bees wax) to the Spirit Owners of the animals. This is *wanore* pure and simple. The gourds of coca and snuff – the 'fertility gourds' – must be kept filled continually, and while the shaman performs his life-sustain
ing work he mentally visits these houses and entertains their owners with food and other offerings, a compensation offered to the Spirit Owners in return for their gifts of fish and game.

The pact of reciprocity implied by the relationship between men and animals is clearly expressed in the ideas about disease. By failing to bless animal food, people in effect refuse to return the life-sustaining and regenerative powers of the animals to their birth houses, thereby denying the species its capacity to reproduce. Similarly, by neglecting to offer coca and snuff to the Spirit Owners of the animals, an evil or incompetent shaman manifestly refuses to reciprocate the gift of life-sustaining foods given to people. In revenge, the animals capture human souls and take them to their houses in the rivers and forests. This predatory incursion by the animal spirits into the human life world manifests itself among people as sickness and death. Disease, then, is a punishment for failed reciprocity.

4 These notions of punishment and revenge point to the fourth domain of Makuna shamanism, the destructive sorcery (*rohare*) perpetrated by malevolent shamans and sorcerers (*yaia*). *Rohare* is a kind of ontological concomitant to the procreative and life-sustaining *wanore* shamanism and the reverse of curing. In his predatory capacity to send sickness and death – just as in his capacity to heal and restore life – the shaman-sorcerer acts as a god among humans, manipulating the forces of life and death.

As opposed to the person-centred and actively asocial role of the shaman-sorcerer (*yai*), the protective shaman (*cumu*) plays an explicitly social and community-oriented role in Makuna society. The *cumu* is said to sustain or maintain the world. He mediates between human beings and other life forms, and has the capacity to communicate with the powerful Spirit Owners of the animals. The shamanic work of *wanore* therefore, is best rendered as a kind of 'cosmonomics'. The protective shaman is a cosmic manager controlling the relationships of predation and exchange among different life forms and communities – human and non-human. It is his task to supervise the pact between men and animals and to guarantee the well-being of people by ensuring the reproduction of the non-human life forms on which humans rely for a living.

DEATH AND RE-AWAKENING

The protective shaman also has more important duties than those immediately associated with hunting, fishing and food shamanism. He plays a key role in the major life-cycle rituals – at birth, initiation and death. A few observations on Makuna notions of death and afterlife shed further light on their eco-cosmology and shamanic system.

Every human being is believed ultimately to be killed and consumed by the gods – directly by a divine predatory attack, or indirectly through the agency of malevolent sorcerers or avenging animal spirits. The primary role of the *cumu* is to protect human beings from the dangers inherent in life and help them evade, as long as possible, their ultimate and unavoidable destiny. When death finally comes, the soul separates from the body and travels to the spirits in the Sky World. Here, say Makuna shamans, the gods cook and consume the dead person, thereby reconstituting the dead as a spirit person in the birth house of the clan. During this other-worldly process the officiating shaman acts in complicity with the gods. When he has established that the soul is irretrievably lost to the body it is his duty to supervise its journey to the skies, deliver it into the hands of the gods, and ensure its ultimate reconstitution – its re-awakening – as a complete spirit person. In fact, the shamanic labour in connection with death may best be envisaged as a performative simulation of the divine work of the gods as they capture the soul of the dead and finally return it to its house of origin.

At birth the newborn child is given the name of a deceased grandparent, implying a notion of spiritual continuity between the living and the dead; a transmigration of the soul between the houses of the living and the waking-up-houses of the dead. Life and death, then, are stopping points along the cyclical journey of the soul; a continuous and cyclical process of construction, deconstruction and reconstruction of the human person.

Illness is understood as a temporary dissociation of soul from body, usually caused by the consumption of unblessed or improperly handled food, particularly animal food. By means of their lethal 'weapons', the animal spirits have the capacity to capture and carry off the human soul to the houses of the animals. There is thus a constant threat of disorder and predatory violence between the different communities of beings; an inherent instability in the Makuna cosmos which must permanently be combated by protective shamans. Lives may be stolen, the boundaries between life forms transgressed and the integrity of each community abused. The work of the *cumu* aims to ensure the integrity, distinctiveness and reproduction of every life form, since human survival depends on a balanced exchange among them.

Implied in this view is a wholly interactive, interconnected and interdependent cosmic society: human beings depend for their physical survival on fish and game animals (and plant food). But fish and game animals also depend on human ritual and shamanic practice for their reproduction; through the metaphysical work of the shaman, and through ritual singing and dancing, men make the animals breed and multiply in their birth-and-dance houses in the rivers and the forest. Similarly, human beings both supply the gods with food and depend on them for their continuing existence and the ordered reproduction of society. Put differently, men relate to animals as gods to men. In a sense, then, men are – and are expected to act as – gods in relation to animals and plants.

Makuna mortuary rituals and the shamanic activities associated with the killing and consumption of animals appear as variations on a single metaphysical theme: the transformation of death into new life. When the shaman/food blesser returns the 'weapons' of the food animals to their birth houses he performs the same ritual work and seeks to accomplish the same effect as when he – acting as a god among humans – returns the souls of the dead to their waking-up-houses: he ensures the continuous reproduction of the species – of animals in one case, and humans in the other. Food shamanism, then, is the analogue of mortuary ritual, a deconstruction of the animal-person into corporeal substance and spiritual essence to permit its subsequent reconstruction.

Like the shamanic activities in connection with human death, food shamanism thus has a creative aspect and reconstitutive potency: it enables rebirth. In this important respect the metaphysical work of shamans and knowledgeable men is the direct counterpart to the reproductive labour of women as mothers and cultivators. Through the shamanic activities associated with hunting and fishing, human predation becomes a life-giving activity. Without men performing the 'mortuary rituals' for the animals (through food shamanism), the animals would not be able to reproduce. Through their food shamanism men thus symbolically 'plant' and 'cultivate' their animal food, and through hunting and fishing they reap the harvest of their shamanic labours. Hunting, then, is a kind of male gardening, a point which is explicitly made in mythic narratives. This shamanic capacity, and the responsibilities it implies, ultimately distinguish human beings from animals in Makuna thought: through their shamanic knowledge and practice men ensure the reproduction of the life forms on which they depend. Animals have the knowledge to sustain themselves in their particular habitats, but only men have the knowledge to re-create the species on which they rely for a living. In Makuna eco-cosmology, the universe of living beings is made up of different 'peoples', each with its distinct capacity to sustain and defend itself. But humans are singular in that they are given the knowledge and responsibility to maintain the whole.

CONCLUSION

Makuna eco-cosmology is no ethereal, mental construct, devoid of practical significance. It is born from practice and acted out in everyday chores of subsistence and survival. Makuna have neither the social incentive nor the techniques for producing and storing a significant food surplus. The ideology of reciprocity guiding their interaction with the environment imposes strong sanctions against over-exploitation of forest and river resources. Fish and game animals can only be caught and killed beyond the immediate family needs in preparation for ritual feasts when meat and fish are shared among several families and with the explicit approval of shamans. The rule is mandatory, and transgressions are believed to bring death and disease. Elsewhere I have estimated that the Makuna exclude more than half of their river territory from fishing, on mythic grounds (Århem 1993). Areas in the forest are also set off as game 'sanctuaries'. These restrictions are severe in the areas considered to be the breeding places – the birth-and-dance houses – of the animals: salt-licks, hills, rapids and water falls. This mythical mapping of the territory, which assigns to every named site and landmark a cosmological signification and mythical meaning, has far-reaching consequences for human resource use. Myths, in effect, are plans for land use – and extremely efficient ones since they are at once ecologically informed, emotionally charged and morally binding. In all, the Makuna mode of livelihood amounts to a complex but efficient system of resource management, a cosmology turned into ecology.

Through their shamanic practices and their ritually regulated hunting and fishing activities the Makuna continually put their cosmology into practice. But, above all, it is by means of their unceasing narration of myths and through the regular performance of communal rituals that Makuna cosmology is intellectually elaborated and socially reproduced as a persuasive and coherent whole. During dramatic, collective rituals this vision of cosmos is transformed into a powerful, personal experience for the participants, which shapes and reshapes their perceptions of reality and turns them into a normative framework for action in and on the world.

At the centre of this cosmological vision is a particular notion of human–nature relatedness. The Makuna stress the continuity between nature and society, and ultimately the essential unity of all life, as manifest in the notions of *masa* – the 'humanness' of all beings – and *he* – the undifferentiated, transcendental reality beyond all physical differentiation. Human predation – hunting, fishing, and gathering – is construed as exchange, and killing for food is represented as a generative act through which death is harnessed for the renewal of life. Such an ideology has powerful implications for human actions. Animal 'others' are treated as 'equals' and 'persons', parties to a moral pact governing relations within human society as well as the grander society of all beings. Rather than proclaiming the supremacy of humankind over other life forms, thus legitimising human exploitation of nature, Makuna eco-cosmology emphasises man's responsibility towards the environment and the interdependence of nature and society. Human life is geared to a single, fundamental and socially valued goal: to maintain and reproduce the interconnected totality of beings which constitute the living world; 'to maintain the world', as the Makuna say. In fact, this cosmonomic responsibility towards the whole – and the accompanying shamanic knowledge – is, according to the Makuna, the hallmark of humanity.

By relating their encompassing notion of 'nature' to a theory of disease, the Makuna charge their eco-cosmology with existential immediacy and potency. Their ethnoetiology thus relates human illness to environmental abuse; disease is viewed as the result of cosmonomic mismanagement. The notions of health and curing are focused, not narrowly on the individual person, but on the natural and social whole of which the human patient is a part. Such a totalising 'eco-medical' system, with all its bio-medical shortcomings, is a notoriously powerful sanction against environmental abuse. The binding power of such a system is so great that even if individuals do not fully believe in it (which today is the case for at least some, young mission-educated men), they are nevertheless strongly induced to adhere to its rules, since the social and existential costs of not doing so are exceedingly great. To the Makuna hunter and fisherman, the health of his family depends on his wise management of the environment. Respecting the pact with nature is the only way of ensuring human well-being and the continuing fertility of the land.

The Makuna case is far from unique. Remarkably similar traditions abound in the ethnographic record. The themes of predation and reciprocity, revenge and renewal, pervade the Amazonian eco-cosmologies of which we have reliable accounts.[6] Though varying in form and expression, local representations of human–nature relatedness in the Amazon appear to be transformations of a fundamentally similar pattern, characteristic of the region as a whole.[7] Cultural representations of predation as exchange, and notions of disease as 'nature's revenge', however, have an extension which reaches far beyond the region and are, indeed, common among indigenous peoples worldwide.[8] Following Bateson (1979), Bateson and Bateson (1987) and Rappaport (1979, 1994), I think it is possible to see such representations and their integration into totemic, animic, and more complex eco-cosmological models as cultural codifications of deep ecological insights, developed during millennia of intimate practical interaction with the environment.[9] What from the point of view of the individual actors and life forms involved appear as predation and violent consumption, in a systemic and holistic perspective may best be represented as relationships of interdependence, cyclical exchange and reciprocity.[10]

While the 'violence of a Nature maintained by creatures eating each other is apparent to those participating in it', writes Rappaport (1994: 158), 'the order or harmony at the level of the ecosystem of which the participants are parts is not. In transcending them it is concealed from them'. In this view, myth and ritual are precisely what the Makuna say they are: vehicles of knowledge about the unchanging, transcendent order behind appearances. In metaphoric imagery, myth and ritual reveal larger patterns and connections only imperfectly perceived, yet intuitively glimpsed, by ordinary experience. Makuna eco-cosmology depicts society-and-nature as a whole, invests it with value, and thereby makes it real.

ACKNOWLEDGEMENTS

I gratefully acknowledge the constructive comments on earlier drafts of this chapter from Bill Arens, Philippe Descola, Andrew Gray, Joanna Overing, and Dan Rosengren. The notion of 'human–nature relatedness' in the title is borrowed from Bird-David (1993).

NOTES

1 The same can be said of many, if not most, indigenous peoples of the world. The evidence from North America is abundant (see, for example, Martin 1978, Tanner 1979 and Nelson 1983). For Amazonian evidence, see Note 6 and References.
2 The related notion of ecosophy, as defined by Naess (1989), refers to 'a philosophical worldview inspired by the conditions of life in the ecosphere'. In the sense that an ecosophy implies a philosophy based on ecological insight but going beyond detached knowledge to embrace fundamental norms and values it can be seen as a particular modern – individualised and explicitly formulated – variety of eco-cosmology.
3 For a general overview of Makuna ethnography, see Århem (1981, 1990, and 1993).
4 Like most Amazonian Indians, the Makuna are increasingly suffering the dramatic effects of external economic structures, such as the boom-and-bust economies of gold and coca currently sweeping across the Amazon.
5 The polysemic notion of *masa* is central to an understanding of Makuna cosmology and sociology. In different contexts it stands for: living beings

as opposed to non-living things; human beings as opposed to non-human beings; and the patrilineal clan (sib) as a discrete social unit among other equivalent units making up the human life-world. The interconnectedness of these multiple meanings will, I hope, become clear in the course of this chapter.

6 See, for example, Reichel-Dolmatoff 1971, Seeger 1981, Crocker 1985, Brown 1986, Viveiros de Castro 1992, Overing 1993, Descola 1994. Cf. also Isacsson's (1993) detailed account of Emberá cosmology (the Chocó region of Colombia).

7 The careful reader will note profound resonances in the cited literature but also some significant differences in interpretation. My analysis thus challenges the generalised account of Tukanoan cosmology in Reichel-Dolmatoff (1976) and suggests alternative interpretations of the rich Jivaro material furnished by Brown (1986) and Descola (1994), bringing the Tukanoan and Jivaroan eco-cosmologies closer to one another than implied by Descola's (1992) comparative analysis. I hope to develop these points in a different context.

8 In his recent attempt to formulate a general theory of religion Bloch (1992) discusses a number of such strikingly similar representations of 'rebounding violence', mainly from Southeast Asian ethnography (the Buid, Orokaiva, and Ma'Betisek). The conclusions he draws from the material are very different from those arrived at here.

9 I have in mind here something more precise than the very general relationship between practical knowledge and mental representation which is characteristic of the 'science of the concrete' and classificatory thought in general (Lévi-Strauss 1966); rather, I conjecture that cultural processes have the capacity to develop a kind of 'systems view' of reality which reaches beyond consciously articulated, individual awareness to capture an 'integrative dimension of experience' (Bateson and Bateson 1987: 2).

10 After all, the imagery of indigenous eco-cosmologies – including that of the Makuna – is not that different in kind from the concepts and metaphors used by ecological science to grasp the complexities of biological reality (i.e. food webs, nutrient cycles, communities, mutualism, antagonism), all implying subtle forms of interaction and interconnectedness among different life forms.

REFERENCES

Århem, K. (1981) *Makuna Social Organization: A Study in Descent, Alliance, and the Formation of Corporate Groups in the North-Western Amazon*, Uppsala: Acta Universitatis Upsaliensis.

— (1990) 'Ecosofía Makuna', in F. Correa (ed.) *La Selva Humanizada: Ecología Alternativa en el Trópico Húmedo Colombiano*, Bogota: Instituto Colombiano de Antropología.

— (1993) *Makuna: An Amazonian People* (Working Papers Series), Department of Social Anthropology, Göteborg University.

Bateson, G. (1979) *Mind and Nature: A Necessary Unity*, New York: Dutton.

— and Bateson, M. C. (1987) *Angels Fear: An Investigation into the Nature and Meaning of the Sacred*, London: Rider.

Bird-David, N. (1993) 'Tribal Metaphorization of Human–Nature Relatedness', in K. Milton (ed.) *Environmentalism: The View from Anthropology*, London: Routledge.

Bloch, M. (1992) *Prey into Hunter: The Politics of Religious Experience*, Cambridge: Cambridge University Press.

Brown, M. F. (1986) *Tsewa's Gift: Magic and Meaning in an Amazonian Society*, Washington, DC: Smithsonian Institution.

Crocker, J. C. (1985) *Vital Souls: Bororo Cosmology, Natural Symbolism, and Shamanism*, Tucson: The University of Arizona Press.

Croll, E. and Parkin, D. (1992) *Bush Base–Forest Farm: Culture, Environment and Development*, London: Routledge.

Descola, P. (1992) 'Societies of Nature and the Nature of Society', in A. Kuper (ed.) *Conceptualizing Society*, London: Routledge.

— (1994) *In the Society of Nature: A Native Ecology in Amazonia*, Cambridge: Cambridge University Press.

Isacsson, S-E. (1993) *Transformations of Existence: On Man and Cosmos in Emberá Thought*, unpublished PhD thesis, Göteborg University.

Lévi-Strauss, C. (1966) *The Savage Mind*, Chicago: University of Chicago Press.

Martin, C. (1978) *Keepers of the Game*, Berkeley: University of California Press.

Naess, A. (1989) *Ecology, Community and Lifestyle: Outline of an Ecosophy*, Cambridge: Cambridge University Press.

Nelson, R. (1983) *Make Prayers to the Raven*, Chicago: University of Chicago Press.

Overing, J. (1993) 'Death and the Loss of Civilized Predation among the Piaroa of the Orinoco Basin', *L'Homme* 126–28, XXXIII, 2–4: 191–211.

Rappaport, R. A. (1979) *Ecology, Meaning and Religion*, Berkeley: North Atlantic Books.

— (1994) 'Humanity's Evolution and Anthropology's Future', in R. Borofsky (ed.) *Assessing Cultural Anthropology*, New York: McGraw Hill.

Reichel-Dolmatoff, G. (1971) *Amazonian Cosmos: The Sexual and Religious Symbolism of the Tukano Indians*, Chicago: University of Chicago Press.

— (1976) 'Cosmology as Ecological Analysis: A View from the Rainforest', *Man* (NS) 11: 307–18.

Seeger, A. (1981) *Nature and Society in Central Brazil*, Cambridge: Harvard University Press.

Tanner, A. (1979) *Bringing Home Animals: Religious Ideology and Mode of Production of the Mistassini Cree Hunters*, London: C. Hurst.

Taylor, A. C. (1993) 'Remembering to Forget: Identity, Mourning and Memory among the Jivaro', *Man* (NS) 28: 653–78.

Viveiros de Castro, E. B. (1992) *From the Enemy's Point of View: Humanity and Divinity in an Amazonian Society*, Chicago: University of Chicago Press.

Willis, R. G. (1990) 'Introduction', in R. G. Willis (ed.) *Signifying Animals: Human Meaning in the Natural World*, London: Unwin Hyman.

Chapter 11

Enraged hunters

The domain of the wild in north-western Europe

Bertrand Hell

Can the study of modern hunting practices in Europe tell us anything about the contested interface between nature and society in western societies? A purely sociological approach will show how hunting reflects the social order of its age. As they follow a strict cynegetic code, today's hunters abide by a wider social charter, just as those Greek and Germanic heroes did when they triumphed over terrifying wild boar, or those medieval knights when they went in search of the white deer. As in war, relations between men and wild animals follow a logic of institutionalised violence wherein, according to a tradition of cynegetic treatises that can be traced back to ancient Greece, the hunter appears as the archetype of the fully accomplished social man.[1] However, hunting also reveals specific conceptualisations of nature. Leach (1964) has shown how, among his fellow British citizens, the linguistic treatment of animal categories reflects the taboos or the ritual values by which they have been marked, thus expressing a cultural code and exhibiting a social distancing. Just as with linguistic categories, hunting techniques reveal a taxonomy of the animal world. In Europe, as much as in Amazonia or Africa, certain animals are either protected, trapped or hunted, while others are highly prized, shunned or destroyed. Their symbolic status thus constitutes an index of ontological boundaries and social classifications.

In this chapter, I propose to discuss the construction of the category of 'wilderness' in north-western Europe as it is expressed in the values attached to the pursuit of wild animals, in particular the 'beasts' of the forest which were seen by the collective European imagination as being *par excellence* the 'wildest' of animals.

Historical documents, folklore and ethnographic data on big game hunting reveal that the nature–culture opposition is mediated in this area by an ambivalent attitude oscillating between, on the one hand, an initially positive hunting compulsion, defining gender status and male hierarchy and, on the other, the ever-present danger of the hunter becoming wild, notably through an excessive contact with the 'black blood' of game. A certain form of mastery of the wild within oneself and in the forest thus constitutes a specific European concept of the ambiguous coexistence of nature and culture.

AN OUTLINE OF EUROPEAN HUNTING

There are the two main types of forest-hunting known in western Europe: the kind that uses beaters and the so-called 'silent hunting' (stalking or lying in wait for the game to approach)[2] and apparently they have nothing in common. When placed within a wider social context, these different techniques appear to involve two quite separate hunting cultures. Indeed, the choice of technique is closely correlated with the type of social structure, the conditions of access to hunting, and the relative density of hunters, as well as the legal code and ethics of hunting. These data are rudimentary in identifying the different conceptions of contemporary hunting.

Over a vast geographical area including all the regions where German dialects are spoken, as well as a number of central European countries (Poland, Hungary and Slovakia), hunters share an identical conception of hunting as 'harvesting'. This conception is embodied in the silent individual approach of the deer – a technique known, both in French and in German, as *pirsch* – in order to obtain a fine trophy. In this hunting-as-harvesting, the hunter claims that he is responsible for the 'management of the animal population'; he watches over and maintains an optimal deer population in his hunting territory by seeing to it that all animal predators are destroyed and that the deer are provided with forage and mineral licks. Through the practice of so-called 'selective shooting', hunters also kill males with irregular or asymmetric antlers; these animals are regarded – falsely according to ethologists – as being poor reproducers. This form of hunting revolves around a fundamental preoccupation: the practice of '*Hege*'. Expressing a concept of conservation and protection, this German term, in use since the fifteenth century, denotes hunting as a quest for the animal which provides the most prestigious trophy. In the case of deer, hunters are haunted by the dream of meeting face to face an animal sporting perfect 'royal' antlers. The whole organisation of hunting is regulated according to a complex appreciation of the trophy, and the annual growth of antlers in the deer community dictates the hunters' strategy. The indispensable *vade-mecum* for hunting is to be found in such practical manuals as *Das Ansprechen des Hirsches* which shows the value of the animal as a function of the morphology of its antlers (for a detailed analysis of the Alsace notion of hunting as harvesting, see Hell 1985: 167–209).

Such a conception of hunting is not without social constraints. In order to manage and harvest his game, the hunter must gain exclusive access to a large territory. Since only an elite can hunt in such conditions, a large body of regulations controls forest hunting. From Austria to Alsace (where a particular code of local law rules hunting), the basic features of the cynegetic jural system are the same: a limitation on the number of lease-holders for each hunting lot, a minimum-surface clause for hunting territories (200 hectares at least), the obligatory adjudication to hunters of small, privately-owned forest plots, and a prohibition on shooting deer that have been beaten out.

By contrast, in southern European countries and in the major part of France, hunting is associated with the notion of a free right of gathering. Hunters reject any idea of reasoned management of the wild fauna, considering that game 'grows on its own'; they prefer the beating method, which is described as an ancient and traditional hunting custom. In this hunting as 'gathering', everything is done to maintain a wide separation between the domestic and the wild. Killing wild animals answers mainly to the real or imaginary necessity of protecting cultivated land, thus becoming an aspect of the farmer's utilitarian logic. In countries where this ethic of hunting prevails, the right to hunt and the right to own individual property are closely linked in the legal system, completely excluding the idea, basic to the jural aspect of hunting as harvest, of a communal approach to the management of landed property.

Two divergent hunting cultures thus coexist in contemporary western Europe, hunting as harvesting and hunting as gathering. One is individualistic and elitist, while the other is open to all and community-oriented, a contrast which is reflected in the rate of hunters per country (see Table 11.1).

This duality is in no way a recent development. The basis for the modern codification of European hunting practices has its origins in the High Middle Ages, as can be seen by comparing the respective status of hunting in the medieval legal corpus of central Italy and the Rhineland (see *La chasse au Moyen Age* 1980: 59–68, 99–113). Hunting in the Italian communal context was entirely controlled by

Table 11.1 The cultural areas of hunting in western Europe: number of hunters as a proportion (per hundred) of the total population, 1981

Hunting as harvesting		*Hunting as gathering*	
Area	*Proportion*	*Area*	*Proportion*
Germany	0.4	Italy	2.6
Alsace	0.6	France	3.6
Austria	1.2	Spain	2.1
Luxembourg	0.6	Greece	3.1

Source: Hell 1994: 23

the demands of the local agricultural and pastoral economy. The village communities sought to preserve the integrity of their cultivated land and their domestic animals against the predatory attacks of wild animals which were considered a 'nuisance'. There was no concern about the protection of wild fauna even if they could be eaten. The legislation appears to be modelled on the Roman tradition to which so many classical authors make reference. Columelle, for instance, thought that game animals were the enemies of agriculture and that hunting was a waste of time (*De Res Rustica*), while Varron saw the pursuit of wild animals as a useless exercise and the cause of unnecessary fatigue. One author in the first century AD remarked that it was much simpler to rear an animal than to chase it for hours in the cold and through thorny undergrowth (*Rerum Rusticarum*). The great hunt, introduced in Italy from the Orient by Scipio of Emilia, never really gained favour with the Roman aristocracy who despised a practice they believed was best left to the care of professional trappers, stewards in charge of agricultural domains, or shepherds defending their herds.

A completely different cynegetic practice was to be found in the Rhineland. Medieval regulations show that strict limitations were imposed on foraging or clearing new plots in the forest and, generally, on increasing the area of cultivated land. All the means used by Italian peasants to protect their plots against the forays of wild animals (enclosures, the use of traps, the possession of dogs, etc.) were prohibited to the peasants of Baden or Alsace. However, there did exist a counterpart: the hunter was obliged to pay an indemnity. Thus in 1549 the German lord Phillip of Hesse was obliged to distribute cereals in order to compensate for the terrible damage caused by wild boar. The profile of the sovereigns of the Carolingian dynasty lies behind these regulatory dispositions. Charlemagne and his celebrated 'Capitulaires', for example, together with the great king-hunters of the eighth and ninth centuries, sought to establish the domain of forest hunting on the basis of detailed regal rights. The hunt was more than a simple 'noble' activity, it was ontologically linked to the civilising function attributed to the king-hero.[3]

Are we to suppose, then, that there exists a radical and absolute opposition between two types of European hunting practices? In my opinion this would be an error. In fact, beyond the apparent cleavage between the two hunting techniques, with their respective ethics and modalities, there is a common underlying symbolic code which structures hunting practice throughout Europe. No type of hunt is totally free from constraints and no spilling of blood is ever regarded as a banal act. Whatever the hunting culture to which they belong, whatever the geographical area in which they live, all European hunters share an identical cultural scheme, that of a flux of wild substances originating from the forest. The circulation of this flux maps the true contours of the natural domain of wilderness.

THE BLACK BLOOD SYSTEM

Cultural representations of hunting in Europe are constructed around the metaphor of the 'black blood', a flux said to impregnate both the body of the hunter and that of the game. The varying degrees of concentration of the black blood constitute a sort of measuring scale by which to judge the degrees of wilderness attributed to forest animals, to hunters, to game meats and, more generally, to social behaviour. Perhaps the most elaborate of these scales is that of the varying degree of the 'fever' which is said to seize hunters and give them their distinctiveness (*Jagdfieber*, or 'hunting fever', as it is called in German-speaking countries).

The scale of fever

European hunters often refer to hunting as 'being in the blood'. In doing so, they establish an absolute natural demarcation between hunters and non-hunters. Hunters do not become so by choice or by chance, their destiny is inscribed in their 'black blood', the ultimate legitimation of their particular status. The effect of the circulation of this specific inner flux is an irresistible desire to kill and to shed the blood of forest game animals, a compulsion which ordinary men do not feel. The exclusion of women from hunting in the forest – a social reality confirmed by statistical data on hunting – is justified on these same grounds: women and black blood are said to be absolutely incompatible. More generally, the absence of hunting fever is taken to indicate the externality of non-hunters to the domain.

Hunters' discourse on scales of fever – or lack of it – is not abstract rhetoric; it is grounded in a set of folk beliefs about human physiology. Among the symptoms indicating the tangible effects on the hunter's body of this singular fever are high body heat, boiling bodily humours and a sharpening of the senses. The levels of concentration of black blood also serve to indicate a relative hierarchy among hunters themselves, personal status being correlated with the fever's strength. Those who are least affected by hunting fever are those who take part in communal hunting teams and who use the collective beating method to hunt. In this highly social context, hunters are careful to keep their passion within strict limits. At the other end of the fever scale are the poachers and above all the 'woodsmen', asocial individuals who live alone in the midst of the forest. These extremely individualistic hunters are seen as having fallen prey to 'rage' because of an excessive fever, i.e. a foaming of the dark blood which has proved too intense. The rest of the hunters (trackers, *pirscheurs*, etc.) adopt the behaviour and the hunting techniques that reflect most closely their own personal level of fever. The less collective the hunting practice, the closer the hunter becomes identified with wild animals.

The scale of warmth of game meat

The next scale in classifying hunters and hunting practices is based on the classification of game meat (mainly deer and wild boar) as a function of its intrinsic body heat, itself a function of the danger these meats present for human consumption. Black blood provokes a drying up of the body and a pernicious fever. This is why an excessive consumption of venison is said to provoke certain physiological side-effects such as vomiting, and the appearance of warts and haemorrhoids, all deemed as classical symptoms of blood contamination. Game flesh, which is reputedly heavy, very 'warm' and has a strong odour, is forbidden to women. The reason for this prohibition is identical to that reported for the Siberian population (Lot-Falck 1953: 185): women are considered unable to withstand the power inherent in wild meat. Venison is thus classified according to the degree of impregnation with black blood. The concentration of black blood decreases with distance from the 'entrails' – a generic term describing a mixture of stagnant blood and sperm and expressing the very seat of an animal's animality – towards the parts of the animal, such as the legs, which are the furthest removed from the focus of his animality. This taxonomy is vividly reflected in variation of the colour of the blood. Because of their position and close relation to the entrails, the giblets are regarded as black meat and very warm. Further on, the ribs, the saddle and shoulders are classified as red meat, and their great warmth still demands a precautionary culinary preparation – the marinade. As they belong to the outer part of the animal, the haunches are regarded as a sweetened wild meat, with the paler colour associated with beef. Inducing only moderate heat, the meat from the outer portions of the animal has acquired the status of a gastronomic dish and can thus be eaten during festive occasions by non-hunters.

The scale of animal savagery

The repertory of colours and smells associated with body parts also functions as a taxonomic device for the classification of forest animals. The folk-taxonomy used by European hunters and contemporary common law is based on a classificatory scheme that can be traced back to the Middle Ages. A distinction between 'red beasts' (roebuck, deer), 'black beasts' (wolves and boar) and 'stinking beasts' (fox, marten, weasel) is found in both ancient German and French hunting treatises. Here also it is the degree of concentration of black blood which structures the taxonomic hierarchy. Contemporary hunters have numerous anecdotes to support their view that the wild boar, that blackest of animals, a dedicated and mischievous loner, is one of the most savage of all the beasts in the forest. Its true nature is said to show when it attacks a man, seeking immediately to emasculate him. Sexuality and colour are closely linked in the evaluation of an animal's savagery. Thus during the rutting season, the black blood is said to boil due to sperm retention, converting 'red game' into 'black game'. During this period even the peaceful roe deer can be transformed into a ferocious animal, quite literally enraged.

The stinking animals embody the very idea of extreme savagery. It is true that they produce smelly glandular secretions, but their stench is above all attributed to specific attributes of their symbolic status. There are two considerations here. First, their meat is regarded as too black; they are carnivorous animals and their small digestive systems do not allow them fully to digest the fresh blood they consume. This is why the consumption of their meat is forbidden while that of the other game animals, herbivores all of them, is permitted. But stinking animals are also associated with uncleanliness since, as carrion-eating animals, they transgress an important biblical taboo – 'Thou shalt not eat of a dead or wounded animal' (Leviticus, XVII). They are, therefore, considered impure.

Levels of edibility

An observation of the consumption of venison shows that decisions about the taste and the cut of meat are not arbitrary. Men are given meat according to the particular level of their fever, a rule imposed by a cultural code which treats the drive to consume black blood as an imperious physiological reality. Fever excites a man to consume meat of various degrees of blackness, according to his strength, while the intrinsic heat of the chosen piece helps to maintain his particular compulsion for the Wild. Thresholds of edibility are thus established. Those who do not hunt and, therefore, do not feel any fever, abstain from eating meat which they regard as indigestible or unhealthy. However, at the other end of the scale, poachers may eat with impunity the blackest flesh of an animal that has been snared (thus not blooded) or they may drink its uncooked blood. As for 'woods-men', they have no misgivings about breaking the common prohibi-tion and eating the flesh of stinking animals – meat which would make other hunters ill. It is imperative, therefore, that they only consume meat that corresponds to their own nature. Knowing his personal limits regarding his ability – or his drive – to consume black blood amounts, for a hunter, to stating his position in the scale of wilderness. This identity is also made manifest in the field of daily social behaviour.

The wild body

The idea that the hunter undergoes a gradual transformation of his nature towards a wild state rests on a series of considerations. To begin with, it is said that his body changes, as the fever which seizes him triggers a development of his 'natural' faculties. Fever sharpens the hearing and the sense of smell and sight and makes the hunter's body insensitive to cold, fatigue and the scratches of thorny undergrowth. The evidence often offered as empirical proof of this is that even when deprived of all technical assistance, in bad weather conditions, poachers have no difficulty surviving in the forest. The vigour and heat associated with a body which has become wild carries a strong sexual connotation. The image of the wild man, covered with hair and endowed with powerful virility is still a common European stereotype, just as it was in the Middle Ages. Everything seems to revolve around the idea that the more savage or wild one's body becomes the more one feels compelled to break with social standards. The figure of the 'woodsman' embodies this lack of sociality: he lives entirely alone, his language becomes limited and he gradually stops worrying about hygiene.

A central scheme structures this conceptualisation of wilderness: driven by their black blood, some men may end up sharing the nature of wild beasts. The notion of the latent danger of black blood lies behind this obsession.[4] There is an ever-present risk that the necessary process of becoming wilder and wilder in order to hunt more and more successfully may result in an uncontrollable bestiality. Until quite recently (the end of the nineteenth century), this threat was seen as a real possibility that could materialise in a dreadful illness: rabies. 'Enraged' people were considered to be wild beasts. They were aggressive, would bark and foam at the mouth; they were reputedly driven to bite because of a desire for blood, and they were notoriously licentious. The collective terror that this eruption of wild behaviour provoked in the centres of towns often resulted in terrible forms of social ostracism. Finally, the enraged person would be killed by suffocation in order to avoid contagion from an effusion of black blood.

THE FUNCTION OF THE WILD

The symbolic layout sketched below is based on a fundamental ambivalence regarding black blood. While on the one hand hunters seek to capture its wild strength (infused in venison meat but also conserved in the trophy), on the other hand they fear the extreme power of metamorphosis which it possesses. This ambivalence not only determines the field of social behaviour associated with hunting, it is also the model for many representations of the Wild in modern European societies. It is the recurring framework, for instance, for popular narratives based on the 'Wild Hunt' theme. Folklorists throughout Europe have shown that these stories were common all over the continent until the end of the nineteenth century. Based on oral tradition, these stories described the cyclical passage of a supernatural hunt in the winter sky. The teams of hunters come from

Blood scale

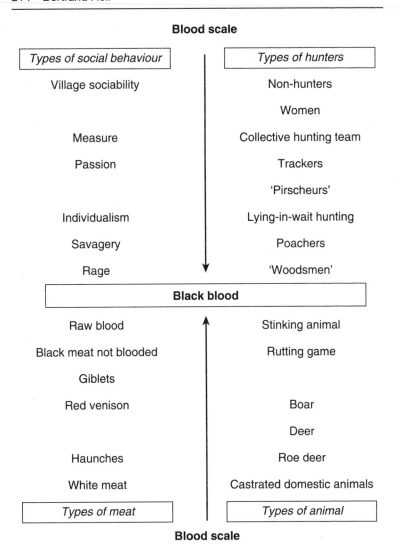

Types of social behaviour		Types of hunters
Village sociability		Non-hunters
		Women
Measure		Collective hunting team
Passion		Trackers
		'Pirscheurs'
Individualism		Lying-in-wait hunting
Savagery		Poachers
Rage		'Woodsmen'

Black blood

Raw blood		Stinking animal
Black meat not blooded		Rutting game
Giblets		
Red venison		Boar
		Deer
Haunches		Roe deer
White meat		Castrated domestic animals
Types of meat		Types of animal

Blood scale

Figure 11.1 The black blood system

the other world and leave behind them bloodied quarters of venison. Unable to resist their attraction, spectators are driven to try and lay hold of the black meat. Sometimes they are lucky and see their portion turned into gold, but in most cases they are seized by the rage and carried off by phantoms.

The Wild Hunt was the object of ambiguous feelings. It was regarded by some farmers as a sacred procession of the deceased which they hoped to see passing over their lands and stables, since it possessed powers of fecundity; but others described it as a sinister hunting pack composed of the damned, which brought in its wake storms and destruction (see Thompson 1958: Motif E 501). This ambivalent image is the basis of certain urban carnival rituals, recorded at the beginning of this century, involving the sudden appearance of masked figures posing as wild animals: deer (in England, Germany and Central Europe), bears (in France and Spain), aurochs (in Poland) or hairy beasts (in Greece and the Balkans). At the beginning of the ritual, the inhabitants welcome these personifications of the Wild with enthusiasm, inviting them to plough a furrow in the middle of the village or to throw wheat on every threshold. However, the convivial atmosphere changes very quickly. The cheerful songs of the masked figures change to obscene ribaldry and the blessings of fecundity turn to threats of rape. In the last part of the ritual, the Wild figures are either symbolically killed (or castrated) or chased beyond the village limits with shouts and stone throwing.[5]

CONCLUSION

The notion that the Wild needs to be confined within strict limits (ritual or otherwise) is part of a wider ideological configuration establishing a clear demarcation between the Wild and the Domestic. The origin of this European *Weltanschauung* can be found at that moment in the Neolithic era when agriculture and animal husbandry established a new order of nature. The relations of sacred companion-ship between men and animals, which obtained during the Palaeo-lithic era – relations which have been observed by anthropologists in hunter-gatherer societies – were supplanted, in both Europe and the Near East, by a mystical solidarity between man and the vegetal domain. With the domestication of plants, a different concept of the global cycle of fecundity and fertility was constructed, a basic symbolic change in the relation to nature, which was later reinforced by Christianity.[6] From then on the blood of sacrificed animals was to be substituted by the blood of the new god, who was identified with an ear of wheat, an explicit metaphor in many sacred texts (The Gospel of St John: 12).

The adoption of agriculture implied a radical and irreversible revolution as much in the use and meaning of symbols as in social organisations and in techno-economic systems. Within this context, the persistence of hunting in European societies can be seen primarily as answering an ideological necessity. According to the archaeologist J. D. Vigne (1993), the social construction of a specific domain defined as wilderness came into effect during the very process of neolithisation. Studying the selective domestication strategies that operated in European societies, he argues that certain animal species, particularly the cervidaes, were deliberately left in their wild state in order to safeguard their appropriation by hunting. This practice thus became the highly symbolic and strictly codified domain of human activity intended to deal with the Wild.

To my mind, contemporary conceptions of the Wild in Europe have to be seen within the context of this very old cultural continuity. Drawing upon Geertz's work on cock-fights in Bali (1973), I propose that the culture of hunting in Europe should be considered as a 'text' revealing a specific 'ethos'. Reference to hunting allows a better understanding of the cultural reason behind contemporary food preferences – 'white' meat, for instance, rather than 'black' meat – and the classification of natural kinds. It allows us also to throw light on a focal point of European cultures, our ambiguous relationship with blood. Within the sphere of the Wild, as expressed in hunting practices, meat is not an objectified commodity, it is not transformed into a quasi vegetable, it is not deprived of sexual and gender connotations.[7] The strictly codified sacrificial rituals of hunting allow for a transgression of the taboo which is so rigorously observed in the domestic space: 'Thou shalt not eat of the blood of any flesh as the soul of every flesh is its blood' (Leviticus, XVII: 14).

NOTES

1   For the Greek world see, for instance, Xenophon 1970; for the French tradition, see Phebus 1971 (1391); for the German tradition, Göchhaussen (1764).
2   Coursing does not exist in Germany and is statistically marginal in France; in the United Kingdom it concerns mainly the fox and the hare.
3   This idea of a close relationship between the sacred, royalty, hunting and the forest is explicitly developed in a work by the English jurist, John Manwood (1592).
4   For the relations between black blood, the rage and other savage furies, see Hell (1994: 99–198).
5   For some wilderness figures in Europe, see Glotz 1975. For a specific ritual, the killing of the bear in the Pyrenees, see Van Gennep (1947: 908–17).

6   Regarding the dramatic schemes that structure mythico-ritual scenarios
    linked to the death and resurrection of a divinity (Osiris, Tammuz,
    Adonis, etc.) see Durand (1960: 339–59). The prehistorian J. Cauvin
    argues (1994) that, in the Near East, a revolution in religious symbolism
    preceded other neolithic technical and social mutations.
7   The status of butchered meat in western societies has been the object of
    numerous works; see, for example, Sahlins (1976), Barrau (1983: 140–
    73), Vialles (1987).

REFERENCES

Barrau, J. (1983) *Les Hommes et Leurs Aliments*, Paris: Messidor.
Cauvin, J. (1994) *Naissance des Divinités, Naissance de L'agriculture*, Paris:
    CNRS.
Durand, G. (1960) *Les Structures Anthropologiques de L'imaginaire*, Paris:
    Dunod.
Geertz, C. (1973) *The Interpretation of Cultures*, New York: Basic Books.
Glotz, S. (1975) *Le Masque dans la Tradition Européenne*, Binche: Musée
    International du Carnaval.
Göchhaussen, F. (1764) *Jagd und Weidwerks-Anmerkungen*, Weimar:
    Hoffmann.
Hell, B. (1985) *Entre Chien et Loup. Faits et Dits de Chasse dans la France de
    L'Est*, Paris: Maison des Sciences de l' Homme.
—— (1994) *Le Sang Noir. Chasse et Mythe du Sauvage en Europe*, Paris:
    Flammarion.
La chasse au Moyen Age, Actes du Colloque de Nice (1980) Paris: Les Belles
    Lettres.
Leach, E. (1964) 'Anthropological Aspects of Language: Animal Categories
    and Verbal Abuse', in E.H. Lenneberg (ed.) *New Directions in the Study of
    Language*, Cambridge, Mass.: MIT Press.
Lot-Falck, E. (1953) *Les Rites de Chasse chez les Peuples Sibériens*, Paris:
    Gallimard.
Manwood, J. (1592) *A Treatise of the Laws of the Forests*, London.
Phebus, G. (1971 [1391]) *Livre de Chasse*, Paris: Seghers.
Sahlins, M. (1976) *Culture and Practical Reason*, Chicago: University of
    Chicago Press.
Thompson, S. (1958) *Motif-Index of Folk-Literature*, Copenhagen: Rosen-
    kilde and Bagger.
Van Gennep, A. (1947) *Manuel de Folklore Français Contemporain*, 1, 3: Paris:
    Picard.
Vialles, N. (1987) *Le Sang et la Chair. Les Abattoirs des Pays de l'Adour*, Paris:
    Maison des Sciences de l'Homme.
Vigne, J. D. (1993) 'Domestication ou Appropriation pour la Chasse: Histoire
    d' un Choix Socio-culturel depuis le Néolithiques. L' exemple des Cerfs', in
    Exploitation des animaux sauvages à travers le temps, Juan-Les-Pins:
    Editions APCDA-CNRS.
Xenophon (1970) *L'art de la Chasse*, Paris: Les Belles Lettres.

Part III

Nature, society and artefact

Chapter 12

When timber grows wild

The desocialisation of Japanese mountain forests

John Knight

INTRODUCTION

'As the mountain trees get taller, the village gets richer.'[1] I heard this expression from a Japanese forest landowner who was commenting ironically on the present-day state of upland decline. Despite the many tall trees all around them, his and other villages had not become rich. The normative relationship between tree growth and village wealth expressed above was not actually working. In fact, the great expanses of tall trees have, in many ways, come to stand for upland degeneration rather than development. The forest around the village is less and less a symbol of wealth and increasingly a 'green desert' (*midori no sabaku*).

This chapter is concerned with how a specific productive initiative has come to be experienced locally as a negative form of environmental change. In post-war upland Japan much mixed natural woodland has been turned into monocultural timber plantations in an attempt to make the mountains a space of domestication able to support modern rural livelihoods. Although a transformation of the mountains has indeed taken place, the new forest that has emerged is not what was promised. Far from extending human control over the natural environment, this industrial forest actually makes for a new, more radical environmental disorder.[2]

CULTIVATION

In recent years the status of ostensibly natural environments has come under greater scrutiny. Hunters and gatherers have long been viewed as 'ecologically passive' and as living in a natural environment, rather than as having any significant effect on or control over it (see Chase

1989: 42 for critique). The implication is that agriculture is the only means of controlling a natural environment. The so-called 'Neolithic Revolution' thus divides human history into two contrasting halves with respect to nature. This assumption is now being challenged by biologists, archaeologists and anthropologists. As Ucko (1989: xii) puts it, 'the actual domestication of plants is a relatively late form of manipulation of the environment and not one which is always adaptively advantageous in the long-term'. The point is that there may be a degree of environmental control or manipulation without actual cultivation, and that this may well exceed the degree of environmental control actually obtained through cultivation.

For anthropologists who study cultivators of one kind or another, this point might usefully be turned around. If hunter-gatherers are not in practice as ecologically passive as represented, are cultivators as ecologically active as they have hitherto tended to appear? If environmental control exists apart from cultivation, cultivation *per se* is no guarantee of environmental control.

Cultivation can be defined as a spatially focused, labour-demanding and ecologically interventionist activity consisting among other things of planting, weeding, and even land clearance (Harris 1989: 17–22). 'Activity' here comprises two things which should be distinguished: particular cultivatory *actions* and the larger cultivation *processes* of which they form part. The former cumulatively make up something larger – eventually, and ideally, a successful process of cultivation. But there is no inevitability about this. It presumes the management of cultivatory actions over time. At the least, this will involve a single cultivator, but also possibly a number of different cultivators. Furthermore, in some cases (notably timber forestry), these different cultivators may temporally be distanced, spread out over a long, even transgenerational span of time.

Cultivation is to be distinguished from production in general because it involves a process of organic growth. It is in terms of this growth that successful cultivatory acts are coordinated. But the longer the time span involved, the greater is the possibility of what might be called productive incompletion. With inorganic production, *incomplete* production will tend to be synonymous with *suspended* production, but this is not the case with organic production, i.e. cultivation. Here production is relatively independent of human producers because growth can continue in the absence of the grower. What emerges is still artificial rather than (pristinely) natural, for the earlier cultivatory acts have irreversibly affected the growth pattern. Yet it is not *fully* artificial; what develops is a partial product whose end-form clearly falls short of what it ought to be in appearance, quality etc. – i.e. what it would have been had the complete set of productive acts duly been applied to it. The grower has lost control of the growth; the 'product' has slipped free of the productive intention that initiated it.

The concern here is with timber forestry. This sort of commercial tree-growing raises two additional complications in relation to cultivation. The first has to do with the time-scale of growth, the second the spatial scale and location of this growth. Trees do not just emerge as different from what they should be; they do so over long periods of time, on a large scale of production, and in particular sorts of places. The consequences of the grower losing control of the growth are not just *inadvertent products* – products alien to the original productive ambition – but also an *unintended environment*. In what follows, a state-promoted attempt to establish widespread timber production in upland Japan is shown to be experienced by mountain villagers, decades later, as a number of disturbing *environmental* changes.

YAMA

In Japanese the word *yama* refers to both mountains and forests, the conceptual distinction between the two being minimal. Mountain forests make up over two-thirds of the national land area, and have long been an important source of symbolism for the Japanese. Mountains are 'symbols of procreation in their volcanic aspect, symbols of fertility in their watershed function, and abodes of the dead in their isolation from the everyday world of man' (Smith 1979: 59). A key feature of the *yama* is their wild character (Kalland 1992: 222). The mountains, like the sea, are a site of the *oku* (or *oki* for the sea), the interior, a wild space associated with *kami* spirits and opposed to the worldly space inhabited by human beings (Berque 1986: 74–76).

For mountain villagers, however, the *yama* constitute a *local* environment. While they are referred to generically, they are experienced as highly differentiated. This is so, first of all, ecologically. Ecological variation was particularly marked on the Kii Peninsula. In Japan it is common to distinguish between the cool, temperate, deciduous forests of north-eastern Japan and the warm, temperate, evergreen, broad-leafed forests of Pacific and south-western Japan (e.g. Ichikawa and Saito 1985: 12–32). However, this must be qualified because, in addition to this regional distinction, there is further variation according to altitude.

In the upland interior of the southern Kii Peninsula both types of forest are found in close proximity, leading some writers to proclaim the special importance of the area's natural environment as the place of the most southerly Japanese beech forest and even the site where Japan's two ecologies meet (Ue 1994: 4–6). Although the typical forest is of the latter, evergreen, broad-leafed kind, there are also deciduous forests of white oak, cherry blossom, maple and chestnut, while from altitudes of 800 metres upwards deciduous beech woodland begins. It must be stressed, however, that this earlier forest was mixed, and already had natural conifer stands, including cryptomeria and Japanese cypress, the two main plantation species conifers that would become so ubiquitous later on.

In Hongū today, although foresters do refer to 'evergreen shiny-leafed forest' (*shōyōjurin*) and 'deciduous broad-leafed forest' (*ochibakōyōrin*) etc., this received scientific classification exists alongside another, older, local classification of trees and forests: 'iron trees', 'shallow trees' and 'black trees' (see Ue 1994: 7). 'Iron trees' (*kanagi*) are those evergreen broad-leafed species such as the evergreen oak used for charcoal-burning. 'Shallow trees' (*asagi*) are those soft trees such as pasania, white oak and cherry blossom, which, while no good for charcoal, nonetheless make for good firewood. 'Black trees' (*kuroki*) are those trees of dark-hued needle-leaves such as hemlock, Douglas fir and silver fir, cryptomeria and Japanese cypress, which were used for building (ibid.).

Second, while for lowland Japanese the *yama* may appear to be a place essentially beyond the sphere of human habitation, for upland dwellers themselves different parts of the mountains serve different purposes. Those parts of the mountains near the village, the *satoyama*, have long been important to village livelihoods as sites of slash-and-burn farming in which wheat, millet and tubers were grown. For much of their history mountain villages have depended on such non-rice cultivation, and rice growing made a relatively minor contribution to local livelihoods. Yukawa (1988) even argues that for mountain villagers the mountains were traditionally the site of production (hunting, gathering and slash-and-burn farming), while the village was the site of consumption (cf. Ue 1994: 7). The later introduction of rice farming meant that the village also became a site of production, but given the paucity of suitable rice farming land, parts of the mountains continued to be cultivated.

In addition to being farming sites themselves, the mountains contributed in important ways to farming in the village. Forest greenery, particularly from the deciduous parts of the mixed woodland, were used for farm fertiliser and for animal fodder. Forest wood was also used for fuel (firewood and charcoal) and building. There is a long history of the manipulation of wood growth in upland Japan. Totman (1989: 247) points out how, at different times, rulers have promoted different sorts of tree growth in the more proximate forest area. In the seventeenth century, for example, the emphasis was on fuel-wood forests and brushy broad-leaf growth was encouraged.

The *yama* was also a direct source of food. Nuts, berries, wild mushrooms and a wide range of *sansai* or edible mountain plants (bracken, fern, butterbur, etc.) were gathered. Upland plants have long been used for medicine, basket materials, fibres (textiles), and as sacred offerings in the home or at festivals (see Shinohara's survey of local plant knowledge, 1990: 205–6). In addition to the felling of natural stands of 'black trees', including cryptomeria and cypress, for building purposes, cryptomeria or cypress trees were also planted and tended deeper in the woods so that in times of need – the wedding of a daughter, the funeral of a parent, etc. – they could be felled and sold. Many forest animals and birds were hunted for their meat, including wild boar, deer, serow, hares, pheasants, turtledoves and sparrows.

Different plants are associated with different parts of the *yama* – such as mountain peaks, ridges, passes, hillsides, ravines, grassland, etc. (see Shinohara 1990: 209–12). Animals too are associated with different parts of the mountains. The wild boar, monkey, and pheasant are traditional farm pests who live in the *sato yama* near the villages. The bear and serow, on the other hand, are animals of the *okuyama*, the remote mountains, and as such are rarely encountered by villagers.

The *yama* is also a place of spirits. While mountains as such have sacred associations in Japan, here too mountain villagers make further distinctions between different parts of the *yama*. The *okuyama* is the abode of dangerous spirits and beings such as fierce-looking demons and tree-dwelling bird-men (*tengu*) found high up near the mountain peaks. There is an overlap between the spirits and the animals of the *okuyama*. In Japan many forest animals are associated with the spirit world as the attendants or messengers of the *kami* spirits. The monkey, for example, was viewed as the mediator between the *yama no kami* (the mountain spirit) and human beings (see Ohnuki-Tierney 1987: 43–45). Images of monkeys, wolves, deer and foxes are to be found at Shinto shrines throughout Japan. The *oku*-dwelling serow is seen as a 'cow demon' (*ushioni*), an animal ghost in the mountains (Kaneko *et al.* 1992: 29).

The traditional characterisation of the *yama* as a wild place in opposition to the village or the plains must be set alongside the fact that parts of the *yama* have long contributed to upland livelihoods. The *yama* was a place of hunting, gathering, farming and forestry, as well as religion, and a highly *differentiated* local knowledge existed of the distribution of plants, animals and spirits within it.

Parts of the *yama* have therefore been incorporated into village life. It does not, however, follow from this that the *yama* was seen as somehow under village control. This could never really be the case because the *yama* was a space of a different order of magnitude from the village. As such, the village remained defensively disposed towards it, routinely preoccupied, for example, with the maintenance of village boundaries. Living in a mountain village, adjacent to the forest, demands an *active* presence that inhibits other, competing forms of life, particularly plant growth. The weeding of village fields forms one front in this struggle. The custom of *michibushin* or village path-clearing undertaken two or three times each year is another. *Michibushin* involves the removal of unwanted plant growth from village paths and the boundary with the forest, while a similar practice takes place in the village cemetery. The *yama* may not be 'wild' in the sense of an environment wholly inhospitable to any human presence in it, yet its association with the mountain spirit and scale difference as a site of organic processes of growth *vis-à-vis* the village make it a dangerous, alien and, ultimately, uncontrollable environment.

GROWING TIMBER

An attempt has been made to bring the *yama* under productive control. In post-war Japan a great expansion in the area of conifer plantations has taken place. The post-war state accorded high priority to restoring the tree cover of the mountainsides after the large scale felling of the pre-war and wartime years. In the post-war years a nationwide afforestation campaign was launched in which special tree-planting days and weeks were designated and annual ceremonies held. A succession of laws were passed promoting afforestation principally through subsidy, but also, if necessary, through compulsion (Fujita 1993: 187, Iguchi 1988: 69–71). There has also been a massive scientific intervention in tree growing through government breeding programmes, the development of chemical fertilisers and pesticides, silvicultural methods, and mechanisation. Against this background of government support, plus the strong demand for wood materials caused by the Korean War and the recovery of the national economy, the prospects for forestry in the 1950s were very promising. This augured well for the future of mountain villagers. Through large-scale, state-supported investment, the mountain forests would become the place of modern, technically advanced, mechanised forest work. The mountain forests would be made more accessible through the development of an enhanced network of roads, the introduction of mechanised saws would increase the efficiency of forest labourers, and advances in science would boost productivity and product quality in forestry. New *industrial* forests would provide forestry jobs for villagers and therefore obviate the need to migrate for work elsewhere.

On the Kii Peninsula timber growing long pre-dated this post-war expansion. Although before the war Japanese timber forestry was largely extractive – involving the felling of primary forest – there also existed regenerative, plantation forestry. If the industrial forest vision is an identifiably post-war one, traditions of timber growing nonetheless existed in the pre-war period and, in some cases, go back much further.[3]

For mountain villagers, growing good timber is a highly prized skill. The term for timber growing is *yamazukuri* – literally, 'mountain-making'. A 'good mountain' (*ii yama*) depends on a number of factors. First of all, north-facing mountainsides make for better timber. Up until the 1950s, it was common to find plantations on north-facing slopes, while the south-facing slopes remained mixed forest. Recently, however, south-facing slopes too have become planted forest. Second, good forest should not be too high up. Up until the 1950s, the timber line did not exceed 800 metres, even for the cypress which is planted higher up the mountainside than the cryptomeria. Now plantations exist even on very high mountainsides.

Successful timber cultivation is a long-term process requiring regular inputs of labour. After the seeds have been gathered, seedlings raised, the soil prepared and the tree saplings planted, at regular intervals the plantation undergrowth of grass and shrubs must be cleared, vine growth such as arrowroot and wisteria removed, and fertiliser and insecticide applied. The growing tree stands should eventually be pruned and thinned. Good *yamazukuri* or forest management is where such care or *te'ire* (literally, 'putting a hand in') has been continuously applied over a fifty- to sixty-year cycle, resulting in the high quality, large diameter, knotless timber suitable for use in building construction.

The length of this production cycle makes *yamazukuri* quite different from *komezukuri* or rice growing. Even though there is no annual harvest, there may nonetheless be an annual appreciation of tree growth. As one retired forest laborer remarked:

> When you have put in a lot of care over many years, affection for the trees is very deep. The enjoyment at looking at each year's growth is very different from that of farm crops which are harvested each year. Instead, you have to wait at least thirty – though on average sixty – years to fell the trees.

(Ue 1984: 17)

This cumulative quality of *yamazukuri* makes trees an important medium for social relations between different generations of villagers, primarily through the family. The Japanese family, known as the *ie*, is ideally a corporate group which continues over time through the succession of the eldest son who co-resides with the parents, ritually cares for the family ancestors, and is responsible for perpetuating the family line down to the next generation. In mountain villages, forest landholdings often form a focal point for these long-term transgenerational family ties.

One large forest landowner in his mid-fifties tends to identify his various mountains according to the ancestor who planted and mostly tended them. At the end of each year, he 'reports' (*hokoku suru*) to the domestic ancestral altar on the plantations felled during the previous year. Most of the felling that occurs, he explains, is of forests planted either by his grandfather or great grandfather (his father died young), and on this end-of-year occasion he expresses his 'gratitude' (*kansha*) for their efforts which have made possible his present-day livelihood, as well as asking for their blessing to ensure that no injuries occur on the family mountains over the coming year.

Family lines other than those of the landowners themselves may also be recognised. In the above example, the father and grandfather of one of the chief forest foremen (*yamaban*) worked with the father and grandfather of the landowner. As his own father died young, the landowner feels particularly close to his foreman's father for this man in effect took on his father's role of passing on *yamazukuri* know-how and details about the various plantations. When the foreman's father died some years ago, the landowner decided to name one of the family mountains after him – the last one which the old man had planted over. To the outsider, aside from their different ages, species and degrees of care, one timber plantation tends to look much like another. But for those who work and manage them, they nonetheless may come to be inscribed with the social relationships that made their successful cultivation possible.

WILD PLANTATIONS?

The post-war vision of the intensive cultivation of the nation's mountain forests has not been fully realised. While the area of *tennenrin* or 'natural forest', already greatly reduced, has diminished further, *jinkōrin* or 'artificial forest' has greatly expanded. In Hongū, where 93 per cent of the land is mountain forest, plantations account for 64 per cent of the forest area, compared with 42 per cent nationally. In turn, 60 per cent of the Hongū plantation area is Japanese cypress and 38 per cent cryptomeria. A great extension of the cultivated area of the forest has taken place, and simultaneous with this change in the natural environment, great social changes have taken place in upland Japan in the post-war period. Large-scale urban outmigration has drastically reduced the population of mountain villages. The population of Hongū fell by well over half between 1955 and 1995.

No attempt is made here to tell the rather more complex story of upland social change in post-war Japan. Two wider national changes should be noted, however. First, in the 1960s the Japanese government removed the ban on wood imports, a move which had an eventual depressing effect on the prices for domestic timber. Second, by the late 1950s a dramatic increase in economic growth in urban Japan transformed the national labour market, exerting a strong pull on the rural population.

Such wider national forces form the background to a particular local experience of change on the part of the mountain villagers of Hongū. As the 1950s vision predicted, it is indeed the new forest which has had the greatest effect on many upland villages in the 1990s. However, for the mountain villagers who live next to it, this forest, far from being the zone of domesticated order originally intended, is a space of radical, multifaceted disorder that threatens the very idea of upland settlement.

Black mountains

The transformation of the earlier mixed woodland into single species timber plantations makes for a strange new landscape. In Hongū a monocultural, rectilinear industrial forest is now the norm. This new forest consists less of trees than of thickening, branchless *trunks* evenly spaced and carefully protected from other forest flora and fauna. This new forest is thus very different from the *zōkibayashi* forest that preceded it, which, typically including deciduous and evergreen, broad-leafed and needle-leafed species, along with a thick undergrowth of weeds and brush, was renowned for its 'dense' (*ussō shita*) quality.

The mountains have been subjected to a thoroughgoing homogenisation. One sign of this is a generalised toponymic obsolescence: local mountains hitherto known for and named after their distinctive patterns of forest growth – 'beech plateau' (*buna no taira*), 'evergreen oakwood mountain' (*kashiomoriyama*), etc. – have all become cypress or cryptomeria forests. The erstwhile altitudinal, areal and species variation of the forest has been lost. The place where Japan's two natural ecologies famously came together is increasingly a place of neither ecology, instead becoming an enormous, monocultural tree farm little different from upland areas throughout the country. The mountain landscape which once contained 'iron trees', 'shallow trees' and 'black trees' now contains 'nothing but black trees' (*kuroki bakari*). Compared with the earlier mixed forest, people complain that these mountains of tall black trees 'feel dark' (*kuraku kanjiru*).

Deterioration

Owing to the state of the market, there is no longer the same economic incentive to tend to the forest that there used to be. This has led many people to sell all or part of their forest land. Others have retained their forests without putting enough care into them, leading to a further loss of value.

Ue points out that most forest landowners are small-scale like him, and cannot make a living full-time from their forests. It is common for such men to work the forests of larger landowners, and return to their own mountains only in their spare time. It is deeply upsetting when he returns to find that the neglect of his own mountains has had irreversible effects. It is as though

you have been occupied with looking after somebody else's child, and have not given enough attention to your own child. When you see the crooked tree, knowing that there is nothing you can do to put it right, you feel nothing but bitterness.

(Ue 1984: 18)

A whole generation of foresters have been in this situation: forced to care for the forests of others to the neglect of their own.

This is also the situation facing the migrant. A key problem in migrant villages like those in Hongū is the neglect of elderly family members that ensues from the migratory displacement of adult children, particularly the first son, the heir, who would otherwise have cared for them. The deleterious effects of this social absence even extend to dead family members. Ancestors without local living descendants to make regular offerings to the family graves are said to become wretched, ghost-like spirits, *muensama*, denied the prospect of progressing to a state of restful buddhahood (*jōbutsu*), and instead condemned to a lonely existence in-between the two worlds.

However, the deleterious consequences of migrant absence are not confined to the social world, but also extend to the natural world. It follows on from the *active* character of the dwelling presence of mountain villagers *vis-à-vis* the natural environment mentioned above that large-scale migrant absence will be expressed in natural (as well as social) disorder. On the one hand, the paths, boundaries and cemeteries of migrant villages are poorly tended and often overgrown, and the village boundary encroached on by the forest. On the other hand, the family forests, planted and tended by a father, even grandfather, will also have suffered neglect in the present generation. Hongū is a place not just of migrant villages but also of *migrant forests*.

Many migrants planted tree saplings upon leaving Hongū in the hope that, with perhaps occasional care thereafter, they would eventually yield a lucrative harvest. Yet for the most part *te'ire*, or regular care, in migrant forests is conspicuously lacking. Migrant forests are thus the saddest sort of forest, poorly tended, unthinned, unpruned, and of greatly diminished market value. Much of this forest is now *senkōrin*, 'incense forest', a forest crowded with thin, weak trees resembling so many incense-sticks stuck into the ground, or again, according to another common expression, *moyashi no yama*, 'a mountain of bean sprouts', where the forest resembles so many sprouts of a soya bean. They are highly vulnerable to damage by snow and wind and, because of the shallowness of their roots, prone to landslides. In the early 1980s it was estimated that more than a third of all plantations in Japan suffered from such neglect (Ue 1984: 21; cf. Ouchi 1988: 48). By 1994, in Hongū at least, the scale of such neglect was deemed much greater. Foresters' estimates of the scale of such neglected forest ranged from half to 90 per cent of all plantations.

In theory, given the long production cycle, the migrant should be able to tend to local trees during his periodic returns to the village, but in practice deterioration often results on account of the inadequacy of interceptive *te'ire*. The forests that emerge are not what was intended, for they bear the durable marks of the other forms of natural growth that have not been impeded. By then, it is too late to do anything about it; a man gets only one chance in life for successful *yamazukuri*. Successful *yamazukuri* is, like 'clean' villages, conditional on local presence. Local absence is a licence for illicit plant growth. Mountains thus tell the story of the villages they surround. Depopulated (*kaso*, literally, sparsely populated) migrant villages tend to be enclosed by (overcrowded, i.e. unthinned) 'incense forests'.

Deterioration may even occur where plantations *are* regularly tended. Deer, serow, bears, hares and wild boar are all serious forest pests (*gaijū*). Bear bark-stripping greatly damages the conifer plantations, leading to defoliation or even the death of the tree. In some areas a majority of the planted trees are affected, leading to great economic loss on the part of the forest landowner. What particularly infuriates landowners is that the bear appears to pick out the best trees in the forest – those maturing trees over twenty years old into which a great deal of labour has already been put (Ue 1983: 362–63). Deer also cause great damage to trees through browsing, bark-stripping, and (with stags) antler cleaning, the effect of which is to retard tree growth, downgrade the quality of timber and diminish its market value, and even cause the death of the tree. The wild boar, too, in its search for arrowroot, lily and bracken roots often creates large holes at the foot of tree stands, something which may cause mature trees eventually to topple over.

A range of measures are employed to minimise this damage, including the burning of animal hair on the plantation (the smell of which keeps animal pests away), the placing of human hair (obtained from the barber) or old clothes on the perimeter of the plantation, modern plantation fencing, battery-powered, scare-noise devices, and pest-extermination programmes. Villagers can now earn money through the hunting and trapping of hares, bears, deer and serow as forest pests, although the protected status of hinds and serow causes great resentment among forest landowners who regularly call for a much larger scale of culling (see, for example, Hirasawa 1985: 57–108).

Encroachment

We have already discussed how the forest has spread to the upper reaches of the mountains. It has also spread in the other direction, and descended the mountains to the very edge of the villages. This new proximity of the forest is a cause of some concern to villagers. The background to this is the shifting geography of upland settlement itself. During this century there has been a gradual change in settlement out of the mountains and towards the main river valleys. As a result, dotted about in the mountains are abandoned villages, which, now overgrown, are said to have 'become mountain' (*yama ni natta*).

The new encroachment of the forest threatens many of the present-day settlements with a similar fate. The first reason for this is that the *satoyama*, the nearby forest, has been turned into timber plantations, and a new, tall, monocultural tree growth has replaced that of an earlier mixed forest. Second, grassland, peripheral rice fields and other fields have been planted over with tree saplings (often by migrants), creating a literal extension of the planted forest. While the intention was that the planted saplings would eventually be felled as timber for a good price, in practice much of this migrant forest, as noted above, has so deteriorated that it is seen as no longer worth harvesting.

The cumulative effect of this trend has been to change the quality of the upland village environment. Migrant villages are, on the whole, *dark* villages. As the mountains are experienced as that much closer, the village becomes, in effect, more *oku* or 'inner' (i.e. remote) in character itself, resembling the more remote abandoned villages that have already been reclaimed by the mountains.

There has long been a tendency for mountain villagers to look downstream, to villages less remote and further away from the mountains than their own. Hence the old expression that 'brides move downstream' (*hanayome wa kawa o kudaru*) (Ue 1984: 209). That the *oku* has never been a desirable place to live is suggested, first, by the refugee origins of many Hongū villages (still commonly cited by villagers), and second, by the fact that local people tend to deny that their village is *oku*, pointing instead to the village further upstream as the *really oku* village. A common local view, however, is that this preference for the downstream, which has become completely freed from logistical control, with the establishment of the road network, has had damaging effects. In Ue's graphic phrase, the neighbouring downstream village has 'turned its back on' the upstream village (Ue 1984: 209–10), and the cumulative effect of this trend has been the radical isolation and extreme depopulation of most *oku* villages.

When represented in this way, the remoteness of upland villages appears to reside in the exogenous forces of urbanisation and downstream bias. What the darkening of the villages due to forest encroachment does is to exacerbate *endogenously* this growing sense of *oku* remoteness. The mountain villages are caught between the lure of the downstream and the tightening grip of the forest.

While forest encroachment affects the village as a whole, it also causes specific damage to village cemeteries, often located on the (upper) edge of the village. The elongating conifer plantations make the graveyard a darker place than before. The plantations form a high, even canopy, creating a uniformly dark forest environment in which undergrowth is largely shaded out. Its new proximity to the forest means that the cemetery comes to share this dark environment. This sort of environment is, however, almost wholly at odds with common local ideas about the normative graveyard environment. In contrast to the cold, dark forest, graves should be in *hiatari no ii tokoro*, 'a place of good sunlight', i.e. a bright location where they can receive direct sunshine.

While villagers refer to the encroachment of the *yama*, it is important to note that the new *yama* is somewhat different from the former. While it is dark, it is not dense. Light is cut down, but there are still clear avenues of space, and, in regularly tended forests, the vegetative density of the mixed forest undergrowth is strikingly absent.

Just as a dark village depresses those who have to live in it, so a dark graveyard is *kimiwarui*, spooky, and highly undesirable for the interred dead. The encroaching plantations may also cause subterranean damage to the village graves, as the roots extend to the buried human remains. As one forester put it, tall trees, like tall people, need to have big feet. Thus the timber plantations that have recently colonised the *satoyama* zone around the villages are seen to have a much greater potential for causing damage to graves than did the earlier proximate mixed forest, which, being regularly cut for fuel wood, did not grow to great heights and therefore did not develop such an extensive root network.

Root damage – especially the penetration of the eye sockets of the skull – is something which is said to greatly disturb the 'sleeping' ancestors, even to the extent of stirring them to cause misfortune to the living descendants who have allowed this situation of extreme posthumous discomfort to arise. In a number of Hongū villages, descendants have taken remedial action by moving the graveyard further into the village (i.e. down the mountainside) into a brighter location clear of the encroaching plantations.

Displacement

The spread of the plantations has major effects on the mountain forests as a whole. It threatens the *tennenrin* or natural forest by extending deep into the mountainous interior. As a result of this ongoing contraction of the area of natural forest, wildlife habitats are eroded, and forest animals find themselves under siege. This altered forest ecology is the background to the reported increase in the damage to farms caused by forest animals in recent years.

Mountain villages have always been vulnerable to such incursions by forest animals, especially the wild boar. So numerous was the boar that it was said to be 'the louse of the mountains' (*yama no shirami*). Ue provides a graphic description of what he calls the 'strategic war' (*kōbōsen*) waged by villagers in earlier decades to defend their farm crops from the autumn invasions of the wild boar, including measures such as regular scare-shouting from the house towards the fields during the night, physically guarding the crops in a field hut, using dogs to guard the crops, leaving oil lamps near the fields, and even building stone 'boar walls' (*shishigaki*) at the perimeter of the village (Ue 1983: 12). In more remote Hongū villages there are wolf shrines at which farmers asked the wolf to protect their fields from boars. The numbers of wild boar have declined, although boar crop damage is still complained about and some farmers still sleep beside their fields (in vans) in the late summer, with their dogs keeping watch over the fields outside. Moreover, crop-raiding by other animals is said to be increasing, and in particular there has been a striking growth in monkey damage (*sarugai*) in recent years. The monkey is known as a traditional thief (*dorobō*) which steals food from humans, but in recent years, as the expansion of the plantations reduces the food available to them, they increasingly come down to the village to feed off persimmon and chestnut trees, rice stalks, mushrooms, sweet potatoes and sweetcorn. Elsewhere there are also reports of the bear becoming a farm pest; although bee-hives are the main target, bears may also opt to feed on the maturing village rice crop (Takahashi 1984: 86–93). Just as the ubiquity of bear damage to the plantations is seen as caused by the displacement of the bear from its high upland habitat by the felling of the upland mixed forest, which causes it to roam the plantations further down the mountains, the descent of the bear to the village is an even starker indication of the *disorder* of the mountains today. The serow – another traditional *oku* dweller – can also be seen near the villages nowadays, a trend also reported in other parts of the country (see Kamata 1992: 17).

The impression is created that the *oku* animals no longer live in the *okuyama*. A migration has taken place *within* the mountains scarcely less momentous than that of the mountain villagers to the cities. Ue makes explicit this parallel:

> For bears and people alike, the place of dwelling has been ruined. Just as the bear must come down from the now bald mountain peak to the plantations, so people must leave the village to work outside.
>
> (Ue 1983: 366–67)

On the one hand, this new ecological disorder mirrors the social disorder of depopulated mountain villages. On the other hand, it exacerbates it: just as the *arboreal* forest is experienced as physically encroaching on the village – threatening to turn it into *yama* – so the village and plantation incursions of the *animal* forest are experienced as undermining the quality of living space.

The sense that the *yama* today has become a place of disorder is further reinforced by the difficulties local people now have in collecting and hunting in the forests. The loss of the forest's natural character is symbolised by the increasing rarity of the pine mushroom (*matsutake*, *Armillaria edodes*). This mushroom lived symbiotically on the roots of the red pine, but in recent years pine rot has seriously affected the number of red pines in the forest. While pine rot is recognised, local people nonetheless tend to associate the decline of the red pines and the prized *matsutake* with the growth of the plantations.[4] Hunters complain about the difficulty of finding game animals in their traditional locations. Certain animals can now be hunted only in very remote *okuyama*. Others, such as the pheasant, now have to be released annually (in the summer) prior to the hunting season.

The spread of the timber plantations may also be seen as affecting the quality of the forest animals. Thus Nomoto reports that other villagers in the region claim that the wild boar they catch in the plantation areas of the forest are smaller and do not taste as good as those they catch in the natural forest (Nomoto 1990: 64). A similar sentiment is to be found in Hongū. Hongū hunters tend to distinguish the good-tasting 'hill boar' (*okashishi*) from the poor-tasting 'valley boar' (*tanishishi*) on the grounds that while the former feed on the nuts and berries of the mixed forest (especially *shiiyama*, forest with many chinquapin trees), the latter feed only on worms, insects and small crabs. The colonisation of the south-facing mountainsides (many of which were known as *shiiyama*) by timber plantations since the 1950s has reduced precisely that habitat which makes for good-tasting wild boar. Not only do the mountains look different with the spread of 'black trees'. They taste different too.

CONCLUSION

In this chapter a formerly domesticated environment has been shown to be experienced as a site of disorder. Instead of the high-grade timber that should have been produced, inadequate care has resulted in low-grade wood unsuitable for the building purpose for which it was intended. This deficient timber crop gives expression to the dishevelled upland social order in which it was produced. In this longest of production cycles, productive control over timber is correlated with intergenerational continuity of the family. To the extent that the family is strong, forestry will be socially encompassed. The disruption of this continuity undermines productive control. As a consequence, the timber stands today represent a *partial* product: the product of human labour, but also of the partiality of its application. The productive efforts of one generation have not been consummated by those of later generations.

Consequently, the normative correlation between tree growth and village prosperity no longer applies. Owing to the deficit of human care applied to it, the tree growth that ought to have expressed a new era of upland prosperity is of an inferior quality and therefore low market value. This post-war tree growth instead takes on a rather different significance. The new forest inverts the correlation between tall trees and rich villages through a number of negative environ-mental effects. If the post-war trend in timber growing, promoted by the state as the economic foundation of an upland modernity, has created a new forest environment, it is one still able to evoke the dangers associated with the *yama*. An ostensibly industrial forest, instead of conferring a new level of material prosperity on the villages, increasingly darkens, invades and encroaches on them. The cultivated forest that the post-war state promised would enrich upland villages now threatens to reclaim them. If the *yama* has always, in some sense, threatened upland settlement with such a fate, the difference today is that this process occurs with a novel, industrial intensity.

NOTES

1   *Yama no kigi ga sukusuku sodatsu to mura wa yutaka ni naru.*
2   Fieldwork was carried out in the mountain village area of Hongū, located on the Kii Peninsula in central Japan, for a twenty-seven-month period between 1987 and 1989 and again for five weeks in the autumn of 1994. The theme of the earlier research was rural depopulation. Upland Japan has been subject to large-scale outmigration since the mid-1950s, resulting in widespread depopulation. Subsequently, research has centred on the way in which this social trend in the villages has been experienced through changes in the surrounding forest. Those who worked in the forests have thus formed one of the main objects of investigation.
3   The Kii Peninsula has its own strong tradition of plantation forestry associated with the Yoshino region to the north. Yoshino forestry developed in the seventeenth century and is distinguished by a highly intensive method of planting and frequent thinning.
4   Fukuoka (1985: 28–29) also argues for such a connection, pointing out that when an area of forest is clear-felled and planted over with cryptomeria trees, small birds will no longer find enough food and will tend to disappear. The disappearance of small birds, in turn, allows the long-horned beetles to flourish, and it is these beetles which are the vectors for the nematodes which attack the red pines. Ichikawa and Saito (1985: 112), on the other hand, stress the dearth of fallen leaves caused by the spread of the plantation as the key factor in the present-day rarity of *matsutake*. The Japanese mountain forests are no longer able fully to supply the seasonal national market for pine mushrooms, and pine mushrooms are now imported annually from South Korea.

REFERENCES

Berque, A. (1986) *Le Sauvage et L'Artifice: Les Japonais devant la Nature*, Paris: Gallimard.
Chase, A. K. (1989) 'Domestication and Domiculture in Northern Australia: A Social Perspective', in David R. Harris and Gordon C. Hillman (eds) *Foraging and Farming: The Evolution of Plant Exploitation*, London: Unwin Hyman.
Fujita, Y. (1993) 'Modern Development of Afforestation in Japan: Process and Results', in A. Mather (ed.) *Afforestation: Policies, Planning and Progress*, London: Belhaven.

Fukuoka, M. (1985) *The Natural Way of Farming: The Theory and Practice of Green Philosophy*, Tokyo: Japan Publications.

Harris, D. R. (1989) 'An Evolutionary Continuum of People–Plant Interactions', in David R. Harris and Gordon C. Hillman (eds) *Foraging and Farming: The Evolution of Plant Exploitation*, London: Unwin Hyman.

Hirasawa, M. (1985) *Kieyuku Yasei to Shizen (Disappearing Wild Nature)*, Tokyo: San'ichi Shobō.

Ichikawa, T and Saitō I. (1985) *Saikō. Nihon no Shinrin Bunkashi (The History of Japanese Forest Culture Reconsidered)*, Tokyo: NHK Books.

Iguchi, T. (1988) 'Afforestation Policies of the Post-World War II Period', in R. Handa (ed.) *Forest Policy on Japan*, Tokyo: Nippon Ringyō Chōsakai.

Kalland, A. (1992) 'Culture in Japanese Nature', in O. Bruun and A. Kalland (eds) *Asian Perceptions of Nature*, Copenhagen: Nordic Proceedings in Asian Studies No.3, NIAS.

Kamata, K. (1992) 'Kumagera no Sumu Hayashi o Mamoru' (Protecting the Forest Where the Black Woodpecker Lives), in M. Nebuka (ed.) *Mori o Kangaeru (Considering the Woodlands)*, Tokyo: Tachikaze Shobo.

Kaneko, H., Konishi, M., Sasaki, K, and Chiba, T. (1992) *Nihonshi no Naka no Dobutsu Jiten (A Dictionary of Animals in Japanese History)*, Tokyo: Tōyōdō Shuppan.

Nomoto, K. (1990) *Kumano Sankai Minzokukō (A Treatise on the Mountain and Coastal Folk Customs of Kumano)*, Kyōto: Jinbun Sho'in.

Ohnuki-Tierney, E. (1987) *The Monkey as Mirror*, Princeton, NJ: Princeton University Press.

Ouchi, Y. (1988) 'Development of the Forest Plan System', in R. Handa (ed.) *Forest Policy on Japan*, Tokyo: Nippon Ringyō Chosakai.

Shinohara, T. (1990) *Shizen to Minzoku: Shin'i no Naka no Doshokubutsu (Nature and Folk Customs: Animals and Plants of the Heart)*, Tokyo: Nihon Editāsukuru Shuppanbu.

Smith, H. (1979) 'Tokyo and London: Comparative Conceptions of the City', in A. M. Craig (ed.) *Japan: A Comparative View*, Princeton, NJ: Princeton University Press.

Takahashi, Y. (1984) *Inakagurashi no Tankyū (Investigating Country Life)*, Tokyo: Soshisha.

Totman, C. (1989) *The Green Archipelago: Forestry in Preindustrial Japan*, Berkeley: University of California Press.

Ue, T. (1983) *Yamabito no Dōbutsushi (A Mountain Villager's Record of Animals)*, Tokyo: Fukuinkan Shoten.

—— (1984) *Yama no Kino Hitorigoto (The Soliloquy of Mountain Trees)*, Tokyo: Shinjuku Shobō.

—— (1989) *Ki no Kuni Kibun (Notes from the Tree Country)*, Tokyo: Shinjuku Shobō.

—— (1994) *Mori no Megumi (The Blessing of the Forest)*, Tokyo: Iwanami Shinsho.

Yukawa, Y. (1988) 'Sato ni Chikazuku Yama: Shiba Mura Omae no Minzoku Hen'yō' (Mountain Descends to the Village: The Transformation of Folkways in Omae, Shiba Village), *Kokuritsu Rekishi Minzoku Hakubutsukan Kenkyu Hokoku* 18: 341–68.

Chapter 13

Xenotransplantation and transgenesis

Im-moral stories about human–animal relations in the West

Eleni Papagaroufali

PIGS FOR THE DESCENDANTS

Western societies tend to treat 'human' and 'animal' as discontinuous and mutually exclusive concepts. The distinctive feature between the two 'worlds' has been the actual and potential possession of mind or 'reason'. Unlike humans, animals and the rest of non-human nature are seen as devoid of rationality. In practice, this anthropocentric stance means that animals are not able to achieve moral goods intentionally, that is, they cannot create culture and, therefore, ought not be granted 'rights' or the status of moral agents (Haraway 1989; Willis 1990; Ingold 1994).

During the last two decades, westerners' certainty of what counts as 'human' and 'animal' nature seems to have been challenged by biotechnological practices, such as xenotransplantation and transgenesis: xenotransplantation involves the transplantation of animal organs and tissues to terminally ill humans. Clinical research includes renal, liver and heart transplants from chimpanzee and baboon donors to humans; basic research involves organ and tissue transplantation from primate to primate, and from pig to baboon, or to mice and other small animals. Transgenesis, on the other hand, entails gene transfers from humans to animals and vice versa. Transgenic manipulations of animals include researchers' plans to insert parts of human genes into fertilised sow eggs to create 'transgenic pigs'. The idea is then to mate these designer pigs to create pigs with human-ready organs and bridge the gap between 'supply' and 'demand' of organs. At the same time, research entailing gene transfers from animals to humans is also included in such plans. Biologists have promoted these experiments in order to overcome rejection of animal organs by human recipient organisms (e.g. Hanson 1992; Cooper 1992; Najarian 1992; Niekrasz *et al.* 1992).

In my attempt to approach transgenesis and xenotransplantation anthropologically, I have realised that such phenomena cause humans to fear that their common human nature, and capacities considered unique to it, might be eliminated. Reactions to this concern include various re-classifications of the criteria that make up human versus animal nature(s), as well as re-evaluations of human–animal relations. Most often, responses of this kind are 'morally' justified through the use of western key-values and related 'projects', such as development, progress, civilisation, domestication. Yet it is an anthropological commonplace that such projects constitute age-old, western and appropriationist, rather 'immoral', tactics against beings considered 'other' – for example, animals and humans in an animal-like state. Through these tactics, the 'other' is subordinated to the 'self' in order to reproduce the original image of the 'same', or the 'one', who is (hu-)Man, of western origin (Haraway 1991: 226–28; see also Wagner 1975; Sahlins 1976; Jordanova 1980; MacCormack 1980).

In this study, I have looked for such morally justified classifications produced by scientific and popular discourses, concerning xenotransplantation and transgenesis, in societies considered 'developed', that is western Europe and the United States, and 'less developed', in this case, Greece. The comparison between the two contexts purports to reveal historically and culturally specific traits of the Greek case, which constitutes the main part of this presentation.

Members of both 'developed' and 'less developed' societies prove to be similar in their effort to reproduce, by any means, stories of an imagined original wholeness seen as unique to humans. Yet disparities between the two contexts, in terms of economic and technological 'development', reveal differences in interpretations concerning the two biomedical practices and underlying conceptions about nature. Indeed, nature, animal or human, is shown to be constructed, and contested, through taxonomies crafted on the basis of historically and culturally specific interests – projected as progressive and, therefore, morally justified. The point this chapter tries to make is that the stories[1] – scientific and popular – westerners tell about themselves and animals are determined by historically specific power relations that develop on a daily basis, within and between nations.

SPECIES BOUNDARIES, BORDERS OF VALUE

Xenotransplantation and transgenesis take place in western Europe and the United States. When it comes to xenotransplantation, western European and American scientists are divided into two broad categories: first, physicians and bioethicists who suggest that great apes and other 'higher' animals should be killed 'humanely' to benefit humans 'who are as a species of more moral worth than are animals' (e.g. Martin 1990; Reemtsma 1990; Caplan 1992). Second, physicians and animal philosophers who argue that, instead of using non-human primates as sources of organs, surgeons should use humans who do not possess – actually or potentially – cognitive and emotional capacities that would make it possible for them to lead individual lives, and, who, therefore, could be considered as less intellectually developed than gorillas and chimpanzees. Inefficient humans suggested to replace primates include those in a state of brain death, as well as anencephalic, comatose, and cortically dead infants (e.g. Kushner and Belliotti 1985; Francione 1990; Singer 1992; Regan 1993).

Taxonomies that stem from the second position are variable. Although they revolve around the basic distinction between animal and human species, classifications are based on the degree of cognition shared by sub-categories of both species – cognition being measured by human standards. Thus, in some cases, inefficient humans, e.g. anencephalic infants, constitute a category of their own, inferior to the one that includes normal or mentally retarded humans and great apes, as well as to the one including 'lesser forms of life' (e.g. fish, reptiles). The moral principle underlying these classifications is that a living being is worthy of protection only if it has some capacity for the self-awareness that makes individual life possible. In other cases, humans who live 'vegetative' lives are classified on a par with plants and/or the 'lower' animals (e.g. insects and worms) that are not attributed with 'individuality' or moral status and are therefore 'replaceable'. The moral principle underlying these classifications is that 'Pigs have rights, but lettuces [and cognitively lower beings] don't' (Singer 1992: 730). The debates between representatives of the two positions are fierce. Public opinion tends to support the latter one: large-scale movements of animal rights activists as well as of vegetarians and ecologists in western Europe and the USA are well known for long-standing fights against researchers.

At first sight, transgenesis, unlike xenotransplantation, involves no species barriers. Molecular biologists view 'species' as heuristic scientific devices, or historical rather than naturally existing entities (e.g. Singleton *et al*.1994). According to them, all living organisms are part of an interwoven 'net' of living beings formed by evolution. Moreover, all living organisms use and are used by other organisms. Moral philosophers have welcomed this stance as anti-anthropocentric: 'Nature as Other is over' exclaims Callicott, professor of philosophy and natural resources (1992: 16).

Yet, despite this egalitarian image of the universe, people involved with transgenesis, like those involved with xenotransplantation, feel the need to name the unmarked human place in nature and describe the equally unmarked nature of human society (Haraway 1991: 93, Midgley 1994: 33). To accomplish this, both philosophers and biologists resort mainly to the image of anthropoid apes: The former describe humans – members of the 'net' – as 'monkeys' that are nevertheless 'big', 'smart', and 'precocious'. The latter, in their effort to prove that transgenesis is an old phenomenon of natural evolution and to justify recent humanly directed transgenesis, stress the genetic similarities between humans and chimpanzees. At the same time, they stress the characteristics unique to humans: in particular, they are considered the only organisms aware of this fabric of nature. Consequently, humans are expected to have the 'moral' obligation to protect and promote knowledge about organisms living 'in the wild', especially great apes who resemble humans phenotypically and genetically, and constitute 'the best sources of scientific clues to human origins and human societal characteristics' (McCarthy and Ellis 1994: 28).

Activists, as well as lawyers and environmental policy makers, are opposed to most transgenic manipulations, especially those entailing the transfer of animal genes into humans – rather than the reverse. They are also worried about the possibility of transgenic organisms being released 'in the wild' and alteration of the 'original' state of the ecosystem (ibid.).

Going through all these different positions, one can notice that although most classifications reveal the fuzziness of 'species' borders, all of them project, implicitly or explicitly, human mental capacities as unique in the universe: living organisms who do not possess reason are classified as 'lower' (regardless of the 'species' they belong to), whereas those who do, even partially (e.g. apes), are classified as 'higher'. Given this evaluation, baboons and chimpanzees are presented as the main source of information about the 'original' state of human nature, the one recognised as pre-social, non-rational and 'wild'. Although this animal-like aspect of human nature is usually rejected (MacCormack 1980; Midgley 1994), its relationship to ape nature is continuously preserved through scientific and popular stories, due to its usefulness: it serves as a secular origin myth for westerners and a moral justification for western scientists' developmental projects, such as xenotransplantation and transgenesis.

GREEK CONCEPTIONS OF RELATIONS TO ANIMALS: PLATONISM, ANTHROPOCENTRISM, HELLINO-CENTRISM

In Greece, one is faced with a rather indifferent attitude to issues concerning animals. The country's 'peripheral' role in scientific research is also expressed by its age-old abstinence from projects promoting the study of human and animal species (see Krimbas 1986, 1993). In fact, Greeks, unlike Euro-Americans, have not been interested in explaining human biological and societal origins through the comparison of humans with animals. On the contrary, Darwinism, neo-Darwinism, sociobiology, as well as ethological and animal psychological theories have ranged from little known to inimical.

According to Krimbas, Greeks, in their effort to define their national identity on the basis of their ancient Greek heredity, have always been platonic, anthropocentric and Hellino-centric, or in other words, negative to natural theories that challenge stories with predefined and foreseen beginnings and endings (ibid.). Indeed, Greeks tend to be concerned more about their historical origins as Greeks than their biological origins as humans. At the same time, they tend to (pre-)define their future evolution in terms involving the protection and preservation (in opposition to change, promotion, and development) of the present state of things.

These tendencies can be discerned in Greek attitudes toward xenotransplantation and transgenesis and underlying conceptions of human–animal nature. The two biomedical practices have only recently been known to the public and their scientific implementation is either non-existent (xenotransplantation) or very limited (transgenesis). Reactions to such foreign phenomena include scattered opinions of physicians and animal rights activists publicised in the form of newspaper articles – as opposed to extensive literature based on locally produced scientific and popular debates.

Greek physicians take a rather negative stance on xenotransplantation and transgenesis: apart from questioning the possibility of developing solid legal and ethical support for such practices (Domenikou 1991), many view such animal experiments as anti-scientific (meaning that such experiments are artificially altering established natural laws), species-ist, and inhumane (Charitakis 1992). The majority, especially those involved in human heart transplantation,[2] consider them 'ineffective' and certainly 'not feasible for countries such as Greece', meaning countries that 'have always followed pan-European scientific achievements instead of experimenting on their own' (Mandros and Kordatos 1991: 52). Given the shortage of human organs, physicians are projecting human living donation, and most of all, artificial organ transplantation, as the only scientifically feasible solutions (ibid.: 58).

Similar attitudes are also shared by animal rights associations, only recently established in Greek cities, on a very small scale. Based on the principle that animals, like humans, feel pain, activists view xenotransplantation and transgenic manipulations of animals as immoral practices that violate animal rights. In fact, the lack of such phenomena in Greece is considered an example of moral superiority on the part of Greeks. According to the president of the Confederation of Greek Animal Rights Associations, also a veterinarian, 'it is more useful to find out about our history than spend the country's money on monkeys' (personal communication).

The activities of Greek animal rights movements in cities include small-scale street protests and prosecutions against practices such as conducting medical experiments with animals, especially when those involve stray dogs and cats;[3] killing stray dogs, instead of finding a person to 'adopt' them; torturing animals in zoos and circuses; abusing pedigree dogs in 'upper-class circles'. According to the President of the Ecological and Animal Rights Union of Greece, most of these practices are not only 'unnatural' but 'foreign', imported from abroad; they are 'age-old habits developed by European (mainly English) colonisers to exploit both humans and animals, either by killing them for profit, or by exposing them, side by side, for pleasure and prestige' (personal communication). This interpretation is implicitly associated with a negative stance towards activities sponsored by foreign animal organisations in Greece, involving the 'racist' and 'elitist' protection of only certain animals

– e.g. turtles, bears, wolves. A similar view can be elicited from Greek Orthodox Church representatives – priests and theologians. Although they support human organ transplantation they oppose xenotransplantation and, especially, transplantation of transgenic human-like organs, because their neo-evolutionist background is considered incompatible with 'the Greek Orthodox Christian spirit' (Karoussos 1987: 46).

At this point, it should be obvious that Greeks, unlike Euro-Americans, are not so intensively and extensively involved with animals, especially 'higher' ones. The absence of apes from the picture seems to reinforce platonic distinctions between human and animal species. Indeed, Greek physicians, as well as activists, and, in particular, church representatives, seem to be concerned more with the preservation of species borders than the breaking of them – though each for different reasons. By the same token, Greeks, unlike Euro-Americans, are not interested in protecting or promoting knowledge about the 'wild' aspect of nature – including human nature – especially the one located in 'exotic' places. On the contrary, both researchers and activists focus on the already known, 'domesticated' environment, that is, on the 'Greek' milieu. The next two sections constitute an attempt to illustrate better the Greek case.

GREEK STRUGGLES AGAINST WORMS

The individuals with whom I discussed xenotransplantation and transgenesis are urban, middle-class, well-educated men and women, aged from the mid-twenties to mid-forties. Most of them are prospective organ or body donors, and have, therefore, developed a special sensitivity to transplantation matters.[4] Both donors and non-donors were well informed about human and artificial organ transplantation, mainly through the mass media. They were less cognisant of xenotransplantation and even less so of transgenic manipulations. Our conversations revolved around the broad question of whether, if they found themselves in a state of terminal illness, they would consent to become recipients of either human, animal, or artificial organs, in order to prolong their lives. No one responded negatively. On the contrary, they all said they would definitely prefer to survive by any means rather than experiencing 'an undignified end', that is, 'being eaten up by dirty worms down there'. These people, while still alive and healthy, already experienced feelings such as pain and shame (i.e. 'loss of human dignity') caused by an imagined struggle against worms. All of a sudden, earthworms, creatures that, compared to humans, are considered of a 'lesser' status in all aspects (cognitively, emotionally, morally), surfaced as the biggest enemies of humans.

More concretely, those who have agreed to donate their organs 'after death' said they have done so because they are appalled by the idea of 'experiencing a death which has such an undignified end'. For these people, bodies devoid of organs become 'empty shells': they have neither senses nor soul nor personality elements. Therefore, when buried 'they would not suffer from being eaten by dirty worms'. Donors of the whole body (to the Medical School) and non-donors also shared these opinions. The former said they had chosen this kind of 'end after death', because they could not stand the idea of being buried and devoured by worms. They believed that through body donation they resisted a 'custom' – that is, burial required by the Church – which is 'insulting to the human personality'. The latter (non-donors) also justified their consent to organ reception through transplantation by their 'fear to be eaten up by filthy worms'. They believed that refusal of this last chance to go on living would equal their 'surrender' to worms, 'those shameless little creatures who wait down there like Charon to devour human flesh'.

It should not come as a surprise that all three categories of discussants (organ donors, body donors, non-donors) said – without having been asked – that they would have preferred their bodies to be cremated rather than buried and exposed to scavenging worms. Cremation – an institution disapproved of by the Greek Orthodox Church[5] – is seen as a 'dignified end after death', because the deceased has a 'fast end', and 'ashes cannot become food for worms'. My interlocutors' fear of being eaten up echoes the death imagery found in Greek funeral laments, still sung in many Greek villages by elderly women. In these age-old, mostly improvised, songs the corpse is depicted as 'food' eaten by the earth, or by Charon, or by animals living outside the grave (e.g. scavengers, blackbirds) or inside the earth, such as snakes, scorpions and worms (Danforth 1982: 101–2, Seremetakis 1991: 185). Given this imagery, death, contrary to Christian views of a rewarding after life, won through patience and perseverance, is marked by darkness, fear, and despair (Danforth 1982: 60; Caraveli 1986: 184; Seremetakis 1991: 185).

Despite their urban background, my interlocutors seem to share the same age-old images of, and feelings about death. Yet, perhaps because of this background, they cannot wait for relatives' lamentation as a form of protest after their death. Faster forms of protest or resistance, ones that anticipate, even prevent, consumption of their bodies by animals, have dominated these urbanite imaginations: prospective organ or body donation, support of cremation, as well as consent to organ reception are but imagined resistance in an imagined – though painfully experienced – struggle between humans and animals, in this case, between Greek urbanities and Greek earthworms!

HUMAN-MADE MACHINES AND HUMANS AGAINST ANIMALS

Given my interlocutors' fear of their body decomposition through consumption by the 'worms of Hades', it should be expected that they would have a positive stance towards transplantation in general, since its purpose is to prolong life and/or postpone death. Yet serious differences surfaced when discussants were called upon to imagine which kind of transplants they would choose for themselves: human – cadaveric or living – organs; animal organs – coming either from normal or transgenic organisms; or artificial ones. This hypothetical question included another hypothesis as well, namely that all kinds of transplants would have equal chances of success or failure. [6]

Apart from a few (they were all prospective organ donors) who would accept 'any sort' of transplant 'as long as their body and soul were saved', the rest could be divided into three categories. Most numerous proved to be those who would prefer artificial over animate organs – human or animal ones of any kind. These people were against killing animals 'to extract only one organ'. Also, they were afraid that human cadaveric or living organs could have been provided by Third World people in need of money, or executed prisoners, or mentally retarded humans. Cadaveric human organs coming from humans in brain death[7] or anencephaly, as well as living ones coming from relatives, were equally out of question, out of fear that the relatives of the donors as well as living donors might 'give them a hard time' by intervening in their lives.

Parallel to these 'rational' justifications, there was disgust felt for any dead or living body part 'full of disgusting fluids', as well as mistrust for these 'pieces of meat' coming either from previously 'inefficient' beings – e.g. anencephalics – or healthy ones but already 'used' and probably 'worn out'. In contrast, artificial organs would be 'clean', 'brand new' – 'like my new pair of glasses' – , 'better monitored', therefore, 'more trustworthy', and 'definitely much closer to living humans, compared to animal or human dead ones'.

Next, in terms of numbers, comes the category of those who 'would have never chosen organs coming from animals', particularly not from genetically altered ones. For these people, animals are 'very different from humans': they are 'inferior creatures to humans, in all aspects' and 'rather disgusting'. For some, accepting animal organs in order to survive was also considered 'insulting to human nature'. Genetically engineered animal donors were also rejected: 'The last thing I want in this short life of mine is to have a monster inside me and perhaps become one,' said one man, laughing loudly. 'These are not natural things,' he added, displaying anger, disgust and horror. Those individuals would rather let doctors decide whether to transplant human or artificial organs. The latter were seen as of equal worth or equally 'close to human nature'. In fact, they would have preferred them to cadaveric human organs, because they would not stem from dead persons.

The high degree of 'naturalness', attributed to artificial organs, by this and the previous category of donors, is based on the fact that they – unlike animals – are constructed by humans. Moreover, confidence is placed in the familiarity of humans – 'at least westerners' – with technology: glasses and contact lenses, drugs, dental seals, pace-makers, intrauterine and prosthetic devices were referred to as cases in which 'artefacts' not only substitute but become human nature. Moreover, the less visible such artefacts are, the more natural they are perceived to become.

Last comes the least numerous category of those who would not have chosen artificial organs – as opposed to animate ones. For these individuals, 'artificial organs have no soul', therefore 'life that comes from animate organs is superior to [life-sustaining] technology'. For some, choosing artificial organs is equated with 'playing God'; in other words, the choice of animate organs – human or animal – 'keeps humans at the level to which they belong'. These individuals said they would let surgeons decide which kind of organ – human or animal – would finally be used. They conceived of both as equally close to human nature due to their possession of 'soul'.[8] The latter is considered necessary for 'better communication' between donors and recipients both before and after the operation. For that matter, though, pets were viewed as better sources of organs than baboons and chimpanzees. Pets and humans are closer to each other, therefore they communicate – and will communicate – better, whereas baboons and chimpanzees are strangers – at least to Greeks.

The same line of thought pervades the distinction between organs donated by living donors as opposed to cadaveric ones. The latter would not have been chosen because they are dead, and thus have no soul; also, there would not have been any previous communication with these donors, when they were alive, because they were strangers. In contrast, living donors, usually close relatives or close friends, are like pets, very familiar, not strangers. Consequently, recipients will be able to communicate with organs equally well as they could with their donors.

At this point, it is worth noting that people of this category were more concerned, even worried, than the others, about the organs coming from genetically altered animals. They gave two reasons for this attitude. First, they saw such organs as 'too artificial, more artificial than artificial organs', therefore, 'completely devoid of soul'. Artificial organs, in comparison with transgenic organs, are seen as 'having more of a soul, metaphorically speaking', because they have 'a direct connection to human hands and mind'; by contrast, in transgenic organisms (and organs) it is 'genes' that 'do the job' through the 'mediation' rather than 'direct' intervention of humans. The fear that their own genetic code might change through accepting this 'thing' inside them, was projected as the second reason for denying this possible choice. Paraphrasing the words of all individuals belonging to this category: genes, like dead donors, like chimpanzees and baboons are (seen as) 'strangers'. The closer one stays to what is more or less 'familiar', the closer one is to one's own nature and self, and the safer, more 'intact' this nature remains.

'HIGHER' ANIMALS, 'LOWER' HUMANS

Common to all the people with whom I discussed xenotransplantation and transgenesis was the conviction that if their life and personality are to be 'prolonged', they must accord with a specific kind (or definition) of nature, which, in their case, is equated with anything familiar, as opposed to foreign. Familiar (or natural) things are perceived as having 'soul' or some other kind of force, that will be transmitted into their terminally ill bodies and 'reanimate', or 'resurrect' them in this life. In fact my interlocutors' preferences parallel those found in the more general context of Greece. Most of them share the Greek physicians' support for artificial substitutes and for human (vs. animal), living (vs. cadaveric) donations. The majority are opposed to animal donations on the basis of views shared by the Greek Church, Greek animal rights activists and many physicians. Finally, those who would accept animal organs show the same preferences as Greek animal rights activists and researchers for 'lower', in particular 'domesticated', 'naturally' living animals (as opposed to transgenic organisms that are seen as 'unnatural').

All these classifications and evaluations (general and particular) lead to two significant realisations. First, that nature, for Greeks, is restricted to what is available in the Greek market (including imported products) and can be consumed (Strathern 1992 makes this point for English people). Hence the variability of definitions of the natural. Yet preferences shown towards one sort of nature (or commodity) over another – e.g. artificial over human/animal – point to a second realisation: that nature is not only variously defined (thus constructed) but contested by Greeks – and likewise by Euro-Americans – leading to the reproduction of the 'original sacred image of the same', or the 'familiar', that is, of the 'whole', or 'complete', or 'efficient' Man – preferably of a Greek origin. It is on the basis of the definition of nature as sameness or familiarity, as well as of completeness or efficiency, that my interlocutors exclude donors who live like vegetables (cases of brain death and anencephaly); feel aversion to animal donors coming from 'exotic' savannahs and jungles, or 'who knows from where' (the case of transgenic animals); avoid and question the quality of organs stemming from people considered 'marginals' (Third World living-organ sellers, executed prisoners, mentally retarded individuals). These exclusions should be seen as part of the classificatory, evaluative, contest-producing process of subordinating the 'other' to the 'same'. When the 'other' is 'altered', 'developed', 'domesticated', 'protected', even 'received' into one's own body – so as to become same/familiar – 'something else' is excluded, evaluated as not natural/familiar/same.

Yet the kinds of 'others', and the tactics chosen to subordinate them to the 'same' or the 'familiar', seem to be analogous to the 'degree' of development – or completeness or efficiency – of the specific context within which such processes take place. In the 'developed' Euro-American context, the role of the 'other' is played by both 'lower' and 'higher' animals, in particular anthropoid apes but also 'ape-like', i.e. mentally inefficient, humans. Western Europeans and Americans have the economic and political power to initiate developmental projects and thereby experiment with and produce the 'novel' and the 'non-familiar' – human-like machines included. Moreover, they present these novelties as 'natural' steps to the evolution, development or progress of Man, and 'familiarise' people *a priori* with their future 'adaptationist' moves. Hominids were shown to play a major role in such evolutionary explanations. Due to their biological similarities with humans, they are constantly used by western scientists to show the western public the state or stage – socioeconomic, political, cultural – in which they would have remained, had they not adopted the developmental projects produced by their countries – in this case xenotransplantation and transgenesis.

In the 'less developed' Greek context, the role of the 'other' is played only by 'lower' animals (from worms to pets) and machines. The former is found within the Greek milieu: it exemplifies and invigorates the platonic, anthropocentric and Hellino-centric nature of Greek relations to 'others', in this case animals. The latter is imported from abroad – and paid for by the European Union's economic assistance to Greece. It is used for the preservation and protection of the present (and future) state of human nature; at the same time, it exemplifies and reinforces the peripheral and dependent nature of Greek relations with Euro-Americans.

The absence of great apes from Greek researchers' and activists' scientific and moral concerns signals the country's lack of economic and political power, necessary for the 'subordination' of 'higher' animals. Greeks, like the inhabitants of 'undeveloped' countries, the home of the great apes, are more interested in the preservation of their national origins than in the study of human origins and the degree to which humans have evolved or 'developed' in divergence from their hominid cousins.

Meanwhile, the European Union cautions Greece that, unless it participates more 'aggressively' in the Europeans' economic and technological struggle against America and Japan, it will be considered 'less' of a member of the Union, meaning that it will be excluded from the Union's activities. The moral justification underlying this classification is that Greece insists on remaining 'peripheral' to the Union's project of 'developmental convergence' (Roumeliotis 1992). In animal terminology, this warning means that, unless Greeks develop relations with 'higher' animals (in addition to worms, pets and stray dogs), they, themselves, will be classified and/or evaluated as 'lower' animals, that is, deprived of 'rights' or the status of moral agents.

Molecular biologists warn us (Singleton *et al.* 1994: 11) that from prokaryotes to humans, we are all only somebody's next meal. Perhaps, this time (the end of twentieth century) Greeks should listen to them. If, at least, they complemented their stories about ancient Greek origins with stories about their origins from chimpanzees, Greeks might become 'wilder' and 'higher', i.e. more European.

NOTES

1   The concept of 'story' is used to stress the narrative, thus orderly, contest-resolving, morality-based, nature of truth claims, made by both laymen and scientists, while representing reality (White 1981) – in this case human and animal nature(s). It is a useful concept for the location of the diverse interpretive versions of phenomena, seemingly governed by 'natural', thus 'objective' and fixed 'laws'.

2   In Greece, human organ and tissue transplantations were initiated in the late 1960s, in a limited number of hospital centres. The first human heart transplantation was undertaken in 1990 whereas the first artificial heart implantation was attempted – and failed – in 1994.

3   In Greece, research with animals is mainly conducted on mice, hamsters, dogs, cats, rabbits, pigs and sheep. A large proportion of dogs were found to be strays (Charitakis 1992).

4   This chapter constitutes part of a wider project on human organ and body donation in Greece. It is based on interviews and long conversations with twenty-five individuals living in the city of Athens. Non-donors include people who have a more or less 'special' relationship with animals, e.g. hunters and pet-owners.

5   Although cremation is legal, such practice is not accepted by the Orthodox Church. It is believed that cremation goes against Christian belief and hope of resurrection (Lekkou 1994: 9, 11).

6   Although it may sound exaggerated to push a hypothetical question thus far, it must be understood that these hypotheses are based on facts: physicians are still experimenting with all three kinds of transplants. On the one hand, human transplants have not turned out to be as successful as was hoped by both physicians and the public. On the other, the shortage of human transplants has contributed to impressive progress in clinical and basic research on animal and artificial transplants.

7   According to research conducted in Greek city hospitals, medical doctors, nurses, and medical students are not only poorly informed about brain death definition but unwilling to face this reality (Dardavessis et al. 1989).

8   Both those interviewees who believe in some sort of an 'after life' (the majority), and those who do not, identify 'soul' with concepts such as 'energy' or 'power', 'spirit' or 'volition', 'feelings', 'consciousness'. All of them are perceived as 'forces' that constitute or sustain life, including life after death.

REFERENCES

Callicott, B. J. (1992) 'La Nature est Morte, Vive la Nature!', *Hastings Center Report* 22, 5: 16–23.

Caplan, A. L. (1992) 'Is Xenografting Morally Wrong?', *Transplantation Proceedings* 24, 2: 722–27.

Caraveli, A. (1986) 'The Bitter Wounding: The Lament as Social Protest in Rural Greece', in J. Dubisch (ed.) *Gender and Power in Rural Greece*, Princeton, NJ: Princeton University Press.

Charitakis, G. (1992) *Doctors' Silence*, Athens: Lygouras and Co.

Cooper, D. K. (1992) 'Is Xenotransplantation a Realistic Clinical Option?', *Transplantation Proceedings* 24, 6: 2393–96.

Danforth, L. (1982) *The Death Rituals of Rural Greece*, Princeton, NJ: Princeton University Press.

Dardavessis *et al.* (1989) 'Survey of Medical and Nursing Personnel with Respect to Brain Death Definition and Transplantations', *Helliniki Iatriki* 55, 2: 142–49.

Domenikou, A. (1991) 'Transplants From Animals', *Ethnos*, 19 November.

Francione, G. L. (1990) 'Xenografts and Animal Rights', *Transplantation Proceedings*, 22, 3: 1044–46.

Hanson, M.G. (1992) 'A Pig in the Poke', *Hastings Center Report* 22, 6: 4.

Haraway, D. (1989) *Primate Visions: Gender, Race and Nature in the World of Modern Science*, New York and London: Routledge.

—— (1991) *Simians, Cyborgs, and Women: The Reinvention of Nature*, New York: Routledge.

Ingold, T. (ed.) (1994) *What is an Animal?*, London and New York: Routledge.

Jordanova, L. J. (1980) 'Natural Facts: A Historical Perspective on Science and Sexuality', in C. MacCormack and M. Strathern (eds) *Nature, Culture and Gender*, Cambridge: Cambridge University Press.

Karoussos, K. (1987) *The Man From the Monkey? An Answer to the Materialist Approach*, Athens: Chrysopigi Publications.

Krimbas, C. (1986) *Darvinika*, Athens: Ermis.

—— (1993) *Mirror Fragments*, Athens: Themelio.

Kushner, T. and Belliotti, R. (1985) 'Baby Face: A Beastly Business', *Journal of Medical Ethics* 11: 178–83.

Lekkou, E. (1994) *Burial Or Cremation?*, Athens: Apostoliki Diakonia Publications.

McCarthy, C. R. and Ellis, G. (1994) 'Developing Policies and Regulations for Animal Biotechnology and the Protection of the Environment', *Hastings Center Report* 24, 1: 24–29.

MacCormack, C. P. (1980) 'Nature, Culture and Gender: A Critique', in C. MacCormack and M. Strathern (eds) *Nature, Culture and Gender*, Cambridge: Cambridge University Press.

Mandros, S. and Kordatos, D. (1991) 'Transplantations Today', *Iatriko Vima* 1991: 47–61.

Martin, J. (1990) 'The Rights of Man and Animal Experimentation: Point of view', *Journal of Medical Ethics* 16: 160–61.

Midgley, M. (1994) 'Beasts, Brutes and Monsters', in T. Ingold (ed.) *What is an Animal?* London and New York: Routledge.

Najarian, J. S. (1992) 'Overview of In Vivo Xenotransplantation Studies: Prospects for the Future', *Transplantation Proceedings* 24, 2: 733–38.

Niekrasz *et al.* (1992) 'The Pig as Organ Donor for Man', *Transplantation Proceedings* 24, 2: 625–26.

Reemtsma, K. (1990) 'Ethical Aspects of Xenotransplantation', *Transplantation Proceedings* 22, 3: 1042–43.

Regan, T. (1983) *The Case for Animal Rights*, Berkeley: University of California Press.

Roumeliotis, P. (1992) *Europe's Tomorrow: On the Threshold of the Twenty-First Century*, Athens: 'Nea Synora'-A.A. Livani.

Salhins, M. (1976) *Culture and Practical Reason*, Chicago: University of Chicago Press.

Seremetakis, N. (1991) *The Last Word*, Chicago and London: University of Chicago Press.

Singer, P. (1992) 'Xenotransplantation and Speciesism', *Transplantation Proceedings* 24, 2: 728–32.

Singleton *et al.* (1994) 'Transgenic Organisms, Science and Society', *Hastings Center Report* 24, 1: 4–14.

Strathern, M. (1992) *After Nature: English Kinship in the Late Twentieth Century*, Cambridge: Cambridge University Press.

Wagner, R. (1975) *The Invention of Culture*, Englewood Cliffs, NJ: Prentice Hall.

White, H. (1981) 'The Value of Narrativity in the Representation of Reality', in W. J. T. Mitchell (ed.) *On Narrative*, Chicago and London: University of Chicago.

Willis, R. (ed.) (1990) *Signifying Animals: Human Meanings in the Natural World*, London: Unwin Hyman.

Chapter 14

The reproduction of nature in contemporary high-energy physics

Detlev Nothnagel

SYMMETRIC ANTHROPOLOGY AND HIGH-ENERGY PHYSICS

In their relation to nature, western societies rely basically on a scientific approach. This approach, characterised by measurement and mathematical expression, has been dominant at least since the Enlightenment.[1] It has also generated some of the key arguments setting western societies apart from what were and sometimes still are called 'primitive societies'. In this perspective, the natural sciences are not only motivated by a quest for truth, at the same time they fulfil a central role in a generally evolutionary classification of cultures. The nature–culture interface thus serves as a structuring device for socio-cultural differentiation.

Given the eminent role of the natural sciences it seems astonishing that the laboratories in which these differences are produced have been systematically excluded from the empirical focus of cultural anthropology. This is one of the reasons why discussions of the differences between 'us' and 'them' have to a large extent remained fruitless and without any firm conclusion. In contrast to anthropological accounts of 'other' societies, there are few ethnographic studies addressing central sub-cultures of western societies. This unbalance, noted by Völger and Welck (1993: 637), is in my view exemplified by Hallpike's (1979) limited comparison; correcting this asymmetry is part of the programme of what is occasionally called 'symmetric anthropology' (see Nothnagel 1989: Chapter 3 and Latour 1991; for examples of promising fields for an anthropology of western societies, see Jackson 1987, Agulhon *et al.* 1989, *L'Homme* 1992, and Nothnagel 1993a). Symmetric anthropology can be regarded as a renewed interest in comparative discussions concerning the relation between scientific, rational, and local forms of knowledge (e.g. magic) which, since Frazer's work, has remained a delicate and unresolved subject in anthropology (see Tambiah 1984). It is certainly not the aim of this approach to negate all differences; instead it wishes to address the empirical question of how far they extend.

One premise of symmetric anthropology is that central issues for modern societies are first tackled within specific, more or less localised, sub-cultures; it is only in a later phase that the results of these elaborations are distributed to a wider range of sub-cultures and other cultures, through processes of 'translation'. Cultural anthropology, which puts fieldwork at the centre of its empirical orientation, should be well suited to address the sub-cultures of western science, particularly when it comes to giving an account of the every day production of knowledge rather than the polished, refined and in most cases written versions intended for public circulation. Acknowledging the asymmetry of anthropology in this respect and the importance of locality in the production of knowledge, some proponents of science studies were thus led to adopt an anthropological approach (the earliest examples are Latour and Woolgar 1979 and Knorr-Cetina 1981; the first field study in high-energy physics was carried out by Traweek 1988).

The following considerations, based on fieldwork at the CERN (Centre Européen de la Recherche Nucléaire) conglomerate of high-energy physics laboratories in Geneva, will furnish an example of the conceptualisation of the nature–culture interface, as conceived by an organisational culture that has profoundly influenced the western approach towards nature as it is taught in schools and communicated in the media, and, thereby, transformed into a crucial element in ideologies of progress and conceptions of linear time.[2] High-energy physics considers itself as a 'frontier science'; it is also 'big science', employing enormous devices combining a wide range of very sophisticated technologies. Its major aim is twofold. It is motivated by research into the fundamental building blocks of matter (particles) and the laws of interaction which 'govern' the complex structures built out of them. But it also searches for a theory describing the origin of the universe, its evolution and final fate, following the dictum that 'physics at very high energy is physics at the very early universe'.

On the experimental side, this requires accelerators in which particles collide at a given point, 'the vertex', with the maximum energy that can presently be handled (and afforded), thereby producing a complex process of interactions characterised by a multitude of traces, the properties of which indicate the type of particle produced. These traces are registered by huge detectors built around the vertex like an onion, with layers of different sub-detectors relating to the various processes relevant for a given experimental scenario. Through often complex 'chains of translation' (Latour 1991), interactions with detecting material are transformed into a signal which can be handled electronically, i.e. written on tape (cassette) and thus 'exported' from the site of the experiment and fed into the computer-based procedures that an analysis in high-energy physics entails. As indicated by this short sketch, quite a number of 'frontiers' have to be crossed and numerous transformations and translations successfully accomplished before the final frontier which distinguishes nature and culture can be 'attacked'.

The fundamental interests of elementary particle physics are frequently expressed in statements like 'we will change the way you look at the world tomorrow'. Superlatives or attributes alluding to size and ambition are often used. High-energy physics has been – up to now – a prestigious science bringing in the (relative) majority of Nobel prizes in physics and playing a decisive role in the competition between nations and/or continents – especially the US and western Europe – in respect to what is called scientific leadership. Elementary particle physics therefore serves as a kind of symbol, indicating the relative technological and scientific status of a specific nation or continent.

The all-embracing, cosmological approach of high-energy physics is exemplified by theories like the 'Grand Unified Theory' or the 'Theory of Everything' (theories pre-dated by Heisenberg's famous 'Weltformel'). Such theories, which attempt to describe the ultimate structure of physical nature in terms of processes of interaction governed by laws of symmetry, are in fact aiming to put an end to all questions by providing a framework that would generate all the answers. This is clearly millenarian, and contradicts all the historical experience of physics; indeed, up to now all 'fundamentalistic' thinking on both the elementary building blocks of matter and all-embracing cosmologies has proved to be wrong.[3]

THE PRODUCTION OF 'NATURAL SYMBOLS'

Nature in modern high-energy physics is reproduced. Its existence is tied to accelerators; its presence is validated by detectors and the theoretical concepts and analytical tools which render the signals delivered meaningful. These instruments are located within a specific environment and characteristic for a specific corporate group for which they make sense. Detectors are the 'eyes' of experimental physics, opening 'windows' and assuring that 'new physics can be seen'. Such metaphors can be regarded as a 'survival' from early times when non-electronic detection techniques were based on visual inspection. In a more general way, these metaphors expressing the mediation between nature and culture relate to the visual orientation that is significant in western societies (see Latour 1986). Detectors are conceived, built and operated through multinational collaborations involving different university and research institutes (research teams working at 'the frontier' included between 100 and over 400 people in the period between 1988 and 1992).[4] The specific conjunction between nature and culture established by these detectors, normally named in an acronymical fashion, is also the distinctive feature signifying specific groups of people such as 'the ALEPH gang' or 'the strange HELIOS people'. The specific conjunction between nature and culture given by a particular detector thus serves as a kind of 'totemic operator' in a Lévi-Straussian sense, dividing experimentalists into groups of people attached to a specific nature–culture interface.

Detectors differ according to the expected products. They are to a large extent an anticipation of the results, translating a theoretical scenario into a technical possibility. In doing this, experimentalists rely heavily on so-called Monte-Carlo simulations, random number generators which double the nature–culture interface by introducing a virtual counterpart. Monte-Carlos provide a simulation of particle decays referring to measured values or future scenarios. They are constructed like a machinery, offering the possibility of choosing parameters or of varying them. In the construction process, Monte-Carlos virtually allow physicists 'to be there' before the first data are taken (see Latour 1987: 248). In the process of analysis, Monte-Carlos also help physicists to refine their expectations and to understand 'what their detector is doing'. For instance, it is said that 'the shape [of a distribution] is well reproduced by the Monte-Carlo which means . . . that we understand the proton-quark fragmentation'.

During 'running time', collisions of particles are registered, written on 'raw data tapes' which are the starting point for the analytical considerations. Analytical processes are very time consuming (judging from my observations, at least a year passes from the last recording of data to the submission of a paper). Results are produced through complex procedures of refinement and classification. In consequence, no empirical result in modern high-energy physics is self-evident. For a long time particles carry their instrumental signature: there are no electrons but CALPAT-electrons or ERIC-electrons and they are 'filtered off' from SLOWSTREAMs or MICRO-DATA-SUMMARY tapes. These electrons tend to differ from one another and only at the end of an analysis does 'the electron' emerge. Thus, the iconic quality of particles is proven *a posteriori* by analytical procedures based on mathematical reasoning. The difficulty one has in choosing the appropriate term does not merely reflect inconsistencies between different semiotic concepts with respect to the definitions of the various sub-categories of a sign, it also indicates the importance of culture. Peirce's (1931) concept of an icon, stressing qualities of 'firstness' and 'similarity', comes close to what is meant here. Nevertheless, the relation of 'icon' and 'index' with respect to what is reconstructed as nature remains complex and resistant to unambiguous definition. This can be interpreted as an indication of the complexity of the nature–culture interface, at least in the context I am referring to here. The decisive factor which influences this reconstructed iconicity is trust in the faithfulness of the 'chain of translation'. Experience with the apparatus and the instruments of the analysis is transformed into a collective conviction of 'being there' as illustrated by the statement that 'normally it takes a lot of time for people to gain confidence in their algorithms'. As iconicity is produced by socio-cultural means, characterised by convention, it has symbolic qualities.

In their intermediary position, particles or decay processes are thus 'natural symbols', to apply a term used by Douglas (1973). This concept relates to the reappraisal of classification which has characterised anthropology since Lévi-Strauss (1962). Structuralist accounts focus on processes transgressing the 'boundary' between nature and culture whereby nature becomes culture (e.g. domestication, education and cooking) or culture becomes nature (e.g. illness, death and war). These mediating processes are part of a complex scenario, involving specific 'arenas' such as the human body and specific persons classified as 'in between', e.g. the healer. In dealing with natural phenomena societies do not only produce or reproduce a classification of them, they re-establish a definition of culture which is conceived as a fragile order based on restriction and moderation. Thus processes of transgression gain a multiple symbolic significance. Given such a view, it is not only society that influences the classification of nature, nature also serves as a means to introduce or to maintain order with respect to the classification of cultural items (see, for instance, Leach 1964, Bulmer 1967, Tambiah 1969, Willis 1972, Ohnuki-Tierney 1987). In this reciprocal modelling process, metaphoric structures of reasoning are of central importance. This close interrelationship between nature and culture led Latour (1991: 128ff) to advocate a symmetrical approach to the anthropology of science that does not accept any *a priori* difference between 'the nature pole' and 'the subject/society pole'.

Analytical procedures in experimental elementary particle physics are very much influenced by theoretical arguments. Theory and experiment are distinguished by different career paths and differences in the social structure of the respective projects. The structures of congresses and the field of publication follow this dualistic pattern. Experiment and theory are opposed in never-ending disputes over prestige and leadership. They are also partially separated by different views on nature: a particle is not quite the same thing for a pure theorist as it is for an experimentalist. For an experimentalist, a particle is primarily a resonance which has to be extracted out of a huge amount of data. For a theorist, in contrast, an hypothetical particle is 'the most economic way to write a theory'. A theorist, especially if he is working on fundamental issues, will never be able fully to understand and appreciate the thinking of an experimentalist, and vice versa. There is a lot of folklore in experimental physics in which this 'uneasy' partnership is discussed. Stories or jokes refer to the question of how far one should trust the work of theorists when elaborating one's discovery strategies. Thus, between experimentalists and theorists there exists a complex structure of relations and alliances ruled by informal commitments or lasting hostilities, giving rise to trades and translations, and multiple marginalities as well as conjunctions between semantic spaces and categories.

Cross-cutting ties are concentrated in a specific group of theorists – called phenomenologists – who present 'pure' and timeless theoretical reasoning in a concrete form by framing testable hypotheses and furnishing experimentalists with usable instruments in the form of calculations or simulation programmes. Experimentalists are thus dependent on a group outside their own sphere of discussions for furnishing products which are usually treated as 'black boxes'. The same holds true for theorists. However, these boundaries are constantly negotiated and the manipulation of these spatio-temporal structures is one of the central factors allowing 'big men' in physics to accumulate power (Nothnagel 1993c). Pure theory then represents the symbolic side – it concentrates on mathematical reasoning based 'on freely invented principles', i.e. culture – while experimental physics represents the 'iconic side'. Both are related by a specific 'in between' group.

The complex process of translation or mediation generates a 'space of negotiation' (*'espace de negotiation'*); this concept – issuing from the French approach to the anthropology of sciences (e.g. Latour 1987, Callon 1991) – is especially valuable here because it precludes any pre-established distinction between content and context and between nature and culture by including all the various items negotiated and translated as well as the various actors negotiating and translating into a common field. Thus a 'space of negotiation' is based on mediating processes and intermediaries passing between the actors and defining their relationship. These mediating links include technical artefacts, literal inscriptions, human beings, and money (Callon 1991:134–35). The 'space of negotiation' changes as a project ages: if the project is successful, i.e. able to present a result, the 'space of negotiation' is almost non-existent and chains of translation

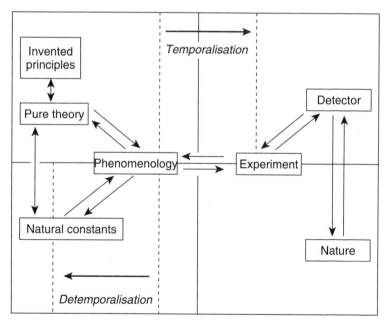

Figure 14.1 Nature–culture interface: 'espace de negotiation'

become irreversible. This obviously depends not only on the object itself but also on the number of human actors involved in the interpretation.[5]

The reproduction of nature as a meaningful sign that can be talked about, is essentially a classificatory activity accompanied and structured by a rich folklore. One of its characteristics is an abundant tableau of tropes such as metaphor, metonymy, synecdoche, etc. (Noeth 1985: 507). For instance, processes of discovery are called 'the hunt' (or 'hunting'). Now, as we know from cultural anthropology, hunting is one of the mediating activities between nature and culture characterised by a very pronounced symbolical value. It entails not only a transformation of nature into culture – converting a wild animal into an edible prey – but also a whole set of socio-cultural values (evidence relating to African studies is given, for example, in Nothnagel 1989: Chapter 2). These values include mechanisms of sharing and distribution as well as mechanisms of power differentiation (gender separation, for instance), since hunting is usually deemed more prestigious than crop cultivation. This marked symbolic value also reveals itself in a 'historical' perspective, insofar as many culture heroes are characterised as hunters (de Heusch 1972, Feierman 1974, Adler 1978). In general terms, one can say that 'wild nature' serves as a reservoir of socio-cultural meaning. Thus, meaning and sense, power and domination are extracted out of these transformational, mediating activities. There are clear parallels with high-energy physics where nature is often constructed as the 'Other', an outside entity. Physicists use an abundance of deictic tropes characterising the 'Other' as something 'out there' from which a signal or 'new physics' has to be 'extracted' or 'dragged out' (the concept of deixis is used here to signify strategies to localise things or persons in space and time – for an outline see Lyons 1977: Chapter 15). It is obvious that these processes are essential for classification. The question of 'what is going on *there*' is solved by establishing categories that discriminate signal from background and produce an 'inside' and an 'outside'. Thereby, numerous borders are created and carefully monitored to ensure that nothing unforeseen 'pops up'.

There is a tendency to conflate issues involving the nature–culture interface with discourses addressing the strange and exotic. In a wide range of societies, the perception of strangers is intimately linked to the relation of humans to nature. The same is true in high-energy physics where everything that is outside the current basis of reasoning, known as the 'Standard Model', is called 'exotics'. The 'exotic' is thus the cognitively abnormal and it is the stability of the boundary between the Standard Model and the exotic that provides an argument for the truth of the former. The hunt which deals with this boundary characterises 'nature' as a living entity that throws up obstacles and hardships and displays resistance. Also, it provides smart people with the appropriate means to overcome these difficulties; for instance, it is said that 'Nature is kind and provides a decay chain with the proper spin-parity sequence' (Telegdi 1990: 9). Thus a skilled and famous 'particle hunter' is also a man of tricks; he knows how to build 'traps' to catch neutrinos, to do an experiment in which efficiencies cancel out, and to vary the pressure of gas chambers to reduce the dispersion provoked by ionisation. The intimacy with, and expertise of, 'nature' characterising the skilled and experienced particle hunter is much like that reported, for instance, for hunters among the Achuar (Descola 1986: 293).

Only the search for 'new physics' is characterised as a hunt. Physics aiming at the refinement of already established values is addressed differently, by metaphors referring to processes of cultivation or machinery. The distribution of prestige which follows this metaphorical classification matches the usual pattern, because only the hunt has the potential for discoveries. The periods of hunting are times of excitement, where passion is translated into extraordinary working hours. The 'experiment' team constantly interacts, grouping around dinner tables, sharing information and discussing rumours. The hunt nearly always takes place under competitive circumstances since there

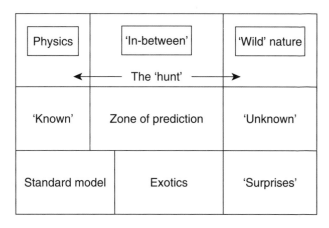

Figure 14.2 Discoveries: the 'landscape' of physics

are always at least two 'hunting campaigns' working in the same temporal regime. This makes time run fast and gives rise to what is called a 'race'. There is no functional reason for this sort of competition because subsequent experiments, which explore the energy domains one step higher, will automatically evaluate what their predecessors found.

The time of the hunt is a time of careful evaluation of the competing environment where one not only tends to play tricks on nature but also on other relevant experiments, for instance by a careful distribution of information. The transgression of the boundary between nature and culture parallels the reinforcement of the boundaries between experimental sub-cultures. Thereby the particular conjunction between nature and culture set up in experiments is transformed into a social disjunction creating an advantage. The aim, as in most scenarios of discovery, is to transform the physical region addressed into a territory – something to which a title can be attached. Parallels between the arenas of discovery addressed in anthropological contexts and those of high-energy physics are striking (Nothnagel 1993c).

DISCIPLINED BODIES AND DISCIPLINED THOUGHTS

The process of the reproduction of nature is represented by metaphors of refinement. From 'raw data tapes' via the establishment of 'candidates' through processes of 'cutting' – separating signal from background – one finally arrives at a 'polished' version to be presented to the public. This transformation is accompanied by a rich tableau of tropes referring to concepts of illness, infection, healing and cleaning. This obviously has to do with the deictic style of reasoning mentioned above. All the conceptual domains alluded to presuppose the existence of borders or boundaries. This is the case when, for instance, concepts of sickness ('there is something sick in ERIC'), intrusion ('the sample is polluted'), and hermeticity ('the leaking in of background') are metaphorically installed. Given the complexity of the nature–culture interface, one of the central issues is to avoid artificial phenomena called 'ghosts', which are dealt with via campaigns called 'ghost busting' or 'ghost killing'. Again, one can see the dualistic logic characterising the processes of classification.

These metaphorical concepts already indicate that the process of analysis is characterised by a productive discrimination. To express it differently, the establishing of borders serves to promote order, a productive 'clearing' of the world, which transforms 'out-thereness' into a theory-laden representation. To a considerable extent, the production of entities via classification refers to the human body, which parallels this process due to its own ambiguous position between nature and culture. The body thus metaphorically models what is happening in the analytic process, hardly an astonishing fact from an anthropological point of view. Distributions have 'shoulders' or 'legs'; 'legs' are 'cut' or can be 'recovered' and a 'shoulder' can look 'sick', 'strange' or 'exotic'. Distributions are also inspected according to their 'behaviour'. They can be 'well behaved' or 'behave beautifully' – that is, in an expected classical way. From another perspective, the installation of the body via metaphorical concepts gives rise to conceptions of a 'hand-based' mastery of nature. For instance one 'gets a handle on' a job, and a technique 'is well in hand'. Thus, the body is used as a manifold conceptual device importing meaning into the everyday analytical discourse of experimental physicists.[6]

The importance of the body is not accidental; it is more or less well documented that the ways of dealing with our external nature also reflect the ways of dealing with our internal nature. A famous example from cultural anthropology involves so-called 'rites of passage', where the propagation of the cultural order is often enacted by the use of 'wild', external nature (Nothnagel 1989: Chapter 2). One can also put it the other way round. In this perspective, the concept of 'wild' nature is regularly redefined by dramatic enactment, i.e. culture. This close link between internal and external nature – which doubles the nature–culture interface – plays an eminent role in the western history of ideas connecting the mastery of internal nature to the mastery of its external complement (Bachelard 1965, Leiss 1972: 57) and vice versa: 'Human domination over nature is also exercised with respect to one's own body' (Lippe 1988: 17).[7]

This becomes clear when referring to specific modes of talk and behaviour indicating the quality of arguments frequently used in high-energy physics. A striking example is given by the expression 'handwaving arguments'. One easily sees how in this evaluative expression notions of restriction and discipline are introduced in favour of a measure indicating the 'goodness' of an argument. Well-founded arguments are ascribed to bodies at rest. The epistemological value of the nature–culture interface established by a certain speaker is thus metaphorically weighted in terms of the mastery of the body. The encultured body is, at least in part, culture-specific and can be read as a significant sign indicating membership and identity. This is alluded to in Bourdieu's (1989) concept of the 'hexis' and its relatedness to corporate identity. The enculturation of the body is also an important part of the professional socialisation of physicists (Traweek 1988, Nothnagel 1993b).[8] The example sketched above contradicts the official western doctrine favouring the separation of mind and body, which was a central ingredient of Enlightenment philosophy and still plays an important role on the official level of science (see Kutschmann 1986).

Comparable mechanisms of argumentative restriction can be found in rhetorical regimes, for instance with respect to strategies of 'being there' with which physicists enfold their arguments, trying to convince others that they can address the promised regions. Physics, for example, has its version of the anthropological 'ethnographic present' (cf. Bazerman 1988). A detemporalisation and a deletion of specific socio-cultural circumstances parallels the transformation of the oral into the written. In structuralist language, a syntagmatic text is thus successively paradigmatised, paving the way for the inclusion of present findings into an actual set of natural constants.

NATURE AS A SOURCE OF SOCIO-CULTURAL MEANING

The discourses of discovery and classification which characterise high-energy physics rely on the assumption of an abundance of meaning. In terms of time, this is translated into an ideology of optimism and open horizons. To establish this as a valuable, working representation of nature in an epistemological framework one has to push aside arguments favouring a circular concept of time. Some theoretical physicists adopt this conception by advocating the 'Anthropic Principle'. The discussion about the Anthropic Principle can be regarded as a philosophical, epistemological reappraisal of the relationship between nature and culture already discussed under the label of 'natural symbols'. In simple terms, the Anthropic Principle alludes to the problematic relationship between two fundamental features of the observation of nature: humans are a product of nature, but they are also a necessary condition for bringing 'nature' into being (for a detailed discussion of the different versions of the Anthropic Principle, see Barrow and Tipler 1988). Thus there is an intimate, twofold relation between the organic and inorganic which raises the question as to whether, in researching into nature, humans only meet themselves. Or, to put it in a teleological perspective: is nature constructed in such a way that the human observer appears as a necessary consequence? In the latter argument, the close relationship between humans and nature justifies the epistemological optimism that even the most 'remote' areas of 'nature' are accessible to human thought. Even though such a position permits a certain optimism, nature cannot be defined as an independent entity, irrespective of how radically the Anthropic Principle is conceived. Hence, nature is no distinct 'Other' and the negation of its 'otherness' introduces a potential circularity. Research into nature is at the same time an inquiry into the identity of humans. Thus, the idea of progress which is at the heart of high-energy physics, is in trouble; the referent, i.e. nature, is hard to define independently.

Anthropic ideas – situated on the outskirts of theory – are regarded as an 'academic exercise' by most physicists, especially those on the experimental side, for whom pure, timeless theory only becomes relevant when translated into measurables (there is at present an animated controversy between a philosophical approach and a more experimental one; cf. Kobbe 1994 for a summary). Thus, the differential distribution of ideas and concepts regarding nature among the various segments of high-energy physics serves several functional ends.

Due to the fact that in high-energy physics it remains uncertain what one is observing and how this can be described, and because one only has theories covering partial aspects, progress is mainly documented via 'technical' parameters. It is therefore the mastery of nature, its productive cultivation, and the related medium-range theories, that are at the heart of the idea of progress. Global and central concepts like the essential nature of an elementary particle or the mass are still not understood. This, however, does not prevent the measurement of masses or the detection of elementary particles.

High-energy physics does not only do something to nature or bodies, it also deals with persons. Making people famous by rewarding them with prizes and medals as well as naming particles, streets and squares after them seems at first glance to be simply a means of creating some sort of culture hero; occasionally one reads or hears sentences like: 'the Planck mass is that mass for which the Compton wavelength ... equals the Scharzschild radius' (Linde 1989: 1). Such a production of famous people, however, also fulfils an important role in relation to the socio-cultural production of time. Again, one is confronted with two, partially different conceptions of time; in giving names to things specific personalities become in some sense immortal, but within a framework of competition names serve as a paradigmatic symbol signifying progress and unlimited horizons of time. It is only at a later stage that a localised sub-culture, constructing a situated view of nature and time embodied in 'big men', can be translated into a key symbol of progress central to whole societies. However, when high-energy physics fulfils this more global symbolic function, it does so through a public image rather different from the type of inside view sketched above.

CONCLUSION

To sum up, nature as it is addressed in high-energy physics' labs is reproduced. It is a representation inscribed in 'techno-facts'. Thus its iconic quality is not a self-evident, given quality, but something that is actively worked out. The cultural, 'local' framework in which this reproduction takes place is characterised by a rich folklore which metaphorically draws on a variety of other nature–culture interfaces, including that of the human body. Nature, as conceived in the culture of high-energy physics, depends on two contradictions: an abundance of meaning and a scarcity of signs, timeless notions and competitive linear time. Both seem to be necessary and short-circuits are prevented by socio-cultural means.

Thus nature, which according to its etymological roots is something that grows independently, hardly exists in the framework I have been considering. Nature is intimately linked to culture, being characterised by a particular organisational structure and distinctive kinds of talk or habitus: 'the physics way', as physicists tend to say. It is only in a second instance that the establishment of nature as a meaningful sign gains importance on a general level. It does so by processes of translation, whereby specific localised versions gain global importance. These processes also serve specific ends, in that they play an important role with respect to what is called 'scientific leadership', producing a ranking of nations (cultures) based on evolutionary and linear conceptions of time. A closer look at the culture of high-energy physics can provide an example, showing the mechanisms which assure the production of linear time.

Nature is in many ways a reservoir for the production of culture; it implies the production of meaning through processes of classification and refinement, technical applications and transformations, the production of specific versions of time, enculturation, disciplined bodies, local identities tied to particular nature–culture interfaces, famous people, and, finally, the 'symbolic' ranking of nations and cultures. In consequence, Eder's somewhat Weberian thesis (1988) that modern conceptions of nature are characterised by their desymbolisation seems to be a simplification. The nature reproduced by physicists is endowed with a number of symbolic features which precisely ensure the continuing interest in this domain, and thus its very existence.

'Nature' – despite being at the centre of all activities – is a term rarely used in physics. It is 'physics' itself that is employed to signify what is being addressed, for instance in such expressions as 'the true physical meaning', 'let's go back to physics', 'we find no physics in the forward direction', etc. 'Nature' only comes into the game when it is time to put an end to the debate, because as physicists often say: 'It is nature that drives us in a certain direction'. The 'natural', however, is invested with cultural meaning, 'determined by those with the power and money to use nature instrumentally' (Pugh 1988: 2). In both western and non-western societies, nature is not only a subject for contemplation and curiosity, it is linked to questions of power and prestige as well as to fundamental problems concerning human identity. The latter feature is stressed by Godelier (1984: 10): 'l'homme a une histoire parce qu'il transforme la nature'. Seen in another perspective this 'productive' feature of the nature–culture interface also reveals a fundamental problem: 'How is it and why is it that men, who are a part of nature, manage to see themselves as other than nature even though, in order to subsist, they must constantly maintain relations with nature?' (Leach 1970: 102).

Physics is not only producing sense in scientific terms; it also takes on a metaphysical quality as it extends questions concerning the 'how', which can be treated on the 'technical' level, to notions concerning the 'why', which transgress the functional, technical level of reasoning. As Kobbe (1994) puts it: 'more than all other disciplines physics reaches the frontiers of the perceivable – and touches the domain of religion'.[9] The metaphysical dimension of the fundamental interests of high-energy physics is without doubt related to the extreme 'out-thereness' that characterises its ultimate aims. It coincides with the extreme distance between the type of questions tackled by physicists and the everyday phenomenal world. This has to do with the methods of physics as much as with its object. The reproduction of nature is linked to complex technical installations, to a variety of sophisticated instruments, a specific dualistic structure of the field and – of course – to physicists who have undergone a long professional socialisation. Without accelerators, without Monte-Carlos, without the 'calibrated eyes' of physicists and the complex relationship between experiment and theory no one would ever know of the existence of 'quarks'. Thus, it is primarily situated knowledge linked to a specific culture which makes this reproduction of nature possible.[10] The delocalisation of this knowledge is only a second step. It implies that 'quarks', which are reproduced in this local environment, are then transformed into a written text which can be circulated, published and finally incorporated into the textbooks which represent scientific knowledge about nature. With this step all the local aspects, the folklore influencing and characterising the reproduction of nature, are lost or – if one prefers – suppressed. Nature has now become a text, ready to serve as a basis for the ranking of nations, for the installation of specific conceptions of time, etc. Nature is implemented into a much wider network of transformations and translations, ready to generate a multitude of further arguments, meanings and interests.

The dichotomy between 'us' and 'them' created in this context of reasoning implicitly supposes a distinction between 'knowledge embedded in society, and knowledge independent of society' (Latour 1987: 213). The former modes of knowledge are usually designated by the prefix 'ethno'. To remind people in western societies that scientific knowledge about nature is also generated in local cultures, dependent on specific circumstances and situated traditions, is one of the central issues of symmetric anthropology. It is in this context that scientific reasoning regains its socio-cultural aspects, thus opening the way for a comparative discussion of the nature–culture interface which does not exclude science.

ACKNOWLEDGEMENTS

I would like to thank the people from CERN, particularly those from UA2, ALEPH, CMS, EAGLE, ASCOT and theory who were willing to answer my questions, invited me to meetings, and sometimes offered me their friendship. I profited very much from these occasions. Additionally, I would like to thank Philippe Descola for his helpful comments and Francis Jarman for checking my English. Potential shortcomings of the article are, however, my own. The University of Bielefeld generously offered me contracts that allowed me to work on my research.

NOTES

1 There are good arguments for casting doubt on the sharp historical distinction between the medieval period and the Enlightenment (see, for instance, Duhem 1906; a synopsis of Duhem's position is provided in Schäfer 1978).

2 Founded in 1954 in Geneva as a European laboratory of fundamental research, the centre has retained its original name even though for several decades now nuclear physics has occupied only a very small part of its research agenda. I was at CERN almost permanently between September 1988 and May 1992.

3 New theories are already predicting the 'compositeness' of quarks (which in the present Standard Model are thought to be elementary) or predicting parallel universes (against the theory of the 'big bang').

4 The overall lifetime of a detector at the high energy frontier is about ten years. Another period of ten years is needed for design and construction.

5 One has to add that the negotiation processes outlined here only include parts of an *'espace de negotiation'* in science. Interests have to be translated into a programme, which has to be translated into a political argument to ensure funding, funding has to be translated into a technical installation, etc. 'Scientists transform texts, experimental apparatus and grants into new texts' (Callon 1991: 141). All this has to be done in order that the observation of 'nature' becomes possible. This process is not unilinear because the object to be found is already there in some form when interests are formulated (Latour 1987: e.g. 287).

6 For reasons of limited space I have to exclude the discussion of ways of reasoning by which the dualistic logic is inversed; that is to say, the question of whether socio-cultural artefacts are conceived in a 'naturalistic' manner. This is, for instance, the case when competition is thought of in terms of 'natural selection' and 'survival of the fittest'.

7 My translation from the German.

8 As physicists are already encultured bodies before undergoing this socialisation, it should be noted that non-verbal ways of expression are also culture and gender specific. A more detailed analysis should take this into consideration.

9 My translation from the German.

10 Cf. Bachelard (1965: 10) who writes: 'En suivant la physique contemporaine, nous avons quitté la nature pour entrer dans une fabrique de phénomènes'.

REFERENCES

Adler, A. (1978) 'Le Pouvoir et l'Interdit', in G. Dieterlen (ed.) *Systèmes de Signes, Textes Réunis en Hommage à Germaine Dieterlen*, Paris: Hermann.

Agulhon, M. *et al.* (1989) *L'autre et le Semblable*, Paris: Presses du CNRS.

Bachelard, G. (1965) *L'Activité Rationaliste de la Physique Contemporaine*, Paris: Presses Universitaires de France.

Barrow, J. D. and Tipler, F. J. (1988) *The Anthropic Cosmological Principle*, Oxford: Oxford University Press.

Bazerman, C. (1988) *Shaping Written Knowledge*, Madison: University of Wisconsin Press.

Bourdieu, P. (1989) *La Noblesse d'État*, Paris: Les Editions de Minuit.

Bulmer, R. (1967) 'Why the Cassowary is not a Bird', *Man* (NS) 2: 5–25.

Callon, M. (1991) 'Techno-Economic Networks and Irreversibility', in J. Law (ed.) *A Sociology of Monsters*, London: Routledge.

Descola, P. (1986) *La Nature Domestique*, Paris: Editions de la Maison des Sciences de l'Homme.

Douglas, M. (1973) *Natural Symbols*, London: Barrie and Jenkins.

Duhem, P. (1906) *La Théorie Physique*, Paris: Chevallier and Rivière.

Eder, K. (1988) *Die Vergesellschaftung der Natur*, Frankfurt: Suhrkamp.

Feierman, S. (1974) *The Shambaa Kingdom*, Madison and London: University of Wisconsin Press.

Godelier, M. (1984) *L'Idéel et le Matériel*, Paris: Fayard.

Hallpike, C.R. (1979) *The Foundations of Primitive Thought*, Oxford: Clarendon Press.

Heusch, L. de (1972) *Le Roi Ivre ou l'Origine de l'Etat*, Paris: Gallimard.

L'Homme (1992) Vol. 121.

Horton, R. and Finnegan, R. (eds) (1973) *Modes of Thought*, London: Faber.

Jackson, A. (ed.) (1987) *Anthropology at Home*, London and New York: Tavistock.

Knorr-Cetina, K. (1981) *The Manufacture of Knowledge*, Oxford: Pergamon.

Kobbe, B. (1994) 'Kosmische Religion', *Bild der Wissenschaften* 1: 72.

Kutschmann, W. (1986) *Der Naturwissenschaftler und sein Körper*, Frankfurt: Suhrkamp.

Latour, B. (1986) 'Visualization and Cognition', in H. Kucklick and E. Long (eds) *Knowledge and Society* Vol. 6, Greenwich, Conn. and London.

— (1987) *Science in Action*, Milton Keynes: Open University Press.

— (1991) *Nous n'avons Jamais été Modernes*, Paris: Éditions la Découverte.

Latour, B. and Woolgar, S. (1979) *Laboratory Life*, Newbury Park: Sage.

Leach, E. (1964) 'Anthropological Aspects of Language', in E. Lenneberg (ed.) *New Directions in the Study of Language*, Cambridge, Mass.: MIT Press.

— (1970) *Claude Lévi-Strauss*, New York: Viking Press.

Leiss, W. (1972) *The Domination of Nature*, New York: G. Braziller.

Lévi-Strauss, C. (1962) *Le Totémisme Aujourd'hui*, Paris: Presses Universitaires de France.

Linde, A. (1989) *Inflation and Quantum Cosmology*, Geneva (CERN Th 5561/89; preprint).

Lippe, R.von (1988) *Vom Leib zum Körper*, Reinbek b. Hamburg: Rowohlt.

Lyons, J. (1977) *Semantics* Vol. 2, Cambridge: Cambridge University Press.

Noeth, W. (1985) *Handbuch der Semiotik*, Stuttgart: Metzler.

Nothnagel, D. (1989) *Der Fremde im Mythos*, Frankfurt: Lang.

— (1993a) 'Anthropologische Feldforschung in Organisationen', *Anthropos* 88: 459–76.

— (1993b) 'Der Gang der Dinge' in S. Helmers (ed.) *Ethnologie der Arbeitswelt*, Bonn: Holos.

— (1993c) *The Death of Time. About the Making of Charismatic Personalities in High-Energy Physics* (unpublished talk; Meeting of the DGV, Leipzig, October).

— (1993d) *Reisen in die Ferne und Reisen in der Zeit* (unpublished talk; Meeting of the DGV-Section for European Anthropology, St Augustin, June).

Ohnuki-Tierney, E. (1987) *The Monkey as Mirror*, Princeton, NJ: Princeton University Press.

Peirce, C. S. (1931) *Collected Papers* Vol. 2, Cambridge, Mass.: Harvard University Press.

Pugh, S. (1988) *Garden – Nature – Language*, Manchester: Manchester University Press.

Schäfer, L. (1978) 'Duhems Bedeutung für die Entwicklung der Wissenschaftstheorie und ihre gegenwärtigen Probleme', in P. Duhem *Ziel und Struktur der physikalischen Theorien*, Hamburg: Meiner.

Tambiah, S. J. (1969) 'Animals are Good to Think and Good to Prohibit', *Ethnology* 8: 423–59.

— (1984) *Magic, Science, Religion, and the Scope of Rationality*, Cambridge: Cambridge University Press.

Telegdi, V. L. (1990) *Mind Over Matter*, Geneva (CERN 90–09, preprint).

Traweek, S. (1988) *Beamtimes and Lifetimes*, Cambridge, Mass.: Harvard University Press.

Völger, G. and Welck, K.von (1993) 'Das Völkerkundemuseum an der Jahrtausendwende', in T. Schweitzer *et al.* (eds) *Handbuch der Völkerkunde*, Berlin: Reimer.

Willis, R. (1972) 'Pollution and Paradigm', *Man* (NS) 7: 369–78.

Chapter 15

New tools for conviviality

Society and biotechnology

Paul Richards and Guido Ruivenkamp

Under what circumstances, and with what consequences, do groups in society become interested in technological futures, and seek to gain some control over the process of technology generation? We pose this basic question in relation to agricultural biotechnologies (defined broadly as procedures that modify agro-biological processes for human material benefit through manipulation of known principles, or more narrowly as modifications that draw upon recent advances in molecular biology).[1]

Technology and social science are often drawn up in an oppositional relationship, reflecting both a Cartesian philosophical heritage in the social sciences and facts of recent technological history. Nuclear technology, developed in conditions of great secrecy by a military-industrial complex, has had a major influence over the agenda for critiques of technology in the post-1945 industrial world (Hall 1986). However, such conceptual polarisation is hard to sustain when attention is paid to the generation of technology as a social process.

New technologies are integral elements within social discourse and practice. They emerge from within institutional settings, and serve as foci for intergroup contestation. For this reason the language of technological change is also a moral discourse (the language of 'ought' rather than 'is'). Different groups envisage the future in different ways, reflecting systematic differences in material culture and social organisation (Douglas and Wildavsky 1982). Perhaps for this reason debates about alternative technologies degenerate into dialogues of the deaf. Our current ambition (as summarised in this paper) is modest – in surveying the field of biotechnology generation, and seeking to identify some of the main organisational actors, we hope to suggest useful ways of beginning to analyse the society–biotechnology interface. This chapter seeks to 'flag' some issues that are likely to become critical points of social contestation, and to comment upon some social science research possibilities. Reference is made mainly to food processing, plant improvement, biotechnology in Third World development, and debates about conservation and sustainable agriculture.

TECHNIQUE AND TECHNOLOGY

Technology is generally taken to mean both a set of processes through which human agency brings about transformations in the material and mental conditions of existence and the knowledge through which such transformations are achieved. Where accounts stress the importance of knowledge some analysts draw a sharp distinction between technique (the practical capacity to attain certain goals) and technology (knowledge of underlying principles abstracted from the transformation process itself in such a way that new potential transformations can be envisaged ahead of any practical competence). On this reckoning, human affairs have been dominated by technique until only recently, but technology (having marched in parallel with advances in scientific knowledge from the seventeenth century) is now a dominant force in the modern world. Indeed, technology is considered in many accounts to be a key factor in modernity.

The modern concept of technology, as knowledge of principles underlying processes of material transformation, is bound up with the rise to prominence of methodological individualism. Teaching programmes in technology, while allowing for specialisation, make it clear that the abstractions of technological principle that count are those that can be internalised by individual human agents. These principles are then deployed by individuals or teams, working in organisations (firms, government research laboratories, universities, etc.), supported by specific institutions (markets, national and international legal codes concerning intellectual property, etc.). The main organisations for technology generation in the modern world are firms, operating in the market-place, but public-sector organisations are important in certain sectors (notably defence and international agriculture).

This conventional account can be challenged in a number of respects. The technique–technology shift as a condition of modernity (Ingold 1988) can be challenged on empirical grounds, at least in the negative sense that it is often hard to prove a lack of appreciation of abstract principle in earlier periods, before the emergence of standard codes for representation and intercultural communication of abstract relationships.

Modern ethnography offers some cautionary tales, in this regard. 'Subsistence' farmers exert selective pressure on plant types at harvest and when replanting; with in-breeding crops it has been shown that this often leads to a solid appreciation of phenotype stabilisation through mass selection, and that some farmers henceforth keep this stabilisation in mind in choosing harvesting and seed storage techniques (Richards 1993). But lacking a framework of evolutionary theory and Mendelian genetics selection principles are often expressed in terms of local abstractions hard for outsiders to decode. These abstractions may invoke concepts of ancestors and witches in which elements of sociological as well as biological concern are inextricably intertwined (Longley and Richards 1993).

A second challenge can be mounted from a Durkheimian perspective. It is neither impossible nor absurd to conceive of technological abstractions that are items of collective rather than individual consciousness. From this perspective, the argument about technological abstraction and modernity is simply one about abstraction at the level of individual agents, and the rise to prominence under capitalism of methodological individualism as the basis for understanding human behaviour and decision making. Critics (ourselves included) detect a self-serving conceptual circularity lurking beneath the alleged historical transition from a world dominated by technique to one dominated by technology. Although technological abstraction might have become increasingly important in modern times the capacity for such abstraction is a species characteristic, and thus latent (at least) in earlier human populations. Emergence of technological abstraction, as an item of cultural self-awareness in the modern western world, may owe a great deal, therefore, to sociological factors.

Sociologists of science successfully demonstrate that scientific sub-fields 'condense' from the elaboration of professional organisations and networks, and that scientific hypotheses need not only evidence but a stable community of believers to achieve success (Latour 1987, Pickering 1992). The same is true for technology. Particular design histories cannot be fully understood without reference to the actor-networks that sustain belief in a given line of technological development (cf. Law and Callon 1992). To point to this ideological 'work', and to attempt to 'unmask' the social interests sustaining particular sets of technological choices is, of course, to run the risk of political controversy. But politics cannot be avoided at this point. To present certain kinds of technological trajectories as 'natural' and 'inevitable' is a manifestation of political power that denies the possibility of choice. It is one of the ironies, and opportunities, of modern bioscience that new developments are seen not only as unavoidable, but also as offering enhanced choices, both to technologists and to society at large.

WHAT IS BIOTECHNOLOGY? A SCHEMATIC OUTLINE

In place of problematic, and perhaps culture-bound, claims built into the technique–technology distinction it is possible to regard biotechnology, in the broad view, as both ancient and modern, and widespread across different cultures. Indigenous biotechnologies include plant and animal selection, bioprocessing of food and drink and other materials (e.g. for fibres) through fermentation, distillation, smoking, leaching (for detoxification), management of soil fertility through use of organic residues, etc. The extent and efficacy of indigenous biotechnology across cultures in the modern world is a matter for ethnographic investigation. The CIKARD network (Center for Indigenous Knowledge for Agriculture and Rural Development, Iowa State University) is active in attempting to record indigenous biotechnological knowledge across about twenty countries in Africa, Asia and Latin America (Indigenous Knowledge and Development Monitor 1994). Other agencies are engaged upon similar inventory and documentation activity.

The recognition that innovation in biotechnology is long-established (Bud 1993) and widely distributed across cultures will be increasingly important in challenging some of the more far-fetched and aggressive claims to intellectual property rights in 'modern' biotechnology (e.g. 'ownership' of plant genomes hitherto largely shaped by farmer selection but latterly modified by new gene transfer methods). The cross-cultural perspective is also important in helping make explicit the social content of biotechnology. An example would be regional cuisine and food preferences as an 'idiom' through which the wider public comes to recognise the social content of technological choices in food processing (Ventura and van der Meulen 1994).

Even allowing for a broad definition of technology many commentators would nevertheless draw a fairly firm line between *traditional, established* and *modern* biotechnologies. An example of a traditional biotechnology would be the production of alcohol from fermentation and distillation of palm wine. Plant breeding drawing upon Mendelian genetics and a knowledge of multivariate statistics would be an example of an established biotechnology. Modern biotechnologies would generally be taken to be those that depend on recent advances in molecular biology (Tait, Chataway and Jones 1990). Before briefly indicating some of these modern technologies, on the grounds that they will perhaps be less familiar to anthropological readers, a warning is in order. Some writers seek to split off 'modern' biotechnology as a distinct sphere specifically because they have in mind the argument that social context is less important than in the case of 'traditional' biotechnologies such as brewing and breadmaking. As we will argue later, this point of view needs to be countered through careful attention to, say, the political economy of investment decisions in the biotechnology industry or the working of actor-networks in shaping laboratory life.

Key initial discoveries in molecular biology were the recognition (by Avery, in 1944) that the genetic material in chromosomes is DNA, and Crick and Watson's unravelling of the three-dimensional structure of this molecule (1953). Two decades later Boyer succeeded in splicing together DNA sequences from two genetic sources (two plasmids of *Escherichia coli*) thus producing the first recombinant (artificially created) DNA.

Recombinant DNA technology is a major element in the repertoire of genetic engineering (the group of techniques that involves altering the natural state of an organism's genome). Genetic engineering depends to a great extent on a knowledge of enzymes that will cut and splice particular gene sequences. Foreign genes can be used in bacteria, e.g. to produce human insulin, to metabolise petroleum (and so 'eat' oil slicks), or to synthesise vaccines (e.g. against Hepatitis B and Epstein-Barr virus). More ambitiously, gene splicing can be used to incorporate permanent genetic change in eukaryotes (amoebae, fungi, plants and animals).

Seemingly, 'transgenic' plants and animals loom larger in public perceptions of biotechnology than their present somewhat limited importance warrants. The major current impact of biotechnology is to be found in bioprocess engineering (the scaling up of enzyme technologies for bulk production of modified organic molecules, in drug manufacture and food processing). It is in food processing, especially, that major socio-economic consequences seem likely to follow from developments in industrial biotechnology (Ruivenkamp 1989, 1994). Enzyme technology offers the food processing industry the possibility of flexible substitution among sources of supply for sugars and edible oils. The resultant restructuring of international food supply chains may have major socio-economic consequences for underdeveloped countries specialising in agricultural commodities such as cane sugar and palm oil.

Recent development of a 'gene gun' technology, however, opens up the possibility of fairly routine production of 'transgenic' crop types at low cost. How likely such transgenic methods are to substitute and displace conventional procedures for improvement of agricultural plants and animals is open to dispute. Some informed sources argue that it is the less dramatic aspects of biotechnology, such as tissue culture and use of molecular markers, that are likely to have the greatest impact on plant and animal improvement, as support rather than replacement for established breeding activities (Simmonds 1983; Thottappilly *et al.* 1992). Whether a gene is transferred through sexual reproduction or through splicing, breeders still face uncertainties about how it will express itself in the phenotype, and how that phenotype will fare within a specific environment.

Nevertheless, bold claims are currently being made for the extent to which new gene transfer technologies will facilitate the transfer of genes, e.g. for herbicide tolerance, into a wide range of 'target' crop plants. Gene-gun patent-holders W. R. Grace and subsidiary Agracetus have recently moved to try and establish patent rights over the genomes of rice and cotton plants modified by this technology. This has, if nothing else, had the effect of focusing considerable international attention on the inappropriateness of existing systems of intellectual property rights (patents, copyright and trade marks) to cover plant genetic resources (Shiva 1994).

One further area of biotechnology development should be mentioned here, in order to complete this brief schematic review of the field. Advances in molecular biology and genetic engineering have considerable implications for human reproduction. Genetic counselling (e.g. in cases of parents at risk of transmitting genes for sickle cell anaemia or cystic fibrosis) may one day be substituted by gene therapy (techniques for curing genetic disease). Perhaps of more immediate relevance are the modern biotechnology-based methods now used in human fertility management, e.g. *in vitro* fertilisation, or new techniques that allow parents to choose the sex of their child. Quite how these extended choices will affect family and other human relationships is not yet clear, but it has been predicted by some that the sense and meaning of the social is at stake (Strathern 1990, 1992).

THE INSTITUTIONAL LANDSCAPE FOR BIOTECHNOLOGY

Two main points might be made about the organisational and institutional framework within which biotechnology is being developed currently. First, biotechnology is dominated by the private sector, and therefore it is essential for analysts to come to terms with sets of issues relating to private-sector institutional culture (e.g. to understand intellectual property rights regimes favoured by businesses). Second, environmental pressure groups are an increasingly important focus for public scrutiny of biotechnology choices. This has implications for Third World control of biotechnology.

Biotechnology and the private sector

Emphasis should be placed on the importance of the private sector, and of multinational companies, in those areas – drugs and food processing – where biotechnology has had its greatest economic impact so far. Compared to the development of nuclear technology post-1945, developed country states apparently see less military-strategic significance in biotechnology (even though, as Bud's 1993 account shows, concern for the possibilities of 'germ warfare' is a relevant factor in public suspicions of genetic engineering). Furthermore, agriculture in these countries is an 'old' and over-protected industry, and the general trend of policy in recent years in both North America and Europe (though with many local variations and short-term reversals) has been towards progressive disengagement of the state from strategic areas such as agricultural research and development (R&D) and management of food surpluses. A striking example was the British government's decision during the 1980s to sell off its public-sector plant breeding research institutes to the private sector. A shift in balance is occurring, therefore, between R&D carried out in public and private sectors, with, potentially, a reduction in funding and institutional support for work undertaken by university laboratories and other public-sector organisations.

The shift in balance between public- and private-sector initiative in biotechnology research may also have major implications for developing countries, where the case for biotechnology R&D in the public sector remains strong, but subject to corrosion by the increasing global influence of private-sector institutional culture. A case in point would be the kinds of intellectual property rights regimes being demanded by the private sector to cover innovation in biotechnology that, if granted, might inhibit activities such as farmer adaptive experimentation significant for the rapid uptake of biotechnology-based agricultural innovations.

More generally, concern has been expressed for the impact on poor countries of the increased capacity of industrial food processors to substitute among sugar and oil sources using enzyme-driven bioprocess engineering techniques. Where once tropical farmers produced distinct commodities – such as oil palm, cocoa and cane sugar – for which they held an environmental comparative advantage, they may end up supplying nothing more than feed-stock for a food processing industry capable of creating, at the processing point, the balance of oils, fats and syrups in demand at that time. In a world in which contract farming is often the norm, this seems set to reduce further poor farmers' already low levels of bargaining power.

Environmental organisations and biotechnology

Although there is no consensus among social scientists and historians about the roots of modern environmentalism in industrial countries, significance is generally accorded to (at least) four kinds of factors: the experience of specific pollution disasters (oil spills, DDT poisoning of bird life, etc.); changes in wealth distribution and the class composition of modern industrial society (environmental activists tend to be middle class and perhaps also particularly dependent on public-sector employment opportunities, see Lowe and Goyder 1986); the rise of environmentally-based leisure pursuits (Hays 1987); and the impact of modern media (especially television).

Douglas and associates (Douglas and Wildavsky 1982) have insisted, however, on a more 'deep structured', and sociologically self-sufficient, approach to explaining how and why campaigning groups pick and choose a relatively narrow set of concerns upon which to focus, from a wide range of uncertainties and dangers afflicting society at any given moment. According to this line of explanation 'environmentalism' is not so much an objective response to an external danger as one of the typical ways in which social groups project internal tensions and concerns for social accountability. There is no denying a strong whiff of the apocalyptic about some environmental activist movements, but it is not yet clear to what extent the 'culture theory' approach of the Douglas school can be integrated as an element within a broader explanation of environmentalism, or whether it stands on its own as a way of accounting specifically for environmentalism's millenarian tendencies.

In whatever way the rise of environmentalism is accounted for, however, the influence of environmental groups in the shaping of biotechnology seems set to grow. Several of the main campaigning 'green' groups in developed countries now have specific standpoints on biotechnology issues, often arrived at through a concern for issues relating to 'sustainable' agriculture. In some cases this has catalysed an interest in global development issues, and alliances between environmental groups and development NGOs may become increasingly important. Environmental groups also focus on bio-hazards, and campaign for controls on transgenic research and safeguards on the release of genetically-modified organisms (GMOs) into the environment. Here they draw on background experience with cases of environmental pollution and campaigns against pesticide abuse. They also exploit effectively the resonances that exist between bio-hazards and public concern about the safety of nuclear energy (radiation hazards, etc.).

Whether or not the industrial biotechnology lobby underestimates the risks associated with bioprocessing and release of GMOs, public suspicion in industrial countries tends to be high, perhaps reflecting the secrecy and lack of consultation surrounding the earlier development of nuclear energy. Bud (1993) reminds us that biotechnology long pre-dates genetic engineering, and was once (and perhaps in future will once again be) a favoured prescription of political radicals for dealing with the dirt and damage of the first industrial revolution, and offering freedom from hunger to developing countries. Modern perceptions, however, were decisively shaped by the fact that the first successful transgenic work was carried out on bacteria, and coincided with the most intense period of student anti-Vietnam War agitation. The legacy of this coincidence is a widespread public perception, among the most highly-educated groups of middle-aged opinion formers in the 1990s in the United States and western Europe in particular, that biotechnology is in some sense a product of 'germ warfare', and indissolubly linked with the power of (in Eisenhower's phrase) 'the military-industrial complex'.

There is an increasing trend in many countries to try and defuse this suspicion through organised dialogue, sometimes by means of regular consultation with environmental groups. In the USA environmental groups are in some cases said to be gaining some of the influence earlier enjoyed by producer/commodity groups in shaping the research agenda of land grant universities and other public-sector research bodies. It remains to be seen if environmental groups will constitute a 'loyal opposition', and steer technology generation in useful new channels, or have a crippling impact on the effective realisation of biotechnology's potential in industrial countries (cf. Rabino 1994).

Meanwhile, there is an important debate beginning to develop about the role of such campaigning groups in underdeveloped countries. Environmental organisations are increasingly important actors on the political stage in a number of African, Asian and Latin American countries (having emerged by imitation, or by local independent invention), but in some cases rivalled by groups developing around more locally-focused eco-cultural and political issues (so-called 'environmental movements of the poor'). Several networks of local environmental groups in Latin America and Asia (fewer in Africa) now campaign for protection of biodiversity. Some link their campaigns to the protection of cultural diversity and the rights of indigenous peoples. Others see a link between agricultural biodiversity and biotechnology, and focus on issues connected with intellectual property rights in bioresources. Some countries with traditions of peasant-activism also have strong indigenous farmers' organisations beginning to scrutinise, and to attempt to exert some control over, the biotechnology agenda (in India, for example). The significance of such groups, whether middle-class dominated conservation movements or 'environmental movements of the poor', is not limited to their potential impact on biotechnology futures in developing countries, but is more generally part of the wider global debate concerning democratisation and civil society (cf. Taylor and Buttel 1992).

SOCIETY–BIOTECHNOLOGY ISSUES: RESEARCH PRIORITIES

Biotechnology innovation as socio-economic process

Much cutting-edge technology – nowhere more so than in the biotechnology field – is elaborated by R&D teams belonging, or contracted to, firms operating within a framework of 'capitalist' institutional culture. Although 'induced innovation' theory (cf. Ruttan 1982), based on the idea that the external environment (e.g.

market trends) signals effectively to R&D teams where innovations are needed, has its proponents and analytical successes, there is considerable dispute about whether established theory in economics is wholly adequate to the task of explaining the real-life innovative behaviour of firms.

Mackenzie (1992), reviewing sociological and economic approaches to technological innovation, suggests the need for a synthesis of approaches. In particular, he points out that R&D decisions in cutting-edge technologies are taken against a background of great economic uncertainty and that this situation of decision making under extreme uncertainty is not unlike the problem addressed by sociologists attempting to explain why certain classes of hypotheses come to be favoured and others rejected, ahead of clear agreement about facts, in laboratory science.

One set of arguments with considerable empirical support is that the key factor 'selecting' for hypotheses ahead of evidence is the extent to which scientists are able to establish stable social networks of consensus and support (cf. Latour 1987, Stichweh 1992, Fujimura 1992). Mackenzie (1992) suggests that this perspective, taking its inspiration from recent studies in the sociology of science (Pickering 1992), may be important in understanding the way in which competing R&D scenarios come to be established, or dispensed with, within and among firms (cf. Webster 1989). He also draws attention to the purely conventional nature of some R&D decision making (based on hunches and arbitrary rules of thumb) and the possible importance of self-fulfilling prophecies in bringing certain lines of development to fruition. He also advocates the importance of ethnographic work in documenting actual decision-making approaches (cf. Latour 1987, Cambrosio et al. 1990), and proposes a potentially useful new subfield of ethno-accountancy (study of how decision makers actually use accountancy data, as distinct from textbook recommendations based on rational-choice ideals). Mackenzie suspects that ethno-accountancy might help pinpoint some subtle differences in the way standardised business decision-making frameworks and procedures are handled cross-culturally.

Empirical support for the kind of programme Mackenzie advocates is already available (Kingery 1991). Mackenzie's programme seemingly would be an interesting and relevant starting point for work on the social construction of biotechnology innovation. In particular, it seems relevant to stress the potential significance of ethnographic insights into the process of scenario building. But it will be equally important to map the terrain, before becoming bogged down in detailed instances. Perhaps a biotechnology equivalent of the International African Institute's ethnographic survey is now needed, as a basis for apprehending the range of cosmologies inhabited by the 'tribes' of biotechnology innovators? If so, we need to discuss what such a survey needs to contain, and debate the categories that might be deployed for data collection. It also needs to be understood that any such ethnographic work cannot be separated from analysis at the level of the global political economy (see the following section), since 'tribes' of innovators thrive or decline according to the position they occupy in an evolving global order (Ruivenkamp 1989).

Political economy approaches to biotechnology impacts

Following in the footsteps of classic analyses, e.g. of the impact of cash cropping and green revolution innovations on agrarian social formations in underdeveloped countries, there have been a number of recent studies of the impact of biotechnology on the international food supply chain. Seemingly enzyme technology in food processing (sugars and vegetable oils especially) will have considerable implications for the international division of agricultural labour. The agricultural labour forces of poor countries seem likely to suffer further disadvantage if food processors' greater ability to substitute among different supply sources for key raw materials leads to unpredictable on-off market engagement in tropical regions specialising in crops such as oil palm. Already, biotechnologists are talking about 'designer oil crops' (Murphy 1994). Third World oil crop outgrowers and contract farmers seem destined to subsist on second-hand reach-me-downs and yesterday's fashions. It seems important for the social sciences to continue to monitor the impact of biotechnology on the distribution of power and agency in agrarian societies. But in addition, more account should be taken of the potential impact of biotechnology on the global political economy of consumption.

One important debate is whether transnational corporations really are transnational, or (as the Coca-Cola company already prefers to believe) multi-local. The implications of the multi-local pursuit of profit are as yet obscure. 'Designer' options on offer from biotechnology may have their primary impact on the international division of labour, but some attention ought also to be paid to whether they will lead to an enhancement of 'bottom-up' consumer choices, and the elaboration of new ranges of consumer items (e.g. low-cost 'regional' food and drink products) tailored to local preferences. The political economy of consumer power is a relatively untilled field. If we are to tackle scenario building in biotechnology seriously then the ethnography of decision making in supermarket chains may be as crucial a step as understanding the internal social dynamics of R&D laboratories on the production side of the equation.

The social shaping of biotechnology

What wider social forces will be brought to bear upon biotechnology? Here we are forced to confront the basic question 'How is society expressed within and through biotechnology?'. *Conventional* analysis sees biotechnology as a largely a-social domain. The key questions, then, are how will biotechnology impact upon society, and how will client and consumer groups react to certain biotechnology developments. *Radical* analysis draws attention to the fact that biotechnology, as a set of practices of certain human groups (laboratory communities and private companies), is inextricably sociological. The inherently hybrid – social-technical – character of biotechnology is nowhere more apparent than in the sphere of new reproductive technologies, where medical personnel and parents work to shape the hitherto natural (or God-given) domains of gender and kinship. But bio-engineers of all kinds attempt to 'shape life', and in so doing uncover profound sociological as well as technical questions. If bio-engineers have begun to mould the basic materials of life in far-reaching ways then society, in turn, can no longer leave the issue of the direction of biotechnology to expert engineers, but must address the questions 'How many hybrid socio-technical processes labelled biotechnology might be envisaged, given current states of knowledge?' and 'What criteria should govern the selection of those advanced for further development?'. This implies an engagement between 'engineers' and 'society' of a kind not seen in the past two or three centuries. It may be helpful briefly to consider the following four issues.

Tailor-made biotechnology

Biotechnology claims to be offering futures by design. This may be rhetoric. There are serious reasons for suspecting that the overall impact of transgenic crops and animals may be rather more limited than currently anticipated. Public opinion, and legislators, may reject transgenics, or severely curtail transgenic experimentation, on ethical or safety grounds. Natural selection may have the last word on many novel organisms. Some years ago Simmonds (1983) argued that the main impact of biotechnology in plant breeding was likely to be in strengthening conventional procedures (through speeding up breeding cycles, in genetic characterisation, etc.) rather than the wholesale replacement of conventional procedures by transgenic manipulation. On the other hand, if some of the claims of biotechnology prove to be more than rhetoric it will be important to ask who calls the shots, and how the possibility of increased choice over biological options will change the world view and every day life of the chooser.

The point has been debated by Strathern (1990, 1992) in relation to the new biotechnologies of reproduction. What happens to social relations and concepts of nature if and when children become the products of their parents' choices as consumers of reproductive technologies? The possibility of tailor-made biotechnologies, especially for harsh environments neglected by conventional plant and animal improvement research (Ruivenkamp and Richards 1994) seemingly proffers a more hopeful (or less troublesome) scenario than the reproductive field surveyed by Strathern. In this first case the relationship between farmer and researcher may usefully be transformed from that of client and patron to that of client and contractor; agricultural biotechnology, if supported in the public sector in poor countries, may offer enhanced scope for implementing the kinds of 'bottom-up' technology generation scenarios espoused by the 'farmer-first' movement in agricultural research (de Boef *et al.* 1993). Work within and on farmers' organisations, however, suggests that, as a prior condition, client groups must have formed some clear understanding of the biotechnology research process and what, realistically, that process might be expected to deliver, before demand-driven, biotechnology-powered, agricultural research becomes a reality. Quite what these understandings might be in specific contexts, how they are formed, and how adequate they might be as a basis for steering research, are questions requiring urgent research attention. In addition, much more information is needed on the way in which, and with what consequences, agricultural research institutions introduced from outside, or designed on external lines, come to be incorporated within local institutional cultures in developing countries (Richards 1994).

Public attitudes to biohazards

There is some research support (Tait 1988) for the view that public attitudes to biotechnology risks either tend to be neutral or rather strongly (and perhaps inappropriately) influenced by 'leakage' of ideas and attitudes from cognate domains (fear of nuclear accidents, concern about a revival of Nazi eugenics, etc.), and that real engagement may await, and will be shaped by, the nature of the first serious biotechnology accidents (e.g. whether these involve escape of GMOs or are industrial accidents in bioprocessing). Social science contributions to risk analysis are now rich and varied (Royal Society 1992), tending to pull in different directions according to differing assessments of the nature of humans as risk assessors (crudely put, whether risk assessments are seen primarily as social or psychological judgements). Possibly a common frame may emerge within cognitive theory (specifically through the study of the cognitive heuristics of risk assessment). Factory cultures of safety in the bioprocessing industry are potential candidates for insightful ethnographic study.

The training of biotechnologists

Skill formation is a crucial 'site' for examination of society–technology interactions. Relevant themes include examination of the history and current character of the higher education institutions graduating bio-engineers, the social background of recruits to bio-engineering, the professionalisation of bio-engineers, and societal debates about the role and status of such professionals. It would be interesting to have comparative information on the background, motivation and career prospects of bio-engineering graduate cohorts in different countries, and biographical profiles of representative or key figures (especially those shaping R&D policy in private firms and major public-sector laboratories). Also we need cross-country information on the content of bio-engineering curricula, and what influence different interest groups exercise on curriculum content. In particular, it is pertinent to ask what social science content, if any, there is and ought to be in the training of bio-engineers. Will society at large increasingly require technologists to be socially sensitive as well as technically competent, and how will education and training institutions respond to this demand for greater social sophistication in engineers (paralleling increased exposure to social issues in the training of doctors and architects)?[2]

Biotechnology and civil society

Increasingly, biotechnology will develop under the sceptical, not to say hostile, scrutiny of activist organisations interested in environmental issues. It is a major research task for social science to understand the rise of environmentalism, and the kinds of organisations and interests present within the environmental movement. The biotechnology industry also seemingly realises that this form of public scrutiny is now a permanent feature of the democratic landscape, with which they will have to come to terms, and much interest is likely to centre on social science studies that purport to be able to decode, explain, predict or manage the public acceptability of different kinds of biotechnology development (Levidow and Tait 1991). An important international equity issue will arise if public pressure in the West limits certain kinds of biotechnology development that might be of great significance to less vocal constituencies in poor countries – for example, if the European Parliament, following trends in Germany (cf. Rabino 1994), moves to limit transgenic research, thus potentially limiting the opportunity for European scientists to contribute to the development of new crop types. Environmental activist groups are not only a feature of developed industrialised countries but are now a worldwide phenomenon. With the spread of global television, satellite communications, fax, e-mail, etc. groups in remote areas find it relatively easy to participate in worldwide networks for exchange of ideas. The debate about global environmental change has itself become global, with a consequent rapid rise in Third World activist organisations. The rich and varied landscape of emergent environmental NGOs urgently requires basic documentation and characterisation. Ethnographic work is needed in order to understand the range and variety of these national and regional NGOs and NGO networks, and to answer questions about their origins and character – the extent to which they represent middle-class 'nationalist' constituencies as distinct, say, from ongoing traditions of peasant resistance ('environmental movements of the poor').

Amid the information overload and welter of activity stemming from the UNCED conference on the global environment in 1992 it is possible to discern one salient central trend. Activist groups worldwide have picked up on a central feature of biotechnology – genes cannot yet be made, they can only be borrowed. If the borrowers then press their case for intellectual property rights in biotechnology then so will the lenders. North–South relations in coming decades seem likely to be increasingly preoccupied with issues revolving around the axis of Southern biodiversity–Northern biotechnology (Seabrook 1993; Kumar 1993). Claims currently being made to intellectual property in genetic resources through genome mapping and novel gene transfer techniques will probably prove to be unsustainable as judges, lawyers and patent inspectors in the western world begin to absorb the full political implications of the Third World opposition currently building up along the biodiversity–biotechnology axis (Shiva 1994). Social scientists interested in these issues may divide broadly into two camps – activists in the struggle over intellectual property resources, and those who attempt to answer the question posed by Marilyn Strathern – what will this struggle over ownership of genetic resources do for our conceptions of nature and ourselves?

CONCLUSION

In this conclusion we wish to stress, above all, the need for *radical* thinking concerning society-biotechnology issues. Thoroughgoing social analysis (e.g. using the perspective of actor-network theory) is essential to make it clear that the understanding of what it is possible to achieve through the application of biotechnology is a product of definite social contexts and working arrangements. Above all, it needs to be understood that biotechnology is a process dominated by venture capital in a fast-elaborating world order of private enterprise, and that this imposes certain constraints on the ways in which the raw material of biotechnology is viewed. Nowhere is this more clear than in the 'interaction' between gene sequencing technology and attempts to secure private property in gene sequences via patent rights. We express, at this juncture, no view on the rights and wrongs of the issue, except to note that gene patenting finally puts paid to the notion of a gene as some pure a-social product of laboratory investigation. In the world of plant or virus patents the gene is now without doubt a hybrid object constructed from biological facts and lawyers' arguments. The world of biotechnology is full of such hybrid socio-technical objects, and it is the particular task of a sociology of biotechnology (as Latour 1993 suggests in other contexts) to understand the sources and implications of this socio-technical hybridity.

For generations, the social sciences fought against hybridisation of their objects of study. This desire to prevent miscegenation among our categories lies at the root of the long-lived and firmly-defended nature–culture distinction. But as in linguistic studies of mixed languages (creolisation studies) what at first appears negative can in fact be a source of strength and new theoretical insight (Richards 1994). Thus our main point about the coming social revolution triggered by biotechnology is that no longer can either side – professional engineers working for private companies on the one hand, say, and interest groups, whether potential clients or activist groups within civil society, on the other – afford to engage in debate in a one-sided manner. In making property claims over the basic raw materials of life, or in making it possible for parents to choose the sex of their child, bio-engineers presume to enter the inner social sanctum from within which individuals and groups draw their sense of identity. Whether they intend to or not, bio-engineers become social theorists and open themselves to debate about the nature and value of alternative social arrangements. Equally, groups representing social interests can no longer be content to leave technical decisions in capable professional hands. The correct characterisation of the gene is no longer exclusively a matter for arcane ivory tower analysis among biologists, but a vital issue affecting the way in which individuals see themselves in society.

The importance of this point is conceded by the current interest shown in the quality of public understanding of these basic issues (as in the public consensus conference on plant biotechnology sponsored by the UK Biotechnology and Biological Sciences Research Council, November 1994). Some imagine that this process is largely about clearing away misconceptions, in order to allow biotechnologists a clearer field in which to work, but others, with a more far-sighted grasp, sense the laying of the groundwork for an entire new contract between science and society. This new contract would make explicit the hybrid character of all technology generation. It would then require the social assumptions behind all technology scenario building to be laid bare for wider democratic inspection. Choice in science and technology would no longer be dominated by the Henry Ford dictum (you can have any colour so long as it is black). The current equivalent of Ford's 'choice' is the idea that there is only one trajectory for biotechnology development, and that all companies are fated to pursue this single trajectory by the iron laws of business competition. Engineers conscious of their social role, and an informed public alert to the possibility of cognitive pluralism in a world of hybrid bio-social objects, might together pursue radically different agenda for biotechnology research than those currently envisaged, with altogether new and potentially beneficial consequences.

As we have argued elsewhere (Ruivenkamp and Richards 1994), the necessary first step in treating biotechnology not as a threat but as an opportunity may be *to think big, but differently*. To do so one needs deliberately to widen, quite radically, the composition of the group contributing ideas to the scenario-building exercise. Just beyond the present reach of the actor-networks sustaining much of the world's biotechnology stands the pent-up imaginative power of the world's rural poor, the single greatest group of potential beneficiaries from a biotechnology revolution correctly handled. We must seek urgently to explore the new and valuable hybrid conceptions of nature and culture that might be forthcoming were the rural poor to be given a clear voice in debates about the future of biotechnology.

NOTES

1   This is the focus of the research programme of the group for Technology and Agrarian Development at Wageningen Agricultural University.
2   Currently, Harro Maat, a member of our research group, is looking at this range of issues as it affects the training of agricultural and bio-engineers in the Netherlands.

REFERENCES

Bud, R. (1993) *Making Life: A History of Biotechnology*, Cambridge: Cambridge University Press.

Cambrosio, A., Limoges, C. and Pronovost, D. (1990) 'Representing Biotechnology: An Ethnography of Quebec Science Policy', *Social Studies of Science* 20: 195–227.

De Boef, W., Amanor, K., and Wellard, K. (eds) (1993) *Cultivating Knowledge: Genetic Diversity, Farmer Experimentation and Crop Research*, London: IT Publications.

Douglas, M. and Wildavsky, A. (1982) *Risk and Culture: An Essay on the Selection of Technological and Environmental Dangers*, Berkeley: University of California Press.

Fujimura, J. H. (1992) 'Crafting Science: Standardized Packages, Boundary Objects, and "Translation" ', in A. Pickering (ed.) *Science as Practice and Culture*, Chicago: University of Chicago Press.

Hall, T. (1986) *Nuclear Politics: The History of Nuclear Power in Britain*, Harmondsworth: Penguin.

Hays, S. (1987) *Beauty, Health and Permanence: Environmental Politics in the United States 1955–85*, Cambridge: Cambridge University Press.

'Indigenous Knowledge and Development Monitor' (1994) *Communications: IK Resource Centers*, 2.

Ingold, T. (1988) 'Tools, Minds and Machines: An Excursion in the Philosophy of Technology', *Techniques et Culture* 12: 151–76.

Kingery, W. David (ed.) (1991) *Japanese/American Technological Innovation: The Influence of Cultural Differences on Japanese and American Innovation in Advanced Materials*, New York: Elsevier.

Kumar, Patnam V. S. (1993) 'Biotechnology and Biodiversity: A Dialectical Relationship', *Journal of Scientific and Industrial Research* 52: 523–32.

Latour, B. (1987) *Science in Action*, Cambridge, Mass.: Harvard University Press.

—— (1993) *We Have Never Been Modern*, Hemel Hempstead: Harvester Wheatsheaf.

Law, J. and Callon, M. (1992) 'The Life and Death of an Aircraft: A Network Analysis of Technical Change', in W. E. Bijker and J. Law (eds) *Shaping Technology/Building Society: Studies in Sociotechnical Change*, London: MIT Press.

Levidow, L. and Tait J. (1991) 'The Greening of Biotechnology: GMOs as Environment-Friendly Products', *Science and Public Policy* 18, 5: 271–80.

Longley, C. and Richards, P. (1993) 'Selection Strategies of Rice Farmers in Sierra Leone', in W. De Boef, K. Amanor, and K. Wellard (eds) *Cultivating Knowledge: Genetic Diversity, Farmer Experimentation and Crop Research*, London: IT Publications.

Lowe, P. and Goyder, J. (1986) *Environmental Groups in Politics*, London: Allen & Unwin.

Mackenzie, D. (1992) 'Economic and Sociological Explanation of Technical Change', in R. Coombs, P. Saviotti and V. Walsh (eds) *Technological Change and Company Strategies*.

Murphy, D. J. (ed.) (1994) *Designer Oil Crops: Breeding, Processing and Biotechnology*, Weinheim: VCH Verlagsgesellschaft.

Patel, Surendra J. (1993) 'Indigenous Knowledge and Intellectual Property Rights', Conference on Indigenous Knowledge and Intellectual Property Rights, Lake Tahoe, 5–10 October.

Pickering, A. (ed.) (1992) *Science as Practice and Culture*, Chicago: University of Chicago Press.

Rabino, I. (1994) 'How European and US Genetic Engineering Scientists View the Impact of Public Attention to their Field: A Comparison', *Science, Technology and Human Values* 19, 1: 23–46.

RAFI (1994) 'The Patenting of Human Genetic Material', *Communique, Rural Advancement Foundation International*, January/February.

Richards, P. (1993) 'Culture and Community Values in the Selection and Maintenance of African Rice', Conference on Indigenous Knowledge and Intellectual Property Rights, Lake Tahoe, 5–10 October.

—— (1994) 'The Shaping of Biotechnology: Institutional Culture and Ideo-types', *Biotechnology and Development Monitor* 18, March.

Royal Society (1992) *Risk*, Chapter 5 'Risk perceptions'.

Ruivenkamp, G. (1989) *De Invoering van Biotechnologie in Agro-industriele Produktieketen: de Overgang naar een Nieuwe Arbeidsorganisatie*, PhD Thesis, Amsterdam University.

—— (1994) *Biotechnology and Changes in the International Production and Trade of Vegetable Oils and Fats*, TAD/WAU Wageningen, typescript.

— and Richards, P. (1994) 'Drought Tolerance Research as a Social Process', *Biotechnology and Development Monitor* 18, March.

Ruttan, V. (1982) *Agricultural Research Policy*, Minneapolis: University of Minnesota.

Seabrook, J. (1993) 'Biotechnology and Genetic Diversity', *Race and Class* 34, 3: 15–30.

Shiva, V. (1994) 'The Need for *Sui Generis* [seed] Rights', *Seedling* (Genetic Resources Action International), 12, 1: 11–15.

Simmonds, N. W. (1983) 'Plant Breeding: the State of the Art', in Kosiye *et al.* (eds) *Genetic Engineering of Plants*, Davis, Cal.: Plenum Press.

Stichweh, R. (1992) 'The Sociology of Scientific Disciplines: on the Genesis and Stability of the Disciplinary Structure of Modern Science', *Science in Context* 5, 1: 3–15.

Strathern, M. (1990) 'Enterprising Kinship: Consumer Choice and the New Reproductive Technologies', *Cambridge Anthropology* 14, 1: 1–12.

— (1992) *Reproducing the Future: Anthropology, Kinship and the New Reproductive Technologies*, Manchester: Manchester University Press.

Tait, J. (1988) 'Public Perception of Biotechnology Hazards', *Journal of Chemical and Technical Biotechnology* 43, 363–72.

— ,Chataway, J. and Jones S. (1990) 'The Status of Biotechnology-based Innovations', *Technology Analysis and Strategic Management* 2, 3: 293–305.

Taylor, P. J. and Buttel, F. H. (1992) 'How Do We Know We Have Global Environmental Problems?: Science and the Globalization of Environmental Discourse', *Geoforum* 23, 3: 405–16.

Thottappilly, G., Monti, L. M., Mohan Raj, D. R. and Moore, A. W. (eds) (1992) *Biotechnology: Enhancing Research on Tropical Crops in Africa*, Wageningen and Ibadan: CTA and IITA.

Ventura, F. and van der Meulen, H. (1994) 'Transformation and Consumption of High-quality Meat: the Case of Chianina Meat in Umbria, Italy', in J. D van der Ploeg and A. Long (eds) *Born from Within: Practice and Perspectives of Endogenous Rural Development*, Assen: van Gorcum.

Webster, A. J. (1989) 'Privatisation of Public Sector Research: The Case of a Plant Breeding Institute', *Science and Public Policy*, 16, 4: 224–32.

Name index

Subject index